Beginning iPhone Development with SwiftUI

Exploring the iOS SDK

Seventh Edition

Wallace Wang

Apress®

Beginning iPhone Development with SwiftUI: Exploring the iOS SDK

Wallace Wang
San Diego, CA, USA

ISBN-13 (pbk): 978-1-4842-9540-3
https://doi.org/10.1007/978-1-4842-9541-0

ISBN-13 (electronic): 978-1-4842-9541-0

Managing Director, Apress Media LLC: Welmoed Spahr
Acquisitions Editor: Miriam Haidara
Development Editor: James Markham
Coordinating Editor: Jessica Vakili

Distributed to the book trade worldwide by Springer Science+Business Media New York, 1 NY Plaza, New York, NY 10004. Phone 1-800-SPRINGER, fax (201) 348-4505, e-mail orders-ny@springer-sbm.com, or visit www.springeronline.com. Apress Media, LLC is a California LLC and the sole member (owner) is Springer Science + Business Media Finance Inc (SSBM Finance Inc). SSBM Finance Inc is a **Delaware** corporation.

For information on translations, please e-mail booktranslations@springernature.com; for reprint, paperback, or audio rights, please e-mail bookpermissions@springernature.com.

Apress titles may be purchased in bulk for academic, corporate, or promotional use. eBook versions and licenses are also available for most titles. For more information, reference our Print and eBook Bulk Sales web page at http://www.apress.com/bulk-sales.

Any source code or other supplementary material referenced by the author in this book is available to readers on the Github repository: https://github.com/Apress/Beginning-iPhone-Development-with-SwiftUI. For more detailed information, please visit http://www.apress.com/source-code.

Printed on acid-free paper

Table of Contents

About the Author

Wallace Wang is a former Windows enthusiast who took one look at Vista and realized that the future of computing belonged to the Mac. He's written more than 40 computer books, including *Microsoft Office for Dummies, Beginning Programming for Dummies, Steal This Computer Book, Beginning ARKit for iPhone and iPad*, and *Pro iPhone Development with SwiftUI*. In addition to programming the Mac and iPhone/iPad, he also performs stand-up comedy, having appeared on A&E's *An Evening at the Improv* and having performed in Las Vegas at the Riviera Comedy Club at the Riviera Hotel and Casino. When he's not writing computer books or performing stand-up comedy, he also enjoys blogging about screenwriting at his site, `https://15minutemoviemethod.com`, where he shares screenwriting tips with other aspiring screenwriters who all share the goal of breaking into Hollywood.

About the Technical Reviewer

 **Massimo Nardone** has more than 22 years of experience in security, web and mobile development, Cloud, and IT architecture. His true IT passions are security and Android.

He has been programming and teaching how to program with Android, Perl, PHP, Java, VB, Python, C/C++, and MySQL for more than 20 years.

Massimo also holds a Master of Science degree in computing science from the University of Salerno, Italy.

He has worked as a project manager, software engineer, research engineer, chief security architect, information security manager, PCI/SCADA auditor, and senior lead IT security/Cloud/SCADA architect for many years.

His technical skills include security, Android, Cloud, Java, MySQL, Drupal, Cobol, Perl, web and mobile development, MongoDB, D3, Joomla, Couchbase, C/C++, WebGL, Python, Pro Rails, Django CMS, Jekyll, Scratch, etc.

He currently works as Chief Information Security Officer (CISO) for Cargotec Oyj.

He worked as a visiting lecturer and supervisor for exercises at the Networking Laboratory of the Helsinki University of Technology (Aalto University). He holds four international patents (PKI, SIP, SAML, and Proxy areas).

CHAPTER 1

Understanding iOS Programming

Programming involves writing commands for a computer to follow. In iOS programming, the computer is either an iPhone or an iPad. To create apps for an iPhone or iPad, you need to learn three different skills:

- How to write commands in the Swift programming language

- How to use Apple's software frameworks

- How to create user interfaces in Xcode

You need to write commands in the Swift programming language to make your app do something unique. Then you rely on Apple's software frameworks to handle common tasks such as detecting touch gestures or accessing the camera. Finally, you design your app's user interface.

Apple's software frameworks let you perform common tasks without writing (and testing) your own Swift code. By relying on Apple's proven and tested software frameworks, you can focus solely on the unique features of your app rather than the mundane details of making an app access different hardware features of an iPhone or iPad.

Ideally, you want your user interface to look good by adapting to all different screen sizes such as an iPhone or iPad. The user interface lets you display information to the user and retrieve information from the user. The best user interface is one that doesn't require even thinking about.

Essentially, every iOS app consists of three parts as shown in Figure 1-1:

- Your code to make an app do something useful

- A user interface that you can design visually in Xcode

- Access to hardware features of an iOS device through one or more of Apple's iOS frameworks

© Wallace Wang 2023
W. Wang, *Beginning iPhone Development with SwiftUI*, https://doi.org/10.1007/978-1-4842-9541-0_1

Figure 1-1. *The three parts of an iOS app*

Apple provides dozens of frameworks for iOS (and their other operating systems as well such as macOS, watchOS, and tvOS). By simply using Apple's frameworks, you can accomplish common tasks by writing little code of your own. Some of Apple's available frameworks include

- SwiftUI – User interface and touch screen support

- ARKit – Augmented reality features

- Core Animation – Displays animation

- GameKit – Creates multiplayer interactive apps

- Contacts – Accesses the Contacts data on an iOS device

- SiriKit – Allows the use of voice commands through Siri

- AVKit – Allows playing of audio and video files

- Media Library – Allows access to images, audio, and video stored on an iOS device

- CallKit – Provides voice calling features

Apple's frameworks essentially contain code that you can reuse. This makes apps more reliable and consistent while also saving developers' time by using proven code that works correctly. To see a complete list of Apple's available software frameworks, visit the Apple Developer Documentation site (https://developer.apple.com/documentation).

Apple's frameworks can give you a huge head start in creating an iOS app, but you still need to provide a user interface so users can interact with your app. While you could create a user interface from scratch, this would also be tedious, time-consuming, and error-prone. Even worse, if every app developer created a user interface from scratch, no two iOS apps would look or work exactly the same, confusing users.

That's why Apple's Xcode compiler helps you design user interfaces with standard features used in most apps such as buttons, labels, text fields, and sliders. In Xcode, each window of a user interface is called a view. While simple iOS apps may consist of a single view (think of the Calculator app on an iPhone), more sophisticated iOS apps consist of multiple views.

To create user interfaces, Xcode offers two options:

- Storyboards

- SwiftUI

Storyboards let you design user interfaces visually by placing user interface objects at specific locations on the screen as shown in Figure 1-2. Unfortunately, using fixed values to define the position of various objects on a user interface means that storyboard user interfaces do not adapt easily to different-size iOS device screens or orientations (portrait or landscape).

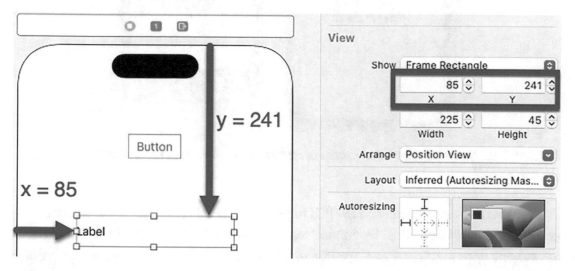

Figure 1-2. *Storyboards use fixed values to define the arrangement of objects on a user interface*

Since fixed values for arranging objects on a user interface won't adapt to different screen sizes, Apple offers a second way to design user interfaces using a framework called SwiftUI. The main idea behind SwiftUI is that you place objects in the center of the user interface and define their position relative to the center.

When the screen size is large, the distance between user interface objects expands. When the screen size is small, the distance between user interface objects shrinks, so the user interface adapts to the screen size automatically as shown in Figure 1-3.

Figure 1-3. *SwiftUI user interfaces can adapt to different screen sizes automatically*

You can use storyboards and SwiftUI together in a single project, or you can use either storyboards or SwiftUI by themselves. Because SwiftUI represents the future for developing apps for all of Apple's products, this book focuses exclusively on creating user interfaces using SwiftUI rather than storyboards.

Learning About Xcode

Learning iOS development is more than just learning how to write code in the Swift programming language. Besides knowing Swift, you must also know how to find and use Apple's different software frameworks, how to use Xcode to design your user interface using SwiftUI, and how to organize, create, and delete files that contain your Swift code. In addition, you must also learn how to write code using Xcode's editor.

Each time you create an Xcode project, you're actually creating a folder that contains multiple files. A simple iOS app might consist of a handful of files, while a complicated app might contain hundreds or even thousands of separate files.

By storing code in separate files, you can quickly identify the file that contains the data you want to edit and modify while safely ignoring other files. No matter how many files a project may hold, Xcode treats them as if all your Swift code were stored in a single file. By breaking up your program into multiple files, you can group different parts of your program in separate files to organize your app.

To further help you organize multiple files in a project, Xcode lets you create separate folders. These folders exist solely for your convenience in organizing your code. Figure 1-4 shows how Xcode can divide an app into folders and files.

Figure 1-4. *Xcode stores your code in files that you can organize in folders*

To get acquainted with iOS app development, let's start with a simple project that will teach you

- How to understand the parts of a project

- How to view different files

- How the different parts of Xcode work

1. Start Xcode. A welcoming screen appears that lets you choose a recently used project or the option of creating a new project as shown in Figure 1-5. (You can always open this welcoming screen from within Xcode by choosing Windows ➤ Welcome to Xcode or by pressing Shift + Command + 1.

Figure 1-5. *The Xcode welcoming screen*

2.   Click the **Create a new Xcode project** option. Xcode displays
     templates for designing different types of apps as shown in
     Figure 1-6. Notice that the top of the template window displays
     different operating systems you can develop apps for such as
     iOS, watchOS, tvOS, and macOS. By selecting different operating
     systems, you can create projects designed for the devices that run
     that particular operating system.

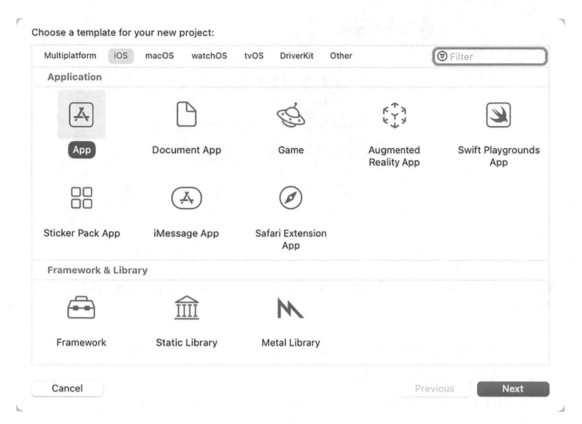

Figure 1-6. *Choosing a project template*

3. Click **iOS** and then click **App**. The App template represents the most basic iOS project.

4. Click the **Next** button. Another window appears, asking for your project name along with an organization name and organization identifier as shown in Figure 1-7. You must fill out all three text fields, but the project name, organization name, and organization identifier can be any descriptive text that you want. Notice that the user interface popup menu lets you choose between SwiftUI and Storyboard. For every project in this book, always make sure you choose SwiftUI.

Figure 1-7. *Defining a project name, organization name, and organization identifier*

5. Click in the Project Name text field and type a name for your project such as MyFirstApp.

6. Click in the Team text field and type your name or company name.

7. Click in the Organization Identifier text field and type any identifying text you wish. Typically this identifier is your website spelled backward such as com.microsoft.

8. Click the Interface popup menu and choose **SwiftUI**. Make sure that all checkboxes are clear. Then click the **Next** button. Xcode displays a dialog for you to choose which drive and folder to store your project in.

9. Choose a drive and folder and click the **Create** button. Xcode displays your newly created project.

The Xcode window may initially look confusing, but you need to see that Xcode groups information in several panes. The far-left pane is called the Navigator pane. By clicking icons at the top of the Navigator pane, you can view different parts of your project as shown in Figure 1-8.

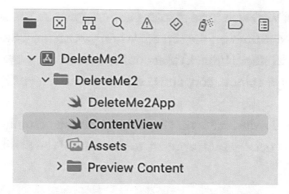

Figure 1-8. *The Navigator pane appears on the far left of the Xcode window*

The main SwiftUI file is called ContentView, which contains Swift code that defines the user interface of an app:

```swift
import SwiftUI

struct ContentView: View {
    var body: some View {
        VStack {
            Image(systemName: "globe")
                .imageScale(.large)
                .foregroundColor(.accentColor)
            Text("Hello, world!")
        }
        .padding()
    }
}

struct ContentView_Previews: PreviewProvider {
    static var previews: some View {
        ContentView()
    }
}
```

The import SwiftUI line lets your app use the SwiftUI framework for designing user interfaces.

The ContentView: View structure displays a single view on the screen. SwiftUI can only display one view at a time on the screen. When you create a SwiftUI iOS app, the default view is a vertical stack (VStack) that contains an Image view and a Text view. The Image view displays a globe icon, and the Text view displays "Hello, world!" on the screen.

The ContentView_Previews: PreviewProvider structure actually displays the user interface in the Canvas pane, which appears to the right of the Swift code as shown in Figure 1-9.

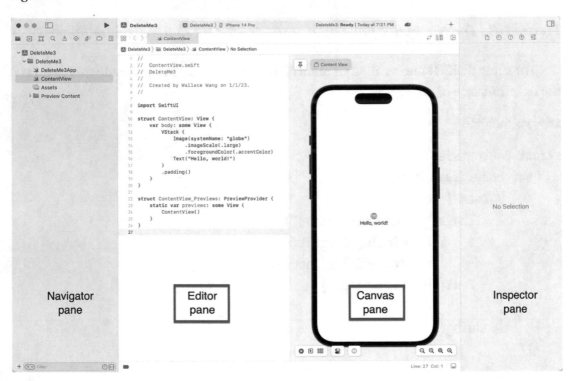

Figure 1-9. *The Editor pane and the Canvas pane*

When the Editor pane and the Canvas pane appear side by side, any changes you make to the Editor pane appear in the Canvas pane and vice versa. If you click the Editor Options icon in the upper-right corner, you can hide or display the Canvas pane as shown in Figure 1-10.

Figure 1-10. *The Editor Options icon lets you toggle between displaying and hiding the Canvas pane*

The Canvas pane serves two purposes. First, it lets you see exactly what your user interface looks like on a simulated iOS device. Besides letting you switch between different simulated iOS devices (such as between different iPhone or iPad models), the Canvas pane also lets you select different settings such as light or dark mode and dynamic type. Changing iOS settings lets you see how your user interface might look under different appearance options.

Switching Between iOS Devices

The Canvas pane emulates a single iOS device such as an iPhone 14 Pro or an iPad Mini. That way you can see how your user interface adapts to the screen sizes of different iOS devices. To make the Canvas pane emulate a different iOS device, follow these steps:

1. Click the name of the currently displayed iOS device at the top of the Xcode window. A list of different iOS devices appears as shown in Figure 1-11.

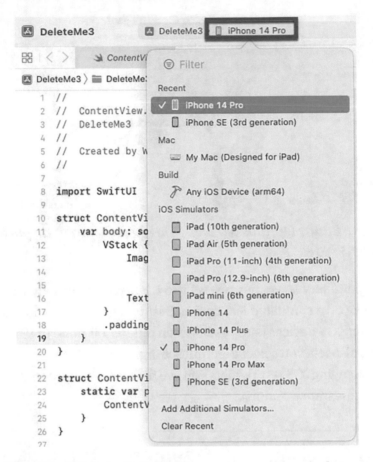

Figure 1-11. *The list of iOS devices the Canvas pane can emulate*

2. Click the iOS device you want to appear in the Canvas pane.

Xcode offers a second way to change the iOS device emulation in the Canvas pane by using the Inspector pane. Follow these steps:

1. Move the cursor in ContentView() inside the ContentView_ Previews: PreviewProvider structure. The Inspector pane appears.

2. Click the Device popup menu and choose an iOS device to appear in the Canvas pane as shown in Figure 1-12.

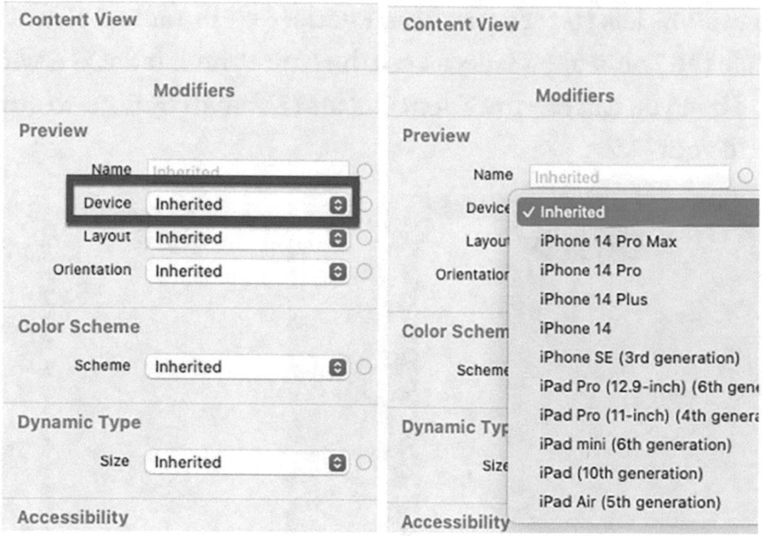

Content View	Content View
Modifiers	Modifiers
Preview	Preview

Figure 1-12. *The Device popup menu can select iOS devices in the Inspector pane*

After you choose a different iOS device for the Canvas pane, you can change the magnification of the Canvas pane by clicking different icons that appear in the bottom-right corner of the Canvas pane as shown in Figure 1-13:

- Zoom Out – Shrinks the size of the iOS device

- Zoom to 100% – Displays the iOS device in its actual size (may cut off parts of the iOS device, especially when emulating an iPad or larger iPhone model)

- Zoom to Fit – Makes the entire iOS device visible

- Zoom In – Expands the size of the iOS device

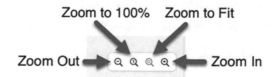

Figure 1-13. *The Zoom icons let you change the magnification of the Canvas pane*

The Zoom to 100% lets you see your user interface on the actual size of the emulated iOS device, while the Zoom to Fit lets you see the entire emulated iOS device as shown in Figure 1-14. Then you can use the Zoom Out and Zoom In options to adjust the size of the iOS device to your liking.

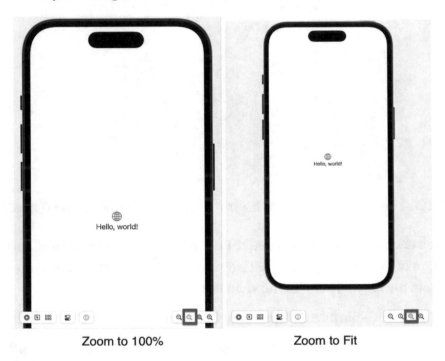

Zoom to 100%   Zoom to Fit

Figure 1-14. *Comparing Zoom to 100% and Zoom to Fit*

Changing the iOS Device Emulation Appearance

Once you've selected an iOS device to emulate in the Canvas pane, you can customize three additional ways to change the appearance of your user interface:

- Color Scheme – Displays either light or dark mode

- Orientation – Displays either portrait or landscape mode

- Dynamic Type – Changes the size of text

To change the appearance of the iOS device emulation in the Canvas pane, follow these steps:

1. Click the Device Settings icon near the bottom of the Canvas pane. A popup window appears as shown in Figure 1-15.

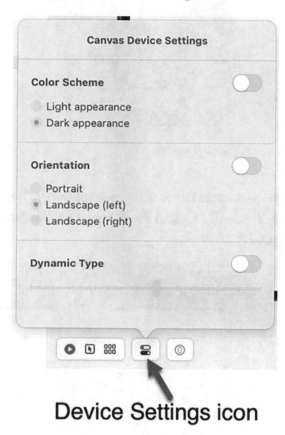

Device Settings icon

Figure 1-15. *The Device Settings window*

2. Click the on/off switch to the right of the setting you want to change such as Color Scheme or Orientation.

3. Click an option to change the iOS device appearance, or drag the slider to change the size of text under the Dynamic Type option.

If you want to compare different options side by side, follow these steps:

1. Click the Variants icon at the bottom of the Canvas pane. A popup menu appears as shown in Figure 1-16.

Variants icon

Figure 1-16. *The Variants popup menu*

2. Choose an option such as Color Scheme Variants or Dynamic Type Variants. Xcode displays all the different options at once as shown in Figure 1-17.

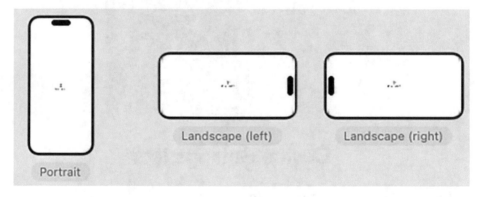

Figure 1-17. *The Orientation Variants displayed*

3. Click the Live icon to view the iOS device back in the Canvas pane again as shown in Figure 1-18.

Live icon

Figure 1-18. *The Live icon*

Selecting User Interface Objects

Once you've placed objects on the user interface, you can only select them by moving the cursor in the Swift code for that object. If you would rather click objects on the user interface using the mouse, you must click the Selectable icon near the bottom of the Canvas pane as shown in Figure 1-19.

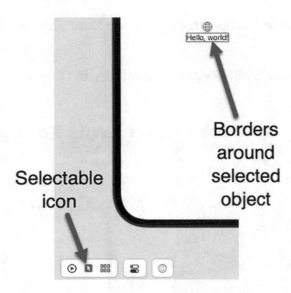

Figure 1-19. *The Selectable icon*

Once you click the Selectable icon and click an object on the user interface, blue borders appear around that object. These blue borders let you see the size of that object. This can be handy for seeing how large an object's background appears if you add a background color.

The Live icon (see Figure 1-18) lets you interact with your user interface to test your app. The Selectable icon makes it easy to edit your user interface.

Manipulating the Xcode Panes

The four Xcode panes (Navigator, Editor, Canvas, and Inspector) serve different purposes. The Navigator pane displays information about your project such as the names of all the files that make up that project. The Editor pane is where you can write and edit Swift code. The Canvas pane is where you can see and test the user interface defined by your Swift code. The Inspector pane displays information about the currently selected object.

You can resize any of the panes by moving the mouse pointer over the pane border and dragging the mouse left or right. If you want, you can toggle between hiding and displaying the Navigator and the Inspector pane. That way you can see more of the Editor and Canvas panes.

To hide/display the Navigator or Inspector pane, you have two options as shown in Figure 1-20:

- Choose View ➤ Navigators/Inspectors ➤ Hide/Show Navigator/ Inspector.

- Click the Show/Hide Navigator/Inspector pane icons.

Figure 1-20. *Hiding or showing the Navigator and Inspector panes*

The Navigator pane lets you select options to display in the Editor pane. The Inspector pane lets you select user interface items to choose different ways to modify them as shown in Figure 1-21.

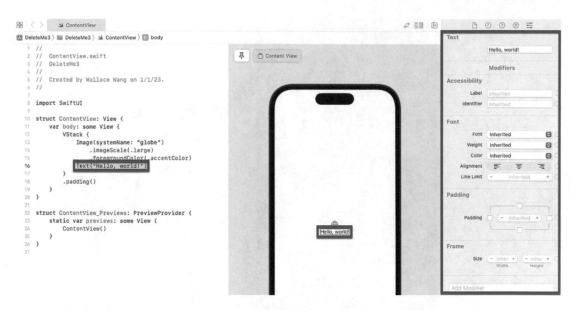

Figure 1-21. *The Inspector pane lists different ways to modify a selected item*

To see how the Inspector pane works, follow these steps:

1. Create a new iOS App project and then click the ContentView file in the Navigator pane. The Editor pane displays the contents of the ContentView file.

2. Move the cursor in the Text("Hello, world!") line.

3. Click the Attributes Inspector icon in the Inspector pane as shown in Figure 1-22. The Inspector pane displays additional ways to modify the currently selected item.

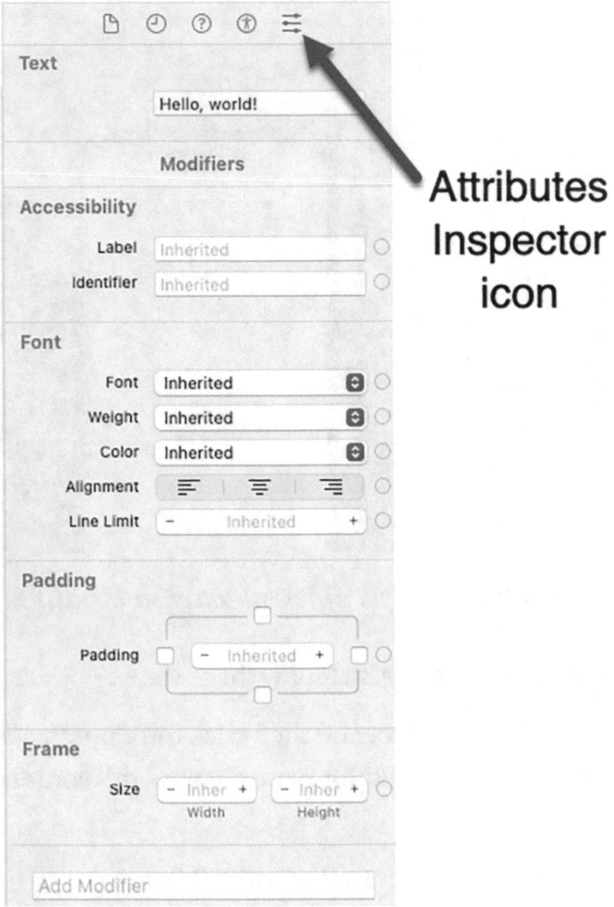

Figure 1-22. *The Attributes Inspector icon lets you view additional ways to modify an item in the Inspector pane*

As you can see, Xcode's panes show different information about a project. The Navigator pane (on the far left) lets you see an overview of your project. Clicking specific items in the Navigator pane displays that item in the Editor pane. The Inspector pane (on the far right) shows additional information about something selected in the Editor pane. The Canvas pane lets you preview the appearance of your user interface.

If you explore Xcode, you'll see dozens of features, but it's not necessary to understand everything at once to start using Xcode. Just focus on using only those features you need and feel free to ignore the rest until you need them.

Summary

Creating iOS apps involves more than just writing code. To help your app access hardware features of different iOS devices, you can use Apple's software frameworks that provide access to the camera or to the address book of an iOS device. The most important framework that all SwiftUI projects use is the SwiftUI framework. By combining your code with Apple's existing software frameworks, you can focus on writing code to make your app work and use Apple's software frameworks to help you perform common functions found on most iOS devices.

Besides writing code, every iOS app also needs a user interface. To create user interfaces, use SwiftUI. Since SwiftUI makes it easy to create user interfaces that adapt to different devices, SwiftUI is fast becoming the preferred way to design user interfaces for apps on all of Apple's platforms (macOS, iOS, iPadOS, watchOS, and tvOS).

The main tool for creating iOS apps is Apple's free Xcode program, which lets you create projects, organize the separate files of a project, and view and edit the contents of each file. Xcode lets you design, edit, and test your app all in a single program. Although Xcode offers dozens of features, you only need to use a handful of them to start creating iOS apps of your own.

Learning iOS programming involves learning how to write commands using the Swift programming language, learning how to find and use Apple's various software frameworks, learning how to design user interfaces in SwiftUI, and learning how to use Xcode. While this might seem like a lot, this book will take you through each step of the way so you'll feel comfortable using Xcode and creating your own iOS apps in the near future.

CHAPTER 2

Designing User Interfaces with SwiftUI

Every app needs a user interface. The basic idea behind SwiftUI is to create a user interface using building blocks known as "views." A view displays a single item on the user interface such as text, an image, or a button as shown in Figure 2-1.

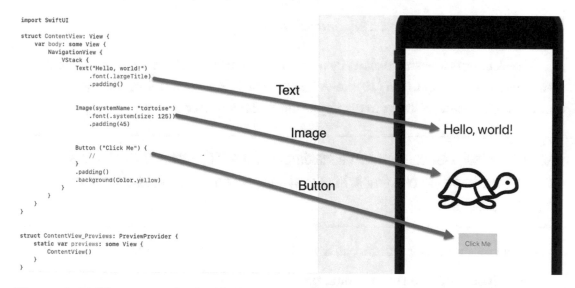

Figure 2-1. *The parts of a SwiftUI user interface*

One limitation of SwiftUI is that it can only display a single view on the screen at a time. To get around this limitation, SwiftUI offers something called "stacks." A stack is considered a single view but lets you combine or stack up to ten additional views. By creating a stack, you can display more than one view on the screen. Stacks can even hold other stacks, essentially letting you display as many views as you want on a single screen.

© Wallace Wang 2023
W. Wang, *Beginning iPhone Development with SwiftUI*, https://doi.org/10.1007/978-1-4842-9541-0_2

There are three types of stacks as shown in Figure 2-2:

- VStack – Vertical stacks that arrange views above and below another view

- HStack – Horizontal stacks that arrange views side by side

- ZStack – A stack that overlays views directly over each other

One
Two
Three

One Two Three

TOnaee

```
VStack {
    Text("One")
    Text("Two")
    Text("Three")
}
```

```
HStack {
    Text("One")
    Text("Two")
    Text("Three")
}
```

```
ZStack {
    Text("One")
    Text("Two")
    Text("Three")
}
```

Figure 2-2. *Vertical, horizontal, and ZStacks*

A stack counts as a single view. By using horizontal (HStack) or vertical (VStack) stacks, you can add up to ten (10) views inside a stack. For greater flexibility, you can embed stacks inside of stacks to display as many views as necessary.

Note   A stack can only contain a maximum of ten (10) views. If you try to store 11 or more views inside of a stack, Xcode will display an error message and refuse to run your program.

When creating a user interface in SwiftUI, you have three options:

- Type Swift code in the Editor pane.

- Drag and drop a view (such as a button) into your Swift code in the Editor pane.

- Drag and drop a view (such as a button) into the Canvas pane.

Typing Swift code in the Editor pane to design a user interface is the fastest and most flexible method, but takes time and requires familiarity with different options. To make typing Swift code to define user interface views easier, Xcode displays a popup menu of options when it recognizes what you're trying to type. By choosing an option and pressing Return, you can create a user interface view quickly as shown in Figure 2-3.

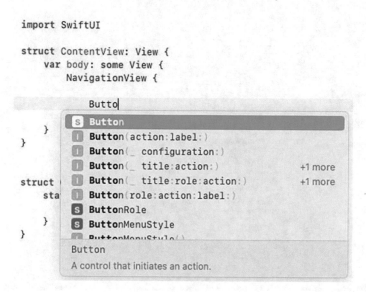

Figure 2-3. *As you type Swift code to define a user interface view, Xcode displays a menu of options*

If you're not familiar with your options for designing a user interface, it's easier to use the Library window, which lists all possible user interface views you can use as shown in Figure 2-4.

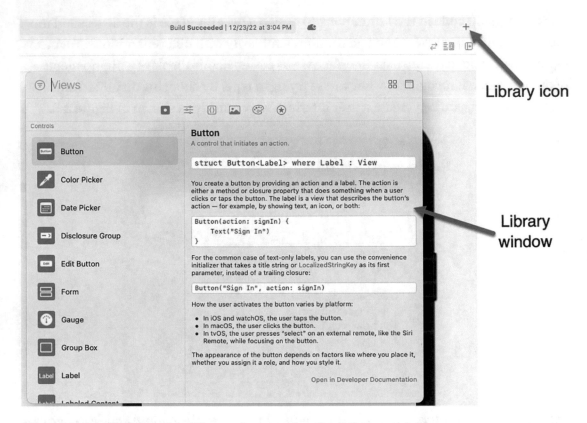

Figure 2-4. *Clicking the Library icon opens the Library window*

Once you open the Library window, you can either

- Drag and drop a user interface view from the Library window into the Editor pane as shown in Figure 2-5.

- Click the Selectable icon and then drag and drop a user interface view onto the simulated iOS device user interface in the Canvas pane as shown in Figure 2-6.

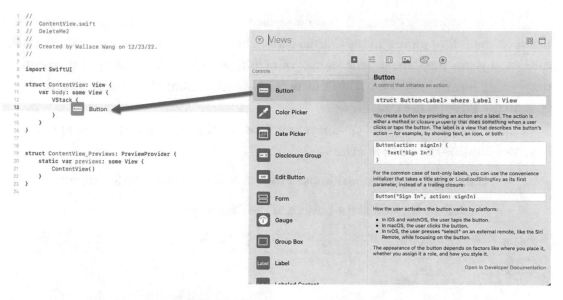

Figure 2-5. *Drag and drop a user interface view into the Editor pane*

Figure 2-6. *Drag and drop a user interface view into the Canvas pane*

No matter how you change the user interface, Xcode keeps all changes synchronized between the Editor pane and the Canvas pane. That means when you type Swift code in the Editor pane, the Canvas pane shows your changes right away. When you drag and drop a user interface view into the Canvas pane, Xcode automatically adds that Swift code in the Editor pane right away.

The Canvas pane displays your user interface, but if you want to test your app, you have two choices as shown in Figure 2-7:

- Click the Run button or choose Product ➤ Run to open the Simulator.

- Click the Live icon at the bottom of the Canvas pane.

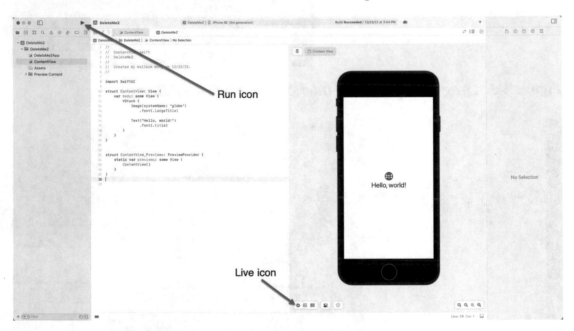

Figure 2-7. *The Run button and the Live Preview icon*

To see how SwiftUI works to create a simple user interface that can respond to the user, follow these steps:

1. Create a new iOS App project, make sure the interface is SwiftUI, and give it a descriptive name (such as SwiftExample).

2. Click the ContentView file in the Navigator pane. The Editor pane displays the contents of the ContentView file.

3. Choose Editor ➤ Canvas. (Skip this step if a check mark already appears in front of the Canvas option.) This opens the canvas so you can preview your user interface.

4. Delete the text "Hello, world!" in the Text command and type the following so the ContentView structure looks like this:

```
struct ContentView: View {
    @State private var message = true
    var body: some View {
        VStack {
            Toggle(isOn: $message) {
                Text("Toggle message on/off")
            }

            if message {
                Text ("Here's a secret message!")
            }
        }
    }
}
```

The preceding Swift code displays a toggle switch on the screen, but you won't be able to see it work unless you run your app in the Simulator (which mimics an iOS device such as an iPhone or iPad) or test it by clicking the Live icon. In most cases, the Live icon offers a faster way to view and test your user interface in the Canvas pane.

5. Click the Live icon to turn on Live Preview. As you click the toggle, notice that the message appears and disappears as shown in Figure 2-8.

Figure 2-8. *Live Preview lets you interact with the user interface in the Canvas pane*

6. Click the Live icon again to turn off Live Preview.

Repeat the preceding steps except click the Run button to open the Simulator. Testing your app in either the Simulator or the Canvas pane is identical. The main difference is that the Canvas pane is usually much faster to use.

Now let's go over this project so you get a rough idea how it works. First, it declares a special State variable called "message," which is initially set to true. Next, the ContentView structure defines a single view as a VStack. That means anything inside this VStack will appear stacked on top of each other.

The first view inside the VStack is a Toggle, which uses a Text view to display the following text to the left of the toggle: "Toggle message on/off". When the Toggle is on, the "message" State variable gets changed to hold a true value. When the Toggle is off, the "message" State variable gets changed to store a false value.

Underneath the Toggle, an if statement appears. If the "message" State variable is true, then it shows a Text view that displays "Here's a secret message!" If the "message" State variable is false, then the Text view does not appear at all.

Modifying the User Interface with the Inspector Pane

Creating a user interface in SwiftUI typically involves two steps. First, you arrange how you want the various user interface views to appear on the screen. Next, you need to customize each user interface view by changing its size, color, or position.

To customize user interface views, you add modifiers. Xcode gives you two ways to add modifiers:

- Type modifiers directly in the Editor pane.

- Click the view you want to modify (either in the Editor pane or after clicking the Selectable icon and then clicking the view in the Canvas pane). Then select a modifier from the Inspector pane as shown in Figure 2-9.

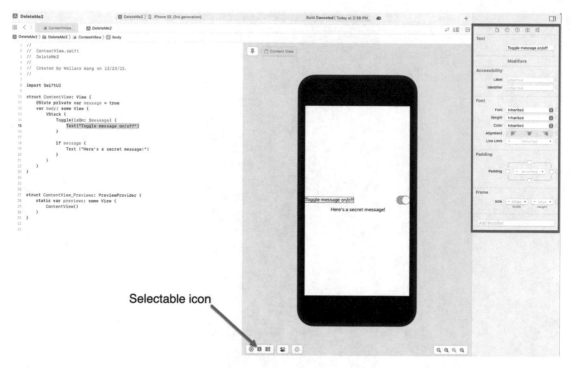

Figure 2-9. *The Inspector pane displays different ways to modify a user interface view*

Typing modifiers directly into the Editor pane requires knowing the names of the modifiers you want to use. As you get more experienced, typing modifiers directly into your Swift code will be fast. However, when you're first getting started, you may not know which modifiers are even available. That's when you might prefer using the Inspector pane.

First, select the user interface view you want to modify. You can do this by moving the cursor into the Swift code that defines that user interface view or by clicking the Selectable icon and then clicking a user interface view in the Canvas pane. When you select a user interface view, the Inspector pane displays modifiers for that particular view.

The Inspector pane displays the most commonly used modifiers such as letting you choose the font, alignment, or color for text. By clicking the Add Modifier button near the bottom of the Inspector pane, you can view a list of additional modifiers as shown in Figure 2-10.

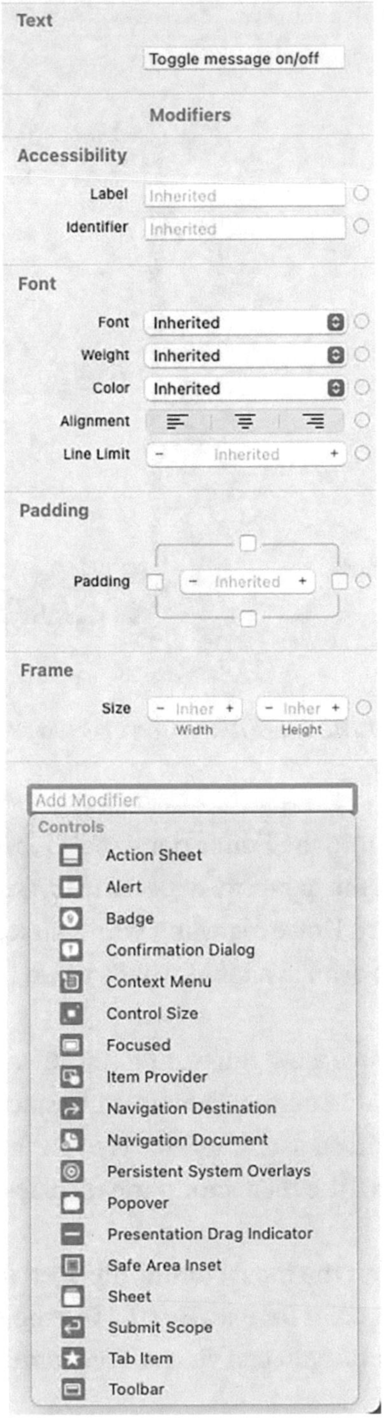

Figure 2-10. *The Add Modifier button displays a list of additional modifiers you can use*

When you see a modifier you want to use from the Add Modifier list, click that modifier. Xcode displays that modifier in the Inspector pane. If you no longer want to see any modifiers you may have added to the Inspector pane, click the Delete button in the upper-right corner of that modifier as shown in Figure 2-11.

Accent Color	Delete
	Blue ⊕

Add Modifier

Figure 2-11. *A Delete button appears to remove modifiers you have added to the Inspector pane*

Keep in mind that the order that you apply modifiers can make a difference. Consider the following Text view with two modifiers, a background and a padding:

```
Text ("Here's a secret message!")
      .background(Color.yellow)
      .padding()
```

This adds a background color of yellow to the Text view and then adds padding (space) around that Text view. Suppose you switched these modifiers around like this:

```
Text ("Here's a secret message!")
      .padding()
      .background(Color.yellow)
```

This order adds padding (space) around the Text view first and then colors the background. Because the background now includes the added space, the background color fills the space around the Text view as well, as shown in Figure 2-12.

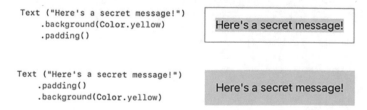

Figure 2-12. *The order of modifiers can make a difference*

No matter which method you use to add modifiers, Xcode keeps everything synchronized. So if you type modifiers in the Editor pane, your changes automatically appear in the Inspector pane. Likewise, if you choose a modifier in the Inspector pane, Xcode automatically adds that modifier to your Swift code in the Editor pane.

To see how to change the appearance of a user interface item, follow these steps:

1. Make sure your SwiftExample project from the previous section is loaded in Xcode. The ContentView file should contain a Toggle and a Text view that appears underneath the Toggle.

2. Click the Selectable icon near the bottom of the Canvas pane. This will let you select views by clicking them directly in the Canvas pane.

3. Click the Toggle in the Canvas pane or move the cursor in the Toggle in the Editor pane. Xcode displays the Inspector pane on the right side of the Xcode window, which shows you the modifiers you can choose to change the appearance of the Toggle.

4. Click the Text view in the Canvas pane that displays "Here's a secret message!" or move the cursor into the Text view in the Editor pane. Notice that the Inspector pane displays modifiers to change the appearance of the Text view.

5. Click the Font popup menu. A list of different font options appears as shown in Figure 2-13.

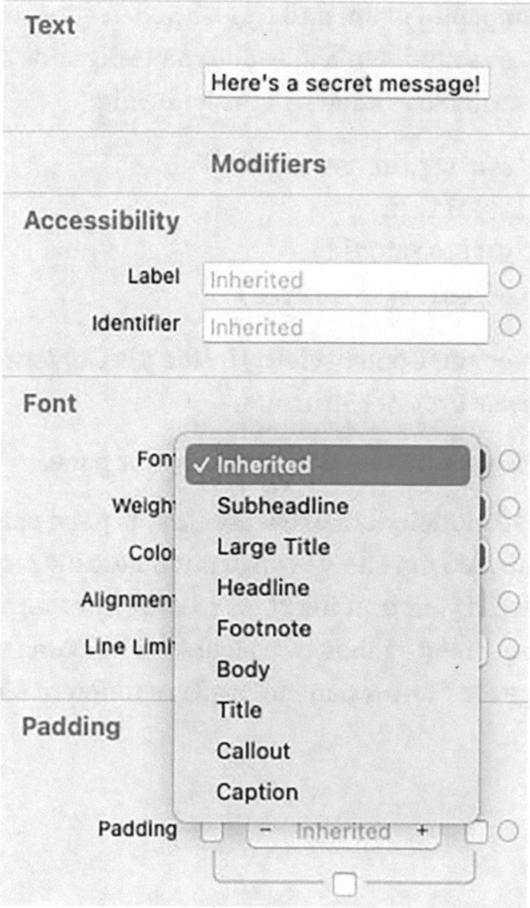

Figure 2-13. *The Font popup menu displays different font options*

6. Choose Large Title. Notice that Xcode automatically adds the
    .font(.largeTitle) command in the ContentView file as shown in
    the following:

```
Text ("Here's a secret message!")
    .font(.largeTitle)
```

7. Click the Weight popup menu and choose Semibold.

8. Click the Color popup menu and choose Red. Notice that each time you choose a modifier, Xcode automatically adds the Swift code to your .swift file as shown in the following:

```
Text ("Here's a secret message!")
    .font(.largeTitle)
    .fontWeight(.semibold)
    .foregroundColor(Color.red)
```

9. Move the cursor into ContentView() inside the ContentView_ Previews: PreviewProvider structure.

10. Click the Device popup menu in the Inspector pane.

11. Choose an iPad model. Notice that the Canvas pane changes to mimic an iPad. Also note how SwiftUI automatically modifies the appearance of your user interface so it appears correctly on a different-size screen as shown in Figure 2-14. (Xcode may take time to change the Canvas pane to display a different iOS device, so be patient.)

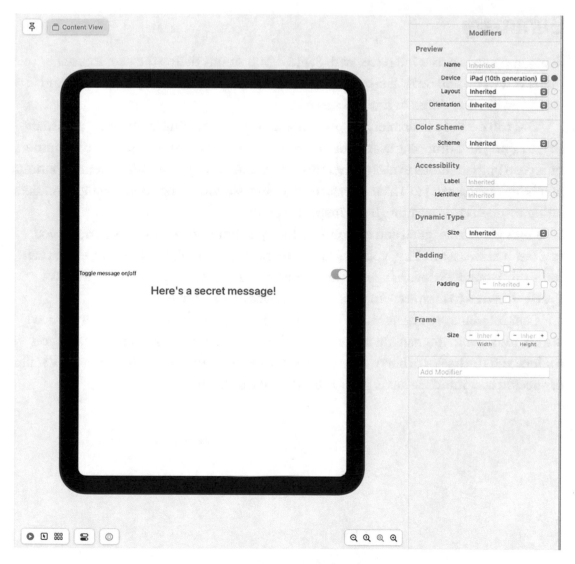

Figure 2-14. *SwiftUI adapts user interfaces to different-size screens*

12. Click the Device popup menu again and choose an iPhone model such as iPhone 11. The canvas now changes to mimic your chosen iPhone model.

The basic idea behind SwiftUI is to let you design your user interface and let Xcode automatically adjust its appearance for different iOS screen sizes. Instead of writing a lot of Swift code to design your user interface, SwiftUI lets you write a minimal amount of Swift code to design your user interface so you can focus your time writing Swift code to make your app do something unique.

Summary

Every app needs a user interface. With SwiftUI, you simply define the user interface items you want, and SwiftUI takes care of making sure your user interface works and looks correctly on different-size iOS screens.

You can design a user interface programmatically (by writing Swift code) or visually (by dragging and dropping user interface items from the Library window). Programmers often use both methods to design their user interface. Once you've added items (buttons, labels, text fields, etc.) to a user interface, you can customize those items using modifiers either through code or through the Inspector pane.

Once you've designed and customized the appearance of your user interface, you can test it in two ways. First, you can run your app in the Simulator program, which can mimic different iOS devices such as an iPhone or iPad. Second, you can use the Live Preview feature to interact with your user interface in the Canvas pane.

User interfaces represent what users see, so it's important that your user interface always looks good no matter what type of iOS device the user runs it on. Now that you understand the basics of how a user interface works, it's time to start learning the details of specific user interface items such as buttons, pickers, and sliders.

CHAPTER 3

Placing Views on the User Interface

When you place a single view on a user interface, SwiftUI centers it in the middle of the screen whether that screen is a small iPhone screen or a much larger iPad screen. As you add more views to your user interface, SwiftUI simply displays those views on top of each other or side by side, depending on whether you arrange them in a vertical or horizontal stack. However, the more views you add to a user interface, the more crowded neighboring views can appear. To solve this problem, SwiftUI offers several ways to place views on the user interface:

- Use the padding modifier.

- Define spacing within a stack.

- Use a spacer between views.

- Define an offset or position location.

You can use one or more of these different methods to arrange views on the user interface so they appear exactly where you want them. Best of all, these positioning methods work on all user interface views in SwiftUI.

Using the Padding Modifier

The padding modifier adds space around a user interface view. By default, the padding modifier adds space around the top, bottom, leading (left), and trailing (right) sides of a view. To use the padding modifier, just add the following after any view:

```
.padding()
```

© Wallace Wang 2023

W. Wang, *Beginning iPhone Development with SwiftUI*, https://doi.org/10.1007/978-1-4842-9541-0_3

Padding serves two purposes. First, it adds space around a view, which changes the background to which you can add color to make the view larger and easier to see. Second, the padding modifier pushes neighboring views further away to make neighboring views easier to see and eliminate crowding.

The simplest padding modifier adds 16 points of spacing on all four sides of a view. If you add a number, you can define the precise spacing you want such as .padding(45) or .padding (3) as shown in Figure 3-1.

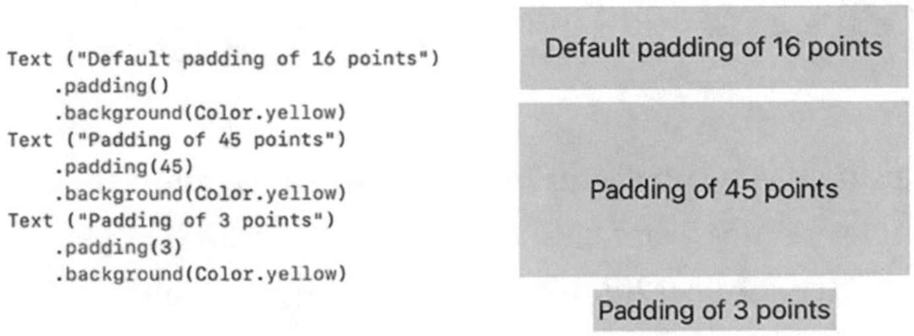

Figure 3-1. *Defining different spacing for the padding modifier*

Notice that the padding modifier adds space around all sides. If you want, you can define spacing to occur in one or more specific areas as shown in Figure 3-2:

- .top

- .bottom

- .vertical (top and bottom)

- .leading (left)

- .trailing (right)

- .horizontal (trailing and leading)

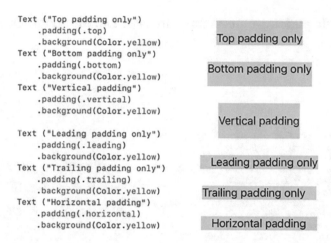

Figure 3-2. *Defining padding around certain areas*

If you don't add a specific value, SwiftUI uses the default 16-point spacing. To define both an area to add padding and a specific spacing, you must define the area to add padding first, followed by a specific value, such as

```
.padding(.top, 30)
```

If you want to add spacing to two or three areas, you can define those areas in square brackets followed by an optional spacing value like this:

```
.padding([.top, .leading])
   .padding([.top, .leading] , 30)
```

This lets you define two areas to add spacing as shown in Figure 3-3.

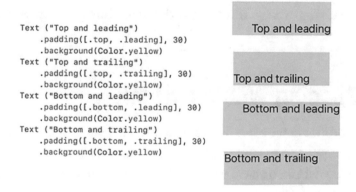

Figure 3-3. *Defining padding around two areas*

You can also add padding around three areas with an optional spacing value as shown in Figure 3-4.

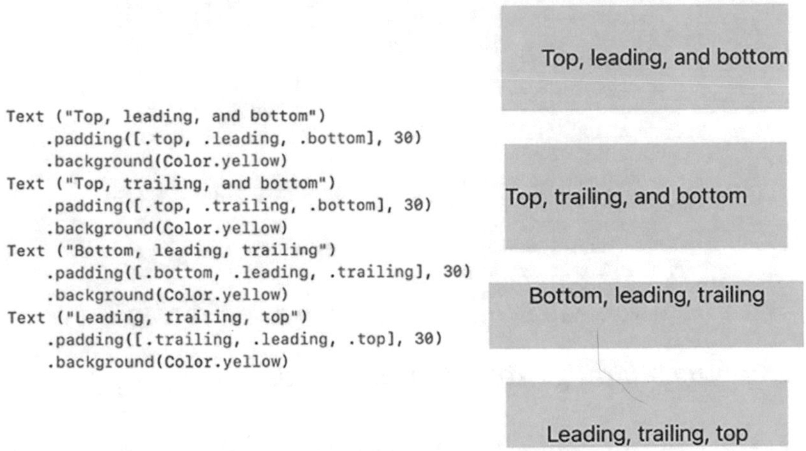
Text ("Top, leading, and bottom")
.padding([.top, .leading, .bottom], 30)
.background(Color.yellow)
Text ("Top, trailing, and bottom")
.padding([.top, .trailing, .bottom], 30)
.background(Color.yellow)
Text ("Bottom, leading, trailing")
.padding([.bottom, .leading, .trailing], 30)
.background(Color.yellow)
Text ("Leading, trailing, top")
.padding([.trailing, .leading, .top], 30)
.background(Color.yellow)
Top, leading, and bottom
Top, trailing, and bottom
Bottom, leading, trailing
Leading, trailing, top

Figure 3-4. *Defining padding around three areas*

Rather than use a fixed numeric value to define a padding's spacing, you can also use a variable that represents a numeric value like this:

```
var distanceSize = 15.0
```

Then you can use this CGFloat variable to define a padding size like this:

```
.padding(CGFloat(distanceSize))
```

Notice that the .padding modifier specifically converts any numeric value into a CGFloat data type. By using a numeric variable to define spacing within a .padding modifier, code can change the value of this variable to change the .padding modifier's spacing.

Defining Spacing Within a Stack

The .padding() modifier can be handy to space different views apart. Without padding, multiple views can appear squashed and crowded together within a stack. By adding padding to each view within a stack, you can separate them so each view is easier to see as shown in Figure 3-5.

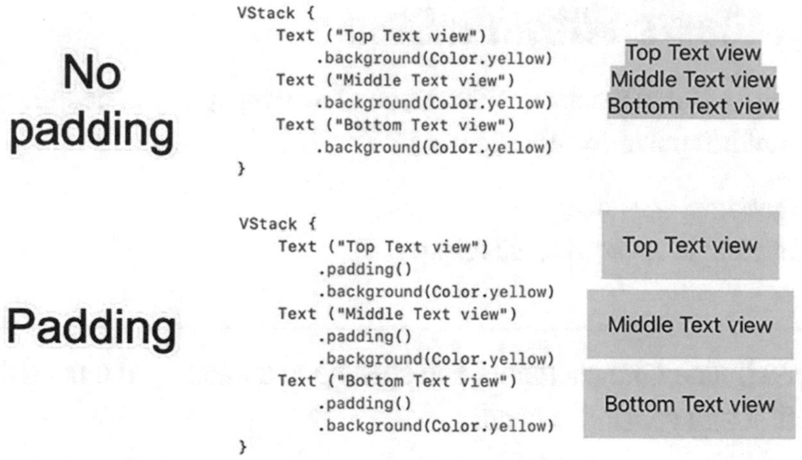

```
VStack {
    Text ("Top Text view")
        .background(Color.yellow)
    Text ("Middle Text view")
        .background(Color.yellow)
    Text ("Bottom Text view")
        .background(Color.yellow)
}
```

No padding

Top Text view
Middle Text view
Bottom Text view

```
VStack {
    Text ("Top Text view")
        .padding()
        .background(Color.yellow)
    Text ("Middle Text view")
        .padding()
        .background(Color.yellow)
    Text ("Bottom Text view")
        .padding()
        .background(Color.yellow)
}
```

Padding

Top Text view

Middle Text view

Bottom Text view

Figure 3-5. *Padding separates views within a stack*

While padding can make each view easier to see, you may want more control over the spacing between views within a stack. To do that, you can define a spacing value when you define a stack such as

```
VStack (spacing: 40) {

}
```

Within a stack, spacing pushes views apart a fixed distance as shown in Figure 3-6.

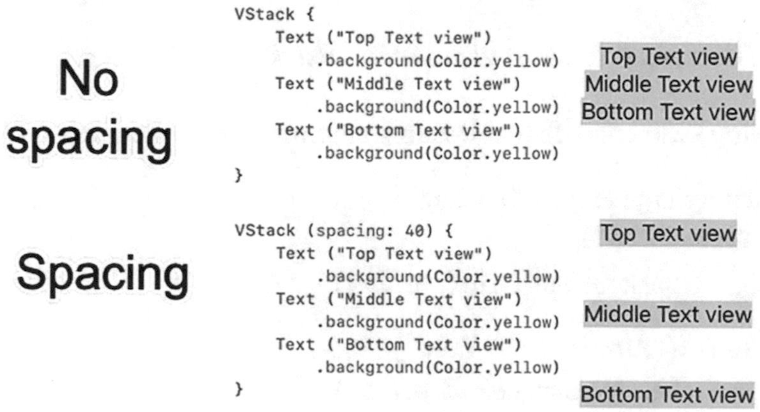

```
VStack {
    Text ("Top Text view")
        .background(Color.yellow)
    Text ("Middle Text view")
        .background(Color.yellow)
    Text ("Bottom Text view")
        .background(Color.yellow)
}
```

No spacing

Top Text view
Middle Text view
Bottom Text view

```
VStack (spacing: 40) {
    Text ("Top Text view")
        .background(Color.yellow)
    Text ("Middle Text view")
        .background(Color.yellow)
    Text ("Bottom Text view")
        .background(Color.yellow)
}
```

Spacing

Top Text view

Middle Text view

Bottom Text view

Figure 3-6. *Spacing creates a fixed distance between all views in a stack*

Aligning Views Within a Stack

When you create a stack (VStack or HStack), you have the option of defining alignment whether you define spacing or not such as

```
VStack (alignment: .leading)
VStack (alignment: .leading, spacing: 24)
```

Note   If you define both alignment and spacing in a stack, you must define alignment first and spacing second.

With VStacks, you have three ways to align views as shown in Figure 3-7:

- .leading (left)

- .center (default setting if no other alignment options are chosen)

- .trailing (right)

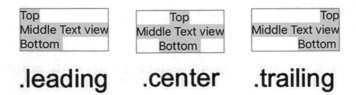

.leading   .center   .trailing

Figure 3-7. *Three ways to align views in a VStack*

The following Swift code defines .leading alignment for a VStack:

```
VStack (alignment: .leading){
    Text ("Top")
        .background(Color.yellow)

    Text ("Middle Text View")
        .background(Color.yellow)

    Text ("Bottom")
        .background(Color.yellow)
}
```

With HStacks, you have five different ways to align views as shown in Figure 3-8:

- .top

- .bottom

- .center (default setting if no other alignment options are chosen)

- .firstTextBaseline

- .lastTextBaseline

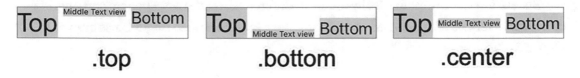

Figure 3-8. *Aligning views in an HStack*

The following Swift code defines .bottom alignment for an HStack:

```
HStack (alignment: .bottom){
    Text ("Top")
        .font(.system(size: 40))
        .background(Color.yellow)

    Text ("Middle Text View")
        .background(Color.yellow)

    Text ("Bottom")
        .font(.largeTitle)
        .background(Color.yellow)
}
```

The .top, .bottom, and .center alignment options work with all types of user interface views. However, if you're specifically working with Text views, SwiftUI offers two additional ways to align Text views based on the baseline. You can align text based on the first view (.firstTextBaseline) or the last view (.lastTextBaseline) as shown in Figure 3-9.

Figure 3-9. *Aligning text in an HStack*

Using Spacers

Using padding and spacing between views in a stack can be handy for arranging views on the user interface. For another way to position views on the user interface, you can also use spacers. A spacer acts like a spring that pushes two views as far apart as possible. A spacer appears in the Editor pane like this:

```
Spacer()
```

Because spacers automatically adapt to different screen sizes, spacers can align views to the edges of the screen no matter what that screen size might be as shown in Figure 3-10.

```
HStack {
    Text ("Left")
        .font(.system(size: 40))
        .background(Color.yellow)
    Spacer()
    Text ("Right")
        .font(.system(size: 40))
        .background(Color.yellow)
}
```

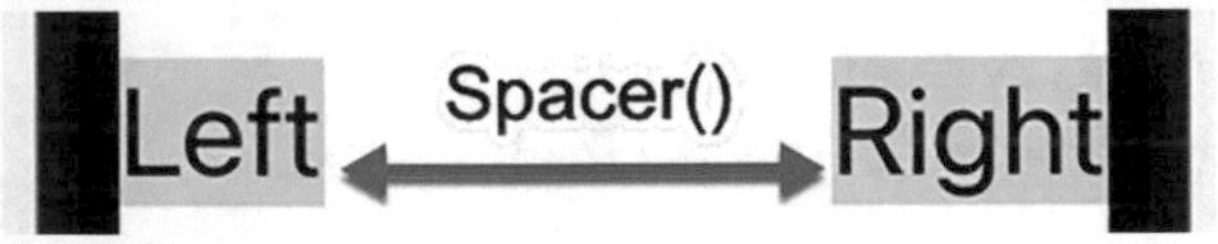

Figure 3-10. *Spacers push views as far apart as possible*

You can combine multiple spacers to push views further apart. For example, consider using a spacer before and after a view to separate them using this Swift code:

```
struct ContentView: View {
    var body: some View {
        VStack {
            Text ("Top")
                .font(.system(size: 40))
                .background(Color.yellow)
            Spacer()
            Text ("Middle")
                .font(.system(size: 40))
                .background(Color.yellow)
```

```
        Spacer()
        Text ("Bottom")
            .font(.system(size: 40))
            .background(Color.yellow)
      }
    }
}
```

The preceding code defines a vertical stack that contains three Text views. A spacer in between each Text view pushes them equally apart as shown in Figure 3-11.

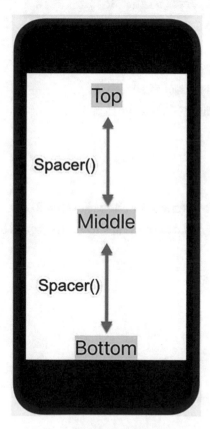

Figure 3-11. *Spacers separate three views equally apart*

If you combine spacers, multiple spacers push views further apart. If we add two spacers in between the Top and Middle views, those two spacers will push the Middle view further down as the following Swift code shows:

```
struct ContentView: View {
    var body: some View {
        VStack {
            Text ("Top")
                .font(.system(size: 40))
                .background(Color.yellow)
            Spacer()
            Spacer()
            Text ("Middle")
                .font(.system(size: 40))
                .background(Color.yellow)
            Spacer()
            Text ("Bottom")
                .font(.system(size: 40))
                .background(Color.yellow)
        }
    }
}
```

Because there are now two spacers in between the Top and Middle views, they push the Middle view further down the screen as shown in Figure 3-12.

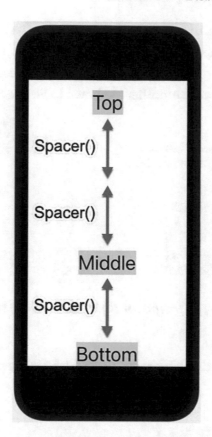

Figure 3-12. *Two spacers push the Middle view further down*

By using multiple spacers, you can adjust views on the user interface relative to the screen size. When the app runs on a larger screen, the spacers push the views further to the boundaries of the screen. When the app runs on a smaller screen, the spacers push the views a shorter distance.

Spacers automatically adjust their size based on screen size. However, you may want to define a minimum length for a spacer to keep it from shrinking too far. To define a minimum length, use the following code:

```
Spacer(minLength: 25.73)
```

Notice that you can define the minimum length as a decimal value (CGFloat) although you could use an integer value as well such as

```
Spacer(minLength: 25)
```

If you do not specify a minimum length, the spacer will simply grow or shrink based on the screen size that the app is running in. If you need to specify a fixed value for a spacer, you can use the .frame modifier. If you're using a spacer within a VStack, you can define a height within the frame modifier as shown in Figure 3-13.

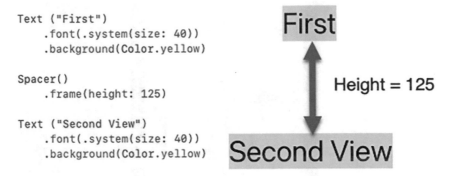

```
Text ("First")
    .font(.system(size: 40))
    .background(Color.yellow)

Spacer()
    .frame(height: 125)

Text ("Second View")
    .font(.system(size: 40))
    .background(Color.yellow)
```

Figure 3-13. *The height of a .frame modifier defines a fixed size for a spacer in a VStack*

When using a spacer in an HStack, define a width for the spacer instead as shown in Figure 3-14.

```
Text ("First")
    .font(.system(size: 40))
    .background(Color.yellow)

Spacer()
    .frame(width: 55)

Text ("Second View")
    .font(.system(size: 40))
    .background(Color.yellow)
```

Width = 55

First ⬌ Second View

Figure 3-14. *The width of a .frame modifier defines a fixed size for a spacer in an HStack*

Using the Offset and Position Modifiers

Spacers, padding, and alignment within a stack can alter the position of views on a user interface, but for another way to position views on the user interface, you can use the offset modifier as well. The offset modifier lets you specify a specific x and y value to move a view from where SwiftUI would normally place it.

In every iOS screen, the origin (0,0) appears in the upper-left corner. The greater the value of x, the further to the right horizontally. The greater the value of y, the further down vertically as shown in Figure 3-15.

Figure 3-15. *The origin and x,y direction on an iOS screen*

The following ZStack places two identical Text views on top of each other. Because both Text views appear in the exact same place, you cannot see both of them at the same time:

```
ZStack {
    Text ("Top")
        .font(.system(size: 40))
        .background(Color.yellow)

    Text ("Top")
        .font(.system(size: 40))
        .background(Color.yellow)
}
```

If we add an offset modifier to one of the Text views, the offset modifier will move the second Text view a fixed distance from where it would normally appear such as

```
ZStack {
    Text ("Top")
        .font(.system(size: 40))
        .background(Color.yellow)
```

```
        Text ("Top")
            .font(.system(size: 40))
            .background(Color.yellow)
            .offset(x: 75, y: 125)
    }
```

This offset pushes the second Text view 75 points to the right and 125 points down as shown in Figure 3-16.

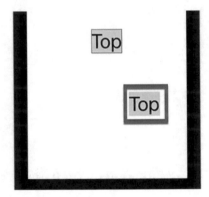

Figure 3-16. *The offset modifier moves a view away from where it would normally appear*

Positive x values move a view to the right, and negative x values move a view to the left. Likewise, positive y values move a view down, and negative values move a view up. Suppose we had an offset modifier as follows:

```
.offset(x: -75, y: -125)
```

This would move the second Text view up and to the left from where it would normally appear as shown in Figure 3-17.

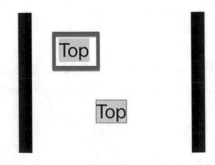

Figure 3-17. *Negative x and y values offset a view to the left and up*

The offset modifier lets you position a view based on where SwiftUI would normally place it. If you'd rather position a view based on the origin (the upper left-hand corner of the screen), use the position modifier instead.

Like the offset modifier, the position modifier needs an x and y value to define the center position of a view. The following Swift code places a Text view 225 to the right and 126 down as shown in Figure 3-18:

```
Text ("Top")
       .font(.system(size: 40))
       .background(Color.yellow)
       .position(x: 225, y: 127)
```

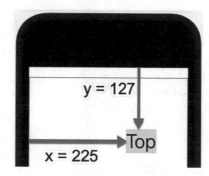

Figure 3-18. *Using the position modifier to place a view on the user interface*

Note   Be careful when using large x or y values with either the offset or position modifier. That's because large values may position a view perfectly on a large screen but position that same view off the edge on a smaller screen.

You can apply the offset and position modifiers to any views. Since stacks are views, you can apply the offset and position modifiers to stacks, which automatically shifts the position of every view inside the stack as well. Consider the following Swift code that applies the offset modifier to an entire VStack:

```
VStack {
    Text ("First")
           .font(.system(size: 40))
           .background(Color.yellow)
```

```
Text ("Second View")
        .font(.system(size: 40))
        .background(Color.yellow)
}.offset(x: 25, y: 125)
```

The preceding code shifts the entire VStack's contents (the two Text views) down and to the right from where they would normally appear as shown in Figure 3-19.

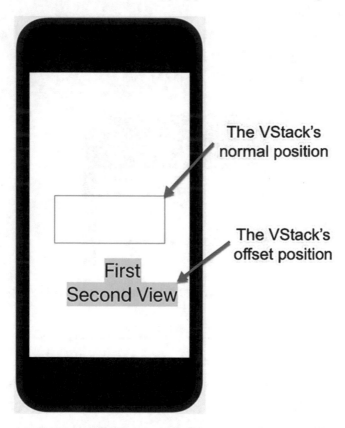

Figure 3-19. *The offset modifier moves an entire stack from where it would normally appear*

The offset modifier shifts the entire VStack from its normal position, but the position modifier places the VStack based on the origin (the upper left-hand corner of the screen). The following Swift code uses the exact same x and y values, but uses the position modifier on the VStack instead:

```
VStack {
    Text ("First")
        .font(.system(size: 40))
        .background(Color.yellow)

    Text ("Second View")
        .font(.system(size: 40))
        .background(Color.yellow)
}.position(x: 25, y: 125)
```

Notice that since the position modifier shifts the VStack from the origin, the x value isn't large enough, and the VStack's contents get cut off by the screen as shown in Figure 3-20.

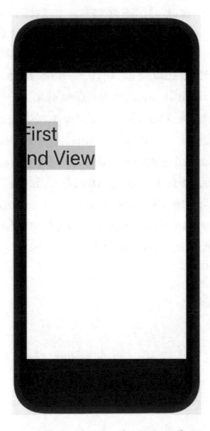

Figure 3-20. *The position modifier places the VStack in relation to the origin*

Summary

Designing a user interface in SwiftUI normally centers views in the middle of the screen. By using the padding modifier, you can increase the space around a view. The padding modifier can affect one, two, three, or all four sides of a view.

When you want to push views apart, use spacers, which act like springs that push views up to the edge of the screen, regardless of the screen's actual size. By using multiple spacers, you can push a view further. You can also define the minimum length that a spacer can shrink to make sure it doesn't shrink beyond a specific length.

Within vertical and horizontal stacks, you can define the spacing between all views within a stack. By using the offset modifier, you can shift a view from where it would normally appear. By using the position modifier, you can precisely place a view on the screen, based on the origin, which is the upper left-hand corner of an iOS screen.

The padding modifier, spacers, spacing within stacks, and the offset/position modifiers let you arrange the placement of views on your user interface. You can apply the padding, offset, and position modifiers on any view, including stacks. By modifying an entire stack, you can modify all views within that stack.

Since stack spacing, the offset modifier, and the position modifier can use fixed numeric values, make sure these values aren't too large where they might push views off the edge of the screen of smaller-size iOS devices. By using padding, spacers, and position and offset modifiers, you can design user interfaces that will look and work identically on different iOS devices. That way you can focus more time on writing code to make your app do something useful and amazing and less time trying to make the user interface adapt to different-size screens and orientations.

CHAPTER 4

Working with Text

Every user interface needs to display information on the screen. While this information can appear in a variety of forms, one common type of information to display on the user interface involves text. If you want to display text on the user interface, you need to define a string to appear in a Text view such as

```
Text("Hello World")
```

For greater flexibility, you can store a string in a variable or constant and then use that variable or constant name in a Text view such as

```
let myString = "Displays a string variable"

Text(myString)
```

By using string variables, you can store different strings in the variable to make the Text view display new text. For more flexibility, a Text view can also display non-string data using string interpolation such as

```
let myString = 46

Text("This is my age = \(myString)")
```

String interpolation allows any non-string data to appear within a string. Best of all, string interpolation doesn't require converting data into a string, so it's a fast and simple way to display data in a Text view.

A Text view can display strings of any length. However, the length of a displayed string can vary depending on the screen size that the app runs in such as the larger iPad screen or the smaller iPhone screen. To customize how strings appear, SwiftUI lets you define the following:

© Wallace Wang 2023
W. Wang, *Beginning iPhone Development with SwiftUI*, https://doi.org/10.1007/978-1-4842-9541-0_4

- Line limits – Defines the maximum number of lines the Text view can display such as 2 or 4

- Truncation – Defines how to truncate or cut off strings if it's not possible to display the entire string

The line limit modifier lets you define the maximum number of lines to display. If you do not specify a line limit value, SwiftUI will display as many lines as possible. To define a line limit, add a lineLimit modifier in Swift code like this:

```
Text("This is my age \(myString). Since I am retired, I am now
    eligible for a pension and Social Security so I can spend the rest
    of my life relaxing and enjoying life without having to work for an
    income anymore.")
        .lineLimit(2)
```

Figure 4-1 shows two identical Text views, but the top Text view does not have a line limit. As a result, it displays all of its text. The bottom Text view has a line limit of 2, so it only shows the first two lines of text.

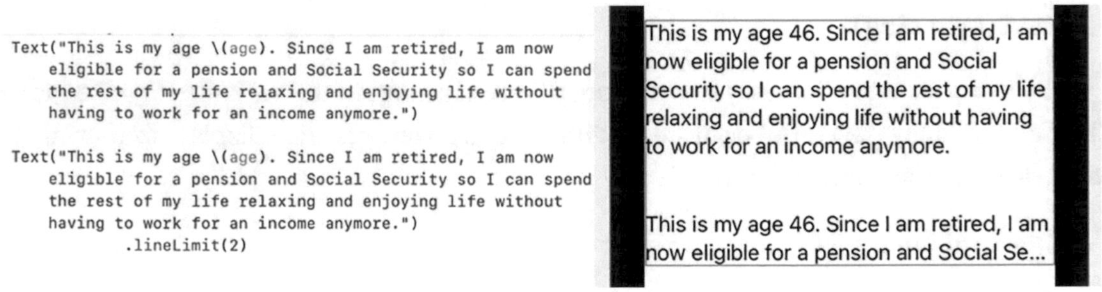

Figure 4-1. *The lineLimit modifier may cut off part of the text*

Rather than type Swift code to define a line limit, you can also click the Text view and open the Inspector. Then you can define a line limit in the Inspector pane as shown in Figure 4-2.

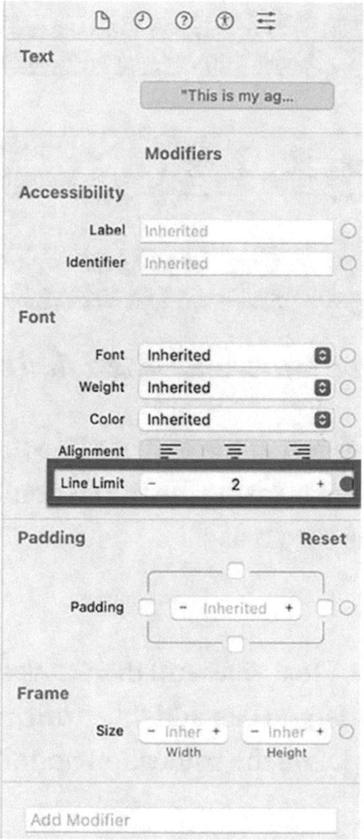

Figure 4-2. *Defining a line limit in the Inspector pane*

If you define a line limit (such as two lines) and your text exceeds that limit (such as displaying three or more lines), SwiftUI will cut off or truncate text. SwiftUI offers three ways to truncate text that exceeds its line limit as shown in Figure 4-3:

- .head – Truncates the beginning of the last line

- .middle – Truncates the middle of the last line

- .tail – Truncates the end of the last line

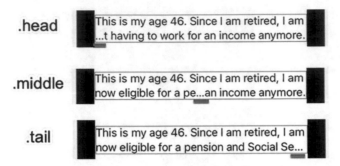

Figure 4-3. *Three different ways to truncate text that exceeds its line limit*

By default, SwiftUI truncates text at the end of a line (tail), but you can define the head or middle truncation option by using the truncationMode modifier with the lineLimit modifier on a Text View such as

```
.truncationMode(.middle)
```

If you move the cursor into a Text view and then click the Add Modifier button at the bottom of the Inspector pane, you can add the Truncation Mode modifier to the Inspector pane. Then you can define the truncation option in the Inspector pane as shown in Figure 4-4.

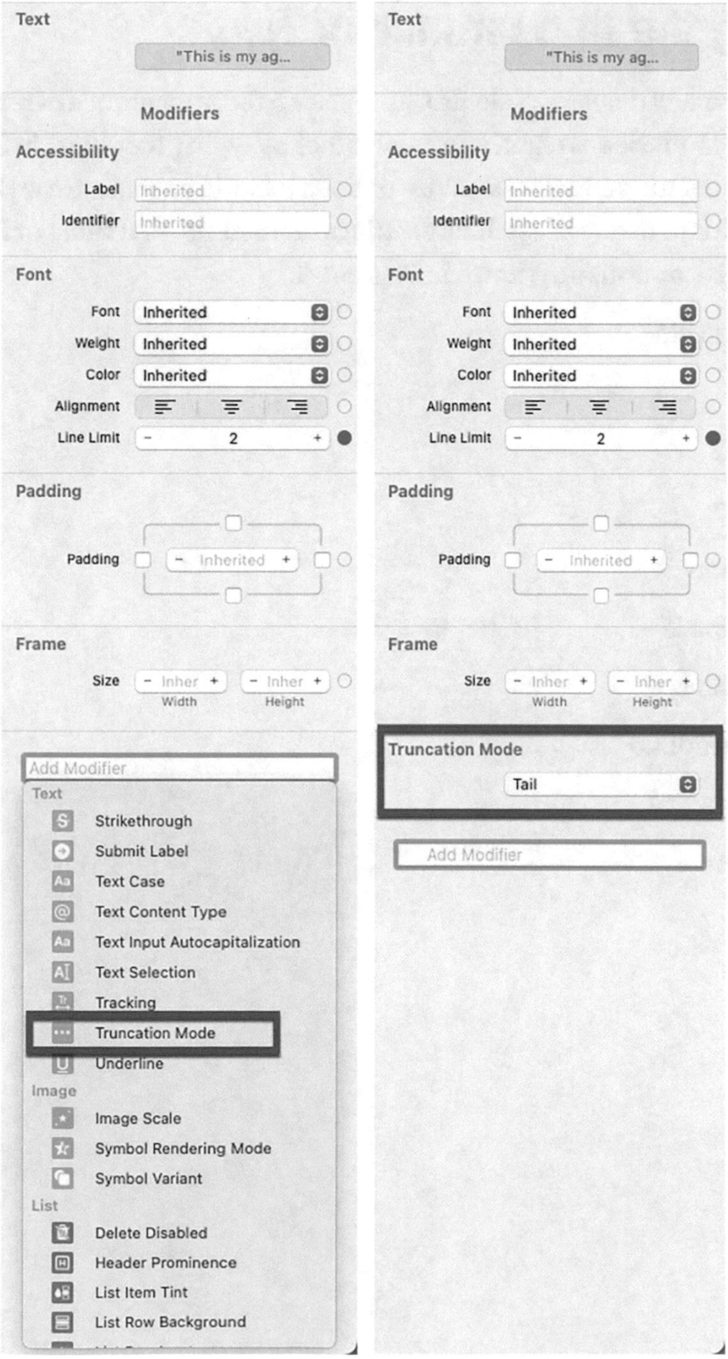

Figure 4-4. *Defining a truncation option in the Inspector pane*

Changing the Appearance of Text

A Text view normally displays plain text. To spice up the appearance of text, SwiftUI lets you define a font size, weight, and color either by typing modifiers in Swift code or through the Inspector pane. The font size options include specific text styles that can automatically adapt to any accessibility settings defined on an iPhone or iPad. The available font size options are shown in Figure 4-5:

- Large Title
- Title
- Title 2
- Title 3
- Caption
- Caption 2
- Headline
- Subheadline
- Callout
- Footnote
- Body

```
Text("Large Title")
    .font(.largeTitle)
Text("Title")
    .font(.title)
Text("Title 2")
    .font(.title2)
Text("Title 3")
    .font(.title3)
Text("Caption")
    .font(.caption)
Text("Caption 2")
    .font(.caption2)
Text("Headline")
    .font(.headline)
Text("Subheadline")
    .font(.subheadline)
Text("Callout")
    .font(.callout)
Text("Footnote")
    .font(.footnote)
Text("Body")
    .font(.body)
```

Figure 4-5. *Different font sizes for displaying text*

In case you want to choose a specific font for a Text view, you can do that using the custom font modifier like this:

```
.font(.custom("Courier", size: 36))
```

In the preceding code, you define the font family followed by the font size. Just keep in mind that Xcode may not support all fonts. If you just want to define a custom font size, you can omit the font name such as

```
.font(.custom("", size: 36))
```

Note   When you define custom fonts and font sizes, the Text view will not automatically resize text based on the user's iOS settings. For that reason, it's best to avoid custom fonts unless you absolutely need them.

In addition to the font size, you can also select a weight, which defines how thin or thick text can appear. The weight options include the following as shown in Figure 4-6:

- Heavy

- Semibold

- Bold

- Regular

- Thin

- Black

- Medium

- Light

- Ultra Light

```
Text("Heavy")
    .font(.largeTitle)
    .fontWeight(.heavy)
Text("Ultra Light")
    .font(.largeTitle)
    .fontWeight(.ultraLight)
Text("Medium")
    .font(.largeTitle)
    .fontWeight(.medium)
Text("Black")
    .font(.largeTitle)
    .fontWeight(.black)
Text("Regular")
    .font(.largeTitle)
    .fontWeight(.regular)
Text("Bold")
    .font(.largeTitle)
    .fontWeight(.bold)
Text("Light")
    .font(.largeTitle)
    .fontWeight(.light)
Text("Semibold")
    .font(.largeTitle)
    .fontWeight(.semibold)
Text("Thin")
    .font(.largeTitle)
    .fontWeight(.thin)
```

Figure 4-6. *Different weights for displaying text*

A third way to modify the appearance of text is to choose a color for text. You can type a color modifier in Swift code or choose a standard color from the Inspector pane such as Red, Green, or Orange as shown in Figure 4-7.

`.foregroundColor(.red)`

Figure 4-7. *Defining color for text*

With color, you can choose a standard color option such as Green, Blue, or Yellow. If you don't want to use a standard color, you can also choose Custom, which lets you define different color values and an opacity value as well from 0 (invisible) to 1 (completely visible). When you choose a custom color option, a color dialog appears for you to choose a nonstandard color as shown in Figure 4-8.

Figure 4-8. *Defining a custom color for text*

Two other ways to define colors include defining

- Hue, saturation, and brightness

- Red, green, and blue (RGB)

The hue value (between 0.0 and 1.0) defines a color based on a color wheel. A value of 0.0 or 1.0 is identical. Other values display different colors from around the color wheel as shown in Figure 4-9.

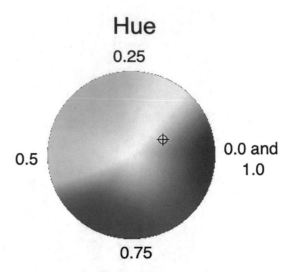

Figure 4-9. *Choosing a color from the color wheel using a hue value*

A saturation value defines how prominent the color appears where a value of 0.0 displays gray, while a value of 1.0 displays the strongest appearance of that color. A brightness value defines how visible the color appears where a value of 0.0 displays no color and a value of 1.0 displays the brightest color.

The red, blue, green (RGB) values let you define a value from 0.0 to 1.0 where 0.0 represents the complete absence of that color. By using different values for red, blue, and green, you can create interesting and unique colors.

To define the hue, saturation, and brightness, use this code:

```
Color(hue: 0.75, saturation: 1.0, brightness: 1.0)
```

To define the red, green, and blue colors, use this code:

```
Color(red: 0.9, green: 0.2, blue: 0.6)
```

Use different values from 0.0 to 1.0 to define each option such as a value of 0.84 for the hue or a value of 0.62 for the green color.

Just like a word processor, SwiftUI also lets you modify text in italics, bold, underline, or strikethrough. To add these effects to text, you can type the following commands:

```
.bold()
.italic()
.underline()
.strikethrough()
```

Rather than type these modifiers, you can also click the Add Modifier popup menu in the Inspector pane as shown in Figure 4-10.

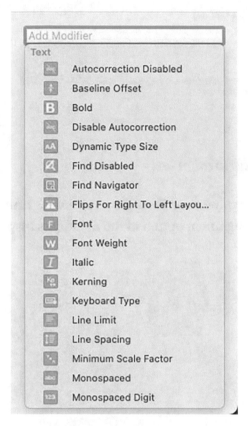

Figure 4-10. *Adding bold, italics, underline, or strikethrough to text*

Another way to modify text is to define its alignment. The three types of alignment are shown in Figure 4-11:

- Leading – Text aligns on the left edge.

- Center – Each line of text appears centered between the left and right edges.

- Trailing – Text aligns on the right edge.

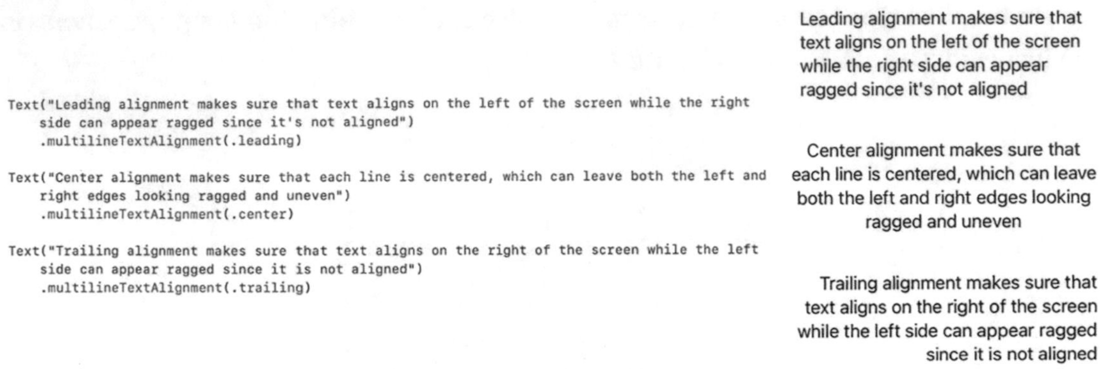

Text("Leading alignment makes sure that text aligns on the left of the screen while the right
side can appear ragged since it's not aligned")
.multilineTextAlignment(.leading)
Text("Center alignment makes sure that each line is centered, which can leave both the left and
right edges looking ragged and uneven")
.multilineTextAlignment(.center)
Text("Trailing alignment makes sure that text aligns on the right of the screen while the left
side can appear ragged since it is not aligned")
.multilineTextAlignment(.trailing)
Leading alignment makes sure that text aligns on the left of the screen while the right side can appear ragged since it's not aligned
Center alignment makes sure that each line is centered, which can leave both the left and right edges looking ragged and uneven
Trailing alignment makes sure that text aligns on the right of the screen while the left side can appear ragged since it is not aligned

Figure 4-11. *Three ways to align text*

You can define text alignment by using the .multilineTextAlignment modifier or through choosing a text alignment option in the Attributes Inspector as shown in Figure 4-12.

Text
Cats are such wonderful c
Modifiers
Accessibility
Label
Inherited
Identifier
Inherited
Font
Font
Inherited
Weight
Inherited
Color
Inherited
Alignment
Line Limit
Inherited

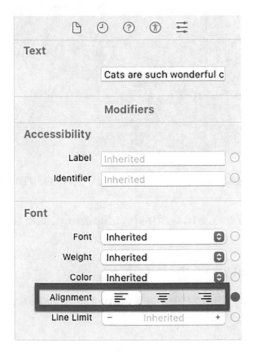

Figure 4-12. *Aligning text in the Inspector pane*

Using the Label View

Similar to the Text view is the Label view. While the Text view just displays a single string of text, the Label view can display both a string and an image side by side as shown in Figure 4-13.

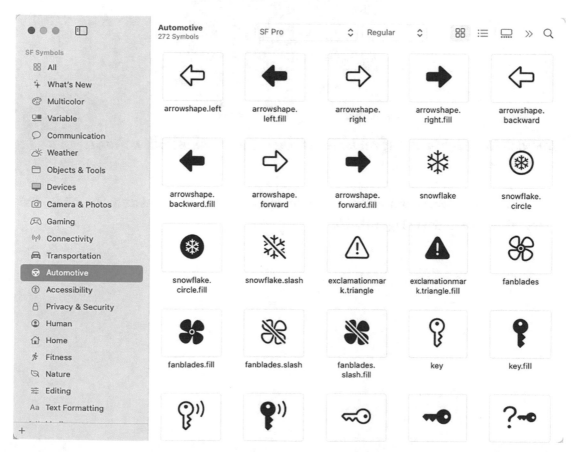

Figure 4-13. *The Label view can display an image and text at the same time*

The Label view can use any image from Apple's free SF Symbols app (`https://developer.apple.com/sf-symbols/`) that displays all available system images as shown in Figure 4-14.

Figure 4-14. *The SF Symbols app displays icons you can include in an Xcode project*

If you want to display an SF Symbol icon in a Label view, you can use this code:

```
Label("Text", systemImage: "SF Symbol image name here")
```

The text can be any string or string variable, while the SF Symbol name must be completely enclosed within double quotation marks such as "creditcard" or "banknote. fill". Make sure you type the SF Symbol icon name exactly as it appears in the SF Symbols app. You can also right-click any icon in the SF Symbols app and, when a popup menu appears, choose Copy Name as shown in Figure 4-15. Then you can paste this name into the Label view.

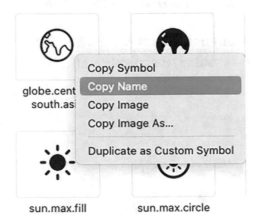

Figure 4-15. *Right-clicking an icon lets you copy its name within the SF Symbols app*

If you want to use your own images, then you'll need to drag and drop them into the Assets folder as shown in Figure 4-16.

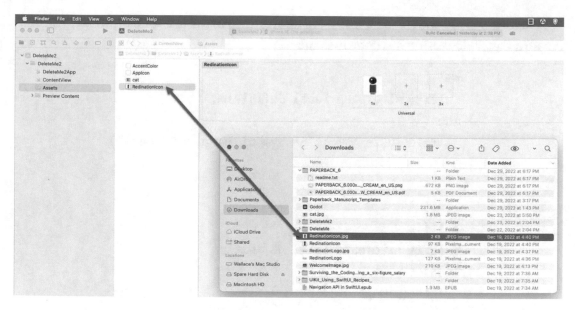

Figure 4-16. *You can drag and drop images into the Assets folder of an Xcode project*

If you want to display an image stored in the Assets folder of your Xcode project, you can use this code:

```
Label("Text", image: "image name here")
```

The text can be any string or string variable, while the image name must exactly match the name of the image file in the Assets folder but without the file extension.

Note   You may want to resize an image before adding it to the Assets folder of your Xcode project. Otherwise, if an image is too large, the Label view will display the image at its original size, which may be far larger than you might want.

The simplest way to define a Label view is to define either a systemImage (from the SF Symbols library) or a regular image stored in the Assets folder:

```
Label("Text", systemImage: "SF Symbol image name here")
Label("Text", image: "image name here from Assets folder here")
```

However, if you want to customize the appearance of the text and/or image, you can create a Label view using this code instead:

```
Label {
    Text("Alternate Label definition")
} icon: {
    Image(systemName: "SF Symbol image name here")
}
```

or

```
Label {
    Text("Alternate Label definition")
} icon: {
    Image("image name here")
}
```

Note   When using an SF Symbol icon, you must define the systemName: parameter within the Image view, but when using an image stored in the Assets folder, you just define the image name with no parameter at all within the Image view.

When you define a Label view using a Text and an Image view, you can customize each individually such as choosing a font for the text and an opacity for the image like this:

```
Label {
    Text("Modifiers")
          .font(.title)
} icon: {
    Image("flag")
          .opacity(0.25)
}
```

The preceding label displays text using the .title font and displays a flag image with an opacity of 0.25 as shown in Figure 4-17.

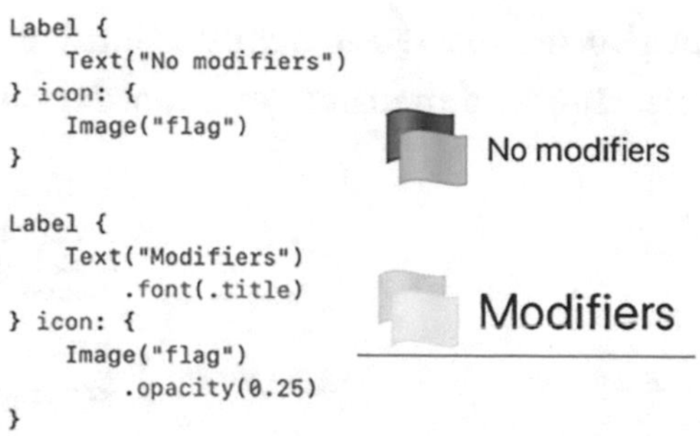

```
Label {
    Text("No modifiers")
} icon: {
    Image("flag")
}
```
No modifiers

```
Label {
    Text("Modifiers")
        .font(.title)
} icon: {
    Image("flag")
        .opacity(0.25)
}
```
Modifiers

Figure 4-17. *Modifying text and an image in a Label view*

When creating a Label view, you have three options as shown in Figure 4-18:

- Text and icon (default)

- Text only

- Icon only

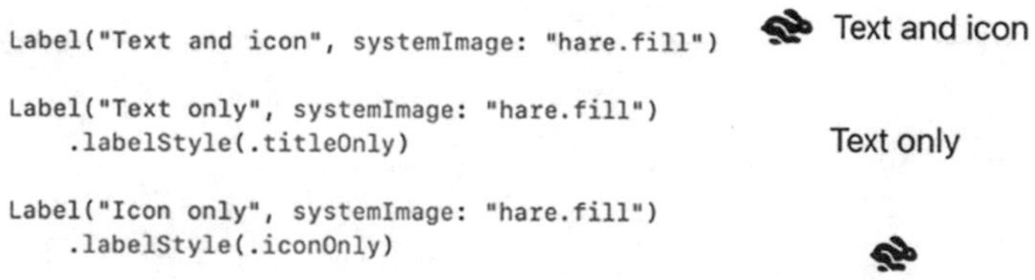

```
Label("Text and icon", systemImage: "hare.fill")
```
Text and icon

```
Label("Text only", systemImage: "hare.fill")
    .labelStyle(.titleOnly)
```
Text only

```
Label("Icon only", systemImage: "hare.fill")
    .labelStyle(.iconOnly)
```

Figure 4-18. *Three different ways the Label view can display information*

Adding a Border Around a Text or Label View

To highlight both a Text and a Label view, you can add a border around them. A border can consist of a color and a width such as

```
.border(Color.red, width: 3)
```

When you use the .border modifier with a Text or Label view, the border closely wraps around the text inside as shown in Figure 4-19.

```
Text("A border around a Text view")
    .border(Color.red, width: 3)
```
A border around a Text view

```
Label("A border around a Label view", systemImage: "folder.fill")
    .border(Color.green, width: 4)
```
A border around a Label view

Figure 4-19. *Borders closely wrap around text inside a Text or Label view*

In case you don't want a border to wrap so tightly around text, you can add padding around the Text or Label view first and then apply the .border modifier as shown in Figure 4-20.

```
Text("A border around a Text view")
    .padding(4)
    .border(Color.red, width: 3)

Label("A border around a Label view", systemImage: "folder.fill")
    .padding()
    .border(Color.green, width: 4)
```

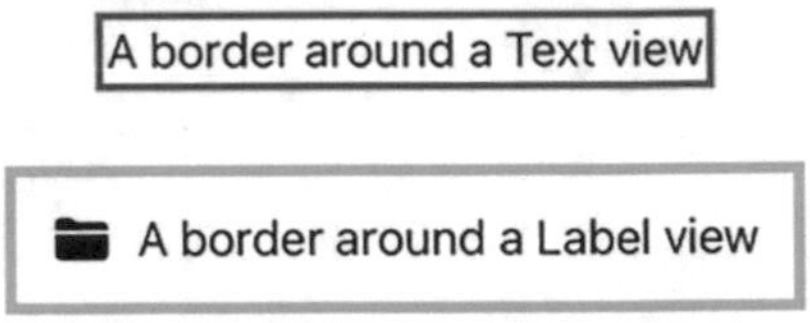

A border around a Text view

📁 A border around a Label view

Figure 4-20. *The padding modifier can add space for borders around a Text or Label view*

Note   Make sure you apply the .padding modifier before the .border modifier. Otherwise, if the .border modifier appears first, SwiftUI will draw the border and then apply the padding around the Text or Label view.

Summary

Text views are handy for displaying any type of textual information on the user interface. Even if you need to display numbers, dates, or any other data types, you can use string interpolation to display data in a Text view. Similar to a Text view is the Label view.

Where the Text view simply displays text, the Label view can display an image and text side by side. The Label view can display either icons listed in the SF Symbols app or any images you add to the Assets folder of your Xcode project. By applying different styles to a Label view, you can display text and icons, text only, or icon only. By using either the Text or Label view, your app can display information on the user interface for the user to view.

CHAPTER 5

Working with Images

Most user interfaces consist of text, but text alone can appear plain. That's why the second most common type of information to display on the screen are images. Images can serve purely for decorative purposes, or they can help the user navigate through a user interface.

The most common type of images to display are icons. The SF Symbols app (`https://developer.apple.com/sf-symbols`) lists all the available icons you can include on your app's user interface. Besides these icons, you can also include any images you drag and drop into the Assets folder of an Xcode project. In addition, you can also include common shapes such as rectangles or circles that can appear on the screen.

Images give you a way to spice up the appearance of any user interface by displaying colorful or informative graphics on the screen. Any time you create a user interface, think of how you can add graphic images to make your user interface more visually appealing to the user.

Displaying Shapes

The simplest image to add to a user interface are common geometric shapes. Geometric shapes can be used alone or placed in the background behind other types of views (such as a Text view) for decorative purposes. The five common geometric shapes are shown in Figure 5-1:

- Capsule
- Circle
- Ellipse
- Rectangle
- Rounded rectangle(cornerRadius: x)

© Wallace Wang 2023
W. Wang, *Beginning iPhone Development with SwiftUI*, https://doi.org/10.1007/978-1-4842-9541-0_5

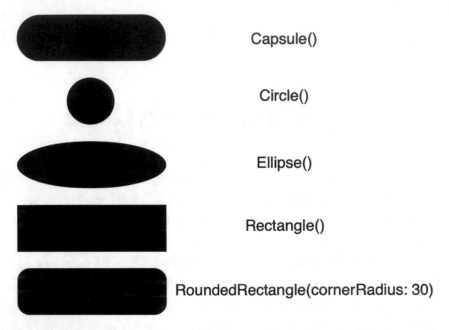

Figure 5-1. *The five different types of geometric shapes available in SwiftUI*

To create any of these geometric shapes, just state the name of the shape you want such as Circle(). The only exception is the rounded rectangle that requires a corner radius value that defines how curved the corners appear. The lower the value is, the sharper the corners appear where a corner radius of 0 creates a 90-degree corner just like an ordinary rectangle. The higher the corner radius value is, the more the rounded rectangle starts to resemble a capsule.

You can define a rounded rectangle in two ways:

- By corner radius

- By defining width and height of the curve

Defining a rounded rectangle by its corner radius requires a numeric value. A low value (such as 10) makes the corners barely rounded. A high value (such as 100) creates a smoother and more prominent rounded curve at each corner of the rectangle as shown in Figure 5-2.

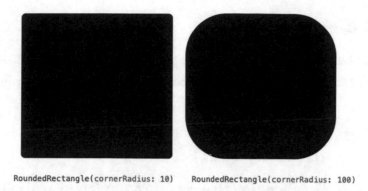

RoundedRectangle(cornerRadius: 10)   RoundedRectangle(cornerRadius: 100)

Figure 5-2. *Changing the corner radius value changes the rounded corners*

A second way to define rounded corners on a rectangle is to define the width and height of the rounded curve like this:

```
RoundedRectangle(cornerSize: CGSize(width: 100, height: 25))
```

The width defines the length of the curve along the X-axis (horizontally), while the height defines the size of the curve along the Y-axis (vertically). By choosing different width and height values, you can create asymmetrically shaped rounded corners for a rectangle as shown in Figure 5-3.

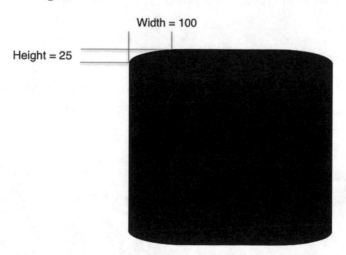

Figure 5-3. *Defining rounded corners using a width and height*

Coloring a Shape

Since the default color of every geometric shape is black, you may want to choose a different color for your shapes. To add color to a shape, you can use the fill modifier like this:

```
Capsule()
    .fill(Color.yellow)
```

In case you don't like using any of the standard colors (green, red, yellow, blue, etc.), you can also define your own colors by defining red, green, and blue values or hue, saturation, and brightness values like this:

```
Circle()
        .fill(Color(red: 1.0, green: 0.0, blue: 0.0, opacity: 1.0))
```

or

```
Ellipse()
        .fill(Color(hue: 1.7, saturation: 2.9, brightness: 0.58))
```

Two additional ways to change the appearance of shapes are

- Opacity

- Shadows

Opacity defines how solid or transparent a shape might be where a low opacity value makes a shape nearly transparent, while a high opacity value makes a shape appear more solid as shown in Figure 5-4.

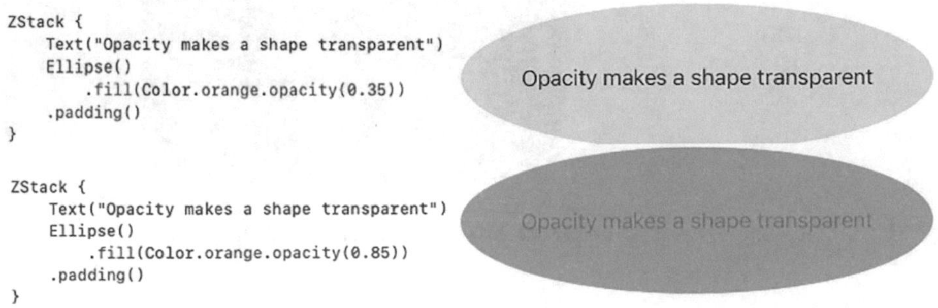

```
ZStack {
    Text("Opacity makes a shape transparent")
    Ellipse()
        .fill(Color.orange.opacity(0.35))
    .padding()
}

ZStack {
    Text("Opacity makes a shape transparent")
    Ellipse()
        .fill(Color.orange.opacity(0.85))
    .padding()
}
```

Figure 5-4. *Opacity can make a shape appear transparent or solid*

To define an opacity for a shape, just add the .opacity modifier after defining a color such as

```
.fill(Color.purple.opacity(0.25))
.fill(Color(hue: 1.7, saturation: 2.9, brightness: 0.58).opacity(0.79))
```

Another way to alter the appearance of a shape is to use shadows. Shadows can appear around the outside or inside edges of a shape as shown in Figure 5-5.

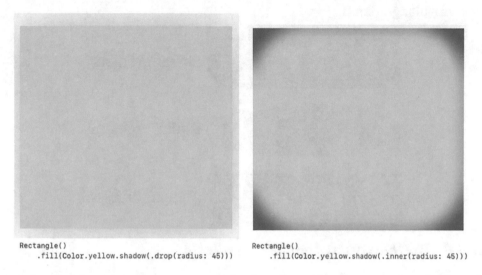

```
Rectangle()                              Rectangle()
    .fill(Color.yellow.shadow(.drop(radius: 45)))      .fill(Color.yellow.shadow(.inner(radius: 45)))
```

Figure 5-5. *Shadows can appear outside the edges of a shape or inside the edges of a shape*

To make shadows appear outside a shape, use the .shadow modifier and define a drop radius. A high drop radius value makes the shadow larger, while a low drop radius value makes the shadow smaller but also more distinct. The drop modifier looks like this:

```
.fill(Color.yellow.shadow(.drop(radius: 15)))
```

To make shadows appear inside a shape, use the .shadow modifier and define an inner radius. A high inner radius makes the shadow larger, while a low inner radius makes the shadow smaller. The inner modifier looks like this:

```
.fill(Color.yellow.shadow(.inner(radius: 145)))
```

Coloring a Shape with Gradients

Another way to add color is to use gradients that spread two or more colors in different ways. SwiftUI offers three types of gradients you can use as shown in Figure 5-6:

- Linear gradients

- Radial gradients

- Angular gradients

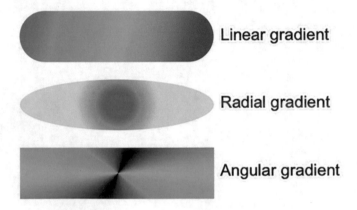

Figure 5-6. *The three types of gradients available*

A linear gradient requires defining two or more colors along with a start point and an end point. The colors get stored within square brackets, and the start and end points can define one of the following positions as shown in Figure 5-7:

- bottom

- bottomLeading

- bottomTrailing

- center

- leading

- top

- topLeading

- topTrailing

- trailing

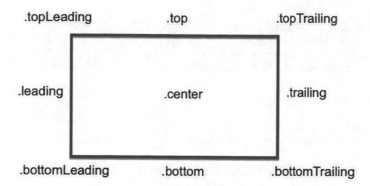

.topLeading   .top   .topTrailing

.leading   .center   .trailing

.bottomLeading   .bottom   .bottomTrailing

Figure 5-7. *Positions of different starting/ending points for a linear gradient*

To create a linear gradient, simply define two or more colors along with a start and end point like this:

```
Capsule()
        .fill(LinearGradient(gradient: Gradient(colors: [.blue,
        .green, .pink]), startPoint: .topLeading, endPoint:
        .bottomTrailing))
```

The radial gradient draws a circular color at a specific location defined by the center parameter such as .center or .top. If you choose a value such as .top, then the gradient center will begin at the top center of a shape as shown in Figure 5-8.

```
Ellipse()
    .fill(RadialGradient(gradient:
        Gradient(colors: [.blue,
        .yellow]), center: .top,
        startRadius: 10, endRadius: 65))
```

Figure 5-8. *The center parameter defines where the center of the radial gradient begins*

The size of the first color is defined by the startRadius. The smaller the startRadius value, the smaller the radius of the first color. The larger the endRadius value is compared with the startRadius value, the more diffuse the colors will blend together. The smaller the endRadius value is compared with the startRadius, the sharper the boundaries between colors as shown in Figure 5-9.

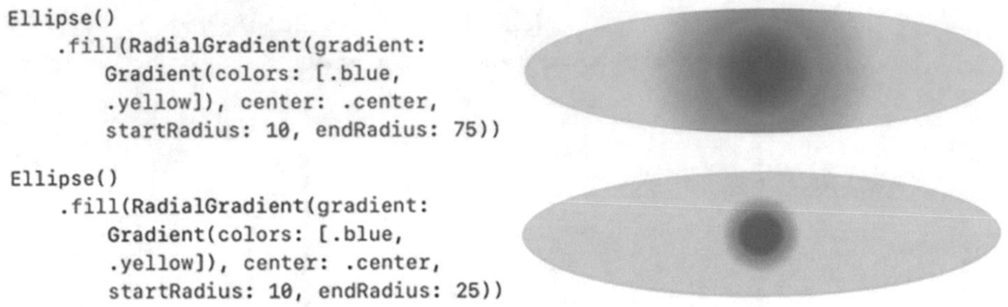

```
Ellipse()
    .fill(RadialGradient(gradient:
        Gradient(colors: [.blue,
        .yellow]), center: .center,
        startRadius: 10, endRadius: 75))
Ellipse()
    .fill(RadialGradient(gradient:
        Gradient(colors: [.blue,
        .yellow]), center: .center,
        startRadius: 10, endRadius: 25))
```

Figure 5-9. *Comparing the startRadius and endRadius values in a radial gradient*

To create a radial gradient, define two or more colors, where the center of the gradient should appear (such as .center or .topLeading), and the startRadius and endRadius like this:

```
Ellipse()
    .fill(RadialGradient(gradient: Gradient(colors: [.blue,
    .yellow]), center: .top, startRadius: 10, endRadius: 65))
```

While the linear and radial gradients can work just fine with two colors, the angular gradient works best with a larger number of colors. If you just define two colors for the angular gradient, SwiftUI will display the two colors side by side and then where they gradually merge as shown in Figure 5-10.

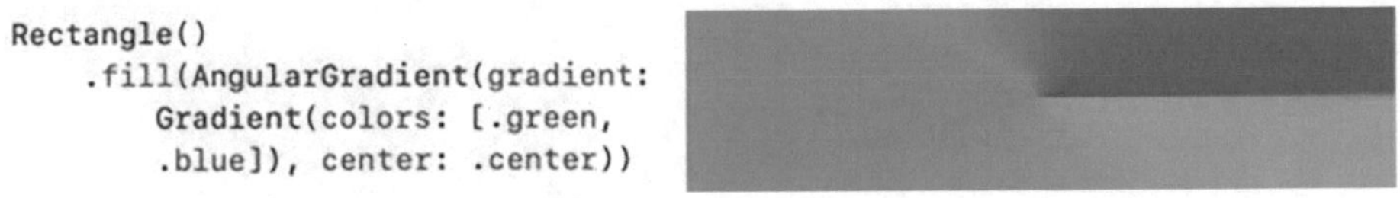

```
Rectangle()
    .fill(AngularGradient(gradient:
        Gradient(colors: [.green,
        .blue]), center: .center))
```

Figure 5-10. *An angular gradient displaying just two different colors*

The more colors you define in an angular gradient, the more they can all blend together. Besides defining multiple colors, you just need to define the center of the angular gradient such as .center or .bottomTrailing. To create an angular gradient, define multiple colors or the same colors multiple times (as shown in Figure 5-11) along with the center such as

```
Rectangle()
    .fill(AngularGradient(gradient: Gradient(colors: [.green,
    .blue, .black, .green, .blue, .black, .green]), center:
    .center))
```

```
Rectangle()
    .fill(AngularGradient(gradient:
        Gradient(colors: [.green, .blue,
        .black, .green, .blue, .black,
        .green]), center: .center))
```

Figure 5-11. *An angular gradient displaying the same colors multiple times*

Displaying Images

Just as the Text view lets you display text on the user interface, the Image view lets you display icons and graphic files on the user interface. If you want to display an icon stored in the SF Symbols app, you can use Swift code like this:

```
Image(systemName: "hare.fill")
```

When you want to display an SF Symbol icon, you must use the systemName parameter. Since icons are small, you may want to enlarge them. The simplest way to enlarge an icon is to define a larger font such as .largeTitle or .custom as shown in Figure 5-12.

```
Image(systemName: "tortoise.fill")
```

```
Image(systemName: "tortoise.fill")
    .font(.largeTitle)
```

```
Image(systemName: "tortoise.fill")
    .font(.custom("", size: 46))
```

Figure 5-12. *Modifying the size of an SF Symbol icon by changing font size*

To display an image, you must first drag and drop it into the Assets folder. Then to display an image stored in the Assets folder, you can use the Image view and specify the image name like this:

```
Image("flag")
```

Images can be of any size, but if they're too large or too small, the Image view will display them at their original size. Since you may need to resize an image to fit on the user interface, you'll need to use the following three modifiers on an Image view:

- .resizable()

- .aspectRatio(contentMode: z)

- .frame(width: x, height: y)

The .resizable() modifier lets an Image view change the size of a displayed image. If an Image view lacks this .resizable() modifier, then the image retains its original size no matter what the size of the Image view might be.

The .frame(width: x, height: y) modifier lets you define the size of the Image view. When used with the .resizable() modifier, the .frame modifier lets you define a fixed width and height of an image.

Since stretching the width and height of an Image view can warp the image displayed inside, the .aspectRatio modifier lets you define how the image should react. The .fill option expands an image to the largest width or height defined by the .frame modifier. The .fit option shrinks an image to the smallest width or height defined by the .frame modifier as shown in Figure 5-13.

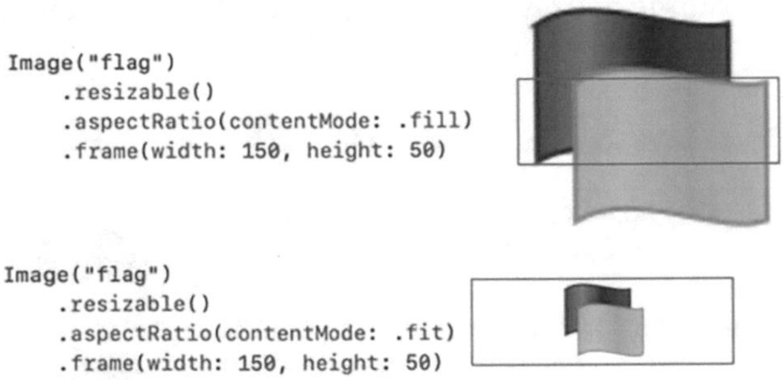

```
Image("flag")
    .resizable()
    .aspectRatio(contentMode: .fill)
    .frame(width: 150, height: 50)
```

```
Image("flag")
    .resizable()
    .aspectRatio(contentMode: .fit)
    .frame(width: 150, height: 50)
```

Figure 5-13. *Using the .fill and .fit aspect ratio on an image*

If you want to further refine the aspect ratio, you can include an aspect ratio value such as

```
Image("flag")
    .resizable()
    .frame(width: 150, height: 150)
    .aspectRatio(0.5, contentMode: .fill)
```

This aspect ratio defines the width to height ratio, so a value of 0.5 would be a 1:2 width to height ratio, while a value of 0.75 would be a 3:4 width to height ratio.

Instead of using the .aspectRatio modifier and defining a contentMode of .fill or .fit, Swift offers two other alternatives:

- .scaleToFill()

- .scaleToFit()

Simply replace the .aspectRatio modifier with the .scaleToFit or .scaleToFill modifier like this:

```
Image("flag")
    .resizable()
    .frame(width: 150, height: 150)
    .scaleToFill()
```

Clipping Images

An Image view can display clip art images that someone has drawn, but it can also display photographs captured with a digital camera. Normally, an Image view displays any picture in the rectangle defined by the .frame modifier. However, to create more unique visual effects, you can clip images by overlaying them with a geometric shape by using the .clipShape modifier.

The .clipShape modifier accepts any common geometric shape such as

```
.clipShape(Circle())
```

When using other geometric shapes such as Ellipse() or Capsule(), make sure the frame width is wide enough. If a frame's width and height are identical, then the Ellipse() and Capsule() shapes simply look like a Circle(). Figure 5-14 shows how the .clipShape(Circle()) modifier changes the appearance of an image that would normally appear as a rectangular image.

```
Image("Cats")
    .resizable()
    .scaledToFill()
    .frame(width: 350, height: 350)
```

```
Image("Cats")
    .resizable()
    .scaledToFill()
    .frame(width: 350, height: 350)
    .clipShape(Circle())
```

Figure 5-14. *Using the .clipShape() modifier*

Adding Shadows to Images

Another way to highlight the appearance of an Image view is to use the .shadow
modifier, which adds a shadow around a view. You can adjust how much the shadow
appears around a view by defining its radius such as

```
.shadow(color: .red, radius: 46, x: 0, y: 0)
```

The .shadow modifier requires the following parameters:

- Color – Defines the shadow's color.

- Radius – Defines the shadow's size around the view.

- X – Defines the x (horizontal) offset of the shadow. A value of 0
  centers the shadow in the horizontal direction around the view.

- Y – Defines the y (vertical) offset of the shadow. A value of 0 centers
  the shadow in the vertical direction around the view.

If the x and y values are nonzero, then the shadow shifts away from the Image view. If the x and y values are both 0, then the shadow appears evenly around all four edges of the Image view as shown in Figure 5-15.

```
Image("kitty")
    .resizable()
    .scaledToFill()
    .frame(width: 250, height: 250)
    .shadow(color: .red, radius: 46, x: 0, y: 0)
```

```
Image("kitty")
    .resizable()
    .scaledToFill()
    .frame(width: 250, height: 250)
    .clipShape(Circle())
    .shadow(color: .green, radius: 46, x: 90, y: 50)
```

Figure 5-15. *Adding a shadow to an Image view with different x and y values*

Adding a Border Around Images

To further highlight an Image view, you can add a border around it using the .overlay modifier like this:

```
.overlay(Rectangle().stroke(Color.blue, lineWidth: 10))
```

The .overlay modifier requires the following parameters:

- Shape – Defines the shape of the border to match the shape of the Image view

- Color – Defines the color of the border

- lineWidth – Defines the thickness of the border line around the Image view

Figure 5-16 shows two uses of the .overlay modifier that use different shapes, colors, and line widths.

```
Image("kitty")
    .resizable()
    .scaledToFill()
    .frame(width: 250, height: 250)
    .shadow(color: .red, radius: 46, x: 0, y: 0)
    .overlay(Rectangle().stroke(Color.blue, lineWidth: 10))


Image("kitty")
    .resizable()
    .scaledToFill()
    .frame(width: 250, height: 250)
    .clipShape(Circle())
    .shadow(color: .green, radius: 46, x: 90, y: 50)
    .overlay(Circle().stroke(Color.purple, lineWidth: 20))
```

Figure 5-16. *Using different values for the .overlay modifier*

Defining the Opacity of an Image

Another way to modify the appearance of an image is to define its opacity. An opacity of 0 means the image is invisible. An opacity of 1 means the image appears with no changes whatsoever. The closer the opacity is to 0, the fainter the image. The closer the opacity is to 1, the sharper the image.

To use the opacity modifier, just define an opacity value from 0 to 1 like this:

```
.opacity(0.75)
```

Figure 5-17 shows how different opacity values modify the appearance of an image.

```
Image("goodCat")
    .resizable()
    .scaledToFill()
    .frame(width: 250, height: 250)
    .opacity(0.75)

Image("goodCat")
    .resizable()
    .scaledToFill()
    .frame(width: 250, height: 250)
    .opacity(0.5)

Image("goodCat")
    .resizable()
    .scaledToFill()
    .frame(width: 250, height: 250)
    .opacity(0.25)
```

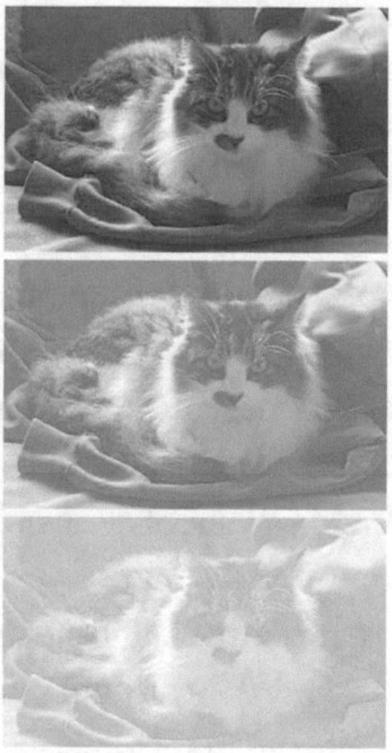

Figure 5-17. *Using different values for the .opacity modifier*

By changing the opacity of different views, you can stack them on top of each other within a ZStack to create interesting visual effects as shown in Figure 5-18.

```
ZStack {

    Image("goodCat")
        .resizable()
        .scaledToFill()
        .frame(width: 250, height: 250)
        .opacity(0.5)

    ZStack {
        RoundedRectangle(cornerRadius: 25)
            .fill(Color.green)
            .frame(width: 350, height: 50)
            .offset(x: 0, y: 90)
            .opacity(0.25)

        Text("Norwegian Forest Cat")
            .offset(x: 0, y: 90)
        .font(.largeTitle)
    }

}
```

Figure 5-18. *The .opacity modifier combined with the ZStack can create visual effects*

Summary

Images are another way to provide information on the user interface. Images can be common geometric shapes such as circles, ellipses, and rounded rectangles, icons that you can find in the SF Symbols app, graphic images, or digital photographs you drag and drop into the Assets folder of an Xcode project.

If you're creating geometric shapes, you can fill them with solid colors, custom colors, or gradients to create an interesting visual blend of multiple colors. If you're using SF Symbol icons, you can adjust their size using the .font modifier. If you're using images stored in the Assets folder of your Xcode project, you can use the .resizable, .frame, and .aspectRatio/.scaleToFit/.scaleToFill modifiers to define the size and appearance of an image.

To create extra visual effects, you can clip images into geometric shapes such as circles, add borders around images, add shadows around images, and modify the opacity. With so many different ways to adjust the appearance of images, you should be able to define an image to appear exactly the way you want it to look on your user interface.

CHAPTER 6

Responding to the User with Buttons and Segmented Controls

Every user interface needs to display information to the user whether that information may be text or images. However, another feature of a user interface is to accept commands from the user. The simplest way to accept commands through a user interface is through buttons.

Buttons represent a single command that can be as simple as a confirmation such as OK or Cancel. To create a button, you need to define

- The title that displays text on the button

- Swift code that runs when the user taps the button

SwiftUI gives you two ways to create a button. The simplest way just defines the text to appear on the title followed by the Swift code to run when the user selects the button like this:

```
Button("Click here") {
    // code to run
}
```

A second way to create a button gives you more flexibility in modifying the appearance of the text on the button such as

```
Button {
    // code to run
} label: {
    Text("Click here")
```

© Wallace Wang 2023
W. Wang, *Beginning iPhone Development with SwiftUI*, https://doi.org/10.1007/978-1-4842-9541-0_6

```
            .font(.largeTitle)
            .foregroundColor(.green)
            .padding()
            .border(Color.red, width: 6)
    }
```

This second method uses a Text view to define the text that appears on the title. Then it uses the .font modifier to define the font size, the .foregroundColor modifier to display the text in green, the .padding modifier to add space around the Text view, and the .border modifier to add a red border with a width of 6 points around the Text view.

Instead of using a Text view to define the button's title, you can also use a Label view to display both text and an icon like this:

```
Button {
    // code to run
} label: {
    Label("Image button", systemImage: "hare.fill")
        .font(.largeTitle)
        .foregroundColor(.purple)
        .padding()
        .border(Color.blue, width: 6)
}
```

This Label view defines text and an icon to appear and then uses the .font modifier to define the size of both the text and the icon. It uses the .foregroundColor modifier to display the text and icon in purple, adds space around the Label view using the .padding modifier, and uses the .border modifier to display a blue border with a width of 6 points around the Label view.

You can also use an Image view to make an image appear as a button like this:

```
Button {
    // code to run
} label: {
    Image("browncat")
        .resizable()
        .frame(width: 150, height: 150)
```

```
        .clipShape(Circle())
        .overlay(Circle().stroke(Color.yellow, lineWidth: 4))
}
```

This Image view uses an image (called "browncat") stored in the Assets folder and then uses the .frame modifier to squeeze the image into a square with a width and height of 150. Then it uses the .clipShape modifier to display the image within a circle followed by the .overlay modifier that displays a yellow border with a line width of 4.

By using this second method to define the title of a button, you can see how you have more control over the appearance of the button's title, especially compared with the simple way of defining a button with plain text as shown in Figure 6-1.

```
Button ("Plain text button") {                                    Plain text button
    // code to run
}

Button {
    // code to run
} label: {
    Text("Custom text button")
        .font(.largeTitle)                                   Custom text button
        .foregroundColor(.green)
        .padding()
        .border(Color.red, width: 6)
}

Button {
    // code to run
} label: {
    Label("Image button", systemImage: "hare.fill")          Image button
        .font(.largeTitle)
        .foregroundColor(.purple)
        .padding()
        .border(Color.blue, width: 6)
}

Button {
    // code to run
} label: {
    Image("kitty")
        .resizable()
        .scaledToFill()
        .frame(width: 150, height: 150)
        .clipShape(Circle())
        .overlay(Circle().stroke(Color.green, lineWidth: 8))
}
```

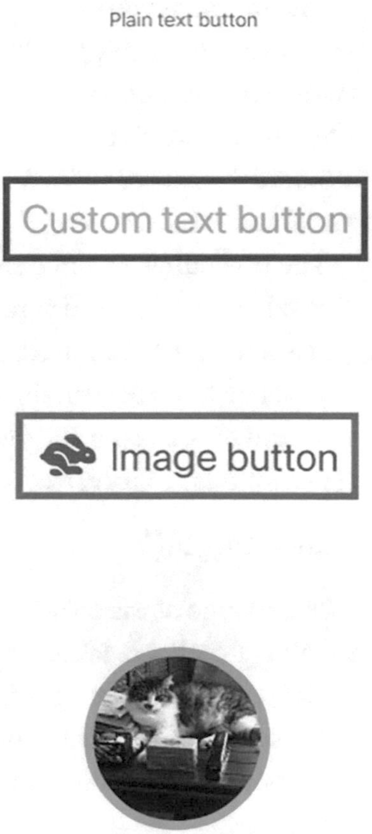

Figure 6-1. *Using a Text view, Label view, or an Image view to define a button's title*

Running Code in a Button

You can store any code to run when the user taps a button. One common type of code to run inside of a button is code that changes a state. In SwiftUI, you can declare special variables as State variables like this:

```
@State var colorMe = false
```

When you store updated data in an ordinary variable, any other part of your program that uses that variable has no idea that the data has been updated. To make sure every part of your program receives any updated data stored in a variable can be tedious and error-prone. That's why SwiftUI offers State variables to solve this problem.

The moment you change the value of a State variable, anything that uses that State variable automatically gets the latest data stored in that State variable without the need to write any extra code. When a variable holds one value, it's in one state, and when that same variable holds a different value, that's another state. SwiftUI State variables simply automate the process of making sure every part of your program knows about changes in a variable's value or state.

The preceding example creates a State variable by using the @State keyword followed by a variable declaration (var) that defines a variable's name (colorMe), data type (Boolean type inferred), and initial value (false).

When using State variables that represent Boolean data types, one common command to use is the .toggle() command, which changes a Boolean variable from true to false (or false to true) such as

```
colorMe.toggle()
```

If the value of the colorMe State variable is true, then the .toggle() command changes the colorMe value to false. If the value of the colorMe State variable is false, then the .toggle() command changes the colorMe value to true.

Boolean State variables are often used to make if-else decisions. Normally, modifiers just contain a single value such as

```
.fill(Color.green)
```

However, if you embed an if-else ternary operator in a modifier, you can duplicate the traditional if-else statement in a single line like this:

```
.fill(colorMe ? Color.green : Color.gray)
```

The preceding Swift code checks the Boolean value of the "colorMe" variable. If it's true, then it uses the color green. Otherwise, it uses the color gray.

Let's see how to put together State variables, the .toggle() command, and the if-else ternary operator to make a button respond to the user.

1. Create a new SwiftUI iOS App project and give it any name you wish such as "Buttons."

2. Click the ContentView file in the Navigator pane.

3. Add a State variable underneath the struct ContentView: View line like this:

```
struct ContentView: View {
    @State var colorMe = false
    var body: some View {
```

This defines a State variable called colorMe (the exact name is arbitrary) and sets its initial value as false, defining it to hold only Boolean data types.

4. Create a VStack with a spacing value of 28 inside the var body: some View like this:

```
struct ContentView: View {
    @State var colorMe = false
    var body: some View {
        VStack (spacing: 28) {

        }
    }
}
```

The spacing of 28 will separate all views inside the VStack so they don't appear crowded together.

5. Type the following inside the VStack:

```
Rectangle()
    .fill(colorMe ? Color.green : Color.gray)
    .frame(width: 250, height: 100)
```

This creates a rectangle where the .frame modifier defines its
width as 250 and its height as 100. Notice that the .fill modifier
uses the colorMe Boolean State variable to determine which color
to display. If colorMe is true, then the rectangle appears green. If
colorMe is false, then the rectangle appears gray.

6. Type the following underneath the Rectangle() inside the VStack
   to create a plain button:

```
Button("Plain text button") {
    colorMe.toggle()
}
```

This defines a button that displays plain text. Each time the user
taps this Button, it uses the .toggle() command to change the
value of colorMe from true to false (or false to true).

7. Type the following underneath the Button inside the VStack to
   create a button that uses a customized Text view to display its title:

```
Button {
    colorMe.toggle()
} label: {
    Text("Custom text button")
        .font(.largeTitle)
        .foregroundColor(.green)
        .padding()
        .border(Color.red, width: 6)
}
```

This defines a button that also uses the .toggle() command to
change the Boolean value of the colorMe variable. However, it
uses a Text view to display the Button's title. The .font modifier
changes the size of the Text view, the .foregroundColor modifier
displays the text in green, the .padding modifier adds space
around the Text view, and the .border modifier displays a red
border, with a width of 6, around the Text view.

8. Type the following underneath the previous Button inside the
    VStack to define a button's title using a Label view:

```
Button {
    colorMe.toggle()
} label: {
    Label("Image button", systemImage: "hare.fill")
        .font(.largeTitle)
        .foregroundColor(.purple)
        .padding()
        .border(Color.blue, width: 6)
}
```

This defines a button that uses the .toggle() command to change
the Boolean value of the colorMe variable. However, it uses a
Label view to display text ("Image button") along with an icon
called "hare.fill". Then it uses the .font modifier to enlarge the text
and icon and the .foregroundColor modifier to display the text and
icon in purple. Finally, it uses the .padding modifier to add space
around the Label view and places a blue border with a width of 6
around the Label view.

9. Type the following underneath the previous Button inside the
    VStack to define a button's title using an Image view:

```
Button {
    colorMe.toggle()
} label: {
    Image("browncat")
        .resizable()
        .frame(width: 150, height: 150)
        .clipShape(Circle())
        .overlay(Circle().stroke(Color.yellow, lineWidth: 4))
}
```

This defines a button that uses the .toggle() command to change the Boolean value of the colorMe variable. Instead of displaying text for the Button's title, the Image view assumes there's an image (called "browncat") that's been stored in the Assets folder of the Xcode project. Then it uses the .resizable and .frame modifiers to resize the image into a box 150 in width and 150 in height. Finally, it uses the .clipShape modifier to shape the image in a circle and uses the .overlay modifier to place a yellow circle border around the image with a line width of 4.

The entire SwiftUI code should look like this:

```
import SwiftUI

struct ContentView: View {
    @State var colorMe = false
    var body: some View {
        VStack (spacing: 28) {

            Rectangle()
                .fill(colorMe ? Color.green : Color.gray)
                .frame(width: 250, height: 100)

            Button("Plain text button") {
                colorMe.toggle()
            }

            Button {
                colorMe.toggle()
            } label: {
                Text("Custom text button")
                    .font(.largeTitle)
                    .foregroundColor(.green)
                    .padding()
                    .border(Color.red, width: 6)
            }
```

```
        Button {
            colorMe.toggle()
        } label: {
            Label("Image button", systemImage: "hare.fill")
                .font(.largeTitle)
                .foregroundColor(.purple)
                .padding()
                .border(Color.blue, width: 6)
        }

        Button {
            colorMe.toggle()
        } label: {
            Image("browncat")
                .resizable()
                .frame(width: 150, height: 150)
                .clipShape(Circle())
                .overlay(Circle().stroke(Color.yellow,
                lineWidth: 4))
        }
      }
    }
}

struct ContentView_Previews: PreviewProvider {
    static var previews: some View {
        ContentView()
    }
}
```

10. Click the Live icon in the Canvas pane.

11. Click any of the buttons. Notice that each time you click a button,
     it toggles the colorMe Boolean variable to alternate displaying
     green or gray in the rectangle.

Storing Code to Run in a User Interface View

When you create a button or similar type of user interface view that interacts with users, you'll need to write Swift code to make that user interface view respond. The simplest way is to write code directly in the same file that defines the user interface such as

```
Button("Plain text button") {
    colorMe.toggle()
}
```

When there are just a few lines of code, this can be fine. However, if you need to store dozens of lines of code to define how a user interface view responds to the user, this can make an entire .swift file harder to understand. Such a file will consist of Swift code to both design the user interface and respond to the user's actions.

Rather than cram multiple lines of code in the code that defines the user interface, it's much better to store the code in a separate function. That way the user interface code just calls a single line of code like this:

```
Button("Click Me") {
    callMyFunction()
}
```

Such an approach will help keep the Swift code that performs an action from the Swift code that defines the user interface. One place to store a function is within the same file that contains the Swift code that defines the user interface such as near the bottom of the structure that defines the user interface as shown in Figure 6-2.

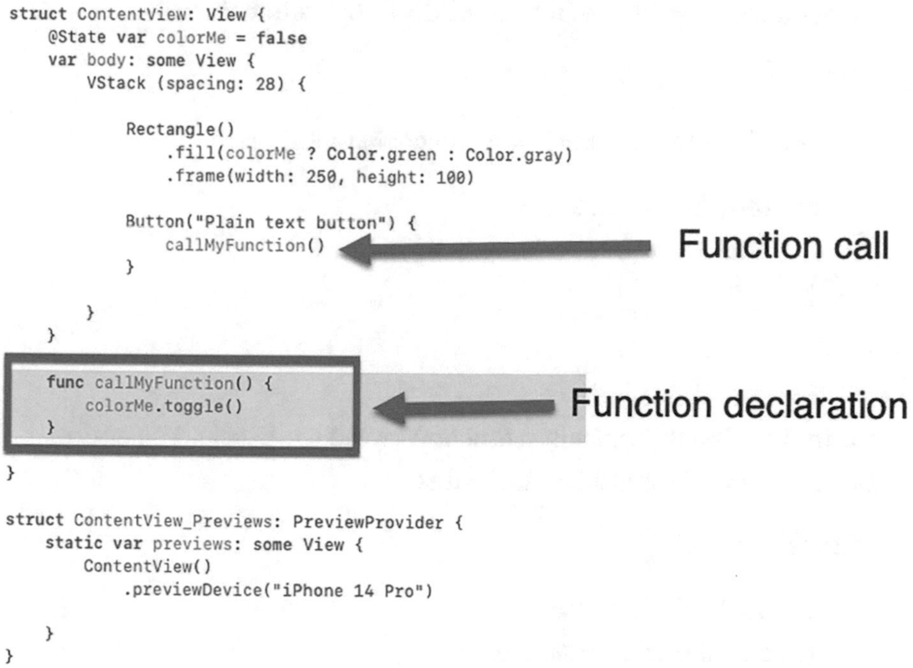

```
struct ContentView: View {
    @State var colorMe = false
    var body: some View {
        VStack (spacing: 28) {

            Rectangle()
                .fill(colorMe ? Color.green : Color.gray)
                .frame(width: 250, height: 100)

            Button("Plain text button") {
                callMyFunction()          ◀━━━━━━━━  Function call
            }

        }
    }

    func callMyFunction() {
        colorMe.toggle()                ◀━━━━━━━━  Function declaration
    }
}

struct ContentView_Previews: PreviewProvider {
    static var previews: some View {
        ContentView()
            .previewDevice("iPhone 14 Pro")
    }
}
```

Figure 6-2. *A function can appear inside the same structure that defines the user interface*

Storing a function in the same file that contains Swift code that defines the user interface keeps everything in one place. However, if a function contains a large amount of code, this approach can still be messy since the file contains both code to define the user interface and code to make the user interface responsive.

A better solution is to store functions in a completely separate file. That way one file contains Swift code for defining the user interface, and another file contains Swift code (stored in functions) that performs specific tasks. To see how to store functions in a separate file, follow these steps:

1. Create a new iOS App project, make sure the interface is SwiftUI, and give it a descriptive name such as CodeFile.

2. Create a State variable called randomNumber like this:

   ```
   @State var randomNumber = 0
   ```

3. Create a Text view and a Button inside a VStack like this:

```
VStack (spacing: 28) {

    Text("Random number = \(randomNumber)")

    Button("Roll dice") {
        randomNumber = rollDice()
    }

}
```

Notice that the Button calls a function called rollDice(). The entire ContentView file should look like this:

```
import SwiftUI

struct ContentView: View {
    @State var randomNumber = 0
    var body: some View {
        VStack (spacing: 28) {

            Text("Random number = \(randomNumber)")

            Button("Roll dice") {
                randomNumber = rollDice()
            }

        }
    }
}

struct ContentView_Previews: PreviewProvider {
    static var previews: some View {
        ContentView()
    }
}
```

4. Choose File ➤ New ➤ File. A window appears as shown in Figure 6-3.

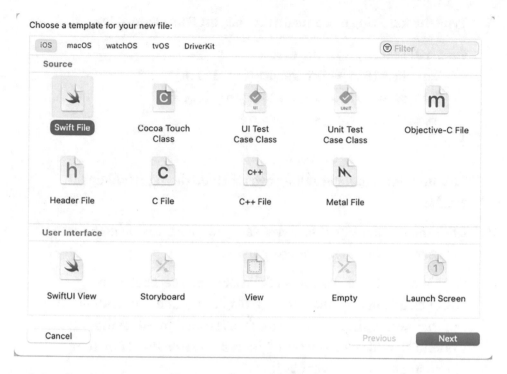

Figure 6-3. *Creating a new file for an Xcode project*

5. Click the iOS tab and then click Swift File.

6. Click the Next button. A window appears, asking you to choose a name for your file.

7. Type a descriptive name, such as StoreFunctions, and click the Create button. Xcode creates a new .swift file in the Navigator pane.

8. Click the newly created .swift file. The only code in a newly created .swift file is the following:

import Foundation

The Foundation framework provides basic functionality for creating apps throughout all of Apple's operating systems including iOS, macOS, watchOS, and tvOS.

9. Type the following underneath the "import Foundation" line:

```
func rollDice() -> Int {
    let firstDie = Int.random(in: 1...6)
    let secondDie = Int.random(in: 1...6)
    return firstDie + secondDie
}
```

This function simulates rolling two six-sided dice and adding the results.

10. Click the ContentView file in the Navigator pane. Xcode displays the user interface in the Canvas pane.

11. Click the "Roll dice" Button on the user interface. Each time you click this Button, the Text view displays a different random number, which shows that the rollDice() function call in the ContentView file can successfully access the rollDice() function stored in a separate .swift file.

Note   One advantage of storing functions in separate files is that you can easily copy a .swift file from one project and paste it in another project. This makes it easy to reuse code between projects.

Using a Segmented Control

A button represents a single command, so if you want to offer the user a choice between multiple commands, you need to use multiple buttons. Unfortunately, multiple buttons can be cumbersome to cram onto a user interface. To get around this problem, SwiftUI offers a segmented control.

Note   Although a segmented control can theoretically display a large number of options, the more options displayed, the more cluttered the segmented control will look. As a general rule, if a segmented control contains too many options, consider using a different way to offer users multiple choices to select such as through a wheel or menu picker as explained in Chapter 8.

The main idea behind a segmented control is to display two or more options in a condensed space rather than use multiple buttons. To create a segmented control, you need the following:

- A State variable to represent which segment (option) the user chose

- A Picker view that lists two or more options

- A tag property linked to each option

- The SegmentedPickerStyle modifier

To display options on a segmented control, the simplest way is to use multiple Text views like this:

```
Picker("", selection: $selectedItem) {
    Text("Fish")
    Text("Tortoise")
    Text("Hare")
    Text("Bird")
}.pickerStyle(.segmented)
```

This would create a segmented control displaying the Text view items in order, so the furthest item on the left will be "Fish" and the furthest item on the right will be "Bird" as shown in Figure 6-4.

```
Picker("", selection: $selectedItem) {
    Text("Fish")
    Text("Tortoise")
    Text("Hare")
    Text("Bird")
}.pickerStyle(.segmented)
```

| Fish | Tortoise | Hare | Bird |

Figure 6-4. *Creating a simple segmented control*

Putting multiple Text views inside a Picker view can define the options that appear, but there's no way for the segmented control to know which option a user selected. If you define the options in a Picker view by using multiple Text views, you need to add a .tag property after each Text view.

This .tag property provides the actual data that represents each item on the segmented control. The .tag property can be any data type (such as String or Int), but every .tag property should contain the same data type.

To see how to use a segmented control that displays options in a Picker view through multiple Text views and .tag properties, follow these steps:

1. Create a new SwiftUI iOS App project and give it any name you wish such as "SegmentedControl."

2. Click the ContentView file in the Navigator pane.

3. Add a State variable underneath the struct ContentView: View line like this:

```
struct ContentView: View {
    @State private var selectedColor = Color.gray
    var body: some View {
```

This creates a State variable called selectedColor. Notice that the "private" keyword is optional, which simply means this variable can only be used within this ContentView structure. The initial value of this selectedColor variable is Color.gray, which means its inferred data type is Color.

4. Create a VStack with a spacing value of 28 inside the var body:
    some View like this:

```
struct ContentView: View {
    @State private var selectedColor = Color.gray
    var body: some View {
        VStack (spacing: 28) {

        }
    }
}
```

The spacing value can be any number you wish, but it adds
spacing between any views you add inside the VStack so they
don't appear crowded together on the user interface.

5. Type the following to create a colored rectangle inside the VStack:

```
Rectangle()
    .fill(selectedColor)
```

This creates a rectangle that contains the color defined by the
selectedColor State variable. Initially, this rectangle is filled with
Color.gray.

6. Type the following to create a segmented control inside
    the VStack:

```
Picker("Favorite Color", selection: $selectedColor) {
    Text("Red").tag(Color.red)
    Text("Green").tag(Color.green)
    Text("Blue").tag(Color.blue)
}.pickerStyle(.segmented)
```

This creates a Picker view that lists three options ("Red", "Green",
and "Blue") displayed on the segmented control. After each
option is a .tag that's linked to each option. While the user sees
the options displayed by the three Text views ("Red", "Green", and
"Blue"), the selectedColor State variable is actually storing the .tag

values, which are Colors (.red, .green, and .blue). The .pickerStyle modifier displays the Picker view as a segmented control by defining .segmented (instead of .wheel or .menu).

The entire SwiftUI code should look like this:

```
import SwiftUI

struct ContentView: View {
    @State private var selectedColor = Color.gray
    var body: some View {
        VStack (spacing: 28) {
            Rectangle()
                .fill(selectedColor)

            Picker("Favorite Color", selection: $selectedColor) {
                Text("Red").tag(Color.red)
                Text("Green").tag(Color.green)
                Text("Blue").tag(Color.blue)
            }.pickerStyle(.segmented)
        }
    }
}

struct ContentView_Previews: PreviewProvider {
    static var previews: some View {
        ContentView()
    }
}
```

7. Click the Live icon in the Canvas pane.

8. Click the "Red," "Green," and "Blue" options on the segmented control. Each time you choose a different option from the segmented control, the selectedColor State variable changes. Then this State variable automatically changes the color of the rectangle as shown in Figure 6-5.

Figure 6-5. *The complete user interface for the segmented control*

Note   If you omit the .pickerStyle(.segmented) modifier, the Picker view will display the three options ("Red", "Green", and "Blue") in a menu as shown in Figure 6-6.

Figure 6-6. *The Picker view appearance without the .pickerStyle modifier displays a menu*

Typing multiple Text views to populate a segmented control can work, but repetition is almost always a sign that code can be simplified. In the case of a Picker view, you can replace multiple Text views by using an array and a ForEach loop instead like this:

```
Picker("", selection: $selectedItem) {
    ForEach(animalArray, id: \.self) {
        Text($0)
    }
}.pickerStyle(.segmented)
```

This ForEach loop identifies an array that contains the options to appear on the segmented control (such as an array called "animalArray") and uses the id property to identify each array item to display in a single Text view. This Text view uses the $0 shorthand argument name to represent each array item.

Besides reducing the need of using multiple Text views to define the options on a segmented control, the ForEach loop also eliminates the need for separate .tag properties for each item. Instead, the array items themselves represent both the options that appear on the segmented control and the choice the user selected.

To see how to use a segmented control that uses a ForEach loop to populate a Picker view, follow these steps:

1. Create a new SwiftUI iOS App project and give it any name you wish such as "SegmentedControlForEach."

2. Click the ContentView file in the Navigator pane.

3. Add a State variable underneath the struct ContentView: View line like this:

```
@State var selectedItem = ""
```

This creates a State variable called selectedItem. The initial value of this selectedItem variable is an empty string, which means its inferred data type is String.

4. Create a VStack inside the var body: some View like this:

```
struct ContentView: View {

    @State var selectedItem = ""
    let animalArray = ["Fish", "Tortoise", "Hare", "Bird"]

    var body: some View {
        VStack {

        }
    }
}
```

5. Type the following to create a Picker view and a Text view inside the VStack:

```
VStack {
    Picker("", selection: $selectedItem) {
        ForEach(animalArray, id: \.self) {
            Text($0)
        }
    }.pickerStyle(.segmented)

    Text(selectedItem)
}
```

This uses a ForEach loop to populate the segmented control created by the Picker view. The Text view displays the choice the user selected.

The entire SwiftUI code should look like this:

```
import SwiftUI

struct ContentView: View {
```

```
@State var selectedItem = ""
let animalArray = ["Fish", "Tortoise", "Hare", "Bird"]

var body: some View {
    VStack {
        Picker("", selection: $selectedItem) {
            ForEach(animalArray, id: \.self) {
                Text($0)
            }
        }.pickerStyle(.segmented)

        Text(selectedItem)
    }
}
}

struct ContentView_Previews: PreviewProvider {
    static var previews: some View {
        ContentView()
    }
}
```

6.   Click the Live icon in the Canvas pane.

7.   Click the "Fish," "Tortoise," "Hare," and "Bird" options on the
     segmented control. Each time you choose a different option from
     the segmented control, the selectedItem State variable changes.
     Then this State variable automatically changes what appears in
     the Text view.

Running Code from a Segmented Control

By just selecting options on a segmented control, the segmented control can only change
a State variable. If you want to run code based on which option the user selected on a
segmented control, you need to add an .onChange modifier as follows:

```
.onChange(of: stateVariable) { newValue in
    // code to run
}
```

Each time the user selects a different option on a segmented control, it changes a State variable. The .onChange modifier runs code each time this State variable changes. The newValue variable contains this latest change and can then run code. To see how this works, follow these steps:

1. Create a new SwiftUI iOS App project and give it any name you wish such as "SegmentedControl Code."

2. Click the ContentView file in the Navigator pane.

3. Add a State variable underneath the struct ContentView: View line like this:

```
struct ContentView: View {
    @State private var message = ""
    var body: some View {
```

This creates a State variable called message. Notice that the "private" keyword is optional, which simply means this variable can only be used within this ContentView structure. Its initial value is an empty string, so its data type is inferred to be String.

4. Create a VStack with a spacing value of 28 inside the var body: some View like this:

```
struct ContentView: View {
    @State private var message = ""
    var body: some View {
        VStack (spacing: 28) {

        }
    }
}
```

The spacing value can be any number you wish, but it adds spacing between any views you add inside the VStack so they don't appear crowded together on the user interface.

5. Type the following to create a Text view inside the VStack:

```
Text(message)
```

This creates a Text view that displays the contents of the message State variable.

6. Type the following to create a segmented control inside the VStack:

```
Picker("", selection: $message) {
    Text("Happy").tag("happy")
    Text("Sad").tag("sad")
    Text("Bored").tag("bored")
}.pickerStyle(.segmented)
```

This creates a Picker view that lists three options ("Happy", "Sad", and "Bored") displayed on the segmented control. After each option is a .tag that's linked to each option. While the user sees the options displayed by the three Text views ("Happy", "Sad", and "Bored"), the message State variable is actually storing the .tag values, which are strings ("happy", "sad", "bored"). The .pickerStyle modifier displays the Picker view as a segmented control by defining .segmented.

7. Type the following after the .pickerStyle modifier:

```
.onChange(of: message) { newValue in
    switch newValue {
    case "happy": message = "Be happy and joyous"
    case "sad": message = "Life can be a struggle at times"
    case "bored": message = "Look for your purpose"
    default:
        break
    }
}
```

The .onChange modifier runs code as soon as it detects a change
in the message State variable, which occurs when the user selects
a different option on the segmented control. When the user
selected a different option, the newValue variable stores that
selected option (such as .tag("happy")).

Based on the value of newValue, a switch statement determines
which text to store in the message State variable. As soon as the
message State variable gets a new value, it gets displayed in the
Text view.

The entire SwiftUI code should look like this:

```swift
import SwiftUI

struct ContentView: View {
    @State private var message = ""
    var body: some View {
        VStack (spacing: 28) {
            Text(message)

            Picker("", selection: $message) {
                Text("Happy").tag("happy")
                Text("Sad").tag("sad")
                Text("Bored").tag("bored")
            }.pickerStyle(.segmented)
                .onChange(of: message) { newValue in
                    switch newValue {
                    case "happy": message = "Be happy and joyous"
                    case "sad": message = "Life can be a struggle at times"
                    case "bored": message = "Look for your purpose"
                    default:
                        break
                    }
                }
        }
    }
}
```

```
struct ContentView_Previews: PreviewProvider {
    static var previews: some View {
        ContentView()
    }
}
```

8. Click the Live icon in the Canvas pane.

9. Click the "Happy," "Sad," and "Bored" options on the segmented control. Each time you choose a different option from the segmented control, the message State variable changes. Then the .onChange modifier runs code to change the message State variable. This new text then appears in the Text view as shown in Figure 6-7.

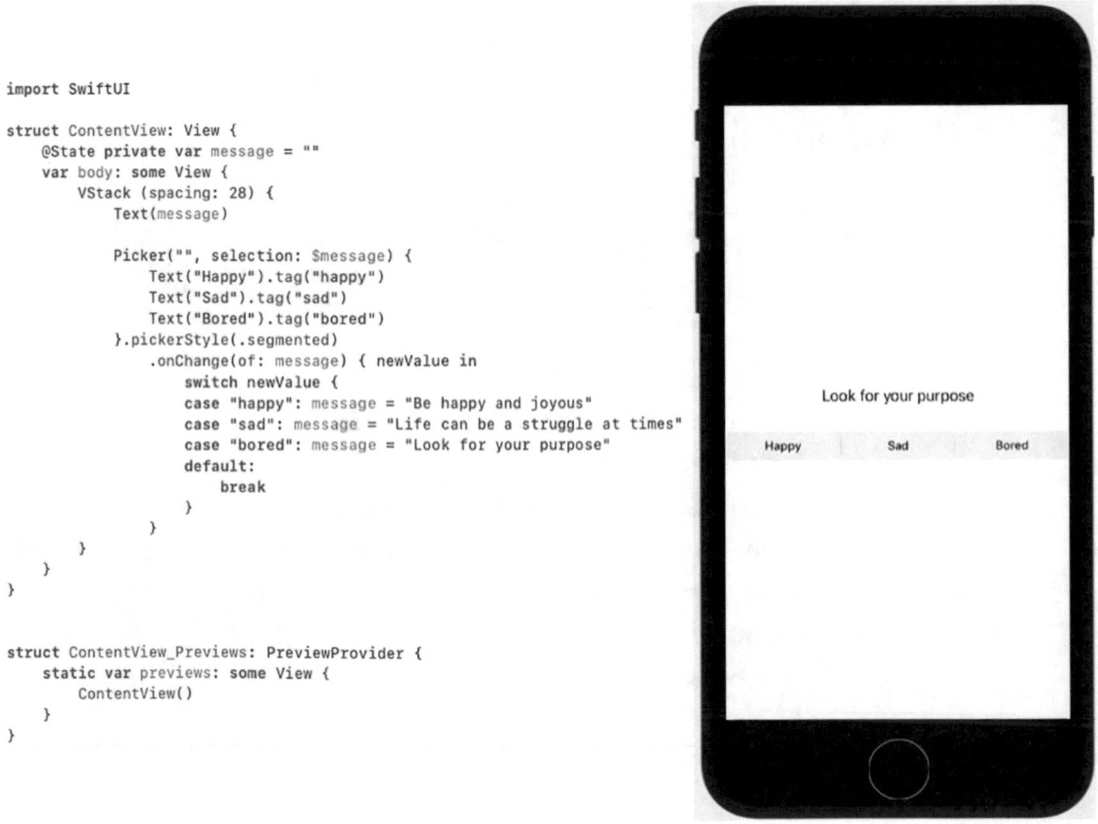

Figure 6-7. *The .onChange modifier can display different texts in the Text view*

By using the .onChange modifier with a segmented control, you can run any Swift code you want when the user chooses a different option on the segmented control. The preceding example uses multiple Text views and .tag properties to populate a Picker view. Here's the code that duplicates that project except using an array and a ForEach loop instead:

```swift
import SwiftUI

struct ContentView: View {

    @State var selectedItem = ""
    @State var message = ""
    let moodArray = ["Happy", "Sad", "Bored"]

    var body: some View {
        VStack {
            Text(message)

            Picker("", selection: $selectedItem) {
                ForEach(moodArray, id: \.self) {
                    Text($0)
                }
            }.pickerStyle(.segmented)
                .onChange(of: selectedItem) { newValue in
                    switch newValue {
                    case "Happy": message = "Be happy and joyous"
                    case "Sad": message = "Life can be a struggle at times"
                    case "Bored": message = "Look for your purpose"
                    default:
                        break
                    }
                }
        }
    }
}
```

```
struct ContentView_Previews: PreviewProvider {
    static var previews: some View {
        ContentView()
    }
}
```

Summary

Buttons represent the simplest way to let the user give commands to a program. At the simplest level, a button consists of text and a list of code to run each time the user selects that button. To customize a button, you can use a Text view or Label view with modifiers or an Image view that can display images such as icons or digital photographs.

A segmented control acts like two or more buttons crammed together in a single control. By using a segmented control, you can display multiple options to the user in a much smaller space than by using multiple buttons.

When working with buttons and segmented controls, you'll often have to create a State variable. When any part of your program changes the value of a State variable, that updated data automatically appears throughout your entire program.

While buttons can run one or more lines of Swift code each time the user selects the button, segmented controls can only run code when combined with the .onChange modifier. Both buttons and segmented controls let you display different options for the user to select on a user interface.

CHAPTER 7

Retrieving Text from Text Fields and Text Editors

User interfaces often need to retrieve text from the user. Sometimes this text can be a single word or short phrase, but other times this text might consist of several paragraphs. To retrieve text from the user, SwiftUI offers three types of views:

- Text Field

- Secure Field

- Text Editor

A Text Field lets the user type in a single line of text such as a name or an address. Optionally, Text Fields can display placeholder text that appears in light gray and is used to explain what type of information the Text Field expects.

A Secure Field works exactly like a Text Field except that it masks any text the user types in. That can be useful when asking the user to type in sensitive information such as credit card numbers.

A Text Editor appears as a large box where the user can type and edit several lines of text such as multiple paragraphs.

Since Text Fields, Secure Fields, and Text Editors need to store data, they need to work with a State variable that can hold a String data type such as

```
@State private var message = ""
```

Using Text Fields

The main purpose of a Text Field is to accept a short amount of text from the user. This can be a single word or a short sentence. To prod the user into typing the expected text, a Text Field can display placeholder text that appears in light gray as shown in Figure 7-1.

© Wallace Wang 2023
W. Wang, *Beginning iPhone Development with SwiftUI*, https://doi.org/10.1007/978-1-4842-9541-0_7

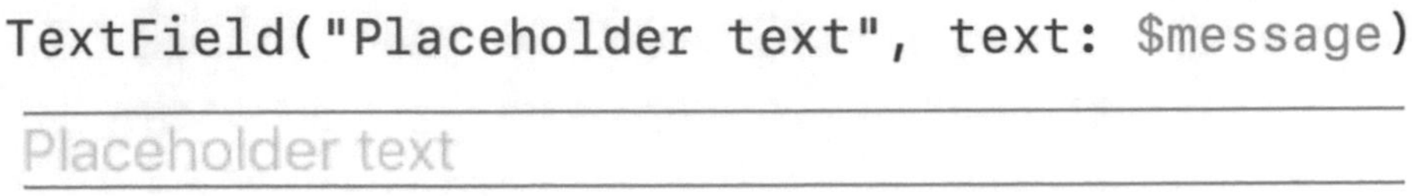

```
TextField("Placeholder text", text: $message)
```

Placeholder text

Figure 7-1. *Text Fields can display placeholder text to guide the user*

When the user types something into a Text Field, that text gets stored in the State variable defined by the text: parameter. In Figure 7-1, this State variable is called "message," and the dollar sign ($) means that the State variable is bound to this Text Field. That means changing the contents of the Text Field automatically changes the message State variable.

Defining Expandable Text Fields

Although a Text Field is meant for accepting a short amount of text, such as an address or a phone number, users can actually type as much text as they want. When a user types too much text, the Text Field can automatically expand either horizontally (the default setting) or vertically.

To define an expandable Text Field, add an axis parameter as either .horizontal or .vertical like this:

```
TextField("Vertical", text: $message, axis: .vertical)
```

When a Text Field expands horizontally, the user can keep typing, and the text appears on a single line until it scrolls out of sight. When a Text Field expands vertically, the width of the Text Field remains fixed, but the height expands to display text on multiple lines as shown in Figure 7-2.

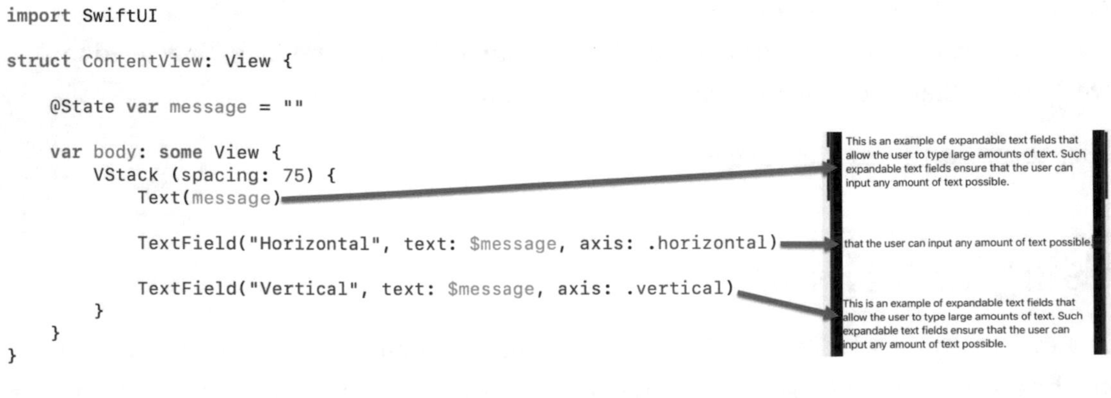

```
import SwiftUI

struct ContentView: View {

    @State var message = ""

    var body: some View {
        VStack (spacing: 75) {
            Text(message)

            TextField("Horizontal", text: $message, axis: .horizontal)

            TextField("Vertical", text: $message, axis: .vertical)
        }
    }
}
```

This is an example of expandable text fields that allow the user to type large amounts of text. Such expandable text fields ensure that the user can input any amount of text possible.

that the user can input any amount of text possible.

This is an example of expandable text fields that allow the user to type large amounts of text. Such expandable text fields ensure that the user can input any amount of text possible.

Figure 7-2. *Text Fields can expand horizontally or vertically*

When a Text Field expands vertically, its height will keep expanding as the user continues typing in text. If you want to define how many lines of text a vertically expanding Text Field can display, use the .lineLimit modifier like this:

```
TextField("Vertical", text: $message, axis: .vertical)
    .lineLimit(3)
```

The preceding code restricts the Text Field to displaying a maximum of three lines of text. When defining a line limit, a vertically expanding Text Field can still allow a large amount of text, but as the user continues typing, the text will scroll up and out of sight.

Rather than define a fixed value to the .lineLimit modifier, you can also define a range such as

```
.lineLimit(2...5)
```

A range means that a Text Field expands and displays the minimum number of text lines and keeps expanding until it reaches the maximum limit. With a .lineLimit(2...5) that defines two to five lines of text, the Text Field will expand to two lines of text. Then if the user keeps adding more text, it will expand to display three lines of text and then four and then finally stop at five. After five lines of text, the Text Field will stop expanding and scroll additional lines of text out of sight.

To see how an expandable Text Field works, follow these steps:

1. Create a new SwiftUI iOS App project and give it any name you wish such as "ExpandableTextField."

2. Click the ContentView file in the Navigator pane.

3. Add a State variable underneath the struct ContentView: View line like this:

```
struct ContentView: View {
    @State var message = ""
```

4. Add a TextField inside the body like this:

```
var body: some View {
    VStack {
        TextField("Vertical", text: $message, axis: .vertical)
            .lineLimit(3)
    }
}
```

The entire ContentView file should look like this:

```
import SwiftUI

struct ContentView: View {
    @State var message = ""

    var body: some View {
        VStack {
            TextField("Vertical", text: $message, axis: .vertical)
                .lineLimit(3)
        }
    }
}

struct ContentView_Previews: PreviewProvider {
    static var previews: some View {
        ContentView()
    }
}
```

5. Click the Live icon.

6. Click in the Text Field and type a large amount of text. Notice that the Text Field expands in height until a maximum of three lines of text appears. Then text starts scrolling up the top of the Text Field.

7. Press the up/down arrow keys to scroll up and down to see any text hidden at the top or bottom of the Text Field.

Changing the Text Field Style

One way to make a Text Field easier to see is to display placeholder text that appears in light gray to let the user know what to type and where to type. A second way to emphasize a Text Field is to add a rounded border around it as shown in Figure 7-3.

Placeholder text

```
TextField("Placeholder text", text: $message)
    .textFieldStyle(.roundedBorder)
    .padding()
```

Figure 7-3. *The appearance of a rounded border around a Text Field*

The .textFieldStyle modifier gives you the option of a .plain or .rounded border:

```
.textFieldStyle(.roundedBorder)
```

While the .roundedBorder displays a border around the Text Field, the .plain modifier eliminates the border and displays the Text Field as if there was no .textFieldStyle modifier at all.

Creating Secure Text Fields

When you type in a Text Field, that text appears visible on the screen. While this can be handy in most cases, it's not appropriate when typing in sensitive information like passwords or credit card numbers. To mask any text that the user types, SwiftUI offers a special text field called a SecureField.

Like a Text Field, a SecureField displays placeholder text and binds itself to a State variable like this:

```
SecureField("Password", text: $message)
```

A SecureField looks identical to a TextField on the user interface. The only difference is that when you type in a SecureField, it masks your text as shown in Figure 7-4.

SecureField

••••••••••|

my password

TextField

Figure 7-4. *The SecureField masks text unlike a Text Field that displays everything the user types*

Any modifier you can use on a Text Field, you can use on a SecureField such as the .textFieldStyle modifier.

Using Autocorrect and Text Content

By default Text Fields use autocorrect, which means as you type, the Text Field tries to guess the word you want to write. In some cases, this can be helpful, but when you're trying to type a name, you don't want autocorrect changing names to common words.

To turn off autocorrect, just add the following modifier:

```
.disableAutocorrection(true)
```

If you want to turn autocorrect back on again, either delete the entire .disableAutocorrection modifier or pass it a false value like this:

```
.disableAutocorrection(false)
```

While disabling autocorrect can stop a Text Field from offering irrelevant suggestions, another solution is to use the .textContentType modifier to define the type of text a Text Field should expect such as a name, email address, or telephone number. To use the .textContentType modifier, you just need to specify the type of text to expect such as

```
TextField("Enter your email address", text: $emailAddress)
        .textContentType(.emailAddress)
```

By defining a specific .textContentType, autocorrect will reduce the number of irrelevant suggestions it makes. The different .textContentType modifier options are

- .URL – For entering URL data

- .namePrefix – For entering prefixes or titles such as Dr. or Mr.

- .name – For entering names

- .nameSuffix – For entering suffixes to names such as Jr.

- .givenName – For entering a first name

- .middleName – For entering a middle name

- .familyName – For entering a family or last name

- .nickname – For entering an alternative name

- .organizationName – For entering an organization name

- .jobTitle – For entering a job title

- .location – For entering a location including an address

- .fullStreetAddress – For entering a complete street address

- .streetAddressLine1 – For entering the first line of a street address

- .streetAddressLine2 – For entering the second line of a street address

- .addressCity – For entering the city name of an address

- .addressCityAndState – For entering a city and a state name in an address

- .postalCode – For entering a postal code in an address

- .sublocality – For entering a sublocality in an address

- .countryName – For entering a country or region name in an address

- .username – For entering an account or login name

- .password – For entering a password

- .newPassword – For entering a new password

- .oneTimeCode – For entering a one-time code

- .emailAddress – For entering an email address

- .telephoneNumber – For entering a telephone number

- .creditCardNumber – For entering a credit card number

- .dateTime – For entering a date, time, or duration

- .flightNumber – For entering an airline flight number

- .shipmentTrackingNumber – For entering a parcel tracking number

Defining Different Keyboards

On a real iOS device, apps display a virtual keyboard that users can tap to type out numbers or characters. Since a Text Field may expect certain types of information such as names, numbers, or email addresses, you can define the specific type of virtual keyboard to use for each Text Field on your user interface. Some of the different virtual keyboards a Text Field can display include

- .default – The virtual keyboard that normally appears unless you specify otherwise

- .asciiCapable – Displays standard ASCII characters

- .numbersAndPunctuation – Displays numbers and punctuation marks

- .URL – Displays a keyboard optimized for URL entries

- .numberPad – Displays a numeric keypad for PIN entry

- .phonePad – Displays a keypad for entering telephone numbers

- .namePhonePad – Displays a keypad for entering a person's name and telephone number

- .emailAddress – Displays a keyboard for typing email addresses

- .decimalPad – Displays a keyboard with numbers and a decimal point

- .twitter – Displays a keyboard for Twitter text entry

- .webSearch – Displays a keyboard for web search terms and URL entry

- .asciiCapableNumberPad – Displays a numeric pad that outputs only ASCII digits

- .alphabet – Displays a keyboard for alphabetic entry

Figure 7-5 shows four different appearances of the virtual keyboard.

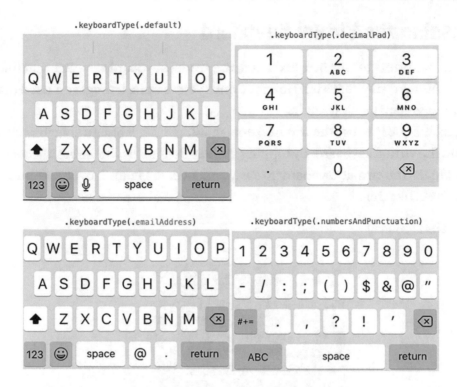

Figure 7-5. *Different appearances of the virtual keyboard*

To define a particular keyboard type for a Text Field, use the .keyboardType modifier like this:

```
TextField("Enter name", text: $message)
    .keyboardType(.phonePad)
```

Note   To view a virtual keyboard, you must test your project in the Simulator or on an actual iOS device. In the Simulator, you can toggle to hide or display the virtual keyboard by choosing I/O ➤ Keyboard ➤ Toggle Software Keyboard or by pressing Command+K. You cannot view the virtual keyboard in the Canvas pane.

Dismissing the Virtual Keyboard

When the user wants to type in a Text Field, the virtual keyboard appears, and the user interface automatically slides up. However, once you're done typing, you need to make the virtual keyboard go away again.

One technique is to use the .submitLabel modifier that defines a specific key to appear on the virtual keyboard. By tapping this key defined by the .submitLabel modifier, users can make the virtual keyboard go away as shown in Figure 7-6. The .submitLabel modifier looks like this:

```
.submitLabel(.done)
```

Figure 7-6. *The .submitLabel(.done) modifier displays a Done button on the virtual keyboard*

If you don't specify a .submitLabel modifier, SwiftUI defaults to displaying a Return button in the bottom-right corner of the virtual keyboard. No matter what label appears on the bottom-right corner key, tapping it will make the virtual keyboard go away.

The different types of buttons the .submitLabel modifier can place on the virtual keyboard include

- .continue – Adds a Continue button

- .done – Adds a Done button

- .go – Adds a Go button

- .join – Adds a Join button

- .next – Adds a Next button

- .return – Adds a Return button

- .route – Adds a Route button

- .search – Adds a Search button

- .send – Adds a Send button

To see how to hide the virtual keyboard by using the virtual keyboard button that you can define, follow these steps:

1. Create a new SwiftUI iOS App project and give it any name you wish such as "DismissKeyboard."

2. Click the ContentView file in the Navigator pane.

3. Add a State variable underneath the struct ContentView: View line like this:

```
struct ContentView: View {
    @State var message = ""
```

4. Add a TextField inside the body like this:

```
var body: some View {
    TextField("Type here", text: $message)
        .submitLabel(.done)
        .padding()
}
```

The entire ContentView file should look like this:

```
import SwiftUI

struct ContentView: View {
    @State var message = ""
    var body: some View {
        TextField("Type here", text: $message)
            .submitLabel(.done)
            .padding()
    }
}
```

```
struct ContentView_Previews: PreviewProvider {
    static var previews: some View {
        ContentView()
    }
}
```

5. Click the Run button or choose Product ➤ Run to run your app in
    the Simulator.

6. Click in the Text Field when your app appears in the Simulator.
    If the virtual keyboard does not appear, press Command+K or
    choose I/O ➤ Keyboard ➤ Toggle Software Keyboard.

7. Click the Done button in the bottom-right corner of the virtual
    keyboard to make the virtual keyboard disappear.

Using a Text Editor

Where a Text Field lets the user type in a word or short sentence, a Text Editor lets the
user type in multiple lines of text, much like a word processor. When you place a Text
Editor on a user interface, it expands to fill all available space. That's why it's best to use
the .frame modifier to define a specific size for the Text Editor.

With a Text Field, tapping the button in the bottom-right corner of the virtual
keyboard makes it go away. Since a Text Editor can hold multiple lines of text, the button
in the bottom-right corner of the virtual keyboard simply moves the cursor to the next
line and always displays the "Return" label.

So if you want to hide a virtual keyboard when using a Text Editor, you need to do the
following:

-   Create a Focus State variable that represents a Boolean value.

-   Add the .focused modifier to the Text Editor and use the Focus State
    variable.

-   Create an additional control, such as a button, that sets the Focus
    State variable to false.

Note   This method of using a Focus State variable with a .focused modifier and a separate control works with Text Fields as well.

First, you need to create a FocusState variable like this:

```
@FocusState var dismissKeyboard: Bool
```

Once you've defined a FocusState variable, you need to use the .focused modifier on a Text Editor (or Text Field) to link to the FocusState variable like this:

```
TextEditor(text: $message)
    .focused($dismissKeyboard)
```

Then you can set the value of the FocusState variable to false through a separate control to make the virtual keyboard disappear like this:

```
Button("Hide Keyboard") {
    dismissKeyboard = false
}
```

To see how Focus State variables work, follow these steps:

1. Create a new SwiftUI iOS App project and give it any name you wish such as "DismissKeyboardTextEditor."

2. Click the ContentView file in the Navigator pane.

3. Create a State variable to hold the contents of a Text Editor, and create a Focus State variable to make the virtual keyboard disappear as follows:

```
struct ContentView: View {

    @State var message = ""
    @FocusState var dismissKeyboard: Bool
```

4. Add a Button and a Text Editor inside of a VStack. To keep the Text Editor from expanding, make sure you add a .frame modifier to the Text Editor. The entire code inside the ContentView file should look like this:

```
import SwiftUI

struct ContentView: View {

    @State var message = ""
    @FocusState var dismissKeyboard: Bool

    var body: some View {
        VStack {
            TextEditor(text: $message)
                .focused($dismissKeyboard)
                .frame(width: 250, height: 150)
                .padding()

            Button("Hide Keyboard") {
                dismissKeyboard = false
            }
        }
    }
}

struct ContentView_Previews: PreviewProvider {
    static var previews: some View {
        ContentView()
    }
}
```

5. Click the Run button or choose Product ➤ Run to run your app in the Simulator.

6. Click in the Text Editor when your app appears in the Simulator. If the virtual keyboard does not appear, press Command+K or choose I/O ➤ Keyboard ➤ Toggle Software Keyboard.

7. Type some text and then click the "Hide Keyboard" Button that you created below the Text Editor. This sets the Focus State variable dismissKeyboard to false, which makes the virtual keyboard go away.

You must use a Focus State variable to make the virtual keyboard go away with a Text Editor.

Summary

One of the most common ways a user can input data into an app is by typing in text. A Text Field can accept a short amount of text such as a name or sentence. By default, a Text Field will expand horizontally, which means the user can keep inputting as much text as they wish and it will appear as a single line.

If you change the Text Field to expand vertically, the height of the Text Field will increase and display multiple lines of text as the user continues inputting text. To keep a Text Field from expanding endlessly, you can use the .lineLimit modifier to define the maximum number of lines to appear in the TextField.

If the user needs to type in sensitive information that shouldn't be displayed on the screen, you can use a Secure Field, which masks anything typed. For displaying multiple lines of text, you can use a Text Editor, which acts like a miniature word processor.

To make typing text easier, use the .contentType modifier to define what type of information a Text Field can expect such as a name or email address. Then use the .keyboardType modifier to define a specific virtual keyboard optimized for inputting in a certain type of information such as telephone numbers or names.

To make a virtual keyboard go away when the user no longer needs it, Text Fields and Secure Fields can rely on the bottom-right corner button to dismiss the virtual keyboard. By using the .submitLabel modifier, you can define common types of titles for this bottom-right corner virtual keyboard button such as Done, Send, or Next.

When creating a Text Editor, it will expand to fill all available space, so you may want to use the .frame modifier to define a specific width and height for the Text Editor. To hide a virtual keyboard when using a Text Editor, use a Focus State variable with the .focused modifier. Then create a separate control, such as a button, to set the Focus State variable to false. This will make the virtual keyboard go away.

Text is the most common way to input data, so make it easy for users to type data into a Text Field, Secure Field, or Text Editor.

CHAPTER 8

Limiting Choices with Pickers

Text Fields are great for letting the user enter any type of information such as names or short answers to questions. The problem is that if the user has the freedom to enter anything, they could accidentally (or on purpose) enter invalid data.

For example, if a Text Field asks for an address, you want the user to have the freedom to type anything. However, if a Text Field asks for a state, language, or gender, you don't want the user to type "dog," "1258dke3," or "I am looking for shoes" because none of this would be valid input, which would likely crash the program.

One solution is to let the user enter any data and then write Swift code to verify that the input is valid. Unfortunately, this would likely take a lot of time and still not be accurate. A far better solution is when there are only a handful of acceptable options; it's best to restrict the user to selecting from a limited range of options.

Pickers display several options and give the user a chance to click to select one option. Since all options are valid, Pickers ensure that users can only enter valid data. An ordinary Picker is fine for letting a user select from a range of text options. For selecting colors or dates, SwiftUI offers special Color Pickers and Date Pickers as well.

Date Pickers even let you define a valid date range. The whole purpose of Pickers is to make sure the user can only input valid data into a program at any given time.

Using a Picker

A Picker displays a list of options defined by multiple Text views. Although a Picker uses text strings to display available options, whatever option the user chooses can actually represent any value such as a string, a decimal number, an integer, or a value defined by an enumeration. (Segmented controls, a special type of Picker view, were introduced in Chapter 6.)

© Wallace Wang 2023
W. Wang, *Beginning iPhone Development with SwiftUI*, https://doi.org/10.1007/978-1-4842-9541-0_8

To create a Picker, use multiple Text views to display the options and attach a .tag modifier to each option. The .tag modifier defines the actual value the user chose such as

```
Picker(selection: $choice, label: Text("Picker")){
    Text("1").tag("one")
    Text("2").tag("two")
    Text("3").tag("three")
    Text("4").tag("four")
    Text("5").tag("five")
}
```

In this example, the available options are numbers, but when the user selects a number, the actual choice is stored as a string such as "three" or "five" as shown in Figure 8-1.

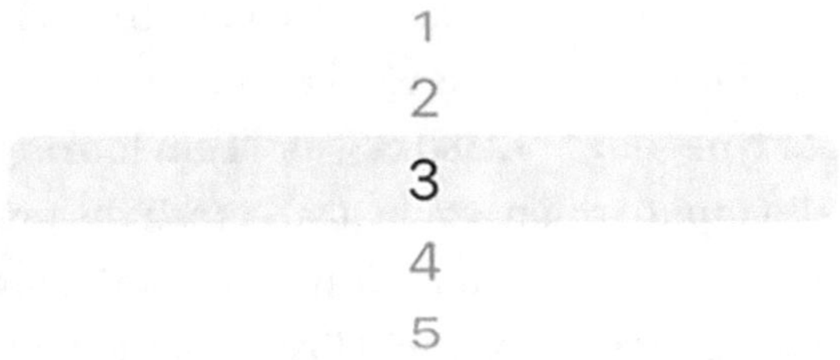

Figure 8-1. *A Picker uses Text views to display choices on the user interface*

The .tag modifier on a Text view can contain any data type, but all .tag modifiers inside the same Picker must be of the same data type that matches the State variable that it's linked to. The following Swift code defines a Picker where multiple Text views display words such as "Cat" or "Bird", but the .tag modifiers store integers such as 0 or 2:

```
Picker("", selection: $choice) {
    Text("Bird").tag(1)
    Text("Cat").tag(2)
    Text("Lizard").tag(3)
    Text("Dog").tag(4)
    Text("Hamster").tag(5)
}
```

Because the .tag modifier contains integers, the "choice" State variable now needs to store Int data types such as

```
@State private var choice = 0
```

To see how a Picker works, follow these steps:

1. Create a new SwiftUI iOS App project and give it any name you wish such as "Picker."

2. Click the ContentView file in the Navigator pane.

3. Add the following State variable under the struct ContentView: View line:

    ```
    struct ContentView: View {
        @State private var choice = 0
    ```

    This creates a State variable that's initially set to 0, which is an integer, so the "choice" State variable is defined to hold Int data types.

4. Create a VStack and create a Picker and a Text view inside the var body: some View line:

    ```
    var body: some View {
        VStack {
            Picker("", selection: $choice) {
                Text("Bird").tag(1)
                Text("Cat").tag(2)
                Text("Lizard").tag(3)
                Text("Dog").tag(4)
                Text("Hamster").tag(5)
            }

            Text("Choice = \(choice)")
        }
    }
    ```

The entire code in the ContentView file should look like this:

```swift
import SwiftUI

struct ContentView: View {
    @State var choice = 0
    var body: some View {
        VStack {
            Picker("", selection: $choice) {
                Text("Bird").tag(1)
                Text("Cat").tag(2)
                Text("Lizard").tag(3)
                Text("Dog").tag(4)
                Text("Hamster").tag(5)
            }

            Text("Choice = \(choice)")
        }
    }
}

struct ContentView_Previews: PreviewProvider {
    static var previews: some View {
        ContentView()
    }
}
```

5. Click the Live icon in the Canvas pane.

6. Select different options in the Picker. Notice that each time you select a different option, the Text view displays "Choice = __" where __ is the .tag value attached to the Text view that the user chose.

7. Change the State variable as follows to hold Double data types:

```swift
@State private var choice = 0.0
```

Because this "choice" State variable has an initial value of 0.0, which is a decimal number, Swift infers that the "choice" variable can now only hold Double data types.

8. Change the .tag modifiers in the Picker as follows:

```
Picker("", selection: $choice) {
    Text("Bird").tag(1.7)
    Text("Cat").tag(2.06)
    Text("Lizard").tag(3.41)
    Text("Dog").tag(4.13)
    Text("Hamster").tag(5.28)
}
```

Because the "choice" State variable has been redefined to hold Double data types, the .tag modifier values must now all represent Double data types as well.

9. Click the Live icon in the Canvas pane.

10. Select different options in the Picker. Notice that each time you select a different option, the Text view displays "Choice = __" where __ is the .tag value as a Double value as shown in Figure 8-2.

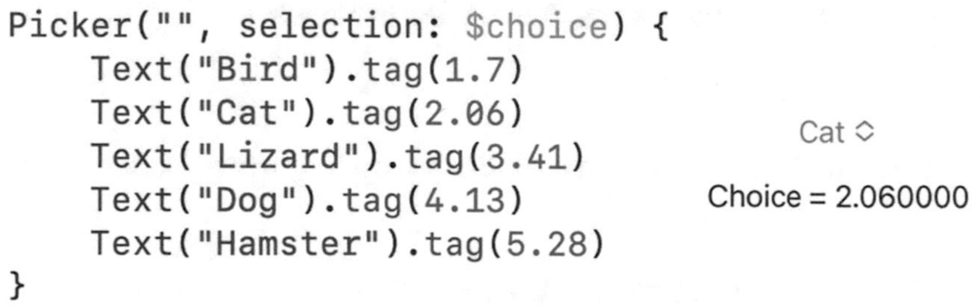

```
Picker("", selection: $choice) {
    Text("Bird").tag(1.7)
    Text("Cat").tag(2.06)
    Text("Lizard").tag(3.41)              Cat ◇
    Text("Dog").tag(4.13)          Choice = 2.060000
    Text("Hamster").tag(5.28)
}
```

Figure 8-2. *A Picker view uses Double values in its .tag modifiers*

By default, a Picker view appears as a menu. However, the .pickerStyle modifier gives you three different ways to display the Picker view as shown in Figure 8-3:

- .pickerStyle(.menu)

- .pickerStyle(.wheel)

- .pickerStyle(.segmented)

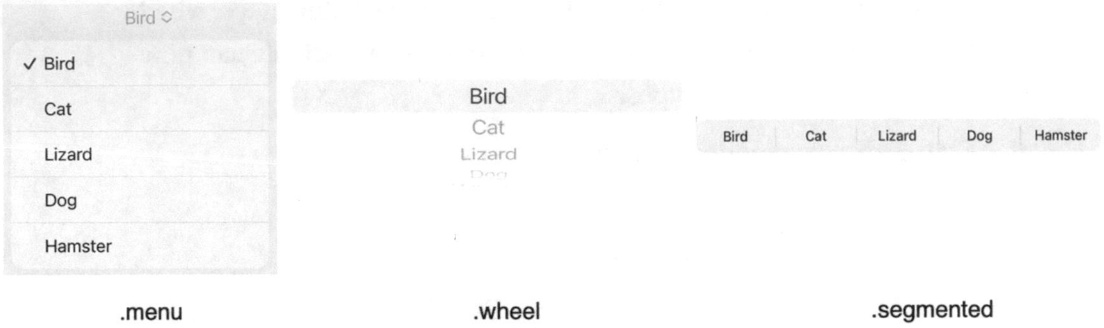

Figure 8-3. *Three different Picker view styles*

Displaying Options in a Picker

The most straightforward way to display options in a Picker is by using multiple Text views. For small numbers of options, this works fine, but if you have a large number of options, especially when displaying options using the .wheel picker style, it's often more convenient to use a ForEach loop to retrieve options from an array.

First, create an array that holds all the options you want to appear in the Picker view such as

```
let myArray = ["Fish", "Tortoise", "Hare", "Bird"]
```

Then create a State variable for the Picker view to access:

```
@State var selectedItem = ""
```

Finally, create the Picker view with a ForEach loop to retrieve each item in the array like this:

```
        Picker("", selection: $selectedItem) {
            ForEach(myArray, id: \.self) {
                Text($0)
            }
        }
```

The ForEach loop needs to know which array to access, and then it uses its id parameter to identify each different array item to display in the Text view. The Text view uses the shortcut $0 to represent each array item.

To see how to use an array and a ForEach loop to populate a Picker view, follow these steps:

1. Create a new SwiftUI iOS App project and give it any name you wish such as "PickerWheel."

2. Click the ContentView file in the Navigator pane.

3. Add the following State variable and array declaration under the struct ContentView: View line:

```
struct ContentView: View {
    let myArray = ["Fish", "Tortoise", "Hare", "Bird"]
    @State var selectedItem = ""
```

4. Create a VStack and put a Picker view inside and use the .wheel option for its picker style. The Picker view must bind to the State variable selectedItem. Inside the Picker view, add a ForEach loop that retrieves each item from the array like this:

```
var body: some View {
    VStack {
        Picker("", selection: $selectedItem) {
            ForEach(myArray, id: \.self) {
                Text($0)
            }
        }.pickerStyle(.wheel)
    }
}
```

5. Above the Picker view, add an Image view, a Text view, and a Spacer like this:

```
        VStack {

            Image(systemName: selectedItem.lowercased())
                .font(.custom("", size: 60))
                .foregroundColor(Color.red)
```

```
Text("You chose = \(selectedItem)")

Spacer()

Picker("", selection: $selectedItem) {
    ForEach(myArray, id: \.self) {
        Text($0)
    }
}.pickerStyle(.wheel)
}
```

The Image view takes the selectedItem State variable and changes it to lowercase. That's because each option displayed in the Picker view (from the array) represents a name of an icon, but each icon name consists of lowercase letters. To make this icon visible, the .font modifier changes the size to 60, and the .foregroundColor modifier changes the color to red.

The Text view displays the name of the item the user selected from the Picker view. The Spacer pushes the Image and Text views to the top of the screen while pushing the Picker view to the bottom as shown in Figure 8-4.

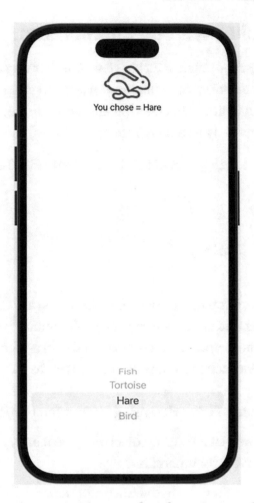

Figure 8-4. *The Image view, Text view, and Picker view on the user interface*

6.   Click the Live icon in the Canvas pane.

7.   Choose an option from the Picker view wheel. Each time you choose a different option, notice that the Text view displays the name of your choice, while the Image view displays the appropriate image with each choice.

Populating a Picker with an Enumeration

An array can be one way to populate a Picker view. Another way can be by retrieving options listed in an enumeration. An enumeration lets you define your own data type with a limited list of valid options. To create an enumeration, you need to define the enumeration name followed by its data type (such as String) such as

```
enum ColorItems: String, CaseIterable, Identifiable {
    case rose
    case grass
    case sky
    var id: Self { self }
}
```

Following the enumeration name (such as ColorItems) are CaseIterable and Identifiable. CaseIterable means we can access the options listed within the enumeration and treat these options (rose, grass, and sky) as data such as Strings. Identifiable means the ForEach loop can count each item in the enumeration, using the id: Self { self } variable.

To see how to populate a Picker view using an enumeration, follow these steps:

1. Create a new SwiftUI iOS App project and give it any name you wish such as "PickerEnumeration."

2. Click the ContentView file in the Navigator pane.

3. Add the following State variables and enumeration declaration under the struct ContentView: View line:

```
struct ContentView: View {
    @State private var selectedColor = ColorItems.rose
    @State var myColor = Color.red

    enum ColorItems: String, CaseIterable, Identifiable {
        case rose
        case grass
        case sky
        var id: Self { self }
    }
```

The selectedColor State variable represents the ColorItems enumeration data type (ColorItems). The myColor State variable represents a Color data type. The ColorItems enumeration defines three valid options: rose, grass, or sky.

4.   Create a VStack and add a Rectangle and a Picker view where the picker style is .wheel. The Picker view must bind to the State variable selectedColor. Inside the Picker view, add a ForEach loop that retrieves each item from the enumeration like this:

```
var body: some View {
    VStack {
        Rectangle()
            .fill(myColor)

        Picker("Favorite Color", selection: $selectedColor) {
            ForEach(ColorItems.allCases, id: \.self) {catFood in
                Text(catFood.rawValue.capitalized)
            }
        }.pickerStyle(.wheel)
    }
}
```

The Rectangle contains the color defined by the myColor State variable. The Picker view uses a ForEach loop to retrieve each item from the ColorItems enumeration. Because the ColorItems enumeration was defined as CaseIterable, the ForEach loop can retrieve each item using .allCases and the id parameter.

The ForEach loop uses an arbitrarily named variable (catFood) to store each item from the enumeration. Then the Text view uses each enumeration item, retrieves its .rawValue (which is the String data type "rose", "grass", and "sky"), and displays the item in the Picker view capitalized ("Rose," "Grass," and "Sky").

5. Add .onChange to the Picker view as follows:

```
.onChange(of: selectedColor) { newValue in
    switch newValue {
    case ColorItems.rose: myColor = Color.red
    case ColorItems.grass: myColor = Color.green
    case ColorItems.sky: myColor = Color.blue
    }
}
```

When .onChange detects that the user selected a different item from the Picker view, it stores that selected item in the newValue variable. The switch statement then checks what option the user selected from the Picker view (rose, grass, or sky). Based on which item the user selected from the Picker view, the switch statement assigns a color to the myColor State variable. The myColor State variable immediately sends the color to the Rectangle.

The entire ContentView file should look like this:

```
import SwiftUI

struct ContentView: View {
    @State private var selectedColor = ColorItems.rose
    @State var myColor = Color.red

    enum ColorItems: String, CaseIterable, Identifiable {
        case rose
        case grass
        case sky
        var id: Self { self }
    }
    var body: some View {
        VStack {
            Rectangle()
                .fill(myColor)
```

```
        Picker("Favorite Color", selection: $selectedColor) {
            ForEach(ColorItems.allCases, id: \.self)
            {catFood in
                Text(catFood.rawValue.capitalized)
            }
        }.pickerStyle(.wheel)
            .onChange(of: selectedColor) { newValue in
                switch newValue {
                case ColorItems.rose: myColor = Color.red
                case ColorItems.grass: myColor = Color.green
                case ColorItems.sky: myColor = Color.blue
                }
            }
        }
    }
}

struct ContentView_Previews: PreviewProvider {
    static var previews: some View {
        ContentView()
    }
}
```

6. Click the Live icon in the Canvas pane.

7. Click the Picker view and choose an option. Whatever option you choose, the related color will appear in the Rectangle.

Using the Color Picker

An ordinary Picker lets you select different options displayed in a Text view. However, what if you want the user to select a particular color? You could list several colors in a Picker, but what if the user wants to select a custom color? That's when you can use the Color Picker.

The Color Picker lets the user select standard colors (red, blue, green, yellow, etc.) or custom colors from a grid or a spectrum or from red, green, and blue sliders as shown in Figure 8-5.

Figure 8-5. *A Color Picker gives you three different options for choosing a custom color*

To create a Color Picker, you must first create a State variable to hold a Color data type such as

```
@State var myColor = Color.red
```

Then you can create a Color Picker by defining a descriptive title followed by a link to the State variable that represents a Color like this:

```
ColorPicker("Pick a color", selection: $myColor)
```

To see how a Color Picker works, follow these steps:

1. Create a new SwiftUI iOS App project and give it any name you wish such as "ColorPicker."

2. Click the ContentView file in the Navigator pane.

3. Add the following State variable under the struct ContentView: View line:

```
struct ContentView: View {
    @State var myColor = Color.gray
```

4. Create a VStack and put a Rectangle inside. Since a Rectangle will expand to fill the entire screen, make sure you put a .frame modifier on it and define its .foregroundColor with the previously defined State variable:

```
var body: some View {
    VStack {
        Rectangle()
            .frame(width: 200, height: 150)
            .foregroundColor(myColor)
    }
}
```

5. Underneath the Rectangle(), define a Color Picker that links or binds to the State variable:

```
ColorPicker("Pick a color", selection: $myColor)
```

The entire ContentView file should look like this:

```
import SwiftUI

struct ContentView: View {
    @State var myColor = Color.gray
    var body: some View {
        VStack {
            Rectangle()
                .frame(width: 200, height: 150)
                .foregroundColor(myColor)
            ColorPicker("Pick a color", selection: $myColor)
        }
    }
}
```

```
struct ContentView_Previews: PreviewProvider {
    static var previews: some View {
        ContentView()
    }
}
```

6. Click the Live icon in the Canvas pane. Notice that since the State variable myColor is given an initial value of gray, the Rectangle initially appears as gray.

7. Click the Color Picker icon, as shown in Figure 8-6, to display the different color options (see Figure 8-4).

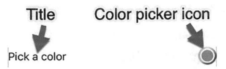

Figure 8-6. *The Color Picker icon*

8. Click a color and then click the close (X) icon in the upper-right corner of the Color Picker dialog to make it go away. Notice that the Rectangle now displays the color you chose.

The Color Picker not only lets users select a color but also an opacity. By default, opacity is turned on, but if you want to turn it off, you can turn it off by changing the supportsOpacity parameter to false like this:

```
ColorPicker("Pick a color", selection: $myColor, supportsOpacity: false)
```

When the supportsOpacity parameter is true (or omitted), the opacity slider appears. When the supportsOpacity parameter is false, the opacity slider does not appear as shown in Figure 8-7.

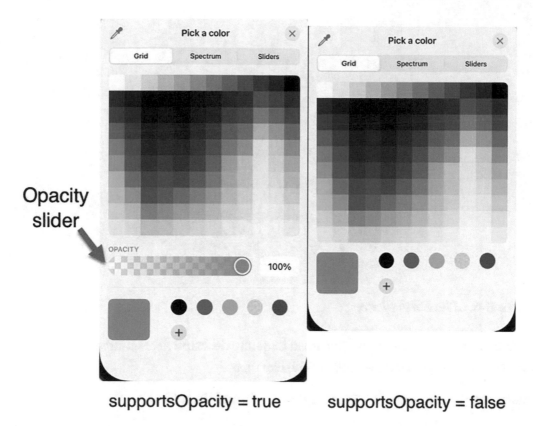

supportsOpacity = true   supportsOpacity = false

Figure 8-7. *The Color Picker with opacity turned on and off*

Using the Date Picker

One common type of data that users need to input are dates and times. However, one person might write a date as "June 14, 2023," and another might write that same date as "6/14/23." When writing a time, one person might type "6:45 p.m." and another might type "18:45."

To make it easy for users to enter dates and times, SwiftUI offers the Date Picker. Instead of typing a date or time, users can simply click the date or time they want as shown in Figure 8-8.

Figure 8-8. *The Date Picker*

To create a Date Picker, you just need to define descriptive text and a State variable to store the user's selected date and/or time like this:

```
DatePicker(selection: $myDate, label: { Text("Date") })
```

Choosing a Date Picker Style

By default, a Date Picker displays a date and time as a field that the user can select. In case you don't like the Date Picker's default, compact format, you can customize the Date Picker's appearance using the .datePickerStyle() modifier as shown in Figure 8-9.

January 2023 >   < >

SUN	MON	TUE	WED	THU	FRI	SAT
1	2	3	4	5	6	7
8	9	10	11	12	13	14
(15)	16	17	18	19	20	21
22	23	24	25	26	27	28
29	30	31				

Date Picker   Jan 15, 2023   7:00 PM

Time   7:26 PM

.compact   .graphical   .wheel

Figure 8-9. *Different styles of the Date Picker*

- .compact – The default way to display a date and time. When the user selects a date, a calendar appears like in the .graphical style. When the user selects a time, different times appear like in the .wheel style.

- .graphical – Displays dates in a calendar but the time as a field. When the user selects a time, different times appear like in the .wheel style.

- .wheel – Displays dates and times in a wheel.

The Swift code for creating a Date Picker requires just adding a State variable to store a date and then using that State variable. In addition, the Date Picker lets you define text to appear when the Date Picker style is .compact:

```
@State var myDate = Date.now

DatePicker(selection: $myDate, label: { Text("Date") })
        .datePickerStyle(.graphical)
```

Displaying a Date and/or Time

Although the Date Picker can let the user select both a date and a time, you may only want the Date Picker to select either a date or a time. To limit the Date Picker to displaying just a date or a time, you can add the displayedComponents parameter and specify either [.date] or [.hourAndMinute] like this:

```
DatePicker(selection: $myDate, displayedComponents: [.date],
label: { Text("Date") })

DatePicker(selection: $myDate, displayedComponents:
[.hourAndMinute], label: { Text("Time") })
```

Restricting a Date Range

When letting users select a date, you may want to restrict the list of valid dates. For example, if you're asking for someone's birthdate, it doesn't make sense to let the Date Picker allow a user to select an outrageously old date of birth such as February 3, 1737.

To restrict a date range for a Date Picker, you must first define the start and end date range such as

```
let dateRange: ClosedRange<Date> = {
    let calendar = Calendar.current
    let startComponents = DateComponents(year: 2024, month: 1, day: 1)
    let endComponents = DateComponents(year: 2024, month: 12, day: 31,
    hour: 23, minute: 59, second: 59)
    return calendar.date(from:startComponents)!
        ...
        calendar.date(from:endComponents)!
}()
```

Notice that a closed range requires defining both a starting date and an ending date. The user can't go further in the past beyond the starting date and can't go further in the future beyond the ending date.

Besides a closed range, you can also choose a partial range. One way is to define a partial range that starts from a specific date such as

```
let dateRange2: PartialRangeFrom<Date> = {
    let calendar = Calendar.current
    let startComponents = DateComponents(year: 2023, month: 1, day: 1)
    return calendar.date(from:startComponents)!...
}()
```

The preceding range starts at January 1, 2023, and allows the Date Picker to choose any date beyond this starting date. Another way to define a partial range is one that goes up to but stops at a specific date such as

```
let dateRange3: PartialRangeThrough<Date> = {
    let calendar = Calendar.current
    let stopComponents = DateComponents(year: 2024, month: 1, day: 1)
    return ...calendar.date(from:stopComponents)!
}()
```

This range lets the Date Picker choose any date up to the specified date (January 1, 2024, in this case). Once you define a date range, you need to add this date range into the Date Picker like this:

```
DatePicker(selection: $myDate, in: dateRange,
displayedComponents: [.date], label: { Text("Date") })
```

This Date Picker uses a State variable called myDate, defines the valid range by the dateRange constant, and only displays dates (and not times). If the Date Picker style is .compact, then it will also display "Date" on the Date Picker.

To see how to use a Date Picker, follow these steps:

1. Create a new SwiftUI iOS App project and give it any name you wish such as "DatePicker."

2. Click the ContentView file in the Navigator pane.

3. Create a State variable to hold a date like this:

```
@State var myDate = Date.now
```

4. Define three date ranges as follows:

```
let dateRange: ClosedRange<Date> = {
    let calendar = Calendar.current
    let startComponents = DateComponents(year: 2023, month:
    1, day: 1)
    let endComponents = DateComponents(year: 2023, month: 12, day:
    31, hour: 23, minute: 59, second: 59)
    return calendar.date(from:startComponents)!
        ...
```

```
            calendar.date(from:endComponents)!
    }()

    let dateRange2: PartialRangeFrom<Date> = {
        let calendar = Calendar.current
        let startComponents = DateComponents(year: 2023,
        month: 1, day: 1)
        let endComponents = DateComponents(year: 2023, month: 12, day:
        31, hour: 23, minute: 59, second: 59)
        return calendar.date(from:endComponents)!...
    }()

    let dateRange3: PartialRangeThrough<Date> = {
        let calendar = Calendar.current
        let startComponents = DateComponents(year: 2023,
        month: 1, day: 1)
        let endComponents = DateComponents(year: 2023, month: 12, day:
        31, hour: 23, minute: 59, second: 59)
        return ...calendar.date(from:startComponents)!
    }()
```

5. Create a VStack to hold a Text view and a Date Picker like this:

```
var body: some View {
    VStack {
        Text("Chosen date = \(myDate)")
            .padding()

        DatePicker(selection: $myDate, in: dateRange3,
        displayedComponents: [.date], label: { Text("Date") })
            .datePickerStyle(.graphical)
            .padding()
    }
}
```

The entire ContentView file should look like this:

```
import SwiftUI

struct ContentView: View {

    @State var myDate = Date.now

    let dateRange: ClosedRange<Date> = {
        let calendar = Calendar.current
        let startComponents = DateComponents(year: 2023,
        month: 1, day: 1)
        let endComponents = DateComponents(year: 2023, month: 12,
        day: 31, hour: 23, minute: 59, second: 59)
        return calendar.date(from:startComponents)!

            ...
            calendar.date(from:endComponents)!
    }()

    let dateRange2: PartialRangeFrom<Date> = {
        let calendar = Calendar.current
        let startComponents = DateComponents(year: 2023,
        month: 1, day: 1)
        let endComponents = DateComponents(year: 2023, month: 12,
        day: 31, hour: 23, minute: 59, second: 59)
        return calendar.date(from:endComponents)!...
    }()

    let dateRange3: PartialRangeThrough<Date> = {
        let calendar = Calendar.current
        let startComponents = DateComponents(year: 2023,
        month: 1, day: 1)
        let endComponents = DateComponents(year: 2023, month: 12,
        day: 31, hour: 23, minute: 59, second: 59)
        return ...calendar.date(from:startComponents)!
    }()
```

```
var body: some View {
    VStack {
        Text("Chosen date = \(myDate)")
            .padding()

        DatePicker(selection: $myDate, in: dateRange,
        displayedComponents: [.date], label: { Text("Date") })
            .datePickerStyle(.graphical)
            .padding()
    }
}

struct ContentView_Previews: PreviewProvider {
    static var previews: some View {
        ContentView()
    }
}
```

6. Click the Live icon in the Canvas pane and click any date. Notice that when you choose a date, it appears above the Date Picker as shown in Figure 8-10.

Chosen date = Sunday, January 15, 2023 at
8:46:10 PM Pacific Standard Time

January 2023 >   ‹   ›

SUN	MON	TUE	WED	THU	FRI	SAT
1	2	3	4	5	6	7
8	9	10	11	12	13	14
15	16	17	18	19	20	21
22	23	24	25	26	27	28
29	30	31				

Figure 8-10.   *The user interface showing a Text view and a Date Picker*

7. Experiment with changing the Date Picker style (.compact,
    .graphical, .wheel) along with choosing the different date ranges
    (dateRange, dateRange2, dateRange3).

Formatting Dates

By default, SwiftUI displays dates with lots of details that you may not want to display. To
display dates within a specific format, you can use the DateFormatter like this:

```
let formatter = DateFormatter()
```

Then you can define a style to display dates and times such as one of the following:

Style	Date	Time
.short	2/15/22	7:15 PM
.medium	Feb 15, 2022	7:15:29 PM
.long	February 15, 2022	7:15:29 PM CST
.full	Tuesday, February 15, 2022	7:15:29 PM Central Standard Time

Note   The locale may change the way dates are actually displayed such as 15 June 2021 or June 15, 2021.

To use a date style, you must define the formatter's dateStyle property like this:

```
formatter.dateStyle = .medium
```

To use a time style, you must define the formatter's timeStyle property like this:

```
formatter.timeStyle = .short
```

Once you've created a DateFormatter and defined its .dateStyle and .timeStyle properties, the final step is to format a date using that formatter and its dateStyle such as

```
formatter.string(from: myDate)
```

To see how to format dates chosen from a Date Picker, follow these steps:

1. Create a new SwiftUI iOS App project and give it any name you wish such as "DatePickerFormat."

2. Click the ContentView file in the Navigator pane.

3. Create a State variable to hold a date like this:

    ```
    @State var myDate = Date.now
    ```

4. Type the following underneath the State variable to define a DateFormatter:

    ```
    let formatter = DateFormatter()
    ```

5. Add a VStack inside the var body: some View line and create a Date Picker inside the VStack like this:

    ```
    VStack {
        Text("Chosen date = \(formatter.string( from: myDate))")
            .padding()

        DatePicker(selection: $myDate, label: { Text("Date") })
    ```

```
}.onAppear() {
    formatter.dateStyle = .full
    formatter.timeStyle = .full
}
```

The Text view displays "Chosen date = " followed by the date, which is stored in the myDate State variable. Notice that the formatter.string command defines how that date is actually displayed.

The Date Picker stores the selected date in the myDate State variable. Then the .onAppear modifier runs Swift code every time the user interface defined by the VStack appears. Inside this .onAppear modifier is the single line that defines the .dateStyle of the formatter to .full. If you change .full to .short, .medium, or .long, you can see how that formats the date differently in the Text view.

The entire ContentView files should look like this:

```
import SwiftUI

struct ContentView: View {

    @State var myDate = Date.now
    let formatter = DateFormatter()

    var body: some View {
        VStack {
            Text("Chosen date = \(formatter.string( from:
            myDate))")
                .padding()

            DatePicker(selection: $myDate, label: { Text("Date") })
        }.onAppear() {
            formatter.dateStyle = .full
            formatter.timeStyle = .full
        }

    }
}
```

```
struct ContentView_Previews: PreviewProvider {
    static var previews: some View {
        ContentView()
    }
}
```

6. Click the Live icon in the Canvas pane and click any date. Notice
    that when you choose a date, it appears above the Date Picker,
    using the date and time styles defined within the .onAppear
    modifier such as .full or .short.

Creating a MultiDate Picker

An ordinary Date Picker only lets users select a single date. If you want users to be able to
select multiple dates at a time, you can use the MultiDatePicker. Since a MultiDatePicker
lets users select multiple dates, these dates get stored in a set of DateComponents. That
means you need to create a State variable like this:

```
@State var dates = Set<DateComponents>()
```

To create a MultiDatePicker, just define it with the State variable to store the multiple
dates selected like this:

```
MultiDatePicker("Select Dates", selection: $dates)
```

To see how to create a MultiDatePicker, follow these steps:

1. Create a new SwiftUI iOS App project and give it any name you
    wish such as "MultiDatePicker."

2. Click the ContentView file in the Navigator pane.

3. Create a State variable to hold multiple dates in a set like this:

    ```
    @State var dates = Set<DateComponents>()
    ```

4. Add a VStack inside the var body: some View line and create a
    MultiDatePicker inside the VStack like this:

```
VStack {
    MultiDatePicker("Select Dates", selection: $dates)
}
.padding()
```

5. Click the Live icon in the Canvas pane. The MultiDatePicker
    appears.

6. Click two or more dates. Each time you click a date, the
    MultiDatePicker highlights it as shown in Figure 8-11. If you click
    a highlighted date, the MultiDatePicker clears the selection.

Figure 8-11. *The MultiDatePicker lets users select two or more dates*

The entire ContentView file should look like this:

```swift
import SwiftUI

struct ContentView: View {
    @State var dates = Set<DateComponents>()
    var body: some View {
        VStack {
            MultiDatePicker("Select Dates", selection: $dates)
        }
        .padding()
    }
}

struct ContentView_Previews: PreviewProvider {
    static var previews: some View {
        ContentView()
    }
}
```

Once you've created a MultiDatePicker, the next step is to retrieve the multiple dates the user selected. First, all selected dates are stored as a DateComponents data type, which includes lots of different information beyond just the date. To see how dates, stored as DateComponents, look, modify the current project as follows:

1. In the current MultiDatePicker project, add the following State variable:

    ```swift
    @State var message = ""
    ```

2. Add a Button and a TextEditor underneath the MultiDatePicker inside the VStack like this:

    ```swift
    Button("Click Me") {
        for x in dates {
            message += "\(x)" + "\n"
        }
    }

    TextEditor(text: $message)
    ```

The entire ContentView file should look like this:

```
import SwiftUI

struct ContentView: View {
    @State var dates = Set<DateComponents>()
    @State var message = ""
    var body: some View {
        VStack {
            MultiDatePicker("Select Dates", selection: $dates)

            Button("Click Me") {
                for x in dates {
                    message += "\(x)" + "\n"
                }
            }

            TextEditor(text: $message)
        }
        .padding()
    }
}

struct ContentView_Previews: PreviewProvider {
    static var previews: some View {
        ContentView()
    }
}
```

3. Click the Live icon in the Canvas pane.

4. Click multiple dates in the MultiDatePicker.

5. Click the Click Me button. Your selected dates appear in the TextEditor as shown in Figure 8-12.

January 2023 >   **‹   ›**

SUN	MON	TUE	WED	THU	FRI	SAT
1	2	3	4	5	6	7
8	9	10	11	12	13	14
15	16	17	18	19	20	21
22	23	24	25	26	27	28
29	30	31				

Click Me

calendar: gregorian (current) era: 1 year: 2023
month: 1 day: 29 isLeapMonth: false
calendar: gregorian (current) era: 1 year: 2023
month: 1 day: 30 isLeapMonth: false
calendar: gregorian (current) era: 1 year: 2023
month: 1 day: 24 isLeapMonth: false

Figure 8-12. *Selected dates chosen from the MultiDatePicker*

Notice that a date such as January 24, 2023, actually gets stored as year: 2023, month: 1, and day: 24. Such a format likely won't be useful, so what we need to do is access just the date property of the DateComponents structure.

To do this, we need to use the DateFormatter as follows:

1. In the current MultiDatePicker project, add the following underneath the two State variables:

```
let dateFormatter = DateFormatter()
```

2. Modify the Button code as follows:

```
        Button("Click Me") {
            for x in dates {
//                message += "\(x)" + "\n"
```

```
                    message += dateFormatter.string(from:
                    x.date!) + "\n"
                }
            }
```

Rather than display the raw DateComponents data, the for loop
will now use the dateFormatter to display the retrieved date
property in a more familiar appearance.

3. Add the following after the last curly bracket that defines
    the VStack:

```
.onAppear() {
    dateFormatter.dateStyle = .medium
    dateFormatter.locale = Locale(identifier: "en_US")
}
```

This defines a style for displaying dates (.short, .medium, .long,
and .full). In addition, this also defines the locale for displaying
dates such as "en_US".

The entire ContentView file should look like this:

```
import SwiftUI

struct ContentView: View {

    @State var dates = Set<DateComponents>()
    @State var message = ""

    let dateFormatter = DateFormatter()

    var body: some View {
        VStack {
            MultiDatePicker("Select Dates", selection: $dates)

            Button("Click Me") {
                for x in dates {
//                      message += "\(x)" + "\n"
                    message += dateFormatter.string(from:
                    x.date!) + "\n"
```

```
                    }
                }

                TextEditor(text: $message)
            }.onAppear() {
                dateFormatter.dateStyle = .medium
                dateFormatter.locale = Locale(identifier: "en_US")
            }
            .padding()
        }
    }

    struct ContentView_Previews: PreviewProvider {
        static var previews: some View {
            ContentView()
        }
    }
```

4. Click the Live icon in the Canvas pane.

5. Click two or more dates in the MultiDatePicker.

6. Click the Click Me Button. Your chosen dates appear in the
   TextEditor, formatted according to the date style you chose such as
   .medium or .long, as shown in Figure 8-13.

January 2023 >   **< >**

SUN	MON	TUE	WED	THU	FRI	SAT
1	2	3	4	5	6	7
8	9	10	11	12	13	14
15	16	17	18	19	20	21
22	23	24	25	26	27	28
29	30	31				

Click Me

Jan 3, 2023
Jan 12, 2023
Jan 13, 2023
Jan 30, 2023
Jan 5, 2023

Figure 8-13. *Formatted dates chosen from the MultiDatePicker*

Summary

Text Fields can be handy for letting users input data. Unfortunately, users can type anything into a Text Field, even completely nonsensical data. To restrict the user to just a valid range of choices, you can use a Picker. A Picker can provide a list of all valid options. Now it's impossible for the user to enter invalid data through a Picker.

When creating a Picker, you can use a .tag property to assign a specific value to the user's selection in a Picker. The .tag property can hold any type of data such as integers, decimal numbers, or strings. All .tag properties must hold the same data type.

As an alternative to using multiple Text views, you can use a ForEach loop to retrieve the choices for a Picker view, which can be stored in an array or an enumeration. Retrieving options to display on a Picker view can be especially useful when you need to display a large number of choices, such as through a Picker view displayed as a wheel.

Another way to display a list of valid options is through the Color Picker. By using the Color Picker, users can select standard colors such as red, green, or blue or create custom colors.

For selecting dates, SwiftUI offers the Date Picker. You can format the way a date appears, such as 6/15/22 or June 15, 2022. The Date Picker can also appear in three different styles (.compact, .graphical, or .wheel). That way you can make a Date Picker look the way that works best in your app. By using Pickers, you can make it easy for users to input only valid data.

If users need to select multiple dates, use the MultiDatePicker. This stores selected dates in a set, which you may need to format using the DateFormatter. Ultimately, Pickers let you offer a fixed range of valid options for the user to select.

CHAPTER 9

Limiting Choices with Toggles, Steppers, and Sliders

Ideally, you want to limit the user to select only valid options. That keeps the user from entering invalid data such as spelling out a number (such as thirty-seven) instead of typing out the number (37). Three additional ways to restrict the user into selecting only valid data are toggles, steppers, and sliders.

A Toggle gives users exactly two choices such as on or off, yes or no, and true or false. Because a Toggle only offers two choices, it represents a Boolean value (true or false).

A Stepper restricts user input to a range of valid data. Steppers display a minus/plus icon that users can click to increment/decrement a value by a fixed amount, up or down. By using a Stepper, users can define a value without typing a specific number.

Sliders also restrict user input to a range of valid data. Sliders let users drag to input a specific value without any typing whatsoever. Both steppers and sliders can define minimum and maximum values to restrict users into choosing only valid numeric values. For many people, it's easier to click or drag to choose a value than to type that number itself. Both steppers and sliders represent a Double value (decimal number).

The whole purpose of toggles, sliders, and steppers is to make sure the user can only input valid data into a program at any given time.

Using a Toggle

If you look at the settings for an iPhone or iPad, you'll see a list of options that you can turn on or off as shown in Figure 9-1.

© Wallace Wang 2023
W. Wang, *Beginning iPhone Development with SwiftUI*, https://doi.org/10.1007/978-1-4842-9541-0_9

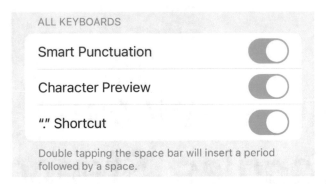

Figure 9-1. *Typical uses for a Toggle*

To create a Toggle, you need to define the text to appear next to the Toggle along with linking or binding a State variable to the Toggle such as

```
Toggle(isOn: $settingValue) {
    Text("Toggle text")
}
```

In this example, the Toggle changes the value of a State variable called settingValue, which should be defined as a Boolean like this:

```
@State var settingValue = true
```

Then the Text view displays "Toggle text" next to the Toggle itself as shown in Figure 9-2.

Toggle text

Figure 9-2. *The appearance of a typical Toggle*

To see how a Toggle works, follow these steps:

1. Create a new SwiftUI iOS App project and give it any name you wish such as "Toggle."

2. Click the ContentView file in the Navigator pane.

3. Add the following State variable under the struct ContentView: View line:

```
struct ContentView: View {
    @State var myToggle = true
```

4. Create a VStack and put a Rectangle inside. Since a Rectangle
    will expand to fill the entire screen, make sure you put a .frame
    modifier on it and define its .foregroundColor with the previously
    defined State variable:

```
var body: some View {
    VStack {
        Rectangle()
            .frame(width: 200, height: 150)
            .foregroundColor(myToggle ? .orange : .green)
    }
}
```

5. Add the Toggle underneath the Rectangle and its modifiers
    like this:

```
Toggle(myToggle ? "Orange" : "Green", isOn: $myToggle)
```

The entire ContentView file should look like this:

```
import SwiftUI

struct ContentView: View {
    @State var myToggle = true
    var body: some View {
        VStack {
            Rectangle()
                .frame(width: 200, height: 150)
                .foregroundColor(myToggle ? .orange : .green)
            Toggle(myToggle ? "Orange" : "Green", isOn: $myToggle)
        }
    }
}

struct ContentView_Previews: PreviewProvider {
    static var previews: some View {
        ContentView()
    }
}
```

6. Click the Live icon in the Canvas pane. Notice that since the State variable myToggle is true, the Rectangle initially appears in orange.

7. Click the Toggle. Notice that each time you click the Toggle, the color of the Rectangle alternates between orange and green, and the text on the Toggle alternates between "Orange" and "Green" as well.

Using a Stepper

When you want the user to input numeric data, you may want to restrict the range of acceptable data. After all, if you ask for the user's age, you don't want –23 or 938478 since both are clearly impossible for someone's age. To make it easy for the user to input numeric data within an acceptable range, you can use a Stepper.

Steppers store a value that users can increment by a fixed increment such as 1 or 2.5. You can define a minimum and a maximum value that the Stepper can represent such as a range between 1 and 10. Furthermore, you can define whether the Stepper wraps or not. Wrapping means if you keep incrementing the Stepper beyond its maximum value, it goes back to its minimum value. Likewise, if you keep decrementing the Stepper below its minimum value, it jumps to its maximum value. This can make it easy for users to choose different values without having to exhaustively step from one extreme value to the other.

To see how a Stepper works, follow these steps:

1. Create a new SwiftUI iOS App project and give it any name you wish such as "Stepper."

2. Click the ContentView file in the Navigator pane.

3. Add the following State variable under the struct ContentView: View line:

```
struct ContentView: View {
    @State var newValue = 0
```

4. Create a VStack inside the var body: some View and add a Stepper
    like this:

```
var body: some View {
    VStack {
        Stepper(value: $newValue) {
            Text("Stepper value = \(newValue)")
        }.padding()
    }
}
```

This defines a simple Stepper that can represent any value and
increases or decreases its value by 1 as shown in Figure 9-3.

Stepper value = 0   − | +

Figure 9-3. *A simple Stepper*

The entire ContentView file should look like this:

```
import SwiftUI

struct ContentView: View {
    @State var newValue = 0

    var body: some View {
        VStack {
            Stepper(value: $newValue) {
                Text("Stepper value = \(newValue)")
            }.padding()
        }
    }
}

struct ContentView_Previews: PreviewProvider {
    static var previews: some View {
        ContentView()
    }
}
```

5. Click the Live icon in the Canvas pane to run your app.

6. Click the – and + icons on the Stepper to decrease or increase
    its value.

Defining a Range in a Stepper

In many cases, you want to define a valid range of values that the Stepper can represent
such as from 1 to 25. To define a range for a Stepper, you need to list the range within the
in: parameter like this:

```
Stepper(value: $newValue, in: 1...10) {
    Text("Stepper value = \(newValue)")
}.padding()
```

To see how to define a range of values that a Stepper can represent, add the
preceding code so the entire ContentView file looks like this:

```
import SwiftUI

struct ContentView: View {
    @State var newValue = 0

    var body: some View {
        VStack {
            // Basic stepper
            Stepper(value: $newValue) {
                Text("Stepper value = \(newValue)")
            }.padding()

            // Stepper in a range
            Stepper(value: $newValue, in: 1...10) {
                Text("Stepper value = \(newValue)")
            }.padding()
        }
    }
}
```

```
struct ContentView_Previews: PreviewProvider {
    static var previews: some View {
        ContentView()
    }
}
```

Click the Live icon in the Canvas pane and click the bottom Stepper. Notice that because its range is restricted between 1 and 10, clicking the – and + icons on the bottom Stepper won't decrease or increase the Stepper's value below 1 or above 10.

Defining an Increment/Decrement Value in a Stepper

Normally, a Stepper increases or decreases its value by 1. Sometimes you might want to increment/decrement by a value other than 1 such as 2 or 5. To define an integer value to increment/decrement a Stepper, you need to define an integer value for the step: parameter like this:

```
Stepper(value: $newValue, in: 1...10, step: 2) {
    Text("Stepper value = \(newValue)")
}.padding()
```

The entire ContentView file should look like this:

```
import SwiftUI

struct ContentView: View {
    @State var newValue = 0

    var body: some View {
        VStack {
            Stepper(value: $newValue) {
                Text("Stepper value = \(newValue)")
            }.padding()

            // Stepper in a range
            Stepper(value: $newValue, in: 1...10) {
                Text("Stepper value = \(newValue)")
            }.padding()
```

```
            // Stepper in a range with increments
            Stepper(value: $newValue, in: 1...10, step: 2) {
                Text("Stepper value = \(newValue)")
            }.padding()

        }
    }
}

struct ContentView_Previews: PreviewProvider {
    static var previews: some View {
        ContentView()
    }
}
```

Click the Live icon in the Canvas pane and click the bottom Stepper. Notice that because its range is restricted between 1 and 10, clicking the – and + icons on the bottom Stepper won't decrease or increase the Stepper's value below 1 or above 10. Yet clicking the – and + icons on the bottom Stepper increments/decrements the Stepper's value by 2.

If you want to define a decimal value for the step: parameter, you'll need to make sure every value used in the Stepper is a decimal value such as

```
        Stepper(value: $decimalValue,
                in: 1.0...10.0,
                step: 0.25) {
            Text("Stepper value = \(decimalValue)")
        }.padding()
```

In the preceding Stepper definition, the range goes from 1.0 (not just 1) up to and including 10.0 (not just 10). Then the step: parameter is defined as 0.25. Finally, the State variable (decimalValue) must also be defined as a decimal value (Double data type) like this:

```
@State var decimalValue: Double = 0
```

The entire ContentView file should look like this:

```
import SwiftUI

struct ContentView: View {
    @State var newValue = 0
    @State var decimalValue: Double = 0

    var body: some View {
        VStack {
            // Basic stepper
            Stepper(value: $newValue) {
                Text("Stepper value = \(newValue)")
            }.padding()

            // Stepper in a range
            Stepper(value: $newValue, in: 1...10) {
                Text("Stepper value = \(newValue)")
            }.padding()

            // Stepper with increment value
            Stepper(value: $newValue, in: 1...10, step: 2) {
                Text("Stepper value = \(newValue)")
            }.padding()

            // Stepper with decimal increment value
            Stepper(value: $decimalValue,
                    in: 1.0...10.0,
                    step: 0.25) {
                Text("Stepper value = \(decimalValue)")
            }.padding()
        }
    }
}
```

```
struct ContentView_Previews: PreviewProvider {
    static var previews: some View {
        ContentView()
    }
}
```

Click the Live icon in the Canvas pane and click the bottom Stepper. Notice that because its range is restricted between 1.0 and 10.0, clicking the – and + icons on the bottom Stepper won't decrease or increase the Stepper's value below 1.0 or above 10.0. Yet clicking the – and + icons on the bottom Stepper increments/decrements the Stepper's value by 0.25.

Using Sliders

Like a Stepper, a Slider lets the user choose a numeric value without typing a specific number. While a Stepper forces users to increment/decrement values by a fixed amount, sliders make it easy for users to choose between a range of values quickly by simply changing the Slider's position. This makes a Slider better suited than a Stepper for letting the user choose from a wide range of values.

Although the Slider can represent any Double data type (decimal number), by default it ranges from 0 to 1 where the far left represents 0 and the far right represents 1.

To see how a Slider works, follow these steps:

1. Create a new SwiftUI iOS App project and give it any name you wish such as "Slider."

2. Click the ContentView file in the Navigator pane.

3. Add the following State variable under the struct ContentView: View line:

   ```
   struct ContentView: View {
       @State var sliderValue = 0.0
   ```

4. Create a VStack inside the var body: some View and add a Text and a Slider like this:

```
var body: some View {
    VStack (spacing: 28){
        Text("Slider value = \(sliderValue)")

        Slider(value: $sliderValue)
    }
}
```

5.   Click the Live icon in the Canvas pane and drag the Slider left and
     right. Notice that the value of this Slider ranges from 0 to 1 as a
     Double value, which displays decimal values.

Changing the Color of a Slider

By default, a Slider displays the color blue as you drag the Slider to the right. If you
want to change that color, you can use the .accentColor modifier like this as shown in
Figure 9-4:

```
Slider(value: $sliderValue)
    .accentColor(.red)
```

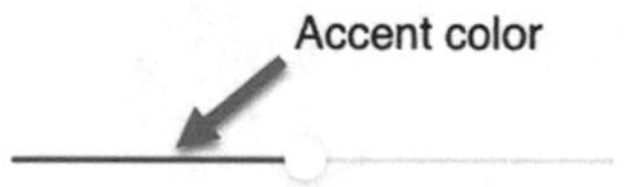

Figure 9-4. *The accent color on a Slider*

Defining a Range for a Slider

By default, a Slider ranges in value from 0 to 1. However, you may want to define a
different range for the Slider such as

```
Slider(value: $sliderValue, in: 1...50)
```

This defines a minimum value for the Slider as 1 and a maximum value as 50. Just
remember that these values are actually decimal values such as 1.0 through 50.0.

Defining a Step Increment for a Slider

If the range of a Slider is greater than 1, dragging the Slider increments/decrements it by 1. To define a different value for the Slider to increment/decrement, you need to define a step: parameter such as

```
Slider(value: $sliderValue, in: 1...50, step: 4)
```

This defines the Slider to change values by 4 such as going from 1 to 5 to 9.

Displaying Minimum and Maximum Labels on a Slider

To make a Slider easier to understand, you can display a minimum and a maximum value label on each end of the Slider. That way you can make it clear what the minimum and the maximum value of a Slider might be such as

```
Slider(value: $sliderValue, in: 1...50, step: 4) {
    Text("Slider")
} minimumValueLabel: {
    Text("1")
} maximumValueLabel: {
    Text("50")
}
```

This defines a Slider that displays 0 at the far left and 50 at the far right as shown in Figure 9-5.

Figure 9-5. *Displaying minimum and maximum labels on a Slider*

To see how all these different sliders work, edit the ContentView file as follows:

```
import SwiftUI

struct ContentView: View {
    @State var sliderValue = 0.0
```

```
var body: some View {
    VStack (spacing: 28){
        Text("Slider value = \(sliderValue)")

        Slider(value: $sliderValue)
            .padding()

        Slider(value: $sliderValue, in: 1...50)
            .padding()

        Slider(value: $sliderValue, in: 1...50, step: 4)
            .padding()

        Slider(value: $sliderValue, in: 1...50, step: 4) {
            Text("Slider")
        } minimumValueLabel: {
            Text("1")
        } maximumValueLabel: {
            Text("50")
        }.padding()
    }
}

struct ContentView_Previews: PreviewProvider {
    static var previews: some View {
        ContentView()
    }
}
```

When you run this project, the top Slider ranges in value from 0 to 1. That means when you drag the other sliders, the top Slider immediately moves all the way to the right. That's because the top Slider can only have a maximum value of 1, while the other sliders range in value from 1 to 50. So dragging the other sliders always pins the top Slider all the way to the right to represent a value of 1, which is the maximum value it can represent.

Summary

When your app needs the user to input numeric data, a text field can work, but it might be clumsy, especially if you only want to accept a limited range of numeric values. To make it easy to input numeric data, use a Stepper or a Slider.

Both a Stepper and a Slider can define a minimum and a maximum value, so that way the user can't input numeric data below a minimum value or above a maximum value. Both steppers and sliders let you define a different increment/decrement value other than 1.

A Stepper takes up less space, but a Slider makes it easier to change values from one extreme to another by simply dragging the Slider from side to side.

By using steppers and sliders, you can make it easy for users to input numeric data. By using a Toggle, you can make it easy for users to choose between exactly two choices such as on/off or yes/no. Steppers, sliders, and toggles simply make it easy for users to enter only valid data.

CHAPTER 10

Providing Options with Links and Menus

At one time, apps just needed buttons to let the user choose commands. As iPhone and iPad apps started getting more sophisticated, the need for alternate ways to allow the user to select commands has grown as well. Two common ways to display commands for users to select are links and menus.

A Link resembles a Button, except that it opens up a browser to display the contents of a website. A Menu lets you display a list of options, which can also include submenus as shown in Figure 10-1

```
Menu("Actions") {
    Button("Duplicate", action: duplicate)
    Button("Rename", action: rename)
    Button("Delete...", action: delete)
    Menu("Copy") {
        Button("Copy", action: copy)
        Button("Copy Formatted", action:
            copyFormatted)
        Button("Copy Library Path", action: copyPath)
    }
}
```

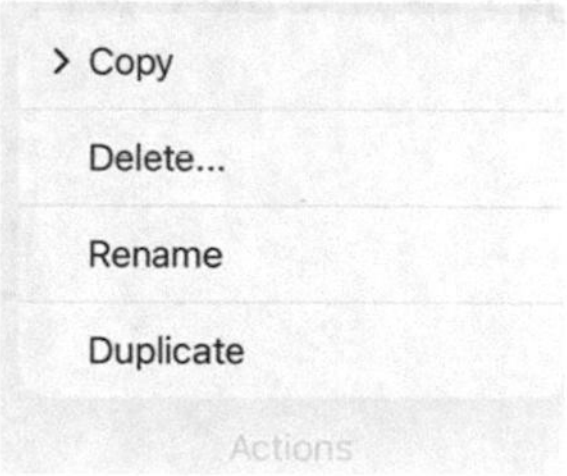

Figure 10-1. *A Menu displaying a list of options including a submenu*

Using Links

Links offer a handy way to give users a chance to visit a website from within an app. A Link defines a website address such as

© Wallace Wang 2023
W. Wang, *Beginning iPhone Development with SwiftUI*, https://doi.org/10.1007/978-1-4842-9541-0_10

```
Link(destination: URL(string: "https://www.apple.com")! ) {
    Text("Apple")
}
```

The Text view defines the text that appears on the link. You can add any modifiers you want to this Text view such as defining a font or background color.

The Link must define a destination as a URL. One way to make sure the website address is accurate is to visit the desired website and then copy its address from your browser and paste it into your Swift code.

Note   To test if the Link successfully loads the website address, you need to test the project either in the Simulator or on an actual iOS device. The Canvas pane cannot open the Safari browser like the Simulator or an iOS device can do.

Using ShareLinks

An ordinary Link acts like a hyperlink to take users to a specific web page. A ShareLink lets users tap on a link that displays a share sheet that gives users options for copying data or sharing it with other apps as shown in Figure 10-2.

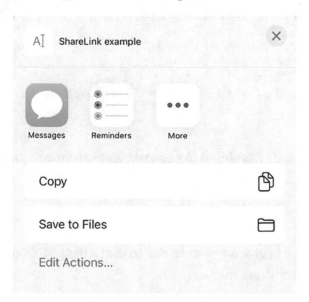

Figure 10-2. *A ShareLink displays a share sheet of options for sharing data with other apps*

The simplest ShareLink simply defines an item to share, which can be a string or URL such as

```
ShareLink(item: "This text will be shared")
ShareLink(item: URL(string: "https://www.apple.com")!)
```

Rather than type a string or URL directly in a ShareLink, you can also use variables such as

```
let shareText = "This text will be shared"
ShareLink(item: shareText)
let url = URL(string: "https://www.apple.com")!
ShareLink(item: url)
```

By default, a ShareLink simply displays a share icon and the word "Share..." as shown in Figure 10-3.

⬆ Share...

Figure 10-3. *The default appearance of a ShareLink displays a share icon and the word "Share..."*

When users click the ShareLink, a share sheet appears (see Figure 10-2), allowing users to share the data in the ShareLink with other apps. To see how this works, follow these steps:

1. Create a new SwiftUI iOS App project and give it any name you wish such as "ShareLink."

2. Click the ContentView file in the Navigator pane.

3. Add the following State variable and constants under the struct ContentView: View line:

    ```
    @State var message = ""
    let shareText = "This text will be shared"
    let url = URL(string: "https://www.apple.com")!
    ```

4. Edit the VStack under the var body: some View line like this:

```
VStack {
    ShareLink(item: "This text will be shared")

    TextField("Placeholder text", text: $message)

    ShareLink(item: URL(string: "https://www.apple.com")!)
}
```

This creates two ShareLinks with a TextField separating them as shown in Figure 10-4.

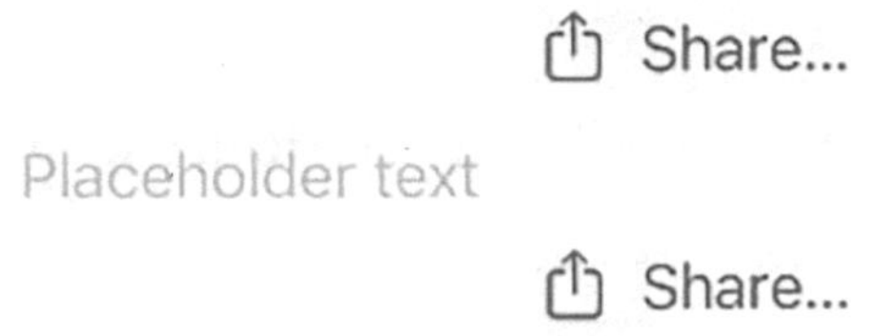

⬆ Share...

Placeholder text

⬆ Share...

Figure 10-4. *The user interface with two ShareLinks and a TextField*

The entire ContentView file should look like this:

```
import SwiftUI

struct ContentView: View {

    @State var message = ""
    let shareText = "This text will be shared"
    let url = URL(string: "https://www.apple.com")!

    var body: some View {
        VStack {
            ShareLink(item: "This text will be shared")

            TextField("Placeholder text", text: $message)

            ShareLink(item: URL(string: "https://www.apple.com")!)
        }
        .padding()
    }
}
```

```
struct ContentView_Previews: PreviewProvider {
    static var previews: some View {
        ContentView()
    }
}
```

5. Click the Live icon in the Canvas pane.

6. Click the top or bottom ShareLink. A share sheet appears (see Figure 10-2).

7. Click Copy on the share sheet. The share sheet disappears.

8. Click in the TextField and hold the left mouse button (or trackpad) down until a Paste menu pops up as shown in Figure 10-5.

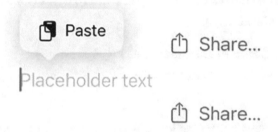

Figure 10-5. *The Paste menu above the TextField*

9. Click Paste. The item defined by the ShareLink appears in the TextField (either "This text will be shared" or `https://www.apple.com`).

Customizing a ShareLink

Rather than display the default share icon and the word "Share...", you can customize the appearance of a ShareLink by defining both the content to share and the appearance of the ShareLink using text, icons, or both.

To display custom text on a ShareLink, you must define the custom text followed by the item to share like this, which creates a ShareLink as shown in Figure 10-6:

```
ShareLink("Custom text here", item: URL(string: "https://www.apple.com")!)
```

⬆ Custom text here

Figure 10-6. *Defining custom text to appear in a ShareLink*

If you copied and pasted the preceding ShareLink, you would share the https://
www.apple.com website address. Notice that the preceding ShareLink still displays the
default share icon. If you don't want to display this share icon, you need to define the text
to appear in the ShareLink using a Text view like this:

```
ShareLink(item: "This text will be shared") {
    Text("Custom ShareLink text")
}
```

The preceding ShareLink will simply display "Custom ShareLink text" on the user
interface but without the share icon. If you just want to display an icon without any text,
you can use an Image view like this:

```
ShareLink(item: "ShareLink example") {
    Image(systemName: "tortoise")
}
```

This ShareLink displays a tortoise icon. You can use any icon you wish from the list
of icons displayed by the free Apple program, SF Symbols (https://developer.apple.
com/sf-symbols).

If you want to display a custom icon and text for a ShareLink, use a Label view that
lets you customize a Text view and an Image view like this as shown in Figure 10-7:

```
ShareLink(item: "ShareLink example") {
    Label {
        Text("Custom ShareLink text")
    } icon: {
        Image(systemName: "hare")
    }
}
```

 Custom ShareLink text

Figure 10-7. *Customizing a ShareLink with both an icon and text*

ShareLinks will share whatever the item: parameter defines, such as a string ("ShareLink example") or a URL ("www.apple.com").

1. Create a new SwiftUI iOS App project and give it any name you wish such as "ShareLink Custom."

2. Click the ContentView file in the Navigator pane.

3. Add the following State variable under the struct ContentView: View line:

```
@State var message = ""
```

4. Edit the VStack under the var body: some View line like this:

```
VStack (spacing: 55) {
    ShareLink(item: "This text will be shared") {
        Text("Custom ShareLink text")
    }

    ShareLink(item: "Just an icon to share") {
        Image(systemName: "tortoise")
    }

    ShareLink(item: "Custom icon and text") {
        Label {
            Text("Custom ShareLink text")
        } icon: {
            Image(systemName: "hare")
        }
    }

    TextField("Placeholder text", text: $message)
}
```

This creates three ShareLinks and a TextField. The first ShareLink displays only text, the second ShareLink displays only an icon, and the third ShareLink displays both a custom icon and text.

The entire ContentView file should look like this:

```
import SwiftUI

struct ContentView: View {
    @State var message = ""
    var body: some View {
        VStack (spacing: 55) {
            ShareLink(item: "This text will be shared") {
                Text("Custom ShareLink text")
            }

            ShareLink(item: "Just an icon to share") {
                 Image(systemName: "tortoise")
             }

            ShareLink(item: "Custom icon and text") {
                Label {
                    Text("Custom ShareLink text")
                } icon: {
                    Image(systemName: "hare")
                }
            }

            TextField("Placeholder text", text: $message)
        }
        .padding()
    }
}

struct ContentView_Previews: PreviewProvider {
    static var previews: some View {
        ContentView()
    }
}
```

5.   Click the Live icon in the Canvas pane.

6.   Click any of the ShareLinks. A share sheet appears (see Figure 10-2).

7.   Click Copy. The share sheet disappears.

8.   Click in the TextField and hold down the left mouse button (or trackpad) until a Paste menu pops up (see Figure 10-5).

9.   Click Paste. The text from your chosen ShareLink now appears in the TextField.

Using Menus

Sometimes you may want to offer the user multiple choices. Cramming multiple buttons on the screen can be clumsy, and even a segmented control can be too limiting. When you need to display multiple options in a small space, that's when you can use a Menu.

A Menu simply appears as a Button on the user interface. When the user taps it, the Menu displays a list of options (see Figure 10-1). Now the user can tap an option or open an additional submenu to see even more options. Menus make it easy to hide multiple options in a limited amount of space.

The simplest Menu consists of a title and a list of options defined by Buttons like this:

```
Menu("Options") {
    Button("Open ", action: openFile)
    Button("Find", action: findFile)
    Button("Delete...", action: deleteFile)
}
```

The preceding code would display a Menu on the screen with the word "Options" displayed. When the user taps "Options," a menu appears listing three choices – Open, Find, and Delete... – as shown in Figure 10-8.

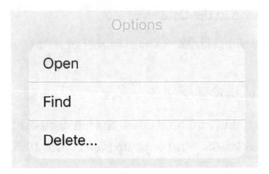

Figure 10-8. *A Menu displays a list of Buttons in a drop-down menu*

When the user taps a Button, that Button calls a function such as openFile, findFile, or deleteFile. Notice that these function calls do not include a parameter list such as openFile(). To see how to create a simple Menu, follow these steps:

1. Create a new SwiftUI iOS App project and give it any name you wish such as "MenuSimple."

2. Click the ContentView file in the Navigator pane.

3. Add the following State variable under the struct ContentView: View line:

```
@State var message = ""
```

4. Modify the VStack under the var body: some View line like this:

```
var body: some View {
    VStack {
        Text(message)
            .padding()

        Menu("Options") {
            Button("Open ", action: openFile)
            Button("Find", action: findFile)
            Button("Delete...", action: deleteFile)
        }

        Spacer()
    }
}
```

All three Buttons call functions to do something. So we need to create functions to make these Buttons work.

5. Right above the last curly bracket in the struct ContentView: View, add the following three functions:

```
func openFile() {
    message = "Open chosen"
}

func findFile() {
    message = "Find chosen"
}

func deleteFile() {
    message = "Delete chosen"
}
```

The entire ContentView file should look like this:

```
import SwiftUI

struct ContentView: View {
    @State var message = ""
    var body: some View {
        VStack {
            Text(message)
                .padding()

            Menu("Options") {
                Button("Open ", action: openFile)
                Button("Find", action: findFile)
                Button("Delete...", action: deleteFile)
            }
        }
    }

    func openFile() {
        message = "Open chosen"
    }
```

```
    func findFile() {
        message = "Find chosen"
    }

    func deleteFile() {
        message = "Delete chosen"
    }

}

struct ContentView_Previews: PreviewProvider {
    static var previews: some View {
        ContentView()
    }
}
```

6. Click the Live icon in the Canvas pane.

7. Click the Options button in the middle of the simulated iOS
    device. A menu appears listing the three options defined by the
    three Button views: Open, Find, and Delete...

8. Click any option. Notice that whatever option you choose, it displays
    a slightly different message in the Text view above the Menu.

Notice that each Button in the Menu calls a function defined by the action:
parameter. Rather than call a function, you can just enclose one or more commands
within curly brackets like this:

```
    Menu("Options") {
        Button("Open ", action: {
            message = "Open chosen"
        })
        Button("Find", action: {
            message = "Find chosen"
        })
        Button("Delete...", action: {
            message = "Delete chosen"
        })
    }
```

Formatting Titles on the Menu and Buttons

A Menu lets you define a title that appears like a standard Button. However, if you want to format the title, there's an alternate way to define a Menu. Instead of just defining the text to appear as a title, you can define a label: parameter where you can use either a Text or Label view like this:

```
Menu {
    Button("Open ", action: {
        message = "Open chosen"
    })
    Button("Find", action: {
        message = "Find chosen"
    })
    Button("Delete...", action: {
        message = "Delete chosen"
    })
} label: {
    Text("Options")
        .font(.largeTitle)
        .foregroundColor(.purple)
        .italic()
}
```

This example displays the Menu's title using the .largeTitle font, the color purple, and italics. Rather than use a Text view, you can also use a Label view to display an icon side by side with text such as

```
Menu {
    Button("Open ", action: {
        message = "Open chosen"
    })
    Button("Find", action: {
        message = "Find chosen"
    })
```

```
            Button("Delete...", action: {
                message = "Delete chosen"
            })
        } label: {
            Label("Options", systemImage: "pencil.circle")
        }
```

By using the label: parameter to define a Menu's title, you have more options for customizing a Menu's title in multiple ways. Using the preceding Label view displays the Menu with an icon and text as shown in Figure 10-9.

⊘ Options

Figure 10-9. *A Label view displays an icon and text for the Menu's title*

You can also format a Button title using a Label view instead of a Text view like this:

```
Menu {
    Button(action: {
        message = "Open chosen"
    }) {
        Label("Open", systemImage: "book")
    }
    Button(action: {
        message = "Find chosen"
    }) {
        Label("Find", systemImage: "magnifyingglass")
    }
    Button(action: {
        message = "Delete chosen"
    }) {
        Label("Delete", systemImage: "trash")
    }
} label: {
    Label("Options", systemImage: "pencil.circle")
}
```

The preceding code displays a Menu list as shown in Figure 10-10.

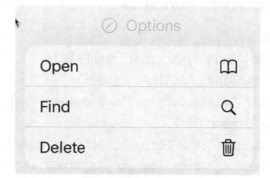

Figure 10-10. *Displaying Buttons in a Menu list using the Label view*

Adding a Submenu

A Menu can display a list of options defined by Buttons. However, a Menu can also display submenus that list additional, related commands as shown in Figure 10-11.

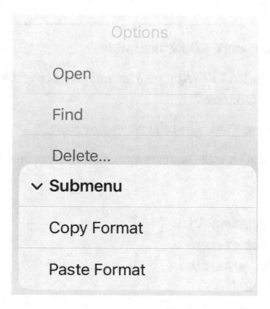

Figure 10-11. *Displaying a submenu*

To create a submenu, just define another Menu instead of a Button. Then include additional Buttons inside the submenu like this:

```
Menu("Options") {
    Button("Open ", action: openFile)
    Button("Find", action: findFile)
    Button("Delete...", action: deleteFile)
    Menu("Submenu") {
        Button("Copy Format", action: copyFormat)
        Button("Paste Format", action: pasteFormat)
    }
}
```

Note   It's possible to create submenus inside of submenus. As a general rule, use only one level of submenus, or else so many lists of options can look confusing to the user.

To see how submenus work, follow these steps:

1. Create a new SwiftUI iOS App project and give it any name you wish such as "Submenu."

2. Click the ContentView file in the Navigator pane.

3. Edit the ContentView file so its entire contents look like this:

```
import SwiftUI

struct ContentView: View {
    @State var message = ""
    var body: some View {
        VStack {
            Text(message)
                .padding()

            Menu("Options") {
                Button("Open ", action: openFile)
                Button("Find", action: findFile)
```

```
                Button("Delete...", action: deleteFile)
                Menu("Submenu") {
                    Button("Copy Format", action: copyFormat)
                    Button("Paste Format", action: pasteFormat)
                }
            }
            Spacer()
        }
    }

    func openFile() {
        message = "Open chosen"
    }

    func findFile() {
        message = "Find chosen"
    }

    func deleteFile() {
        message = "Delete chosen"
    }

    func copyFormat() {
        message = "Copy format chosen"
    }

    func pasteFormat() {
        message = "Paste format chosen"
    }
}

struct ContentView_Previews: PreviewProvider {
    static var previews: some View {
        ContentView()
    }
}
```

4.   Click the Live icon in the Canvas pane.

5.   Click Options defined by the Menu. This displays a list of options including the submenu identified by a > symbol as shown in Figure 10-12.

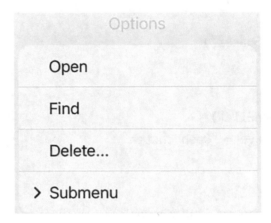

Figure 10-12.   *The > symbol identifies a submenu*

6.   Click the submenu to see an additional list of options appear.

Submenus make it easy to group related options together, but since these options are initially hidden from view, use submenus sparingly to avoid confusing the user.

Summary

Links and menus are two additional ways a user interface can display options for the user to select. A Link opens a browser and jumps to a specific website. A ShareLink lets you share information with another app. Menus display a list of options defined by Buttons and other Menus that define submenus.

By using the Label view in a Menu, you can combine an icon with text side by side. By using the Text view in a Menu, you can customize the appearance of text that appears on the user interface such as choosing a font or color. Menus give you a way to display multiple options to the user without taking up a lot of space on the screen.

CHAPTER 11

Touch Gestures

Allowing the user to control an app through buttons, toggles, or menus is handy, but all of these controls take up space on the screen. To eliminate the need for extra objects on the user interface, your app can also detect and respond to touch gestures that allow direct manipulation of items displayed on the screen.

The different types of touch gestures that an iOS app can detect and respond to include

- Tap – A fingertip touches the screen and lifts up.

- Spatial tap – One or more fingertips touching the screen and reporting the tap location.

- Pinch – Two fingertips come together or move apart.

- Rotation – Two fingertips rotate left or right in a circular motion.

- Pan – A fingertip slides in a dragging motion across the screen.

- Swipe – A fingertip slides up, down, left, or right across the screen and lifts up.

- Long press – A fingertip touches and presses down on the screen.

You can apply touch gestures to any view such as an Image view, a Text view, or a shape like a Rectangle or Ellipse.

Detecting Tap Gestures

Tap gestures simply detect when a user taps the screen. By default, a tap gesture recognizes a single tap by one fingertip, but you can define multiple taps by two or more fingertips.

© Wallace Wang 2023
W. Wang, *Beginning iPhone Development with SwiftUI*, https://doi.org/10.1007/978-1-4842-9541-0_11

To see how to detect tap gestures, follow these steps:

1. Create a new SwiftUI iOS App project and give it any name you wish such as "TapGesture."

2. Click the ContentView file in the Navigator pane.

3. Add the following State variable under the struct ContentView: View line:

```
@State var changeMe = false
```

4. Add a VStack inside the body along with a Rectangle like this:

```
var body: some View {
    VStack {
        Rectangle()
            .frame(width: 175, height: 125)
            .foregroundColor(changeMe ? .red : .yellow)
            .onTapGesture {
                changeMe.toggle()
            }
    }
}
```

This creates a Rectangle that fills up the entire screen. Then the .frame modifier restricts its width to 175 and its height to 125. The .foregroundColor modifier uses the changeMe State variable to decide whether to color the Rectangle with red or yellow.

The .onTapGesture modifier lets the Rectangle detect a single tap gesture. When it detects a tap gesture, it toggles the value of the changeMe State variable from true to false (or false to true). The entire ContentView file should look like this:

```
import SwiftUI

struct ContentView: View {
    @State var changeMe = false
    var body: some View {
```

```
        VStack {
            Rectangle()
                .frame(width: 175, height: 125)
                .foregroundColor(changeMe ? .red : .yellow)
                .onTapGesture {
                    changeMe.toggle()
                }
        }
    }
}

struct ContentView_Previews: PreviewProvider {
    static var previews: some View {
        ContentView()
    }
}
```

5. Click the Live icon in the Canvas pane.

6. Click the Rectangle. Notice that each time you click the Rectangle, the .onTapGesture modifier toggles the changeMe State variable, which alternates the Rectangle color between red and yellow.

By default, the .onTapGesture modifier detects a single tap gesture. If you want to detect multiple taps such as a double or triple tap, you can define the count: parameter like this:

```
.onTapGesture(count: 2)
```

A value of 2 defines a double tap, while a value of 3 would define a triple tap.

Detecting Spatial Tap Gestures

A spatial tap gesture is like an ordinary tap gesture except it's most useful for detecting the location of one or more taps. To detect a tap location, you need a State variable that can store CGPoint data types like this:

```
@State var tapLocation: CGPoint = .zero
```

Then you need to define a spatial tap gesture to detect locations like this:

```
var spatialTapGesture: some Gesture {
    SpatialTapGesture()
        .onEnded { event in
            tapLocation = event.location
        }
}
```

The event.location detects the location of tap gestures and stores the x and y data in the tapLocation State variable where tapLocation.x contains the horizontal distance from the origin (upper-left corner of an object) and tapLocation.y contains the vertical distance from the origin. The origin is defined by the object that the spatial tap gesture is attached to.

Once you can detect the tap location, then you can respond based on the area where the user tapped. By default, the spatial tap gesture only detects a single tap, but you can define how many taps needed such as two by defining the count parameter like this:

```
var spatialTapGesture: some Gesture {
    SpatialTapGesture(count: 2)
        .onEnded { event in
            tapLocation = event.location
        }
}
```

To see how to use a spatial tap gesture, follow these steps:

1. Create a new SwiftUI iOS App project and give it any name you wish such as "SpatialTapGesture."

2. Click the ContentView file in the Navigator pane.

3. Add the following State variable and constant under the struct ContentView: View line:

   ```
   @State var tapLocation: CGPoint = .zero
   let dimension: CGFloat = 360
   ```

4. Add a spatial tap gesture variable underneath the State variable and constant like this:

```
var spatialTapGesture: some Gesture {
    SpatialTapGesture()
        .onEnded { event in
            tapLocation = event.location
        }
}
```

In this example, the spatial tap gesture name is "spatialTapGesture," but it can be any name you want. The name of your spatial tap gesture will later be used to attach it to an object.

5. Add a VStack inside the body along with a Rectangle and two Text views like this:

```
VStack {
    Rectangle()
        .foregroundStyle(tapLocation.y > dimension / 2.0 ? Color.
        orange : Color.purple)
        .overlay(Text("Tap Me").font(.largeTitle).
        foregroundColor(tapLocation.x > dimension / 2.0 ? Color.
        black : Color.white))
        .frame(width: dimension, height: dimension)
    .gesture(spatialTapGesture)

    Text("Tap x location = \(tapLocation.x)")
    Text("Tap y location = \(tapLocation.y)")
}
```

This creates a Rectangle with a width and height defined by the "dimension" constant, which is set to 360. The .foregroundStyle modifier changes color based on where the user taps (clicks) on the Rectangle. If the user clicks in the bottom half of the Rectangle (tapLocation.y > dimension/2.0), then the Rectangle's color is orange. Otherwise, the Rectangle's color is purple.

Overlaid over the Rectangle is a Text view where the foreground color of the text will appear as black if the user clicks (taps) the right half of the Rectangle (tapLocation.x > dimension/2.0) or appear white if the user clicks (taps) the left half of the Rectangle.

The two Text views underneath the Rectangle simply display the x and y location where the user tapped (clicked) where the origin (0,0) is the upper-left corner of the Rectangle.

The entire ContentView file should look like this:

```
import SwiftUI

struct ContentView: View {
    @State var tapLocation: CGPoint = .zero
    let dimension: CGFloat = 360

    var spatialTapGesture: some Gesture {
        SpatialTapGesture()
            .onEnded { event in
                tapLocation = event.location
            }
    }

    var body: some View {
        VStack {
            Rectangle()
                .foregroundStyle(tapLocation.y > dimension / 2.0 ?
                Color.orange : Color.purple)
                .overlay(Text("Tap Me").font(.largeTitle).
                foregroundColor(tapLocation.x > dimension / 2.0 ?
                Color.black : Color.white))
                .frame(width: dimension, height: dimension)
            .gesture(spatialTapGesture)

            Text("Tap x location = \(tapLocation.x)")
            Text("Tap y location = \(tapLocation.y)")
        }
    }
}
```

```
struct ContentView_Previews: PreviewProvider {
    static var previews: some View {
        ContentView()
    }
}
```

6.   Click the Live icon in the Canvas pane.

7.   Click in the upper-left corner, upper right, bottom right, and
     bottom left of the Rectangle. Notice that each time you click in
     a different area, the two Text views identify the location where
     you clicked. The location where you click on the Rectangle also
     defines how the Rectangle and text color may change.

Try adding a count parameter to the SpatialTapGesture like this and testing the app
again to double-click before the spatial tap gesture will be recognized:

```
SpatialTapGesture(count: 2)
```

Detecting Long Press Gestures

A long press gesture occurs when the user presses one or more fingertips on the screen
for a fixed amount of time where the fingertips don't move very far. To define a long
press, you can modify the following properties:

- minimumDuration – Defines how long one or more fingertips must
  press down on the screen until the long press is recognized

- maximumDistance – Defines how far fingertips can move before the
  long press gesture fails

The simplest .onLongPressGesture modifier looks like this:

```
.onLongPressGesture {
    //  Code to run
}
```

If you want, you can add the minimumDuration: and maximumDistance: parameters like this:

```
.onLongPressGesture(minimumDuration: 3,
maximumDistance: 2) {
    // Code to run
}
```

The preceding version of the .onLongPressGesture modifier forces the user to hold a press for a minimum of 3 seconds. If you want to do something while the user presses down, you can use the pressing: parameter like this:

```
.onLongPressGesture(minimumDuration: 2, maximumDistance: 2,
pressing: {stillPressed in
    // Code to run while the long press occurs
}) {
    // Code to run after detecting the long press gesture
}
```

To see how to detect a long press gesture, follow these steps:

1. Create a new SwiftUI iOS App project and give it any name you wish such as "LongPressGesture."

2. Click the ContentView file in the Navigator pane.

3. Add the following State variables under the struct ContentView: View line:

```
@State var changeMe = false
@State var message = ""
```

4. Add a Text view inside the VStack like this:

```
var body: some View {
    VStack {
        Text(message)
    }
}
```

5. Add a Rectangle underneath the Text view:

```
Rectangle()
    .frame(width: 175, height: 125)
    .foregroundColor(changeMe ? .red : .yellow)
```

6. Add the .onLongPressGesture modifier to the Rectangle like this:

```
.onLongPressGesture(minimumDuration: 2, maximumDistance: 2,
pressing: {stillPressed in
    message = "Long press in progress: \(stillPressed)"
}) {
    changeMe.toggle()
}
```

The pressing: parameter displays true while the long press gesture is in progress. Then it displays false as soon as the long press gesture is completed. As soon as the long press gesture is completed, it toggles the changeMe State variable from false to true (or true to false).

The entire ContentView file should look like this:

```
import SwiftUI

struct ContentView: View {
    @State var changeMe = false
    @State var message = ""
    var body: some View {
        VStack {
            Text(message)
            Rectangle()
                .frame(width: 175, height: 125)
                .foregroundColor(changeMe ? .red : .yellow)
                .onLongPressGesture(minimumDuration: 2,
                maximumDistance: 2, pressing: {stillPressed in
                    message = "Long press in progress: \
                    (stillPressed)"
                }) {
```

```
                            changeMe.toggle()
                    }
            }
        }
    }

    struct ContentView_Previews: PreviewProvider {
        static var previews: some View {
            ContentView()
        }
    }
```

7. Click the Live icon in the Canvas pane.

8. Move the mouse pointer over the Rectangle and hold down the
    left mouse button to simulate a press gesture. Notice that the Text
    view displays "Long press in progress: true".

9. Keep holding the left mouse button down until the Rectangle
    changes color. This indicates that the minimumDuration of 2 has
    been reached and the long press gesture recognized.

Detecting Magnification Gestures

A magnification gesture (also known as a pinch gesture) occurs when the user holds
two fingertips on the screen and moves the fingertips apart or closer together. This
magnification gesture often occurs when the user wants to zoom in on an image or zoom
out to see more of something such as a larger view of a map.

Since the magnification gesture changes the size of a view, you need to define two
State variables that represent the current size and the final size as CGFloat data types
like this:

```
@State private var tempValue: CGFloat = 0
@State private var finalValue: CGFloat = 1
```

To resize a view, the magnification gesture needs to work with the .scaleEffect modifier on the view you want to resize such as

```
Image(systemName: "star.fill")
    .font(.system(size: 200))
    .foregroundColor(.green)
    .scaleEffect(finalValue + tempValue)
```

Then you need to attach the .gesture modifier to the view you want to resize using the magnification gesture like this:

```
.gesture(

)
```

Inside the parentheses of the .gesture modifier is where you define the magnification gesture. You need to detect when the magnification gesture changes and when it finally ends like this:

```
.gesture(
    MagnificationGesture()
        .onChanged { amount in
            //  Code to run
        }
        .onEnded { amount in
            //  Code to run
        }
)
```

The .onChanged modifier measures how far the user moves two fingertips apart or closer together. The .onEnded modifier measures the distance between the two fingertips when the user ends the magnification gesture by lifting both fingertips off the screen.

To see how to detect a magnification gesture, follow these steps:

1. Create a new SwiftUI iOS App project and give it any name you wish such as "MagnificationGesture."

2. Click the ContentView file in the Navigator pane.

3. Add the following State variables under the struct ContentView:
    View line:

```
@State private var tempValue: CGFloat = 0
@State private var finalValue: CGFloat = 1
```

4. Add a VStack with an Image inside the body like this:

```
var body: some View {
    VStack {
        Image(systemName: "star.fill")
            .font(.system(size: 200))
            .foregroundColor(.green)
            .scaleEffect(finalValue + tempValue)
    }
}
```

This displays a star in an Image view with a font size of 200
and filled with the color green. Notice the .scaleEffect modifier
defines the size of the star image as the combination of the two
State variables. A size of 1 represents the current size of the
image where a smaller value shrinks the image and a larger value
expands the image.

5. Add a .gesture modifier to the Image since that's what we want to
    resize using the magnification gesture like this:

```
var body: some View {
    VStack {
        Image(systemName: "star.fill")
            .font(.system(size: 200))
            .foregroundColor(.green)
            .scaleEffect(finalValue + tempValue)
            .gesture(

            )
    }
}
```

This allows the Image view to recognize a gesture. Now we just need to define which gesture to recognize.

6. Add the MagnificationGesture inside the .gesture () parentheses along with defining .onChanged and .onEnded modifiers like this:

```
var body: some View {
    VStack {
        Image(systemName: "star.fill")
            .font(.system(size: 200))
            .foregroundColor(.green)
            .scaleEffect(finalValue + tempValue)
            .gesture(
                MagnificationGesture()
                    .onChanged { amount in
                        tempValue = amount - 1
                    }
                    .onEnded { amount in
                        finalValue += tempValue
                        tempValue = 0
                    }
            )
    }
}
```

The .onChanged modifier measures the distance between the two fingertips and subtracts 1 to calculate the value of the tempValue State variable. If the user moves two fingertips apart, the value of amount will be greater than 1, so subtracting 1 will leave the additional amount to resize the Image.

The .onEnded modifier uses the last distance defined by the user's two fingertips and stores that value in the finalValue State variable. Then it clears the tempValue State variable to 0.

The entire ContentView file should look like this:

```swift
import SwiftUI

struct ContentView: View {
    @State private var tempValue: CGFloat = 0
    @State private var finalValue: CGFloat = 1

    var body: some View {
        VStack {
            Image(systemName: "star.fill")
                .font(.system(size: 200))
                .foregroundColor(.green)
                .scaleEffect(finalValue + tempValue)
                .gesture(
                    MagnificationGesture()
                        .onChanged { amount in
                            tempValue = amount - 1
                        }
                        .onEnded { amount in
                            finalValue += tempValue
                            tempValue = 0
                        }
                )
        }
    }
}

struct ContentView_Previews: PreviewProvider {
    static var previews: some View {
        ContentView()
    }
}
```

7. Click the Live icon in the Canvas pane.

8. Hold down the Option key and click on the simulated iOS device screen displayed in the Canvas pane. Holding down the Option key while clicking the left mouse button displays two gray circles that simulate pressing two fingertips on the screen as shown in Figure 11-1.

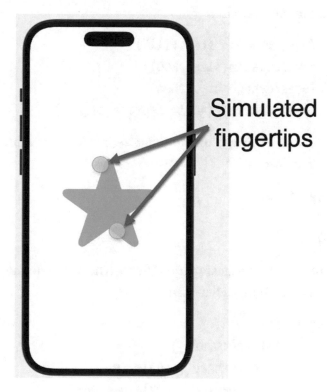

Figure 11-1. *Mimicking a two-finger press gesture in the Canvas pane*

9. While holding down the Option key, drag the mouse to simulate moving the two fingertips closer or farther apart. Notice that as you drag the mouse, the star image shrinks or expands to match the magnification gesture.

Detecting Rotation Gestures

A rotation gesture is similar to a magnification gesture because they both use two fingertips. The main difference is that a rotation gesture detects when the two fingertips move in a circular motion clockwise or counterclockwise.

Since the rotation gesture changes the angle of a view, you need to define one State variable that measures the angle of rotation as a Double data type like this:

```
@State private var degree = 0.0
```

To rotate a view, the rotation gesture needs to work with the .rotationEffect modifier on the view you want to rotate such as

```
Image(systemName: "star.fill")
    .font(.system(size: 200))
    .foregroundColor(.green)
    .rotationEffect(Angle.degrees(degree))
```

Then you need to attach the .gesture modifier to the view you want to rotate using the rotation gesture like this:

```
.gesture(

)
```

Inside the parentheses of the .gesture modifier is where you define the rotation gesture and detect when it changes like this:

```
.gesture(
    RotationGesture()
        .onChanged({ angle in
            degree = angle.degrees
        })
)
```

The .onChanged modifier measures how far the user rotates two fingertips clockwise or counterclockwise. To see how to detect a rotation gesture, follow these steps:

1. Create a new SwiftUI iOS App project and give it any name you wish such as "RotationGesture."

2. Click the ContentView file in the Navigator pane.

3. Add the following State variable under the struct ContentView: View line:

```
@State private var degree = 0.0
```

4. Add a VStack with an Image inside the body like this:

```
var body: some View {
    VStack {
        Image(systemName: "star.fill")
            .font(.system(size: 200))
            .foregroundColor(.green)
            .rotationEffect(Angle.degrees(degree))
    }
}
```

This defines an Image view that displays a star at a font size of 200 and a color of green. Then it uses the .rotationEffect modifier to rotate the Image.

5. Add a .gesture modifier to the Image since that's what we want to rotate using the rotation gesture like this:

```
var body: some View {
    VStack {
        Image(systemName: "star.fill")
            .font(.system(size: 200))
            .foregroundColor(.green)
            .rotationEffect(Angle.degrees(degree))
            .gesture(

            )
    }
}
```

6. Add the RotationGesture inside the .gesture () parentheses along with defining an .onChanged modifier like this:

```
var body: some View {
    VStack {
        Image(systemName: "star.fill")
            .font(.system(size: 200))
            .foregroundColor(.green)
            .rotationEffect(Angle.degrees(degree))
```

```
                    .gesture(
                        RotationGesture()
                            .onChanged({ angle in
                                degree = angle.degrees
                            })
                    )
            }
        }
```

The .onChanged modifier measures the angle that the user rotates the two-fingertip gesture on the screen. The entire ContentView file should look like this:

```
import SwiftUI

struct ContentView: View {
    @State private var degree = 0.0

    var body: some View {
        VStack {
            Image(systemName: "star.fill")
                .font(.system(size: 200))
                .foregroundColor(.green)
                .rotationEffect(Angle.degrees(degree))
                .gesture(
                    RotationGesture()
                        .onChanged({ angle in
                            degree = angle.degrees
                        })
                )
        }
    }
}
```

```
struct ContentView_Previews: PreviewProvider {
    static var previews: some View {
        ContentView()
    }
}
```

7. Click the Live icon in the Canvas pane.

8. Hold down the Option key and click inside the green star displayed in the Canvas pane. Holding down the Option key while clicking the left mouse button displays two gray circles that simulate pressing two fingertips on the screen (see Figure 11-1).

9. While holding down the Option key, drag the mouse to simulate moving the two fingertips rotating. Notice that as you drag the mouse, the star image rotates to match the rotation gesture.

Detecting Drag Gestures

A drag gesture occurs when the user presses and slides a fingertip across the screen. The drag gesture often moves an item on the screen to a new location.

Since the drag gesture changes the location of a view, you need to define one State variable that measures this location as a CGPoint like this:

```
@State private var circlePosition = CGPoint(x: 50, y: 50)
```

To move a view, the drag gesture needs to work with the .position modifier on the view you want to move such as

```
Circle()
    .fill(Color.blue)
    .frame(width: 100, height: 100)
    .position(circlePosition)
```

Then you need to attach the .gesture modifier to the view you want to move using the drag gesture like this:

```
.gesture(

)
```

Inside the parentheses of the .gesture modifier is where you define the drag gesture and detect when it changes like this:

```
.gesture(DragGesture()
    .onChanged({ value in
        //  Code to run
    }))
```

The .onChanged modifier measures how far the user drags a fingertip across the screen. To see how to detect a drag gesture, follow these steps:

1. Create a new SwiftUI iOS App project and give it any name you wish such as "DragGesture."

2. Click the ContentView file in the Navigator pane.

3. Add the following State variables under the struct ContentView: View line:

```
@State private var circlePosition = CGPoint(x: 50, y: 50)
@State private var circleLabel = "50, 50"
```

4. Add a VStack with a Text view and a Circle inside the body like this:

```
var body: some View {
    VStack {
        Text(circleLabel)
            .padding()
        Circle()
            .fill(Color.blue)
            .frame(width: 100, height: 100)
            .opacity(0.8)
            .position(circlePosition)
    }
}
```

This defines a Text view that displays the contents of the circleLabel State variable and defines a Circle colored blue. This Circle uses the .position modifier to work with the drag gesture.

5. Add a .gesture modifier to the Circle since that's what we want to move using the drag gesture like this:

```
var body: some View {
    VStack {
        Text(circleLabel)
            .padding()
        Circle()
            .fill(Color.blue)
            .frame(width: 100, height: 100)
            .opacity(0.8)
            .position(circlePosition)
            .gesture(

            )
    }
}
```

6. Add the DragGesture inside the .gesture () parentheses along with defining an .onChanged modifier like this:

```
var body: some View {
    VStack {
        Text(circleLabel)
            .padding()
        Circle()
            .fill(Color.blue)
            .frame(width: 100, height: 100)
            .opacity(0.8)
            .position(circlePosition)
            .gesture(DragGesture()
                        .onChanged({ value in
                circlePosition = value.location
                circleLabel = "\(Int(value.location.x)), \
                (Int(value.location.y))"
            }))
    }
}
```

The .onChanged modifier measures the location of the user's fingertip on the screen. Then it stores the x and y location values in the circleLabel to appear inside the Text view. The entire ContentView file should look like this:

```
import SwiftUI

struct ContentView: View {
    @State private var circlePosition = CGPoint(x: 50, y: 50)
    @State private var circleLabel = "50, 50"

    var body: some View {
        VStack {
            Text(circleLabel)
                .padding()
            Circle()
                .fill(Color.blue)
                .frame(width: 100, height: 100)
                .opacity(0.8)
                .position(circlePosition)
                .gesture(DragGesture()
                            .onChanged({ value in
                    circlePosition = value.location
                    circleLabel = "\(Int(value.location.x)), \
                    (Int(value.location.y))"
                }))
        }
    }
}

struct ContentView_Previews: PreviewProvider {
    static var previews: some View {
        ContentView()
    }
}
```

7. Click the Live icon in the Canvas pane.

8. Move the mouse pointer over the Circle on the simulated iOS device in the Canvas pane and then drag the mouse. Notice as you drag the mouse, the Text view constantly updates the x and y location of the Circle.

Defining Priority and Simultaneous Gestures

You can add touch gestures to any view. Since a stack is also a view, that means you can add touch gestures to VStacks, HStacks, and ZStacks as well. If you add a gesture to a view inside of a stack and then add a second, identical gesture to the stack itself, which gesture gets recognized?

When a gesture modifies an entire stack, every view inside that stack can recognize that gesture. However, if a view inside that stack has its own gesture modifier, that gesture modifier will get recognized instead. To see how this works, follow these steps:

1. Create a new SwiftUI iOS App project and give it any name you wish such as "TwoGestures."

2. Click the ContentView file in the Navigator pane.

3. Add the following State variable under the struct ContentView: View line:

   ```
   @State var message = ""
   ```

4. Add a VStack with a Text view, a Circle, and a Spacer inside the body like this:

   ```
   var body: some View {
       VStack {
           Text(message)
               .padding()
           Circle()
               .frame(width: 125, height: 125)
               .foregroundColor(.blue)
           Spacer()
       }.background(Color.yellow)
   }
   ```

This creates a Text view at the top and a blue Circle underneath. Then the Spacer pushes the boundary of the VStack down and colors it yellow to make it easy to see as shown in Figure 11-2.

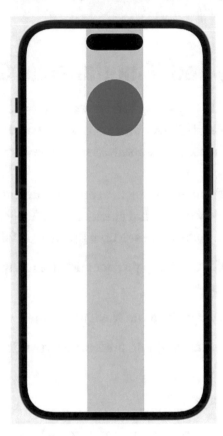

Figure 11-2. *Creating a VStack where a Spacer pushes the boundary to the bottom of the screen*

5. Add a .onTapGesture modifier to the Circle like this:

```
Circle()
    .frame(width: 125, height: 125)
    .foregroundColor(.blue)
    .onTapGesture {
        message = "Circle tapped"
    }
```

When the user taps the Circle, the message State variable will hold the string "Circle tapped".

6. Add a .onTapGesture modifier to the entire VStack like this:

```
var body: some View {
    VStack {
        Text(message)
            .padding()
        Circle()
            .frame(width: 125, height: 125)
            .foregroundColor(.blue)
            .onTapGesture {
                message = "Circle tapped"
            }
        Spacer()
    }.background(Color.yellow)
    .onTapGesture {
        message = "VStack tapped"
    }
}
```

If you click the Circle, the Circle's .onTapGesture modifier ("Circle tapped") will be recognized. If you click anywhere else in the VStack, the VStack's .onTapGesture modifier ("VStack tapped") will be recognized. The entire ContentView file should look like this:

```
import SwiftUI

struct ContentView_Previews: PreviewProvider {
    static var previews: some View {
        ContentView()
    }
}
```

7. Click the Live icon in the Canvas pane and click the blue Circle. Notice "Circle tapped" appears in the Text view. Even though the Circle is inside the VStack, the VStack's .onTapGesture modifier gets ignored.

8. Click the yellow background of the VStack. Notice "VStack tapped" appears in the Text view.

Defining a High-Priority Gesture

The gestures attached to views inside a stack will always be recognized over gestures attached to a stack. If you want a stack's gesture modifier to run instead of a gesture modifier attached to a view inside of that stack, you need to use the .highPriorityGesture modifier.

This .highPriorityGesture modifier simply identifies which gesture should have the higher priority. In this case, we want the stack's gesture modifier to run first, so we need to enclose it within the .highPriorityGesture modifier like this:

```
.highPriorityGesture(
    TapGesture()
        .onEnded { _ in
    message = "VStack tapped"
})
```

Notice that the TapGesture uses the .onEnded modifier to detect when the tap gesture ends so it can store "VStack tapped" in the message State variable.

To see how the .highPriorityGesture modifier works, follow these steps:

1. Create a new SwiftUI iOS App project and give it any name you wish such as "HighPriorityGestures."

2. Click the ContentView file in the Navigator pane.

3. Add the following State variable under the struct ContentView: View line:

```
@State var message = ""
```

4. Add a VStack with a Text view, a Circle, and a Spacer inside the body like this:

```
var body: some View {
    VStack {
        Text(message)
            .padding()
        Circle()
            .frame(width: 125, height: 125)
            .foregroundColor(.blue)
        Spacer()
    }.background(Color.yellow)
}
```

5. Add a .onTapGesture modifier to the Circle like this:

```
Circle()
    .frame(width: 125, height: 125)
    .foregroundColor(.blue)
    .onTapGesture {
        message = "Circle tapped"
    }
```

Normally when the user taps the Circle, the message State variable will hold the string "Circle tapped".

6. Add a .highPriorityGesture modifier to the entire VStack like this:

```
var body: some View {
    VStack {
        Text(message)
            .padding()
        Circle()
            .frame(width: 125, height: 125)
            .foregroundColor(.blue)
            .onTapGesture {
                message = "Circle tapped"
            }
```

231

```
            Spacer()
    }.background(Color.yellow)
        .highPriorityGesture(
            TapGesture()
                .onEnded { _ in
            message = "VStack tapped"
        })
    }
```

If you click the Circle, the Circle's .onTapGesture modifier ("Circle tapped") would normally be recognized. However, the .highPriorityGesture modifier defines the TapGesture on the VStack to get recognized first. The entire ContentView file should look like this:

```
import SwiftUI

struct ContentView: View {
    @State var message = ""

    var body: some View {
        VStack {
            Text(message)
                .padding()
            Circle()
                .frame(width: 125, height: 125)
                .foregroundColor(.blue)
                .onTapGesture {
                    message = "Circle tapped"
                }
            Spacer()
        }.background(Color.yellow)
            .highPriorityGesture(
                TapGesture()
                    .onEnded { _ in
                message = "VStack tapped"
            })
```

```
        }
    }

    struct ContentView_Previews: PreviewProvider {
        static var previews: some View {
            ContentView()
        }
    }
```

7. Click the Live icon in the Canvas pane and click the blue Circle. Notice "VStack tapped" appears in the Text view because of the .highPriorityGesture modifier on the VStack that overrides the Circle's .onTapGesture modifier.

8. Click the yellow background of the VStack. Notice "VStack tapped" still appears in the Text view.

Defining Simultaneous Gestures

Normally, the gesture modifiers attached to an individual view will run instead of any gesture modifiers attached to a stack. If you use the .highPriorityGesture modifier, then you can make a stack's gestures run instead of any gesture modifiers attached to an individual view. However, what if you want both gestures attached to a view and attached to a stack to run?

Then you can use the .simultaneousGesture modifier to make sure that a stack's gesture modifier run at the same time as a gesture modifier attached to an individual view. To define simultaneous gestures to run, enclose the gesture that would normally get ignored within the .simultaneousGesture modifier like this:

```
.simultaneousGesture(
    TapGesture()
        .onEnded { _ in
    message = "VStack tapped"
})
```

To see how the .simultaneousGesture modifier works, follow these steps:

1. Create a new SwiftUI iOS App project and give it any name you wish such as "SimultaneousGestures."

2. Click the ContentView file in the Navigator pane.

3. Add the following State variable under the struct ContentView: View line:

```
@State var message = ""
```

4. Add a VStack with a Text view, a Circle, and a Spacer inside the body like this:

```
var body: some View {
    VStack {
        Text(message)
            .padding()
        Circle()
            .frame(width: 125, height: 125)
            .foregroundColor(.blue)
        Spacer()
    }.background(Color.yellow)
}
```

5. Add a .onTapGesture modifier to the Circle like this:

```
Circle()
    .frame(width: 125, height: 125)
    .foregroundColor(.blue)
    .onTapGesture {
        message += "Circle tapped"
    }
```

Notice that when the Circle recognizes a tap gesture, it adds (+=) "Circle tapped" to the current value of the message State variable.

6. Add a .simultaneousGesture modifier to the entire VStack like this:

```
var body: some View {
    VStack {
        Text(message)
            .padding()
        Circle()
            .frame(width: 125, height: 125)
            .foregroundColor(.blue)
            .onTapGesture {
                message += "Circle tapped"
            }
        Spacer()
    }.background(Color.yellow)
        .simultaneousGesture(
            TapGesture()
                .onEnded { _ in
                message = "VStack tapped"
        })
}
```

If you click the Circle, the Circle's .onTapGesture modifier
("Circle tapped") would normally be recognized. However, the
.simultaneousGesture modifier defines the TapGesture on the
VStack to get recognized first before also recognizing the gesture
modifier on the Circle. The entire ContentView file should look
like this:

```
import SwiftUI

struct ContentView: View {
    @State var message = ""

    var body: some View {
        VStack {
            Text(message)
                .padding()
            Circle()
```

235

```
                        .frame(width: 125, height: 125)
                        .foregroundColor(.blue)
                        .onTapGesture {
                            message += "Circle tapped"
                        }
                    Spacer()
                }.background(Color.yellow)
                    .simultaneousGesture(
                        TapGesture()
                            .onEnded { _ in
                        message = "VStack tapped"
                    })
            }
        }

        struct ContentView_Previews: PreviewProvider {
            static var previews: some View {
                ContentView()
            }
        }
```

7. Click the Live icon in the Canvas pane and click the blue Circle.
    Notice "VStack tappedCircle tapped" appears in the Text view
    because of the .simultaneousGesture modifier on the VStack that
    lets it run before the Circle's .onTapGesture modifier.

8. Click the yellow background of the VStack. Notice "VStack
    tapped" still appears in the Text view.

Summary

Touch gestures give commands to an app without placing an object on the user interface
such as a button. Gestures can often work with one or more fingertips such as a double
or triple tap.

When adding multiple gestures, remember that gestures attached to individual views run instead of gestures attached to stacks. If you want a stack's gesture modifier to run first, enclose it within the .highPriorityGesture modifier. If you want both the stack and individual view's gesture modifiers to run one after another, enclose the stack modifier within the .simultaneousGesture modifier.

Adding gestures to an app can make the user interface less cluttered and more intuitive by letting users directly manipulate objects on the screen.

CHAPTER 12

Using Alerts, Action Sheets, and Contextual Menus

Almost every app needs to display and accept data from the user. The simplest way to display data is through a Text view, but sometimes you need to display data and give the user a way to respond. In that case, you can use an Alert or an Action Sheet. Yet another way to display options to the user are contextual menus.

An Alert pops up on the screen, giving the user a chance to respond. Then users can dismiss the Alert by tapping one or more buttons as shown in Figure 12-1.

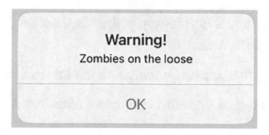

Figure 12-1. An Alert typically displays a message and one or more buttons

An Action Sheet looks nearly identical to an Alert except that an Alert appears in the middle of the screen, while an Action Sheet slides up and appears at the bottom of the screen. Alerts are meant more to grab the user's attention such as warning if you're about to delete data that you won't be able to retrieve or undo later. On the other hand, action sheets are meant more as a reminder that may not be as crucial or destructive.

Contextual menus appear after a long press gesture on a view such as a Text view. Then it pops up as a list of options that the user can select as shown in Figure 12-2.

© Wallace Wang 2023
W. Wang, *Beginning iPhone Development with SwiftUI*, https://doi.org/10.1007/978-1-4842-9541-0_12

Figure 12-2. *A Contextual Menu lists multiple options to select*

Displaying an Alert/Action Sheet

Every user interface needs to display data back to the user. In some cases, this data can be displayed just in a label, but sometimes you need to make sure the user sees certain information. In those situations, you should use an alert controller.

An Alert/Action Sheet appears over an app's user interface and can be customized by changing the following properties:

- Title – Text that appears at the top of the Alert/Action Sheet, often in bold and a large font size

- Message – Text that appears underneath the title in a smaller font size

- One or more buttons – A button that can dismiss the Alert/ Action Sheet

A title typically consists of a single word or short phrase that explains the purpose of the alert controller such as displaying "Warning" or "Log In." To dismiss an Alert/Action Sheet, you need at least one button.

To see how to create a simple Alert/Action Sheet that does nothing but display a title, a message, and a button to dismiss it, follow these steps:

1. Create a new SwiftUI iOS App project and give it any name you wish such as "Alert."

2. Click the ContentView file in the Navigator pane.

3. Add the following State variable under the struct ContentView:
    View line:

```
@State var showAlert = false
```

4. Add a VStack with a Button like this:

```
var body: some View {
  VStack {
      Button("Show Alert") {
          showAlert.toggle()
      }
  }
}
```

5. Add the .alert modifier to the Button like this:

```
.alert(isPresented: $showAlert) {
    Alert(title: Text("Warning!"), message: Text("Zombies
    on the loose"), dismissButton: .default(Text("OK")))
}
```

This .alert modifier shows an Alert when the showAlert State
variable is true. Then it uses a Text view to display "Warning!" and
a second Text view to display "Zombies on the loose". Finally, it
uses a third Text view to display "OK" on a Button.

Note   The Alert uses a dismissButton: parameter to define a single button to
appear. To make the code shorter, you can define the Button's appearance by just
using the style (.default) instead of the longer version like this: Alert.Button.default.

The entire ContentView file should look like this:

```
import SwiftUI

struct ContentView: View {
    @State var showAlert = false
```

```
var body: some View {
    VStack {
        Button("Show Alert") {
            showAlert.toggle()
        }
        .alert(isPresented: $showAlert) {
            Alert(title: Text("Warning!"), message:
            Text("Zombies on the loose"), dismissButton:
            .default(Text("OK")))
        }
    }
}
}

struct ContentView_Previews: PreviewProvider {
    static var previews: some View {
        ContentView()
    }
}
```

6. Click the Live icon in the Canvas pane and then click the Button to display the Alert (see Figure 12-1) in the middle of the screen.

7. Click OK to make the Alert go away.

8. Replace .alert with .actionSheet like this:

```
.actionSheet(isPresented: $showAlert) {
    ActionSheet(title: Text("Warning!"), message: Text("Zombies on
    the loose"), buttons: [.default(Text("OK"))])
}
```

Note   Where the Alert defined a Button using the dismissButton: parameter, the ActionSheet uses the buttons: parameter and encloses one or more buttons inside square brackets [ ] like an array. To make the code shorter, you can define the Button's appearance by just using the style (.default) instead of the longer version like this: ActionSheet.Button.default.

9. Click the Button on the simulated iOS screen. Notice that now an Action Sheet appears at the bottom of the screen.

10. Click the OK button to make the Action Sheet go away.

Creating an Alert or an Action Sheet is nearly identical but with minor differences in defining buttons and whether you use .alert (and Alert) or .actionSheet (ActionSheet).

Displaying and Responding to Multiple Buttons

The simplest Alert/Action Sheet displays a single button that allows the user to dismiss it. However, you may want to give the user more than one option to choose and then respond differently depending on which button the user taps.

An Alert can display up to two buttons called a primaryButton: and a secondaryButton:. An ActionSheet can display up to three buttons. For each button you want to display, you can choose one of three styles as shown in Figure 12-3:

- .default – Displays text in blue

- .destructive – Displays text in red

- .cancel – Displays text in bold

Figure 12-3. *The three different styles for buttons*

To see how to create an Alert that displays two buttons, follow these steps:

1. Create a new SwiftUI iOS App project and give it any name you wish such as "AlertTwoButtons."

2. Click the ContentView file in the Navigator pane.

3. Add the following State variable under the struct ContentView: View line:

    ```
    @State var showAlert = false
    ```

4. Add a VStack and a Button inside the var body: some View like this:

    ```
    var body: some View {
        VStack {
            Button("Show Alert") {
                showAlert.toggle()
            }
        }
    }
    ```

5. Add an .alert modifier to the Button like this:

```
.alert(isPresented: $showAlert) {
    Alert(title: Text("Warning!"),
          message: Text("Zombies on the loose"),
          primaryButton: .default(Text("Default")),
          secondaryButton: .cancel(Text("Cancel")))
}
```

For either the primaryButton or secondaryButton, you can use
the .destructive button type instead just to see how the button's
appearance changes within an Alert. The entire ContentView file
should look like this:

```
import SwiftUI

struct ContentView: View {
    @State var showAlert = false

    var body: some View {
        VStack {
            Button("Show Alert") {
                showAlert.toggle()
            }
            .alert(isPresented: $showAlert) {
                Alert(title: Text("Warning!"),
                      message: Text("Zombies on the loose"),
                      primaryButton: .default(Text("Default")),
                      secondaryButton: .cancel(Text("Cancel")))
            }
        }
    }
}

struct ContentView_Previews: PreviewProvider {
    static var previews: some View {
        ContentView()
    }
}
```

6. Click the Live icon in the Canvas pane and then click the "Show Alert" Button. The Alert appears.

7. Click either the "Default" or "Cancel" Button to make the Alert go away.

To see how to create an Action Sheet that displays three buttons, follow these steps:

1. Create a new SwiftUI iOS App project and give it any name you wish such as "ActionSheetButtons."

2. Click the ContentView file in the Navigator pane.

3. Add the following State variable under the struct ContentView: View line:

```
@State var showAlert = false
```

4. Add a VStack and a Button inside the var body: some View like this:

```
var body: some View {
    VStack {
        Button("Show Action Sheet") {
            showAlert.toggle()
        }
    }
}
```

5. Add an .actionSheet modifier to the Button like this:

```
.actionSheet(isPresented: $showAlert) {
    ActionSheet(title: Text("Warning!"),
                message: Text("Zombies on the loose"),
                buttons: [
                    .default(Text("Default")),
                    .cancel(Text("Cancel")),
                    .destructive(Text("Destructive"))])
}
```

246

The entire ContentView file should look like this:

```
import SwiftUI

struct ContentView: View {
    @State var showAlert = false

    var body: some View {
        VStack {
            Button("Show Action Sheet") {
                showAlert.toggle()
            }
            .actionSheet(isPresented: $showAlert) {
                ActionSheet(title: Text("Warning!"),
                            message: Text("Zombies on the loose"),
                            buttons: [
                                .default(Text("Default")),
                                .cancel(Text("Cancel")),
                                .destructive(Text("Destruc
                                tive"))])
            }
        }
    }
}

struct ContentView_Previews: PreviewProvider {
    static var previews: some View {
        ContentView()
    }
}
```

6. Click the Live icon in the Canvas pane and then click the "Show Action Sheet" Button. The Action Sheet appears at the bottom of the simulated iOS screen.

7. Click the "Default," "Cancel," or "Destructive" Button to make the Action Sheet go away.

Making Alert/ActionSheet Buttons Responsive

Just adding buttons to an Alert or Action Sheet makes those buttons simply dismiss the Alert/Action Sheet when the user selects any of them. Most likely, you'll want buttons to perform some type of action. To do that, you must first create a function that contains code you want to run when the user selects a particular button. Then you must call that function when the user selects a button.

To make a button responsive, you need to add the action: parameter like this:

```
.alert(isPresented: $showAlert) {
    Alert(title: Text("Warning!"),
        message: Text("Zombies on the loose"),
        primaryButton: .default(Text("Default"), action: {
        message = "Default chosen"
    }),
        secondaryButton: .cancel(Text("Cancel"), action:
        cancelFunction))
    }

}
}

func cancelFunction() {
    message = "Cancel chosen"
}
```

The first method to using the action: parameter involves curly brackets where you can type as many lines of code as you wish. However, the more code you type, the more cluttered the entire .alert or .actionSheet will look.

The second method to using the action: parameter is to call a function. That way the action: code is isolated in a separate function while keeping the .alert or .actionSheet code shorter and easier to read.

No matter which method you choose, selecting any button will dismiss the Alert or Action Sheet from the screen. That's why if you omit the action: parameter completely, selecting that button will dismiss the Alert or Action Sheet.

To see how to make buttons responsive in an Alert, follow these steps:

1. Create a new SwiftUI iOS App project and give it any name you wish such as "AlertResponsiveButtons."

2. Click the ContentView file in the Navigator pane.

3. Add the following State variables under the struct ContentView: View line:

```
@State var showAlert = false
@State var message = ""
```

4. Add a VStack in the var body: some View and put a Text view and a Button inside the VStack like this:

```
var body: some View {
    VStack {
        Text(message)
            .padding()
        Button("Show Alert") {
            showAlert.toggle()
        }
    }
}
```

5. Add an .alert modifier to the Button like this:

```
.alert(isPresented: $showAlert) {
    Alert(title: Text("Warning!"),
          message: Text("Zombies on the loose"),
          primaryButton: .default(Text("Default"), action: {
        message = "Default chosen"
    }),
          secondaryButton: .cancel(Text("Cancel"), action:
          cancelFunction))
}
```

6. Add the following function above the last curly bracket in the struct ContentView: View like this:

```
func cancelFunction() {
    message = "Cancel chosen"
}
```

The entire ContentView file should look like this:

```
import SwiftUI

struct ContentView: View {
    @State var showAlert = false
    @State var message = ""

    var body: some View {
        VStack {
            Text(message)
                .padding()
            Button("Show Alert") {
                showAlert.toggle()
            }
            .alert(isPresented: $showAlert) {
                Alert(title: Text("Warning!"),
                      message: Text("Zombies on the loose"),
                      primaryButton: .default(Text("Default"),
                      action: {
                    message = "Default chosen"
                }),
                      secondaryButton: .cancel(Text("Cancel"),
                        action: cancelFunction))
            }
        }
    }

    func cancelFunction() {
        message = "Cancel chosen"
    }
}
```

```
struct ContentView_Previews: PreviewProvider {
    static var previews: some View {
        ContentView()
    }
}
```

7. Click the Live icon in the Canvas pane and then click the Show
    Alert Button. An Alert appears.

8. Click the Cancel or Default Button. Notice that a message appears
    to let you know which Button you chose.

To see how to make buttons responsive in an Action Sheet, follow these steps:

1. Create a new SwiftUI iOS App project and give it any name you
    wish such as "ActionSheetResponsiveButtons."

2. Click the ContentView file in the Navigator pane.

3. Add the following State variables under the struct ContentView:
    View line:

```
@State var showAlert = false
@State var message = ""
```

4. Add a VStack in the var body: some View and put a Text view and a
    Button inside the VStack like this:

```
var body: some View {
    VStack {
        Text(message)
            .padding()
        Button("Show Action Sheet") {
            showAlert.toggle()
        }
    }
}
```

5. Add an .actionSheet modifier to the Button like this:

```
.actionSheet(isPresented: $showAlert) {
    ActionSheet(title: Text("Warning!"),
                message: Text("Zombies on the loose"),
                buttons: [
                    .default(Text("Default"), action: {
        message = "Default chosen"
    }),
                    .cancel(Text("Cancel"), action:
                     cancelFunction),
                    .destructive(Text("Destructive"), action: {
        message = "Destructive chosen"
    })])
}
```

6. Add the following function above the last curly bracket in the
    struct ContentView: View like this:

```
func cancelFunction() {
    message = "Cancel chosen"
}
```

The entire ContentView file should look like this:

```
import SwiftUI

struct ContentView: View {
    @State var showAlert = false
    @State var message = ""

    var body: some View {
        VStack {
            Text(message)
                .padding()
            Button("Show Action Sheet") {
                showAlert.toggle()
            }
```

```
        .actionSheet(isPresented: $showAlert) {
            ActionSheet(title: Text("Warning!"),
                        message: Text("Zombies on the loose"),
                        buttons: [
                            .default(Text("Default"),
                            action: {
                message = "Default chosen"
            }),

                            .cancel(Text("Cancel"), action:
                            cancelFunction),
                            .destructive(Text("Destructive"),
                            action: {
                message = "Destructive chosen"
            })])
        }
      }
    }

    func cancelFunction() {
        message = "Cancel chosen"
    }

}

struct ContentView_Previews: PreviewProvider {
    static var previews: some View {
        ContentView()
    }
}
```

7. Click the Live icon in the Canvas pane and then click the Show
   Action Sheet Button. An Alert appears.

8. Click the Cancel, Default, or Destructive Button. Notice that a
   message appears to let you know which Button you chose.

Displaying TextFields in an Alert

An Alert (but not an ActionSheet) has the option of displaying one or more TextFields where the user can enter data. Then the Alert can retrieve the data the user entered in the TextFields to pass it to another part of the program.

You need to attach the .alert modifier to a user interface item, but instead of creating an Alert dialog, you define TextFields and Buttons separately like this:

```
.alert("Login", isPresented: $showAlert, actions: {
    TextField("Username", text: $username)

    SecureField("Password", text: $password)

    Button("Login", action: {
        message = "login"
    })
}, message: {
    Text("Please enter your username and password.")
})
```

The preceding code creates a simple Alert that displays a text field and a button as shown in Figure 12-4.

Figure 12-4. *Displaying a text field in an Alert dialog*

To see how to make an Alert with text fields, follow these steps:

1. Create a new SwiftUI iOS App project and give it any name you wish such as "AlertTextField."

2. Click the ContentView file in the Navigator pane.

3. Add the following State variables under the struct ContentView:
   View line:

```
@State var showAlert = false
@State var username: String = ""
@State var password: String = ""
@State var message = ""
```

4. Add a VStack in the var body: some View and put three Text views
   and a Button inside the VStack like this:

```
var body: some View {
    VStack (spacing: 50) {

        Text("You clicked the " + message + " button!")
        Text("Your user name is: " + username)
        Text("Your password is: " + password)

        Button("Show Alert") {
            showAlert = true
        }

    }
```

5. Attach an .alert to the closing curly bracket of the Button like this:

```
.alert("Login", isPresented: $showAlert, actions: {
    TextField("Username", text: $username)

    SecureField("Password", text: $password)

    Button("Login", action: {
        message = "login"
    })

    Button("Cancel", role: .cancel, action: {
        message = "cancel"
    })
```

```
}, message: {
    Text("Please enter your username and password.")
})
```

The entire ContentView file should look like this:

```
import SwiftUI

struct ContentView: View {
    @State var showAlert = false
    @State var username: String = ""
    @State var password: String = ""
    @State var message = ""

    var body: some View {
        VStack (spacing: 50) {

            Text("You clicked the " + message + " button!")
            Text("Your user name is: " + username)
            Text("Your password is: " + password)

            Button("Show Alert") {
                showAlert = true
            }
            .alert("Login", isPresented: $showAlert, actions: {
                TextField("Username", text: $username)

                SecureField("Password", text: $password)

                Button("Login", action: {
                    message = "login"
                })

                Button("Cancel", role: .cancel, action: {
                    message = "cancel"
                })
            }, message: {
                Text("Please enter your username and password.")
            })
```

```
            }
        }
    }

    struct ContentView_Previews: PreviewProvider {
        static var previews: some View {
            ContentView()
        }
    }
```

6. Click the Live icon in the Canvas pane.

7. Click the Show Alert Button on the user interface. A Login Alert
   appears as shown in Figure 12-5.

Figure 12-5. *An Alert dialog displaying a TextField and a SecureField*

8. Click in the Username TextField and type a name.

9. Click in the Password SecureField and type a password. Notice
   that the SecureField masks any characters you type.

10. Click the Login Button. The user interface identifies that you
    clicked the Login button and typed in a username and password.

Using Contextual Menus

A Contextual Menu can hide multiple options from the user interface. Then it appears only after detecting a long press gesture on a view such as a Text view. When the Contextual Menu lists options, the user can select one.

A Contextual Menu defines a list of Buttons where each Button displays text and an action to perform if the user selects that Button. The action can call a function or enclose Swift code within curly brackets like this:

```
.contextMenu(menuItems: {
    Button("Red", action: {
        myColor = Color.red
    })
    Button("Purple", action: purple)
    Button("Green", action: green)
    Button("Orange", action: orange)
})
```

In this example, the Button displaying "Red" as its title uses curly brackets to define code to run. The other three Buttons ("Purple", "Green", and "Orange") call functions. Notice that each function call simply uses the function name and does not need a parameter list if it is empty.

To see how to make a Contextual Menu, follow these steps:

1. Create a new SwiftUI iOS App project and give it any name you wish such as "ContextualMenu."

2. Click the ContentView file in the Navigator pane.

3. Add the following State variable under the struct ContentView: View line:

```
@State var myColor = Color.gray
```

4. Add a VStack in the var body: some View and put a Rectangle and a Text view inside the VStack like this:

```
var body: some View {
    VStack {
        Rectangle()
```

```
        .foregroundColor(myColor)
    Text("Pick a color")
        .padding()
    }
}
```

The preceding code defines a Rectangle and colors it based on the myColor State variable, which is initially set to Color.gray. Then it displays a Text view.

5. Add a .contextualMenu modifier to the Text view like this:

```
.contextMenu(menuItems: {
    Button("Red", action: {
        myColor = Color.red
    })
    Button("Purple", action: purple)
    Button("Green", action: green)
    Button("Orange", action: orange)
})
```

6. Add the following functions above the last curly bracket in the struct ContentView: View like this:

```
func purple() {
    myColor = Color.purple
}

func green() {
    myColor = Color.green
}

func orange() {
    myColor = Color.orange
}
```

The entire ContentView file should look like this:

```swift
import SwiftUI

struct ContentView: View {
    @State var myColor = Color.gray

    var body: some View {
        VStack {
            Rectangle()
                .foregroundColor(myColor)
            Text("Pick a color")
                .padding()
                .contextMenu(menuItems: {
                    Button("Red", action: {
                        myColor = Color.red
                    })
                    Button("Purple", action: purple)
                    Button("Green", action: green)
                    Button("Orange", action: orange)
                })
        }
    }

    func purple() {
        myColor = Color.purple
    }

    func green() {
        myColor = Color.green
    }

    func orange() {
        myColor = Color.orange
    }

}
```

```
struct ContentView_Previews: PreviewProvider {
    static var previews: some View {
        ContentView()
    }
}
```

7. Click the Live icon in the Canvas pane.

8. Move the mouse pointer over the "Pick a color" Text view and hold down the left mouse button to mimic a long press gesture. After a moment, the Contextual Menu appears.

9. Click any of the options displayed in the Contextual Menu. Notice that the Rectangle changes color based on the option you chose.

Summary

Alerts display information in the middle of the screen (.alert), while action sheets display information at the bottom of the screen (.actionSheet). An Alert and an Action Sheet can display a title and a message along with at least one button to dismiss the Alert/Action Sheet. However, an Alert can display up to two buttons, while an Action Sheet can display up to three buttons.

Buttons on an Alert/Action Sheet just dismiss the Alert/Action Sheet, but you can attach code to run when the user selects a button. One way is to write the code directly in the .alert/.actionSheet modifier, but a better solution is to call a function and separate code in that function away from the .alert/.actionSheet modifier.

Use alerts when you need to display important information to the user and get immediate feedback, such as verifying if the user wants to delete data. Use action sheets when you need to display information at the bottom of the screen. Use contextual menus when you want to hide multiple options off the user interface but make them available when the user wants to see them.

CHAPTER 13

Displaying Lists

One common way to display lots of related data to the user is through a List (also called a Table view). A List simply shows multiple rows of similar types of data stacked vertically. The simplest type of a List defines one or more Text views that appear in separate rows as shown in Figure 13-1:

```
List {
    Text("Cat")
    Text("Dog")
    Text("Bird")
    Text("Reptile")
    Text("Fish")
}
```

Figure 13-1. *A simple List containing multiple Text views*

© Wallace Wang 2023
W. Wang, *Beginning iPhone Development with SwiftUI*, https://doi.org/10.1007/978-1-4842-9541-0_13

If a List contains more items than can appear on the screen at one time, the List will let users swipe up or down to view all the data. Best of all, this scrolling feature doesn't require any additional coding.

When creating a List, you can use multiple Text views, but if you want to display a large number of items that may grow or shrink over time, manually typing multiple Text views won't work. Instead, you may need to use a loop to retrieve data and display it in a Text view within a List.

To see how to use a loop to create a List and swipe up and down to view all items in a List, follow these steps:

1. Create a new SwiftUI iOS App project and give it any name you wish such as "SimpleList."

2. Click the ContentView file in the Navigator pane.

3. Add a List inside the var body: some View like this:

```
var body: some View {
    List {
        ForEach(1...25, id: \.self) { index in
            Text("Animal #\(index)")
        }
    }
}
```

This code uses a ForEach loop to create 25 separate items. The index variable increments each time the ForEach loop runs, so the value of index will start at 1 and end at 25. The entire ContentView file should look like this:

```
import SwiftUI

struct ContentView: View {
    var body: some View {
        List {
            ForEach(1...25, id: \.self) { index in
                Text("Animal #\(index)")
            }
        }
    }
}
```

```
struct ContentView_Previews: PreviewProvider {
    static var previews: some View {
        ContentView()
    }
}
```

4. Click the Live icon in the Canvas pane. Notice that even though the List contains 25 items, not all items are visible on the screen at once as shown in Figure 13-2.

Figure 13-2. *The appearance of the List defined by a ForEach loop*

5. Drag the mouse up and down to mimic a swipe gesture. Notice that the List automatically scrolls up/down to show you the rest of its contents.

Displaying Array Data in a List

The data displayed in a List is typically stored in an array. The number of items in the array can be fixed, but more often the number of items will vary over time. That means the contents of the List will likely vary as the array grows and shrinks over time.

To see how to display the contents of an array in a List, follow these steps:

1. Create a new SwiftUI iOS App project and give it any name you wish such as "ListArray."

2. Click the ContentView file in the Navigator pane.

3. Define an array under the struct ContentView: some View line like this:

```
var myArray = ["Cat", "Dog", "Turtle", "Ferret", "Parrot",
"Goldfish", "Lizard", "Canary", "Tarantula", "Hamster"]
```

4. Add a VStack inside the var body: some View and create a List like this:

```
var body: some View {
    VStack {
        List {
            ForEach(0...myArray.count - 1, id: \.self) { index in
                Text(myArray[index])
            }
        }
    }
}
```

This creates a List and uses the ForEach loop to count from 0 up to the last item in the array. (Remember, the first item in the array has an index value of 0, so the last item in the array has an index value equal to the total number of items in the array – 1.) Then it uses this index value to retrieve each item from the array to display in the List as shown in Figure 13-3.

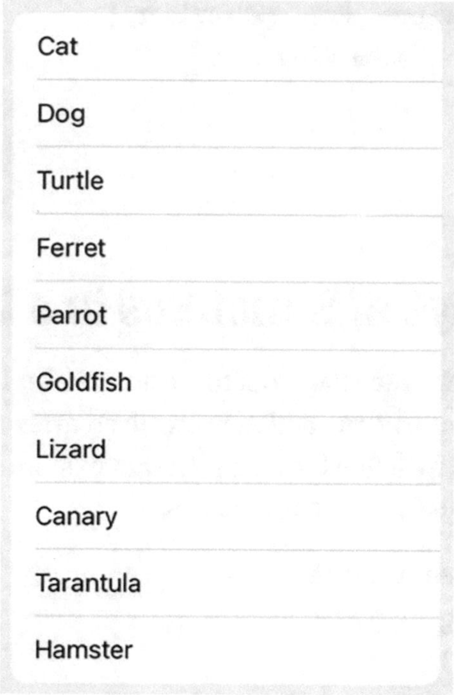

Cat

Dog

Turtle

Ferret

Parrot

Goldfish

Lizard

Canary

Tarantula

Hamster

Figure 13-3. *Displaying the contents of an array in a List*

The entire ContentView file should look like this:

```
import SwiftUI

struct ContentView: View {
    var myArray = ["Cat", "Dog", "Turtle", "Ferret", "Parrot", "Goldfish",
    "Lizard", "Canary", "Tarantula", "Hamster"]

    var body: some View {
        VStack {
            List {
                ForEach(0...myArray.count - 1, id: \.self) { index in
                    Text(myArray[index])
                }
            }
        }
    }
}
```

```
struct ContentView_Previews: PreviewProvider {
    static var previews: some View {
        ContentView()
    }
}
```

Displaying Arrays of Structures in a List

The previous code uses a ForEach loop to retrieve array items by index values. Another way to store data is to use a structure and then create an array of structures.

The purpose for this is to define the data you want to store along with a unique ID that you can use to identify each structure such as

```
struct Animals: Identifiable {
    let pet: String
    let id = UUID()
}
```

Once you define an Identifiable structure, you can store it in an array like this:

```
var myAnimals = [
    Animals(pet: "Cat"),
    Animals(pet: "Dog"),
    Animals(pet: "Turtle"),
    Animals(pet: "Ferret"),
    Animals(pet: "Parrot"),
    Animals(pet: "Goldfish"),
    Animals(pet: "Lizard"),
    Animals(pet: "Canary"),
    Animals(pet: "Tarantula"),
    Animals(pet: "Hamster")
]
```

Not only does this array store a string in the pet field, but it also uniquely identifies each structure with an ID. Now you can use this unique ID to display each item in a List like this:

```
List(myAnimals) {
    Text($0.pet)
}
```

Notice that the preceding code does not require a loop. To see how this code works, follow these steps:

1. Create a new SwiftUI iOS App project and give it any name you wish such as "ListOfStructures."

2. Click the ContentView file in the Navigator pane.

3. Define a structure and an array under the struct ContentView: some View line like this:

```
struct ContentView: View {

    struct Animals: Identifiable {
        let pet: String
        let id = UUID()
    }

    var myAnimals = [
        Animals(pet: "Cat"),
        Animals(pet: "Dog"),
        Animals(pet: "Turtle"),
        Animals(pet: "Ferret"),
        Animals(pet: "Parrot"),
        Animals(pet: "Goldfish"),
        Animals(pet: "Lizard"),
        Animals(pet: "Canary"),
        Animals(pet: "Tarantula"),
        Animals(pet: "Hamster")
    ]
```

4. Add a List inside the var body: some View like this:

```
var body: some View {
    List(myAnimals) {
        Text($0.pet)
    }
}
```

The entire ContentView file should look like this:

```
import SwiftUI

struct ContentView: View {

    struct Animals: Identifiable {
        let pet: String
        let id = UUID()
    }

    var myAnimals = [
        Animals(pet: "Cat"),
        Animals(pet: "Dog"),
        Animals(pet: "Turtle"),
        Animals(pet: "Ferret"),
        Animals(pet: "Parrot"),
        Animals(pet: "Goldfish"),
        Animals(pet: "Lizard"),
        Animals(pet: "Canary"),
        Animals(pet: "Tarantula"),
        Animals(pet: "Hamster")
    ]

    var body: some View {
        List(myAnimals) {
            Text($0.pet)
        }
    }
}
```

```
struct ContentView_Previews: PreviewProvider {
    static var previews: some View {
        ContentView()
    }
}
```

Notice how much shorter the code looks to create a List compared with the previous version that required a ForEach loop.

Creating Groups in a List

If you have many items displayed in a List, it can be hard to scroll through all this data to find the item you want. To solve this problem, lists let you create sections as shown in Figure 13-4.

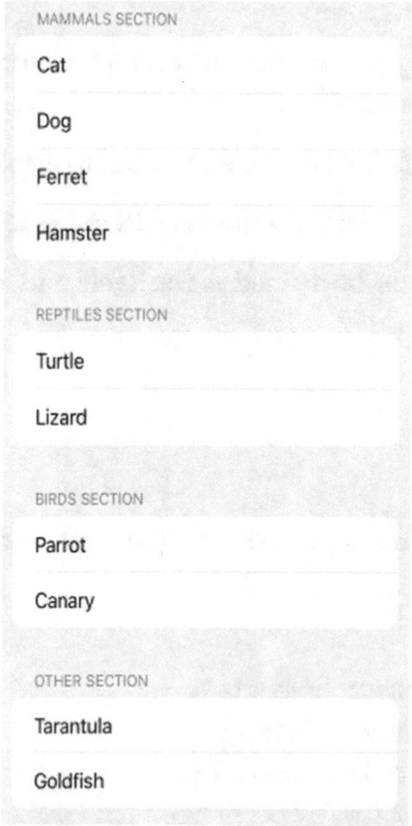

Figure 13-4. *Displaying the contents of a List in sections*

To define sections, you need to create two structures. One structure defines the section headings, and the second structure defines the data you want to display. To define the section headings, you need to define

- A String constant to hold each section's name

- An array constant to hold an array of structures that contain the actual data to display

- An ID that defines a unique ID for each section

The structure name must be defined as Identifiable to create a unique ID such as

```
struct SectionHeading: Identifiable {
    let name: String
    let animalList: [Animals]
    let id = UUID()
}
```

The preceding structure uses "animalList" to store an array of structures called Animals. This Animals structure needs

- A String constant to hold the data you want to display in the List

- An ID that defines a unique ID for each item in the List

This second structure must be defined as Hashable and Identifiable such as

```
struct Animals: Hashable, Identifiable {
    let pet: String
    let id = UUID()
}
```

Finally, you can create an array that defines the sections and the items within each section such as

```
var myAnimals = [
    SectionHeading(name: "Mammals",
                   animalList: [
                     Animals(pet: "Cat"),
                     Animals(pet: "Dog"),
```

```
                    Animals(pet: "Ferret"),
                    Animals(pet: "Hamster")])
    ]
```

Then to display items in a List, you need to use nested ForEach loops. The outer ForEach loop defines the section names such as

```
        ForEach(myAnimals) { heading in
            Section(header: Text("\(heading.name) Section")) {

            }
        }
```

Then the inner ForEach loop defines the items to appear within each section such as

```
            ForEach(heading.animalList) { creature in
                Text(creature.pet)
            }
```

To see how to create a List divided into sections, follow these steps:

1. Create a new SwiftUI iOS App project and give it any name you wish such as "ListSections."

2. Click the ContentView file in the Navigator pane.

3. Define a structure under the struct ContentView: some View line to define the data you want to display in the List like this:

```
struct Animals: Hashable, Identifiable {
    let pet: String
    let id = UUID()
}
```

4. Add a second structure underneath to define the section names to display in the List like this:

```
struct SectionHeading: Identifiable {
    let name: String
    let animalList: [Animals]
    let id = UUID()
}
```

5. Add an array to list the sections and the items to appear within each section like this:

```
var myAnimals = [
    SectionHeading(name: "Mammals",
                   animalList: [
                    Animals(pet: "Cat"),
                    Animals(pet: "Dog"),
                    Animals(pet: "Ferret"),
                    Animals(pet: "Hamster")]),

    SectionHeading(name: "Reptiles",
                   animalList: [
                    Animals(pet: "Turtle"),
                    Animals(pet: "Lizard")]),

    SectionHeading(name: "Birds",
                   animalList: [
                    Animals(pet: "Parrot"),
                    Animals(pet: "Canary")]),

    SectionHeading(name: "Other",
                   animalList: [
                    Animals(pet: "Tarantula"),
                    Animals(pet: "Goldfish")])
]
```

6. Add a List inside the var body: some View like this:

```
var body: some View {
    List {

    }
```

7. Add a ForEach loop inside the List to define the section name
    like this:

```
var body: some View {
    List {
        ForEach(myAnimals) { heading in
            Section(header: Text("\(heading.name) Section")) {

            }
        }
    }
}
```

Notice that a Text view displays the "name" property of each
section, which was previously defined by the array ("Mammals",
"Reptiles", "Birds", and "Other").

8. Add a second ForEach loop to define the actual data to display in
    the List like this:

```
var body: some View {
    List {
        ForEach(myAnimals) { heading in
            Section(header: Text("\(heading.name) Section")) {
                ForEach(heading.animalList) { creature in
                    Text(creature.pet)
                }
            }
        }
    }
}
```

Notice that this second ForEach loop uses the "pet" property that was previously
defined by the array ("Cat", "Dog", "Ferret", "Hamster", "Turtle", "Lizard", "Parrot", "Canary",
"Tarantula", "Goldfish"). The entire ContentView file should look like this:

```
import SwiftUI

struct ContentView: View {

    struct Animals: Hashable, Identifiable {
        let pet: String
```

```
        let id = UUID()
    }

    struct SectionHeading: Identifiable {
        let name: String
        let animalList: [Animals]
        let id = UUID()
    }

    var myAnimals = [
        SectionHeading(name: "Mammals",
                       animalList: [
                        Animals(pet: "Cat"),
                        Animals(pet: "Dog"),
                        Animals(pet: "Ferret"),
                        Animals(pet: "Hamster")]),

        SectionHeading(name: "Reptiles",
                       animalList: [
                        Animals(pet: "Turtle"),
                        Animals(pet: "Lizard")]),

        SectionHeading(name: "Birds",
                       animalList: [
                        Animals(pet: "Parrot"),
                        Animals(pet: "Canary")]),

        SectionHeading(name: "Other",
                       animalList: [
                        Animals(pet: "Tarantula"),
                        Animals(pet: "Goldfish")])
    ]

    var body: some View {
        List {
            ForEach(myAnimals) { heading in
                Section(header: Text("\(heading.name) Section")) {
                    ForEach(heading.animalList) { creature in
```

```
                Text(creature.pet)
            }
        }
      }
    }
  }
}

struct ContentView_Previews: PreviewProvider {
    static var previews: some View {
        ContentView()
    }
}
```

Adding Line Separators to a List

Lists typically display lines in between items. SwiftUI lets you choose to hide or display those lines or tint the lines with a specific color.

To hide or display lines within a List, use the .listRowSeparator modifier with either .visible or .hidden like this:

```
.listRowSeparator(.hidden)
```

To color the lines separating items in a List, use the .listRowSeparatorTint modifier with a color such as .red or .blue like this:

```
.listRowSeparatorTint(.red)
```

You can use both modifiers inside of a List to modify the ForEach loop that defines what to display in a List. To see how to show and color line separators in a List, follow these steps:

1. Create a new SwiftUI iOS App project and give it any name you wish such as "ListLines."

2. Click the ContentView file in the Navigator pane.

3. Add an array under the struct ContentView: View line like this:

```
var myArray = ["Cat", "Dog", "Turtle", "Ferret", "Parrot",
"Goldfish", "Lizard", "Canary", "Tarantula", "Hamster"]
```

4. Add a List inside the VStack under the var body: some View line
    like this:

```
var body: some View {
    VStack {
        List {

        }
    }
}
```

5. Add a ForEach loop inside the List to find all the array items
    starting from 0 up to the total number of items in the array – 1
    like this:

```
var body: some View {
    VStack {
        List {
            ForEach(0...myArray.count - 1, id: \.self) { index in
                Text(myArray[index])
            }
        }
    }
}
```

6. Add a .listRowSeparator modifier to the ForEach loop like this:

```
var body: some View {
    VStack {
        List {
            ForEach(0...myArray.count - 1, id: \.self) { index in
```

```
            Text(myArray[index])
        }.listRowSeparator(.visible)
    }

}
}
```

This .listRowSeparator shows the lines (.visible).

7. Add a .listRowSeparatorTint modifier to the ForEach loop like this:

```
var body: some View {
    VStack {
        List {
            ForEach(0...myArray.count - 1, id: \.self) { index in
                Text(myArray[index])
            }.listRowSeparator(.visible)
            .listRowSeparatorTint(.red)
        }

    }
}
```

You can choose any color you want such as .orange or .purple. The entire ContentView file should look like this:

```
import SwiftUI

struct ContentView: View {
    var myArray = ["Cat", "Dog", "Turtle", "Ferret", "Parrot",
    "Goldfish", "Lizard", "Canary", "Tarantula", "Hamster"]

    var body: some View {
        VStack {
            List {
                ForEach(0...myArray.count - 1, id: \.self) {
                index in
                    Text(myArray[index])
                }.listRowSeparator(.visible)
                .listRowSeparatorTint(.red)
```

```
                }
            }
        }
    }

    struct ContentView_Previews: PreviewProvider {
        static var previews: some View {
            ContentView()
        }
    }
```

8. Click the Live icon in the Canvas pane. Notice that the List displays lines between each item in the color you defined.

Displaying Alternating Colors to a List

A long List can be cumbersome to view. While lines (colored or not) separating items in a List can make lists easier to read, another option is to use alternating colors in list rows as shown in Figure 13-5.

Figure 13-5. *Alternating colors can make lists easier to read*

SwiftUI lets you define colors like this:

```
Color.green
```

One problem with colors is that they may appear so vibrant that they make the text in each row of a List hard to read. To adjust the color strength, we can add an .opacity modifier to make the color less intense. A value of 0 makes the color disappear completely, and a color of 1 makes the color appear in full strength. Therefore, an opacity value less than 1 will lower the color's appearance such as

```
Color.green.opacity(0.4)
```

If an array populates a List, then the array index can be used to alternate rows depending if the array index is odd or even. To determine if an array index (or any number) is even, use the swift modulo operator (%) to divide that number by 2. If the value is 0, then the number is even; otherwise, the number is odd.

So to define the background color of each row in a List, we'll need to use the .background modifier to identify even and odd array index values like this:

```
.background(index % 2 == 0 ? Color.green) : Color.yellow
```

To see how to display alternating colors in a List, follow these steps:

1. Create a new SwiftUI iOS App project and give it any name you wish such as "ListAlternatingColors."

2. Click the ContentView file in the Navigator pane.

3. Add an array under the struct ContentView: View line like this:

   ```
   var myArray = ["Cat", "Dog", "Turtle", "Ferret", "Parrot",
   "Goldfish", "Lizard", "Canary", "Tarantula", "Hamster"]
   ```

4. Add a List inside the VStack under the var body: some View line like this:

   ```
   var body: some View {
       VStack {
           List {

           }
       }
   }
   ```

5. Add a ForEach loop inside the List to find all the array items starting from 0 up to the total number of items in the array – 1 like this:

```
var body: some View {
    VStack {
        List {
            ForEach(0...myArray.count - 1, id: \.self) { index in
                Text(myArray[index])
            }
        }

    }
}
```

If we add a background color to the Text view inside the ForEach loop, all we'll do is highlight just the Text view and not the entire row. What we need to do is embed the Text view inside of an HStack and then add a Spacer() to push the HStack boundary all the way to the edge of the iOS screen.

6. Embed the Text view inside an HStack with a Spacer() like this:

```
var body: some View {
    VStack {
        List {
            ForEach(0...myArray.count - 1, id: \.self) { index in
                HStack {
                    Text(myArray[index])
                    Spacer()
                }
            }
        }

    }
}
```

Now we can add a background color to the HStack, which will include both the Text view and the width of the HStack, which is pushed out to the right with the Spacer().

7. Add a background modifier to the last curly bracket that defines the HStack like this:

```
var body: some View {
    VStack {
        List {
            ForEach(0...myArray.count - 1, id: \.self) { index in
                HStack {
                    Text(myArray[index])
                    Spacer()
                }.background(index % 2 == 0 ? Color.green.
                opacity(0.4) : Color.yellow.opacity(0.4))
            }
        }

    }
}
```

Feel free to choose different colors and opacity values. Notice that if an array index is even, the row will appear in green, but if an array index is odd, then the row will appear in yellow. The entire ContentView file should look like this:

```
import SwiftUI

struct ContentView: View {
    var myArray = ["Cat", "Dog", "Turtle", "Ferret", "Parrot",
    "Goldfish", "Lizard", "Canary", "Tarantula", "Hamster"]

    var body: some View {
        VStack {
            List {
                ForEach(0...myArray.count - 1, id: \.self) {
                index in
                    HStack {
```

```
                         Text(myArray[index])
                         Spacer()
                    }.background(index % 2 == 0 ? Color.green.
                    opacity(0.4) : Color.yellow.opacity(0.4))
                }
            }
        }
    }
}

struct ContentView_Previews: PreviewProvider {
    static var previews: some View {
        ContentView()
    }
}
```

8. Click the Live icon in the Canvas pane. SwiftUI displays
    alternating rows of colors and opacities (see Figure 13-5).

Adding Swipe Gestures to a List

Many common apps such as Mail, Messages, and Photos display items in a List. With
these lists, users can swipe left to right or right to left to display additional options to
choose as shown in Figure 13-6.

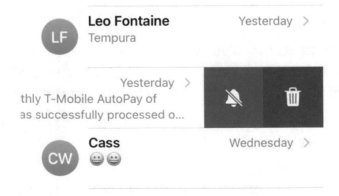

Figure 13-6. *Swiping on a List can reveal additional options*

Two common tasks for lists involve deleting and moving items. Deleting items from a List involves removing the item, typically after the user swipes from right to left. Moving items in a List involves sliding a fingertip on an item to place it in a new location in the List.

Deleting Items from a List

The most common shortcut in iOS for deleting an item in a List involves a right-to-left swipe to reveal a Delete button. As an alternative, the user can continue the right-to-left swipe to delete an item without needing to tap the Delete button at all. Since this swipe to delete gesture is often used, SwiftUI makes it easy to implement.

The first step is to add the .onDelete modifier to the ForEach loop within a List like this:

```
List {
    ForEach(0...myArray.count - 1, id: \.self) { index in

    }.onDelete(perform: delete)
}
```

This calls a delete function that uses the array name that contains the items displayed in a List (called "myArray" in the following example) and calls the remove method like this:

```
func delete(at offsets: IndexSet) {
    myArray.remove(atOffsets: offsets)
}
```

To see how to create a swipe to delete gesture in a List, follow these steps:

1. Create a new SwiftUI iOS App project and give it any name you wish such as "ListDelete."

2. Click the ContentView file in the Navigator pane.

3. Add a State variable array under the struct ContentView line like this:

   ```
   @State var myArray = ["Cat", "Dog", "Turtle", "Ferret", "Parrot",
   "Goldfish", "Lizard", "Canary", "Tarantula", "Hamster"]
   ```

The exact strings you type don't matter just as long as you type several strings to fill the array.

4. Add a List under the var body: some View line like this:

```
var body: some View {
    List {

    }
```

5. Add a ForEach loop inside this List to count from 0 to the total number of items in the array – 1. Then display the array item in a Text view like this:

```
var body: some View {
    List {
        ForEach(0...myArray.count - 1, id: \.self) { index in
            Text(myArray[index])
        }
    }
```

6. Add the .onDelete modifier to the ForEach loop to call a function called delete like this:

```
var body: some View {
    List {
        ForEach(0...myArray.count - 1, id: \.self) { index in
            Text(myArray[index])
        }.onDelete(perform: delete)
    }
```

7. Add the following function above the last curly bracket in the struct ContentView: View like this:

```
func delete(at offsets: IndexSet) {
    myArray.remove(atOffsets: offsets)
}
```

The entire ContentView file should look like this:

```swift
import SwiftUI

struct ContentView: View {
    @State var myArray = ["Cat", "Dog", "Turtle", "Ferret",
    "Parrot", "Goldfish", "Lizard", "Canary", "Tarantula",
    "Hamster"]

    var body: some View {
        List {
            ForEach(0...myArray.count - 1, id: \.self) { index in
                Text(myArray[index])
            }.onDelete(perform: delete)
        }
    }

    func delete(at offsets: IndexSet) {
        myArray.remove(atOffsets: offsets)
    }

}

struct ContentView_Previews: PreviewProvider {
    static var previews: some View {
        ContentView()
    }
}
```

8. Click the Live icon in the Canvas pane.

9. Swipe right to left on any item in the List. Notice that the .onDelete
    modifier automatically displays the Delete button as shown in
    Figure 13-7.

Figure 13-7. *The Delete button created by the .onDelete modifier*

10. Tap the Delete button. Notice that the row containing that item disappears.

Moving Items in a List

Another common way to use lists is to rearrange or move items within a List. In iOS, this is usually a two-step process. First, you must edit the List to display three-horizontal line icons to the right of each item in the List. Second, you slide a List item using the three-horizontal line icon to place that item in a new location as shown in Figure 13-8.

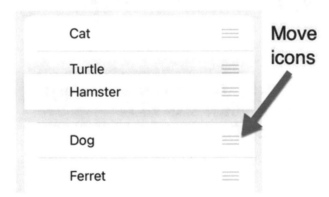

Figure 13-8. *Move icons appear to the right of items in a List*

The first step is to add the .onMove modifier to the ForEach loop within a List like this:

```
ForEach(0...myArray.count - 1, id: \.self) { index in

}.onMove(perform: move)
```

This calls a move function that uses the array name that contains the items displayed in a List (called "myArray" in the following example) and calls the move method like this:

```
func move(from source: IndexSet, to destination: Int) {
    myArray.move(fromOffsets: source, toOffset: destination)
}
```

To see how to display move icons in a List, follow these steps:

1. Create a new SwiftUI iOS App project and give it any name you wish such as "ListMove."

2. Click the ContentView file in the Navigator pane.

3. Add a State variable array under the struct ContentView line like this:

   ```
   @State var myArray = ["Cat", "Dog", "Turtle", "Ferret", "Parrot", "Goldfish", "Lizard", "Canary", "Tarantula", "Hamster"]
   ```

   The exact strings you type don't matter just as long as you type several strings to fill the array.

4. Add a NavigationView under the var body: some View line like this:

   ```
   var body: some View {
       NavigationView {

       }
   ```

   The NavigationView is necessary to display an Edit button in the upper-right corner of the screen.

5. Add a List inside the NavigationView like this:

   ```
   var body: some View {
       NavigationView {
           List {

           }
       }
   }
   ```

6. Add a ForEach loop inside this List to count from 0 to the total
    number of items in the array – 1. Then display the array item in a
    Text view like this:

```
var body: some View {
    NavigationView {
        List {
            ForEach(0...myArray.count - 1, id: \.self) { index in
                Text(myArray[index])
            }
        }
    }
}
```

7. Add the .toolbar modifier to the List like this:

```
var body: some View {
    NavigationView {
        List {
            ForEach(0...myArray.count - 1, id: \.self) { index in
                Text(myArray[index])
            }
        }.toolbar {
            EditButton()
        }
    }
}
```

This .toolbar { EditButton() } code adds an Edit button in the
upper-right corner of the NavigationView.

8. Add the .onMove modifier to the ForEach loop to call a function
    called move like this:

```
var body: some View {
    NavigationView {
        List {
```

```
      ForEach(0...myArray.count - 1, id: \.self) { index in
          Text(myArray[index])
      }.onMove(perform: move)
  }.toolbar {
      EditButton()
  }
}
```

9. Add the following function above the last curly bracket in the struct ContentView: View like this:

```
func move(from source: IndexSet, to destination: Int) {
    myArray.move(fromOffsets: source, toOffset: destination)
}
```

The entire ContentView file should look like this:

```
import SwiftUI

struct ContentView: View {
    @State var myArray = ["Cat", "Dog", "Turtle", "Ferret",
    "Parrot", "Goldfish", "Lizard", "Canary", "Tarantula",
    "Hamster"]

    var body: some View {
        NavigationView {
            List {
                ForEach(0...myArray.count - 1, id: \.self) {
                index in
                    Text(myArray[index])
                }.onMove(perform: move)
            }.toolbar {
                EditButton()
            }
        }
    }
```

```
        func move(from source: IndexSet, to destination: Int) {
            myArray.move(fromOffsets: source, toOffset: destination)
        }

    }

    struct ContentView_Previews: PreviewProvider {
        static var previews: some View {
            ContentView()
        }
    }
```

10. Click the Live icon in the Canvas pane.

11. Tap the Edit button in the upper-right corner of the screen. The three–horizontal line icons appear to the right of each item in the List (see Figure 13-8). Notice that when you tap the Edit button, it changes into a Done button.

12. Slide any of the horizontal line icons up or down to move an item to a new location in the List.

13. Tap the Done button in the upper-right corner of the screen to hide the horizontal line icons to the right of each item in the List.

Creating Custom Swipe Actions for a List

SwiftUI also allows custom left-to-right and right-to-left gestures on List items. The first step is to add a .swipeActions modifier to the view that displays items in a List such as a Text view. Then define whether you want a .leading (left-to-right) or .trailing (right-to-left) swipe gesture like this:

```
.swipeActions(edge: .trailing)
```

Each .swipeActions modifier needs to define a Button (including the Button's title and code to run when selected) along with a .tint modifier to display a specific color when selected such as

```
.swipeActions(edge: .trailing) {
    Button {
        //  Code to run
    } label: {
        //  Icon to display
    }.tint(.red)
```

To see how to create a custom swipe action in a List, follow these steps:

1. Create a new SwiftUI iOS App project and give it any name you wish such as "ListCustomSwipes."

2. Click the ContentView file in the Navigator pane.

3. Add a State variable and a State variable array under the struct ContentView line like this:

```
@State var myArray = ["Cat", "Dog", "Turtle", "Ferret", "Parrot",
"Goldfish", "Lizard", "Canary", "Tarantula", "Hamster"]

@State var message = ""
```

4. Add a VStack, Text view, and a List under the var body: some View line like this:

```
var body: some View {
    VStack {
        Text("\(message)")
        List {

        }
    }
}
```

5. Add a ForEach loop inside this List to count from 0 to the total number of items in the array – 1. Then display the array item in a Text view like this:

```
var body: some View {
    VStack {
        Text("\(message)")
        List {
            ForEach(0...myArray.count - 1, id: \.self) { index in
                Text(myArray[index])
            }
        }
    }
}
```

6. Add multiple .swipeActions modifiers to the Text view inside the
   ForEach loop like this:

```
var body: some View {
    VStack {
        Text("\(message)")
        List {
            ForEach(0...myArray.count - 1, id: \.self) { index in
                Text(myArray[index])
                    .swipeActions(edge: .trailing) {
                        Button {
                            message = "Item = \(myArray[index]) --
                            Index = \(index)"
                        } label: {
                            Image(systemName: "calendar.circle")
                        }.tint(.yellow)
                    }

                    .swipeActions(edge: .trailing) {
                        Button {
                            message = "Green button selected"
                        } label: {
                            Image(systemName: "book")
                        }.tint(.green)
                    }
```

```
                .swipeActions(edge: .leading) {
                    Button {
                        message = "Left to right swipe"
                    } label: {
                        Image(systemName: "graduationcap")
                    }.tint(.purple)
                }
            }
        }
    }
}
```

The entire ContentView file should look like this:

```
import SwiftUI

struct ContentView: View {
    @State var myArray = ["Cat", "Dog", "Turtle", "Ferret",
    "Parrot", "Goldfish", "Lizard", "Canary", "Tarantula",
    "Hamster"]

    @State var message = ""

    var body: some View {
        VStack {
            Text("\(message)")
            List {
                ForEach(0...myArray.count - 1, id: \.self) {
                index in
                    Text(myArray[index])
                        .swipeActions(edge: .trailing) {
                            Button {
                                message = "Item = \(myArray
                                [index]) -- Index = \(index)"
                            } label: {
                                Image(systemName: "calendar.
                                circle")
```

```
                                        }.tint(.yellow)
                                    }

                                    .swipeActions(edge: .trailing) {
                                        Button {
                                            message = "Green button selected"
                                        } label: {
                                            Image(systemName: "book")
                                        }.tint(.green)
                                    }

                                    .swipeActions(edge: .leading) {
                                        Button {
                                            message = "Left to right swipe"
                                        } label: {
                                            Image(systemName: "graduationcap")
                                        }.tint(.purple)
                                    }

                            }
                        }
                    }
                }
            }

            struct ContentView_Previews: PreviewProvider {
                static var previews: some View {
                    ContentView()
                }
            }
```

7. Click the Live icon in the Canvas pane.

8. Swipe left to right to see the .leading swipe gesture Button appear as shown in Figure 13-9.

Figure 13-9. The appearance of a List item after a left-to-right swipe gesture

9.   Tap the purple graduation cap icon. The message "Left to right swipe" appears near the top of the screen.

10. Swipe right to left to see the two .trailing swipe gesture Buttons appear as shown in Figure 13-10.

Figure 13-10. The appearance of a List item after a right-to-left swipe gesture

11. Tap the green book icon. The message "Green button selected" appears.

12. Swipe right to left to see the two .trailing swipe gesture Buttons appear (see Figure 13-10).

13. Tap the yellow calendar circle icon. The name of the item and its index position in the array appear at the top of the screen.

Note   If you create a custom right-to-left swipe gesture, it will override the .onDelete gesture.

Searching a List

Since lists often display large amounts of data, scrolling through a long List can be cumbersome. To make searching for specific data in a large List easier, you can add a search bar. Now users can type one or more characters to filter a long List so they only see the relevant data they want.

To add a search bar to a List, you need to embed a List inside a NavigationView and add a .searchable modifier to a List like this:

```
NavigationView {
    List (arrayName, id: \.self) { x in
        Text(x)
    }.searchable(text: $stateVariable)
```

In this example, you would need to replace "arrayName" with the actual array name containing the List items. Then you need to replace "stateVariable" with the name of a State variable that holds a String data type.

To see how to search a List, follow these steps:

1. Create a new SwiftUI iOS App project and give it any name you wish such as "ListSearch."

2. Click the ContentView file in the Navigator pane.

3. Underneath the "import SwiftUI" line, add a function that returns an array of Strings like this:

```
func newList() -> [String] {
    return ["Automobile", "Bicycle", "Skateboard",
    "Boat",  "Scooter", "Airplane", "Skates"]
}
```

This function simply returns an array of Strings. This function will later be used to refresh the entire List after a user finishes searching the List.

4. Add two State variables underneath the struct ContentView line like this:

```
@State var search = ""
@State var transportation = newList()
```

The search State variable will store data typed from the search bar. The transportation State variable stores an array of Strings, which it retrieves by calling the newList() function.

5. Add a NavigationView inside the VStack like this:

```
var body: some View {
    VStack {
        NavigationView {

        }
    }
}
```

6. Add a List inside the NavigationView like this:

```
var body: some View {
    VStack {
        NavigationView {
            List (transportation, id: \.self) { x in
                Text(x)
            }
        }
    }
}
```

This populates the List with the items stored in the transportation State variable, which contains an array of Strings.

7. Add the .searchable modifier to the last curly bracket of the List like this:

```
var body: some View {
    VStack {
        NavigationView {
            List (transportation, id: \.self) { x in
                Text(x)
            }.searchable(text: $search)
        }
```

```
        }
    }
```

This adds a search bar to the top of the screen. Whatever the user types in the search bar will get stored in the search State variable. Right now this search bar won't work, so we need to add an .onChange modifier to it.

8. Add the .onChange modifier to the List like this:

```
var body: some View {
    VStack {
        NavigationView {
            List (transportation, id: \.self) { x in
                Text(x)
            }.searchable(text: $search)
                .onChange(of: search) { newValue in
                    if !newValue.isEmpty && newValue.count >= 1 {
                        transportation = transportation.filter {
                            $0.lowercased().hasPrefix(newValue.
                            lowercased())
                        }
                    } else {
                        transportation = newList()
                    }
                }
        }
    }
}
```

The .onChange modifier runs each time the content of the search bar changes. If the search bar is completely empty, then the .onChange modifier runs the newList() function to repopulate the List. If the search bar is not empty and contains at least one character, then the search bar uses a filter to match what the user typed to each List item. The .hasPrefix modifier simply checks if what the user typed matches part or all of the letters that make up each List item.

The entire ContentView file should look like this:

```swift
import SwiftUI

func newList() -> [String] {
    return ["Automobile", "Bicycle", "Skateboard",
    "Boat",  "Scooter", "Airplane", "Skates"]
}

struct ContentView: View {

    @State var search = ""
    @State var transportation = newList()

    var body: some View {
        VStack {
            NavigationView {
                List (transportation, id: \.self) { x in
                    Text(x)
                }.searchable(text: $search)
                    .onChange(of: search) { newValue in
                        if !newValue.isEmpty && newValue.
                        count >= 1 {
                            transportation = transportation.
                            filter {
                                $0.lowercased().hasPrefix(
                                newValue.lowercased())
                            }
                        } else {
                            transportation = newList()
                        }
                    }
            }
        }
    }
}
```

```
struct ContentView_Previews: PreviewProvider {
    static var previews: some View {
        ContentView()
    }
}
```

9. Click the Live icon in the Canvas pane. The items appear in the
   List with a search bar on top as shown in Figure 13-11.

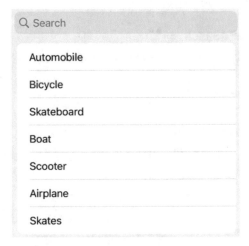

Figure 13-11. *The initial appearance of the search bar and the List of items*

10. Click in the search bar and type a "b". Notice that the List now
    filters out all items except the ones that start with a "b" like "Boat"
    and "Bicycle" as shown in Figure 13-12.

Figure 13-12. *The search bar filters out all items that fail to match text typed in
the search bar*

11. Click Cancel or the close icon (x). Notice that the List displays all
    items once more.

Summary

Lists are common ways to display multiple, related items in one place. To help organize items in a List, you can group related items together.

Besides displaying items in a List, you can also detect swipe gestures from left to right or right to left. By using the .onDelete modifier, you can allow users to delete items from a List. By using a NavigationView and an Edit button, you can use the .onMove modifier to allow users to move items within a List.

You can also define custom swipe gestures to appear on a List. When you create custom swipe gestures, you can define an icon and a color to appear for each button. By using swipe gestures with lists, users can modify List items in different ways.

To make lists easier to read, consider adding lines to separate items or use alternating colors. A search bar can also make it easy for users to find the item they want, especially if a List contains a large number of items. By using lists, you can display organized information for the user to view and select.

CHAPTER 14

Using Forms and Group Boxes

When you fill out paper forms, you may notice that the paper forms group related items together. For example, the form may ask for your name, address, and phone number in one area of the form and ask for your gender, racial background, and marital status in another area of the form. Paper forms make it easy to enter related data in one area.

A SwiftUI Form works in a similar way by grouping related views together that offer options and settings that the user can select. Forms consist of an optional header, optional footer, and content inside defined by views such as Text, Slider, or Toggle views as shown in Figure 14-1.

```
Form {
    Section(header: Text("Header"), footer: Text("Footer"),
            content: {
        Text("Text inside form")
        Toggle(isOn: $toggleOn) {
            Text("Volume On/Off")
        }
        Slider(value: $sliderValue)
    })
}
```

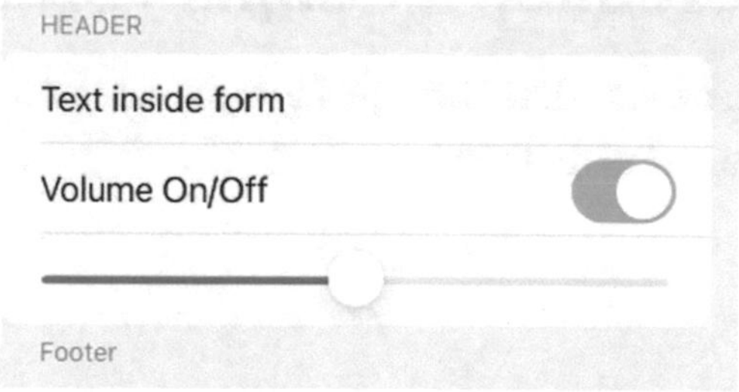

Figure 14-1. *The typical parts of a Form*

A Form groups related views together like a stack. The difference is that a Form also visually groups views together on the user interface. All views within a Form appear together, while any views not in the Form appear separated by a gray area as shown in Figure 14-2.

© Wallace Wang 2023
W. Wang, *Beginning iPhone Development with SwiftUI*, https://doi.org/10.1007/978-1-4842-9541-0_14

This is in the Form

Also in the Form

```
Form {
    Text("This is in the Form")
    Text("Also in the Form")
}
Text("Outside the Form")
```

Outside the Form

Figure 14-2. *Forms group views together on the user interface*

Similar to forms are group boxes, which give you a simpler way to visually group related views together on the user interface. When you need to group views together, you can choose between a Form and a Group Box.

Creating a Simple Form

The simplest Form just groups one or more views together. To create a Form, you just need to do this:

```
Form {
    //
}
```

To see how to create a simple Form, follow these steps:

1. Create a new SwiftUI iOS App project and give it any name you wish such as "SimpleForm."

2. Click the ContentView file in the Navigator pane.

3. Add two State variables under the struct ContentView: View line like this:

```
@State var messageOne = ""
@State var messageTwo = ""
```

4.   Add two Forms and two Text views inside the VStack like this:

```
var body: some View {
    VStack {
        Form {
            Text("This is the first Form")
            TextField("Type here", text: $messageOne)
        }
        Form {
            Text("This is the second Form")
            TextField("Type here", text: $messageTwo)
        }
        Text("Form #1 = \(messageOne)")
        Text("Form #2 = \(messageTwo)")
    }
}
```

The entire ContentView file should look like this:

```
import SwiftUI

struct ContentView: View {
    @State var messageOne = ""
    @State var messageTwo = ""
    var body: some View {
        VStack {
            Form {
                Text("This is the first Form")
                TextField("Type here", text: $messageOne)
            }
            Form {
                Text("This is the second Form")
                TextField("Type here", text: $messageTwo)
            }
```

```
                Text("Form #1 = \(messageOne)")
                Text("Form #2 = \(messageTwo)")
            }
        }
    }

    struct ContentView_Previews: PreviewProvider {
        static var previews: some View {
            ContentView()
        }
    }
```

This code creates a user interface that displays two forms on the screen along with two Text views that are not part of either Form as shown in Figure 14-3.

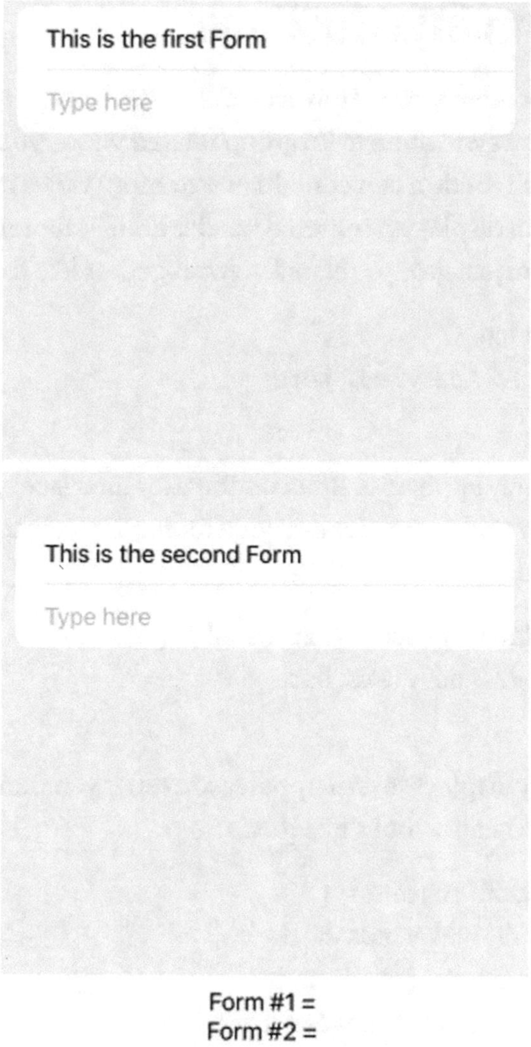

This is the first Form

Type here

This is the second Form

Type here

Form #1 =
Form #2 =

Figure 14-3. *Two forms appear on the user interface*

5. Click the Live icon in the Canvas pane.

6. Click in the top Text Field and type some text. Notice that this text now appears in the Text view ("Form #1 =") at the bottom of the screen.

7. Click in the middle Text Field and type some text. Notice that this text now appears in the Text view ("Form #2 =") at the bottom of the screen.

Dividing a Form into Sections

A Form can hold one or more views. However, the more views in a Form, the more crowded all of those views will appear. To group related views, you can divide a Form into sections where each Section can contain one or more views to display on the screen. In addition, sections can display an optional header and/or footer.

The simplest Section just groups related views together like this:

```
Section {
    // Add views here
}
```

While a Section visibly appears distinct on the user interface, you can further distinguish a Section by using a header and/or a footer. If you just want to define a header, you can use code like this:

```
Section("Header text here") {
    // Add views here
}
```

This method simply displays text in uppercase even if you don't type it that way. Another way to define a header looks like this:

```
Section(content: {
    // Add views here
}, header: {
    // Define header text here
}
```

You can also use this method to define just a footer like this:

```
Section(content: {
    // Add views here
}, footer: {
    // Define footer text here
}
```

Note   The text in a footer appears exactly as you type it, unlike a header that automatically displays text in all uppercase.

If you want to define both a header and a footer, you can use this code:

```
Section {
    // Add views here
} header: {
    // Define header text here
} footer: {
    // Define footer text here
}
```

To see how to create headers and footers in sections, follow these steps:

1. Create a new SwiftUI iOS App project and give it any name you wish such as "HeaderFormSections."

2. Click the ContentView file in the Navigator pane.

3. Add a Form inside the var body: some View like this:

```
var body: some View {
    Form {

    }
}
```

4. Add four Sections defined in different ways inside the Form like this:

```
var body: some View {
    Form {
        Section {
            Text("This Section has no header")
        }

        Section("Just a Header") {
            Text("This Section uses a simple header")
        }
```

```
        Section {
            Text("This Section uses a simple footer")
        } footer: {
            Text("Just a Footer")
        }

        Section {
            Text("This Section uses both a header and footer")
        } header: {
            Text("The header")
        } footer: {
            Text("The footer")
        }
    }
}
```

The entire ContentView file should look like this:

```
import SwiftUI

struct ContentView: View {

    var body: some View {
        Form {
            Section {
                Text("This Section has no header")
            }

            Section("Just a Header") {
                Text("This Section uses a simple header")
            }

            Section {
                Text("This Section uses a simple footer")
            } footer: {
                Text("Just a Footer")
            }
```

```
        Section {
            Text("This Section uses both a header and footer")
        } header: {
            Text("The header")
        } footer: {
            Text("The footer")
        }
    }
}

struct ContentView_Previews: PreviewProvider {
    static var previews: some View {
        ContentView()
    }
}
```

The preceding code creates a Form with four different Sections as shown in Figure 14-4.

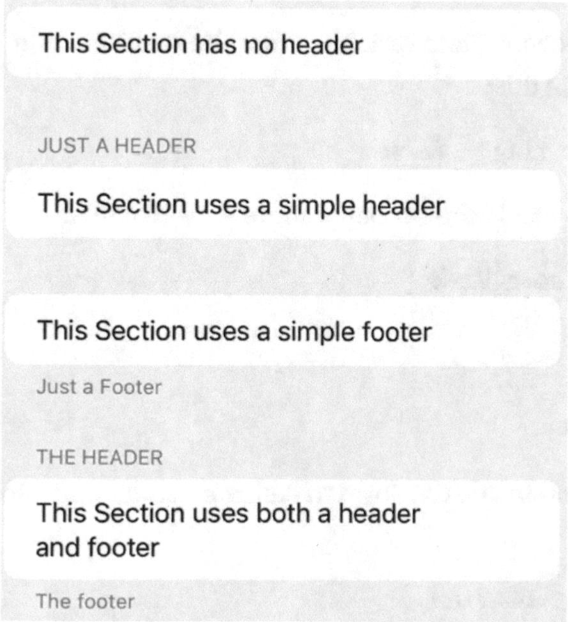

This Section has no header

JUST A HEADER

This Section uses a simple header

This Section uses a simple footer

Just a Footer

THE HEADER

This Section uses both a header and footer

The footer

Figure 14-4. *Four different ways to display a Section*

Disabling Views in a Form

Often times a paper form might ask a series of questions. Based on your answer, another group of questions may not be relevant. For example, if a paper form asks if you're married or single, you might answer "married." In this case another part of the paper form might ask about your spouse's name and contact information.

However, if you answer "single," there's no point in answering any additional questions about a spouse. With SwiftUI forms, you can selectively disable views within a Form based on a Boolean value by using the .disabled modifier like this:

```
.disabled(flag)
```

If the value of the Boolean variable is true, then the .disabled modifier prevents the user from interacting with the selected view. If the Boolean variable is false, then the .disabled modifier allows the user to interact with the selected view.

To see how to use the .disabled modifier within a Form, follow these steps:

1. Create a new SwiftUI iOS App project and give it any name you wish such as "FormDisable."

2. Click the ContentView file in the Navigator pane.

3. Add the following State variable under the struct ContentView: View line like this:

    ```
    @State var flag = false
    ```

4. Add a Form inside the var body: some View like this:

    ```
    var body: some View {
        Form {

        }
    }
    ```

5. Add a Section inside the Form to define a header and a footer like this:

    ```
    var body: some View {
        Form {
            Section {
    ```

```
        } header: {
            Text("Header")
        } footer: {
            Text("Footer")
        }
    }
}
```

6. Add a Toggle and a Button inside the Section like this:

```
var body: some View {
    Form {
        Section {
            Toggle(isOn: $flag) {
                Text("Are you married?")
            }
            Button(flag ? "Disabled" : "Click Me") {

            }.disabled(flag)
        } header: {
            Text("Header")
        } footer: {
            Text("Footer")
        }
    }
}
```

Notice that the .disabled modifier affects the Button. If the flag
Boolean variable is true, then the Button will be disabled. If the
flag Boolean variable is false, then the Button will be enabled.
The entire ContentView file should look like this:

```
import SwiftUI

struct ContentView: View {
    @State var flag = false
```

```
    var body: some View {
        Form {
            Section {
                Toggle(isOn: $flag) {
                    Text("Are you married?")
                }
                Button(flag ? "Disabled" : "Click Me") {

                }.disabled(flag)
            } header: {
                Text("Header")
            } footer: {
                Text("Footer")
            }
        }
    }
}

struct ContentView_Previews: PreviewProvider {
    static var previews: some View {
        ContentView()
    }
}
```

7. Click the Live icon in the Canvas pane. Notice that the Button
   displays the title "Click Me" in blue.

8. Click the Toggle. This changes the flag State variable from false
   to true (or true to false). When the flag State variable equals
   true, then the .disabled modifier grays out the Button, making it
   impossible for the user to select.

Using Group Boxes

Group boxes offer a simpler way to organize related views together. Although similar to a Form, a Group Box can display a label and visually displays multiple views within a gray rectangle, while a Form displays multiple views within a white rectangle as shown in Figure 14-5.

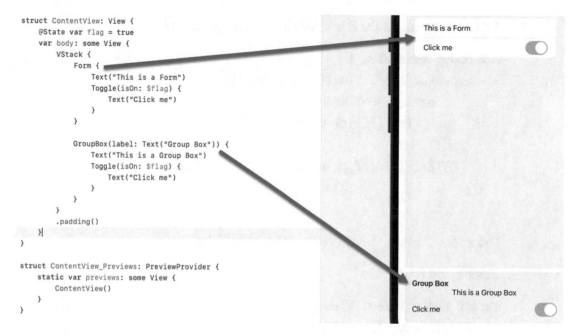

Figure 14-5. *The visual differences between a Form and a Group Box*

To see how to use a Group Box, follow these steps:

1. Create a new SwiftUI iOS App project and give it any name you wish such as "GroupBox."

2. Click the ContentView file in the Navigator pane.

3. Add the following State variables under the struct ContentView: View line like this:

```
struct ContentView: View {
    @State var flag = true
    @State var message = ""
```

4. Add a Group Box inside the var body: some View like this:

```
var body: some View {
    GroupBox(label: Text("Group Box")) {

    }
}
```

5. Add a Toggle and a Text Field inside the Group Box like this:

```
var body: some View {
    GroupBox(label: Text("Group Box")) {
        Toggle(isOn: $flag) {
            Text("Click me")
        }
        TextField("Type here", text: $message)
    }
}
```

The entire ContentView file should look like this:

```
import SwiftUI

struct ContentView: View {
    @State var flag = true
    @State var message = ""

    var body: some View {
        GroupBox(label: Text("Group Box")) {
            Toggle(isOn: $flag) {
                Text("Click me")
            }
            TextField("Type here", text: $message)
        }
    }
}
```

```
struct ContentView_Previews: PreviewProvider {
    static var previews: some View {
        ContentView()
    }
}
```

The preceding code creates a Group Box as shown in Figure 14-6.

Figure 14-6. *The appearance of a Group Box*

Summary

Forms let you visually group related views together on the user interface. To further differentiate views on a Form, you can divide a Form into multiple sections where each Section lets you define an optional header and/or optional footer. A Section can have a header, a footer, both a header and a footer, or nothing at all.

Depending on how the user responds to the user interface, you may want to disable one or more views to prevent the user from interacting with them. Disabling one or more views prevents the user from inputting unnecessary data.

Both forms and group boxes are simply two different ways to group and organize related views together to make your app's user interface easier to understand.

CHAPTER 15

Using Disclosure Groups, Scroll Views, and Outline Groups

Many apps contain lots of information such as names and addresses. However, you may not want to view all stored information at once to avoid cluttering up the screen. When you want to give users the option of selectively hiding or displaying information, that's when you can use a Disclosure Group or an Outline Group.

A Disclosure Group can appear in two states. First, it can appear as a single line of text that represents a link. Second, when the user taps this link, it expands to reveal one or more additional views as shown in Figure 15-1.

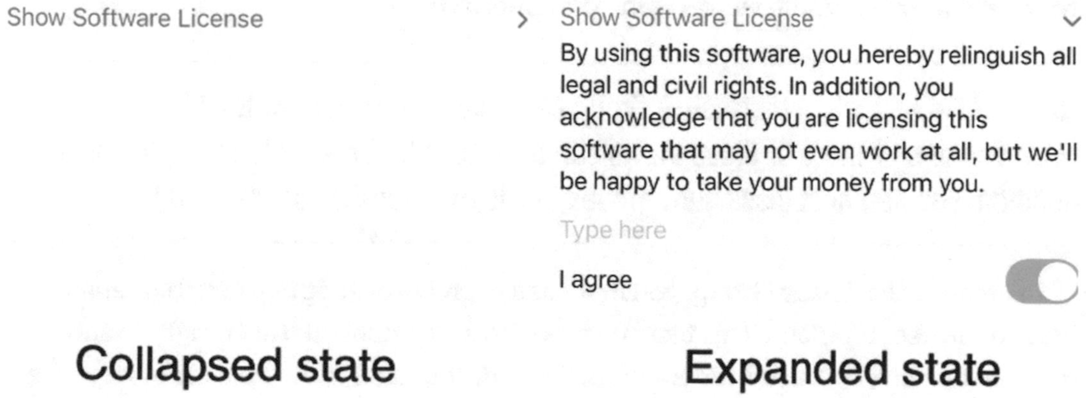

Show Software License   ❯   Show Software License   ∨
By using this software, you hereby relinquish all legal and civil rights. In addition, you acknowledge that you are licensing this software that may not even work at all, but we'll be happy to take your money from you.

Type here

I agree

Collapsed state   **Expanded state**

Figure 15-1. *The two states of a Disclosure Group*

While a Disclosure Group can selectively hide or show a group of related views, an Outline Group can selectively hide or show groups of text within a List (see Chapter 13) as shown in Figure 15-2.

© Wallace Wang 2023
W. Wang, *Beginning iPhone Development with SwiftUI*, https://doi.org/10.1007/978-1-4842-9541-0_15

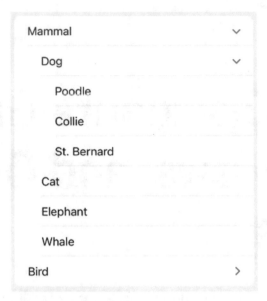

Figure 15-2. *The appearance of an Outline Group*

Using a Disclosure Group

A Disclosure Group is designed to hide one or more views (Text, Slider, Toggle, etc.) until the user taps the Disclosure Group name to expand it. When expanded, a Disclosure Group reveals one or more views on the user interface.

Note   Like a stack, a Disclosure Group can hold a maximum of ten (10) views. However, one or more of those views can be stacks that can hold multiple views. In addition, you can nest disclosure groups inside of other disclosure groups.

To create a Disclosure Group, you first need to create descriptive text that represents a link on the user interface. This text appears with a > symbol on the far right to show users that this link contains hidden items. Second, you need to create a list of views (up to ten) that will appear when the user selects the Disclosure Group link.

To see how to create a Disclosure Group, follow these steps:

1. Create a new SwiftUI iOS App project and give it any name you wish such as "DisclosureGroup."

2. Click the ContentView file in the Navigator pane.

3. Add three State variables under the struct ContentView: View line like this:

```
@State var sliderValue = 0.0
@State var message = ""
@State var flag = true
```

4. Add a DisclosureGroup inside the var body: some View like this:

```
var body: some View {
    DisclosureGroup("Expand Me") {

    }.padding()
}
```

5. Add the following inside the DisclosureGroup:

```
var body: some View {
    DisclosureGroup("Expand Me") {
        Text("You typed = \(message)")
        TextField("Type here", text: $message)
            .padding()

        Text(flag ? "Toggle = true" : "Toggle = false")
        Toggle(isOn: $flag) {
            Text("Toggle")
        }.padding()

        Text("The slider value = \(sliderValue)")
        Slider(value: $sliderValue, in: 0...15)
            .padding()
    }.padding()
}
```

The entire ContentView file should look like this:

```
import SwiftUI

struct ContentView: View {
    @State var sliderValue = 0.0
    @State var message = ""
    @State var flag = true

    var body: some View {
        DisclosureGroup("Expand Me") {
            Text("You typed = \(message)")
            TextField("Type here", text: $message)
                .padding()

            Text(flag ? "Toggle = true" : "Toggle = false")
            Toggle(isOn: $flag) {
                Text("Toggle")
            }.padding()

            Text("The slider value = \(sliderValue)")
            Slider(value: $sliderValue, in: 0...15)
                .padding()
        }.padding()
    }
}

struct ContentView_Previews: PreviewProvider {
    static var previews: some View {
        ContentView()
    }
}
```

6. Click the Live icon in the Canvas pane.

7. Click the Expand Me Disclosure Group link to reveal all the views hidden inside as shown in Figure 15-3.

Figure 15-3. *The expanded Disclosure Group*

8. Click in the Text field and type some text. Notice that whatever you type appears in the Text view that displayed "You typed =".

9. Click the Toggle. Notice that each time you click the Toggle, the Text view above the Toggle displays either "Toggle = true" or "Toggle = false".

10. Drag the Slider left and right. Notice that as you drag the Slider, its numeric value appears in the Text view above the Slider that displays "The slider value = ".

11. Click the Disclosure Group link again to hide all the views. Each time you click the Disclosure Group link, it alternates between showing all the views inside the Disclosure Group and hiding them.

Using a Scroll View

When you arrange multiple views within a VStack, those views remain fixed on the user interface. If you display more views than the user interface can show, part of those views will be cut off or hidden out of sight. To fix this problem, SwiftUI offers a special container called a Scroll View.

Like a stack, a Scroll View can hold multiple views. Unlike a stack, a Scroll View lets users scroll vertically or horizontally to view the entire contents of the Scroll View. Scroll views can work anywhere you might use a stack, including within a Disclosure Group.

The simplest way to create a Scroll View is to define a ScrollView like this:

```
ScrollView {
    // Multiple views here
}
```

This lets you scroll vertically with a scroll indicator on the right side. The scroll indicator lets you see how close or how far away you may be to/from the beginning or end of the list of items as shown in Figure 15-4.

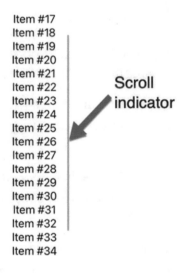

Figure 15-4. *The scroll indicator appears on the right of a vertically scrolling Scroll View*

Another way to create a Scroll View is to define a direction to scroll (Axis.Set. horizontal or Axis.Set.vertical) along with whether to show the scroll indicator or not (showsIndicators: parameter) like this:

```
ScrollView(Axis.Set.horizontal, showsIndicators: false, content: {

}
```

To see how the Scroll View works, follow these steps:

1. Create a new SwiftUI iOS App project and give it any name you
   wish such as "ScrollView."

2. Click the ContentView file in the Navigator pane.

3. Add a ScrollView under the var body: some View line like this:

```
var body: some View {
    VStack {
        ScrollView(Axis.Set.vertical, showsIndicators: true,
        content: {

        })

    }
    .padding()
}
```

To shorten the ScrollView code, you could just do this:

```
var body: some View {
    VStack {
        ScrollView {

        }
    }
}
```

4. Add a ForEach loop inside the ScrollView like this:

```
var body: some View {
    VStack {
        ScrollView(Axis.Set.vertical, showsIndicators: true,
        content: {
            ForEach(0..<50) {
                Text("Item #\($0)        ")
            }
        })

    }
    .padding()
}
```

The entire ContentView file should look like this:

```
import SwiftUI

struct ContentView: View {
    var body: some View {
        VStack {
            ScrollView(Axis.Set.vertical, showsIndicators: true,
            content: {
                ForEach(0..<50) {
                    Text("Item #\($0)      ")
                }
            })

        }
        .padding()
    }
}

struct ContentView_Previews: PreviewProvider {
    static var previews: some View {
        ContentView()
    }
}
```

5. Click the Live icon in the Canvas pane.

6. Scroll up and down on the list of "Item #" items displayed on the user interface. Notice that as you scroll up or down, you can see the slider indicator on the right side (see Figure 15-4).

Jumping to a Specific Location

A ScrollView can display a large number of items. However, the more items are displayed, the harder it can be to find any one particular item. Rather than force users to endlessly scroll, SwiftUI offers the ability to jump to a specific location in a ScrollView.

So if a ScrollView displays 100 items, you can jump to a specific position such as the 54th item or the 12th item in the ScrollView. This makes it easy for users to rapidly jump to a specific numeric position among a large list of items in a ScrollView.

When jumping to a specific position in a ScrollView, you have a choice of where to display or anchor that item: .top, .center, or .bottom. The .top anchor displays the selected item at the top of the screen, the .center anchor displays the selected item in the center of the screen, and the .bottom anchor displays the selected item at the bottom of the screen.

To see how to jump to a specific location in a ScrollView, follow these steps:

1. Create a new SwiftUI iOS App project and give it any name you wish such as "ScrollViewJumpTo."

2. Click the ContentView file in the Navigator pane.

3. Add two State variables underneath the struct ContentView line like this:

```
@State var sliderValue = 0.0
@State var anchorPosition = UnitPoint.center
```

4. Add a ScrollViewReader under the var body: some View line like this:

```
var body: some View {
    ScrollViewReader { scrollView in

    }
}
```

5. Add an HStack inside the ScrollViewReader and put a Text view and a Slider inside the HStack like this:

```
var body: some View {
    ScrollViewReader { scrollView in
        HStack {
            Text("\(Int(sliderValue))")
            Slider(value: $sliderValue, in: 0...99)
        }
    }
}
```

The Text view displays the Slider's value as an integer because the Slider's value is a Double data type. The Slider ranges in value from 0 to 99.

6. Add a Button underneath the HStack. This Button will let us scroll to a specific location in the ScrollView list where the location is defined by the Slider:

```
var body: some View {
    ScrollViewReader { scrollView in
        HStack {
            Text("\(Int(sliderValue))")
            Slider(value: $sliderValue, in: 0...99)
        }
        Button("Scroll to slider value") {
            withAnimation{
                scrollView.scrollTo(Int(sliderValue), anchor:
                anchorPosition)
            }
        }
    }
}
```

The Button takes the value stored in the Slider and jumps to that position in the ScrollView. withAnimation makes the ScrollView move gradually to the location defined by the anchor.

7. Add a Picker underneath the Button like this:

```
var body: some View {
    ScrollViewReader { scrollView in
        HStack {
            Text("\(Int(sliderValue))")
            Slider(value: $sliderValue, in: 0...99)
        }
        Button("Scroll to slider value") {
            withAnimation{
```

```
                scrollView.scrollTo(Int(sliderValue), anchor:
                anchorPosition)
            }
        }

        Picker("Location", selection: $anchorPosition, content: {
            Text("Top").tag(UnitPoint.top)
            Text("Center").tag(UnitPoint.center)
            Text("Bottom").tag(UnitPoint.bottom)
        }).pickerStyle(.segmented)
    }
}
```

The Picker displays a segmented control with three choices: Top,
Center, and Bottom. That way the user can decide which type of
anchor to use for scrolling to a specific item in the ScrollView.

8. Add the ScrollView underneath the Picker view like this:

```
var body: some View {
    ScrollViewReader { scrollView in
        HStack {
            Text("\(Int(sliderValue))")
            Slider(value: $sliderValue, in: 0...99)
        }
        Button("Scroll to slider value") {
            withAnimation{
                scrollView.scrollTo(Int(sliderValue), anchor:
                anchorPosition)
            }
        }

        Picker("Location", selection: $anchorPosition, content: {
            Text("Top").tag(UnitPoint.top)
            Text("Center").tag(UnitPoint.center)
            Text("Bottom").tag(UnitPoint.bottom)
        }).pickerStyle(.segmented)
        ScrollView {
```

```
            }
        }
    }
```

9. Add a ForEach loop inside the ScrollView to create a list of items:

```
var body: some View {
    ScrollViewReader { scrollView in
        HStack {
            Text("\(Int(sliderValue))")
            Slider(value: $sliderValue, in: 0...99)
        }
        Button("Scroll to slider value") {
            withAnimation{
                scrollView.scrollTo(Int(sliderValue), anchor:
                anchorPosition)
            }
        }

        Picker("Location", selection: $anchorPosition, content: {
            Text("Top").tag(UnitPoint.top)
            Text("Center").tag(UnitPoint.center)
            Text("Bottom").tag(UnitPoint.bottom)
        }).pickerStyle(.segmented)
        ScrollView {
            ForEach(0..<100) { index in
                Text("Item # \(index)")
                    .id(index)
            }
        }
    }
}
```

Notice that the Text view inside the ScrollView contains an .id modifier, which tracks the index value from 0 up to but not including 100 (99). This .id value is what the .scrollTo command will use to jump to specific items in the ScrollView. The user interface should look as shown in Figure 15-5.

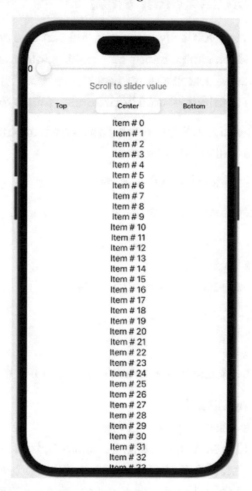

Figure 15-5. *The complete user interface*

10. Click the Live icon in the Canvas pane.

11. Drag the Slider to a large value such as 67.

12. Click the Scroll to slider value Button. Notice that your chosen position appears centered in the screen.

13.   Click the segmented control and choose Top or Bottom and click
      the Scroll to slider value Button. Your chosen value appears near
      the top or bottom of the screen.

Defining a Horizontal Scroll View

ScrollViews, by default, scroll vertically. However, you can also change the scroll
direction to horizontal, which can be handy for scrolling information that may be too
wide to be visible on the screen such as large amounts of text.

   To see how to make a ScrollView scroll horizontally, follow these steps:

1.   Create a new SwiftUI iOS App project and give it any name you
     wish such as "ScrollViewHorizontal."

2.   Click the ContentView file in the Navigator pane.

3.   Add a ScrollViewReader under the var body: some View line
     like this:

```
var body: some View {
    ScrollViewReader { scrollView in

    }
}
```

4.   Add the ScrollView inside the ScrollViewReader like this:

```
var body: some View {
    ScrollViewReader { scrollView in
        ScrollView (.horizontal, showsIndicators: true){
            Text("This is a long amount of text that won't fit
            within the narrow width of an iPhone. That way you can
            see how to scroll horizontally.")
        }
    }
}
```

5.   Click the Live icon in the Canvas pane. The text appears cut off on
     the right side of the simulated iOS device as shown in Figure 15-6.

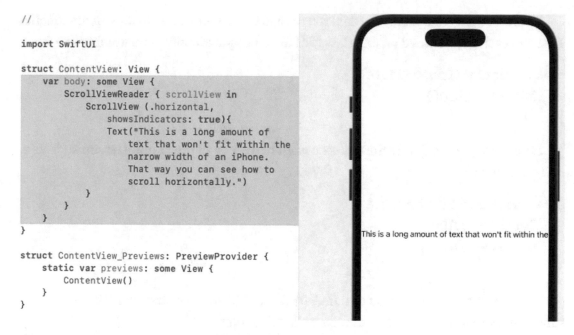

```
//

import SwiftUI

struct ContentView: View {
    var body: some View {
        ScrollViewReader { scrollView in
            ScrollView (.horizontal,
                showsIndicators: true){
                Text("This is a long amount of
                    text that won't fit within the
                    narrow width of an iPhone.
                    That way you can see how to
                    scroll horizontally.")
                }
            }
        }
}

struct ContentView_Previews: PreviewProvider {
    static var previews: some View {
        ContentView()
    }
}
```

This is a long amount of text that won't fit within the

Figure 15-6. *Horizontal scrolling lets you view text cut off by the boundaries of the iOS screen*

6. Move the mouse pointer over the text and drag left and right to see how the text can scroll horizontally.

Using an Outline Group

An Outline Group acts like a super Disclosure Group. The main difference is that a Disclosure Group can only display up to ten views, while an Outline Group can display an endless number of items defined within a separate class. In addition, an Outline Group automatically indents categories to make it easier to see the hierarchical relationship between items (see Figure 15-2).

Outline groups display arrays of objects that define relationships. To use an Outline Group, you need to do the following:

*   Create a class that holds the data you want to display.

*   Create an array that holds multiple objects defined by the class.

*   Create an Outline Group that displays the data stored in the objects.

To create a class that holds the data you want to display, you need to make it Identifiable. That way each object based on that class will have a unique identification number like this:

```
class Species: Identifiable {
    let id = UUID()
}
```

Next, you need to define the data you want to display in the Outline Group such as a string like this:

```
class Species: Identifiable {
    let id = UUID()
    var name: String
}
```

The next step is to create an optional array for holding subcategories. These subcategory items must also be the same class like this:

```
class Species: Identifiable {
    let id = UUID()
    var name: String
    var classification: [Species]?
}
```

Finally, the class needs an initializer since none of the class's properties have an initial value. That means each time you create an object, you must assign a value to its property. In this case, the only property that needs a value is the "name" property that holds a String data type that's absolutely necessary. The other property, called "classification", can hold an array of objects but can also be a nil value:

```
class Species: Identifiable {
    let id = UUID()
    var name: String
    var classification: [Species]?

    init(name: String, classification: [Species]? = nil) {
        self.name = name
        self.classification = classification
    }
}
```

After defining a class, the next step is to define an array that holds objects based on that class like this:

```
var Animals: [Species] = [
    Species(name: "Mammal", classification: [
        Species(name: "Dog", classification: [
            Species(name: "Poodle"),
            Species(name: "Collie"),
```

Notice that this array is defined to hold objects based on the defined class ("Animals" in this example). Each object in the array needs a name (such as "Mammal" or "Collie"). Some objects do not hold a list of subcategories, but for those that do, you need to specify an array of objects based on the same class ("Species"). In the preceding example, the "Dog" object defines an array of objects that hold "Poodle" and "Collie".

The third step is to define an Outline Group:

```
OutlineGroup(Animals, id: \.id, children: \.classification) {
creature in
    Text(creature.name)
}
```

This defines the array to use (Animals) and to display each item in the array using a unique ID (defined by UUID() within the class declaration). If there are any children or subcategories stored within an object, that's identified by the children: parameter. Finally, the Text view within the OutlineGroup displays the name property of each object.

To see how to use an Outline Group, follow these steps:

1. Create a new SwiftUI iOS App project and give it any name you wish such as "OutlineGroup."

2. Click the ContentView file in the Navigator pane.

3. Add the following class declaration under the import SwiftUI line like this:

```
class Species: Identifiable {
    let id = UUID()
    var name: String
    var classification: [Species]?
```

```
    init(name: String, classification: [Species]? = nil) {
        self.name = name

        self.classification = classification
    }
}
```

4. Add the following array underneath the struct ContentView: View line like this:

```
struct ContentView: View {
    var Animals: [Species] = [
        Species(name: "Mammal", classification: [
            Species(name: "Dog", classification: [
                Species(name: "Poodle"),
                Species(name: "Collie"),
                Species(name: "St. Bernard"),
            ]),
            Species(name: "Cat"),
            Species(name: "Elephant"),
            Species(name: "Whale"),
        ]),
        Species(name: "Bird", classification: [
            Species(name: "Canary"),
            Species(name: "Parakeet"),
            Species(name: "Eagle"),
        ]),
    ]
```

5. Add the OutlineGroup underneath the var body: some View line like this:

```
var body: some View {
    List {
        OutlineGroup(Animals, id: \.id, children:
        \.classification) { creature in
            Text(creature.name)
        }
```

```
        }
    }
```

The entire ContentView file should look like this:

```
import SwiftUI

class Species: Identifiable {
    let id = UUID()
    var name: String
    var classification: [Species]?

    init(name: String, classification: [Species]? = nil) {
        self.name = name

        self.classification = classification
    }
}

struct ContentView: View {
    var Animals: [Species] = [
        Species(name: "Mammal", classification: [
            Species(name: "Dog", classification: [
                Species(name: "Poodle"),
                Species(name: "Collie"),
                Species(name: "St. Bernard"),
            ]),
            Species(name: "Cat"),
            Species(name: "Elephant"),
            Species(name: "Whale"),
        ]),
        Species(name: "Bird", classification: [
            Species(name: "Canary"),
            Species(name: "Parakeet"),
            Species(name: "Eagle"),
        ]),
    ]
```

```swift
    var body: some View {
        List {
            OutlineGroup(Animals, id: \.id, children:
            \.classification) { creature in
                Text(creature.name)
            }
        }
    }
}

struct ContentView_Previews: PreviewProvider {
    static var previews: some View {
        ContentView()
    }
}
```

6. Click the Live icon in the Canvas pane.

7. Click any of the items in the Outline Group that displays a >
    character on the far right. This indicates that the item contains
    additional lists that can be displayed (see Figure 15-2).

Outline groups can be handy for storing and displaying lists of items that the user can
hide or display. Since outline groups use arrays, there's no limit to the number of items
you can display in an Outline Group (unlike the ten-view limit of a Disclosure Group).

Summary

Disclosure groups can be handy for hiding one or more views temporarily out of sight. By
clicking the Disclosure Group title, you can toggle between seeing additional views and
hiding them. Think of disclosure groups as a collapsible list of views.

While disclosure groups make it easy to hide or view data, scroll views make it easy to
scroll up or down (or left and right) to view additional data. You can even use scroll views
inside of disclosure groups as well.

If you need to display data in a hierarchy, consider using the Outline Group. An Outline Group requires defining a class that contains the properties you want to store along with a UUID() to automatically create distinct ID numbers for each chunk of data. Then you need to create an array of objects, based on the class you defined. Finally, you can use an OutlineGroup to display data on the screen.

Disclosure groups, scroll views, and outline groups are just different ways to group related data together. Disclosure groups act like collapsible lists. Scroll views let users see data that might normally get cut off. Outline groups act like multiple disclosure groups that can selectively hide or display data. The whole purpose of all three views is to provide different ways to display information to the user.

CHAPTER 16

Creating Charts

Apps need to display information to users. Whether that information might be text or numbers, large amounts of data can be difficult to understand. That's why many apps convert information into charts that can make it easy to track trends, make comparisons, or identify ratios. Charts simply convert numeric data into colorful images that are easy to understand at a glance.

The key to creating any chart is to identify the data you have and determine what story you want to tell about that data. For example, a list of sales can be used to show how sales are growing (or shrinking), which time periods are most profitable (and which are least profitable), how different salespeople compare, or which products might be selling better than others.

There is no right or wrong way to create a chart from data. Since charts are meant to communicate, the only mistake you can make is creating a chart that doesn't tell the story you want to tell about your data. SwiftUI can create the following types of charts as shown in Figure 16-1:

- Bar
- Point
- Line
- Area
- Rectangle

© Wallace Wang 2023
W. Wang, *Beginning iPhone Development with SwiftUI*, https://doi.org/10.1007/978-1-4842-9541-0_16

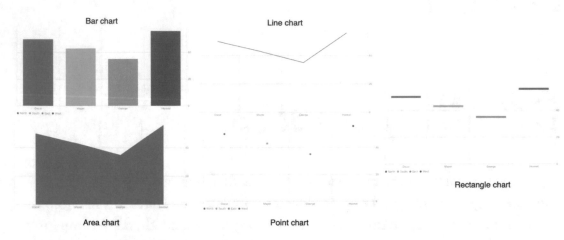

Figure 16-1. *Different types of charts available*

Charts use numeric data to define marks along an axis. The mark visually measures data, while an axis acts like a ruler that helps users determine the quantities that each mark represents. In a bar chart, an individual bar is a mark, while in a line chart, an individual line is a mark as shown in Figure 16-2.

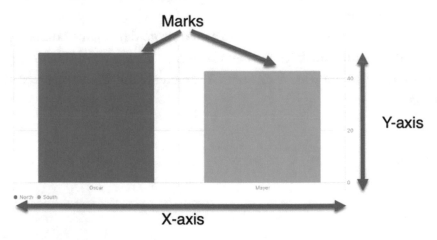

Figure 16-2. *Identifying marks and axes in a chart*

To create charts, you must import the Charts framework like this:

```
import Charts
```

Then you can define a chart within the body like this:

```
Chart {

}
```

Creating a Bar Chart

To create a bar chart, you need to use BarMark to define an x and a y value like this:

```
BarMark(x: .value("Category", "Chart Label"),
        y: .value("Quantity", 0))
```

The x value defines the category of the data (to help you understand what each mark represents) and the label to display on the chart. The y value defines the quantity of the data followed by a numeric value as shown in Figure 16-3.

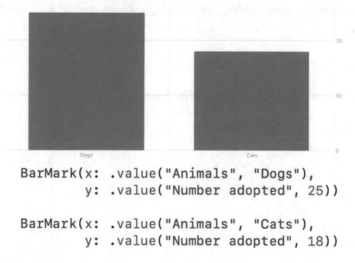

```
BarMark(x: .value("Animals", "Dogs"),
        y: .value("Number adopted", 25))

BarMark(x: .value("Animals", "Cats"),
        y: .value("Number adopted", 18))
```

Figure 16-3. *How a BarMark defines a bar chart*

Notice that in Figure 16-3, the texts "Dogs" and "Cats" appear under each mark, and the numeric values 25 and 18 define the height of each mark. The text "Animals" helps identify the category that "Dogs" and "Cats" fall under, and the text "Number adopted" helps identify what each numeric value means.

Notice that neither "Animals" nor "Number adopted" appears on the chart since this text is meant to help you understand the data each mark displays. Also notice that instead of using fixed numeric values, you could replace one or more with variables instead. That way the chart can change appearance when values change.

To see how to create a simple bar chart, follow these steps:

1. Create a new SwiftUI iOS App project and give it any name you wish such as "BarChartSimple."

2. Click the ContentView file in the Navigator pane.

3. Add the Charts framework underneath the SwiftUI framework like this:

```
import Charts
```

4. Add a State variable under the struct ContentView: View line like this:

```
@State var sliderValue = 50.0
```

5. Add a Chart inside the VStack like this:

```
var body: some View {
    VStack {
        Chart {

        }
    }
}
```

6. Add two BarMarks inside the Chart to define two bars like this:

```
var body: some View {
    VStack {
        Chart {
            BarMark(x: .value("Name", "Oscar"),
                    y: .value("Sales", 50))

            BarMark(x: .value("Name", "Mayer"),
                    y: .value("Sales", Int(sliderValue)))
        }
    }
}
```

This code defines a bar chart with two vertical bars.

7. Add the following HStack underneath the Chart like this:

```
var body: some View {
    VStack {
        Chart {
            BarMark(x: .value("Name", "Oscar"),
                    y: .value("Sales", 50))

            BarMark(x: .value("Name", "Mayer"),
                    y: .value("Sales", Int(sliderValue)))
        }
        HStack {
            Text("\(Int(sliderValue))")
            Slider(value: $sliderValue, in: 1...100)
        }.padding()
    }
}
```

The HStack displays a Text view and a Slider where the Text view displays the current value of the Slider, which can range from 1 to 100. The entire ContentView file should look like this:

```
import SwiftUI
import Charts

struct ContentView: View {
    @State var sliderValue = 50.0
    var body: some View {
        VStack {
            Chart {
                BarMark(x: .value("Name", "Oscar"),
                        y: .value("Sales", 50))

                BarMark(x: .value("Name", "Mayer"),
                        y: .value("Sales", Int(sliderValue)))
            }
            HStack {
```

```
                        Text("\(Int(sliderValue))")
                        Slider(value: $sliderValue, in: 1...100)
                }.padding()
            }
        }
    }

    struct ContentView_Previews: PreviewProvider {
        static var previews: some View {
            ContentView()
        }
    }
```

8. Click the Live icon in the Canvas pane.

9. Drag the Slider to see how the value of the Slider adjusts the
    height of the second bar. As you drag the Slider to change its value,
    notice how the Charts framework automatically adjusts the values
    of the Y-axis up to a maximum of 100.

Defining Charts with Loops and Arrays

For small charts, it's easy to define one or more marks, such as BarMarks. However, if
you need to chart large amounts of data, defining each mark can be cumbersome. Even
worse, you may not know the exact number of marks you want for a chart based on data
that can change in size.

For that reason, it's better not to define marks individually but instead rely on data
structures and loops to define the number and height of each mark in a chart. First, we
need to define a structure to hold the data to chart:

```
struct SalesPeople: Identifiable {
    var name: String
    var sales: Int
    var id: String { name }
}
```

A structure lets you define the two types of data to define your chart. In this example, it's a String (name) and an Int (number of sales). The structure needs an ID to identify it, so the entire structure must be defined as Identifiable, and the ID is defined as a String based on the name property.

Second, we need to create an array of the structure we just defined like this:

```
var mySalesArray: [SalesPeople] = [
    .init(name: "Oscar", sales: 50),
    .init(name: "Mayer", sales: 43),
    .init(name: "George", sales: 62),
    .init(name: "Hormel", sales: 26)
]
```

Once we have an array of structures where the array defines a category (name) and a value (sales), we can use that within a chart. That means defining the array name that contains the chart data and an arbitrary variable name that temporarily stores each array item like this:

```
Chart (mySalesArray) { x in

}
```

Finally, we need to define a BarMark that accesses the name and sales properties of each array item like this:

```
Chart (mySalesArray) { x in
    BarMark(x: .value("Name", x.name),
            y: .value("Sales", x.sales))
}
```

To see how to use an array of structures to define a bar chart, follow these steps:

1. Create a new SwiftUI iOS App project and give it any name you wish such as "BarChartArray."

2. Click the ContentView file in the Navigator pane.

3. Add the Charts framework underneath the SwiftUI framework like this:

   ```
   import Charts
   ```

4. Add a structure underneath the "import Charts" line like this:

```
struct SalesPeople: Identifiable {
    var name: String
    var sales: Int
    var id: String { name }
}
```

5. Add an array underneath the structure like this:

```
var mySalesArray: [SalesPeople] = [
    .init(name: "Oscar", sales: 50),
    .init(name: "Mayer", sales: 43),
    .init(name: "George", sales: 62),
    .init(name: "Hormel", sales: 26)
]
```

6. Add a Chart inside the VStack like this:

```
        VStack {
            Chart (mySalesArray) { x in

            }
        }
```

7. Add a BarMark inside the Chart like this:

```
        VStack {
            Chart (mySalesArray) { x in
                BarMark(x: .value("Name", x.name),
                        y: .value("Sales", x.sales))
            }
        }
```

The entire ContentView file should look like this:

```
import SwiftUI
import Charts
```

```
struct SalesPeople: Identifiable {
    var name: String
    var sales: Int
    var id: String { name }
}

var mySalesArray: [SalesPeople] = [
    .init(name: "Oscar", sales: 50),
    .init(name: "Mayer", sales: 43),
    .init(name: "George", sales: 62),
    .init(name: "Hormel", sales: 26)
]

struct ContentView: View {
    var body: some View {
        VStack {
            Chart (mySalesArray) { x in
                BarMark(x: .value("Name", x.name),
                        y: .value("Sales", x.sales))
            }
        }
    }
}

struct ContentView_Previews: PreviewProvider {
    static var previews: some View {
        ContentView()
    }
}
```

8. Click the Live icon in the Canvas pane. Notice that the Chart
   has created four different marks (bars) that display a label
   underneath (name). The height of each mark (bar) represents its
   numeric value.

Defining Colors for a Bar Chart

Normally a bar chart displays each mark (bar) in a default color of blue. However, you can choose a different color by using the .foregroundStyle modifier like this:

```
BarMark(x: .value("Name", x.name),
        y: .value("Sales", x.sales))
.foregroundStyle(.orange)
```

The .foregroundStyle modifier defines a single color. To display marks (bars) in different colors, we need to define a third category. That way each category will appear in its own color. In the previous example, we simply created marks (bars) based on name and sales like this:

```
.init(name: "Hormel", sales: 26)
```

The name identifies each mark (bar), and sales defines how the mark (bar) appears. To create distinct colors, we need to add a third category such as

```
.init(name: "Hormel", department: "West", sales: 26)
```

This new category (department) will define the colors. Each department will get a unique color as shown in Figure 16-4.

```
import SwiftUI
import Charts

struct SalesPeople: Identifiable {
    var name: String
    var department: String
    var sales: Int
    var id = UUID()
}

var mySalesArray: [SalesPeople] = [
    .init(name: "Oscar", department: "North", sales: 50),
    .init(name: "Mayer", department: "South", sales: 43),
    .init(name: "George", department: "East", sales: 62),
    .init(name: "Hormel", department: "West", sales: 26),
    .init(name: "Mike", department: "North", sales: 67),
    .init(name: "Spam", department: "South", sales: 38),
    .init(name: "Jan", department: "East", sales: 47),
    .init(name: "Lundy", department: "West", sales: 53)
]

struct ContentView: View {
    var body: some View {
        VStack {
            Chart (mySalesArray) { x in
                BarMark(x: .value("Name", x.name),
                        y: .value("Sales", x.sales))
                .foregroundStyle(by: .value("Department",
                    x.department))
//                  .foregroundStyle(.orange)
            }
        }

    }
}
```

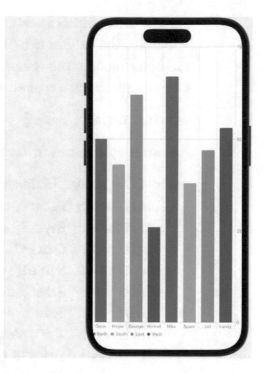

Figure 16-4. *Displaying different colors for each mark (bar)*

To see how to create multiple colors for a bar chart, follow these steps:

1. Create a new SwiftUI iOS App project and give it any name you
   wish such as "BarChartMultipleColors."

2. Click the ContentView file in the Navigator pane.

3. Add the Charts framework underneath the SwiftUI framework
   like this:

   import Charts

4. Add a structure underneath the "import Charts" line like this:

   struct SalesPeople: Identifiable {
       var name: String
       var department: String
       var sales: Int
       var id = UUID()
   }

Notice that we added a new category called "department." Also notice that the ID is set to UUID() to create a unique identifier for each structure. This is essentially equivalent to the previous project structure that created an ID from the name like this:

```
var id: String { name }
```

5. Add an array underneath the structure like this:

```
var mySalesArray: [SalesPeople] = [
    .init(name: "Oscar", department: "North", sales: 50),
    .init(name: "Mayer", department: "South", sales: 43),
    .init(name: "George", department: "East", sales: 62),
    .init(name: "Hormel", department: "West", sales: 26),
    .init(name: "Mike", department: "North", sales: 67),
    .init(name: "Spam", department: "South", sales: 38),
    .init(name: "Jan", department: "East", sales: 47),
    .init(name: "Lundy", department: "West", sales: 53)
]
```

Notice that this array defines different departments: North, South, East, and West. We'll define this department value to display each department in a different color.

6. Add a Chart inside the VStack like this:

```
        VStack {
            Chart (mySalesArray) { x in

            }
        }
```

7. Add a BarMark inside the Chart like this:

```
        VStack {
            Chart (mySalesArray) { x in
                BarMark(x: .value("Name", x.name),
                        y: .value("Sales", x.sales))
            }
        }
```

8.   Add a .foregroundStyle modifier like this:

```
VStack {
    Chart (mySalesArray) { x in
        BarMark(x: .value("Name", x.name),
                y: .value("Sales", x.sales))
        .foregroundStyle(by: .value("Department",
        x.department))
    }
```

The entire ContentView file should look like this:

```
import SwiftUI
import Charts

struct SalesPeople: Identifiable {
    var name: String
    var department: String
    var sales: Int
    var id = UUID()
}

var mySalesArray: [SalesPeople] = [
    .init(name: "Oscar", department: "North", sales: 50),
    .init(name: "Mayer", department: "South", sales: 43),
    .init(name: "George", department: "East", sales: 62),
    .init(name: "Hormel", department: "West", sales: 26),
    .init(name: "Mike", department: "North", sales: 67),
    .init(name: "Spam", department: "South", sales: 38),
    .init(name: "Jan", department: "East", sales: 47),
    .init(name: "Lundy", department: "West", sales: 53)
]

struct ContentView: View {
    var body: some View {
        VStack {
            Chart (mySalesArray) { x in
                BarMark(x: .value("Name", x.name),
```

```
                              y: .value("Sales", x.sales))
                    .foregroundStyle(by: .value("Department",
                    x.department))
//                      .foregroundStyle(.orange)
                }
            }

        }
    }

    struct ContentView_Previews: PreviewProvider {
        static var previews: some View {
            ContentView()
        }
    }
```

9. Click the Live icon in the Canvas pane. Notice that each mark
   (bar) now appears in a different color that's labeled as shown in
   Figure 16-5.

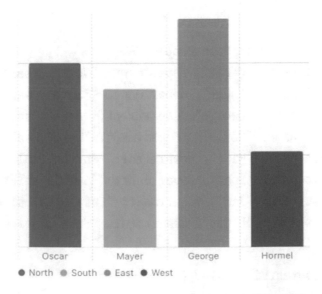

Figure 16-5. *Each mark (bar) is identified by a different color*

Displaying an Average Value with the RuleMark

When you have a large number of marks (bars), it can be hard to compare the different values. Which ones are higher than average? Which ones are lower than average? To make this distinction easy to see, charts offers a RuleMark, which can display a line at the exact average of whatever data you're displaying.

The RuleMark command looks like this:

```
RuleMark (y: .value("Average Sales", (mySalesArray.map{Int($0.sales)}).
reduce(0, +)/Set(mySalesArray.map({$0.sales})).count))
                                .foregroundStyle(.purple)
```

First, we need to define what numeric data appears on the Y-axis. The preceding code assumes that the height of each mark (bar) is defined by a numeric value called "sales," which is part of an array (mySalesArray) of structures.

Second, we need to calculate the average by adding the values of the items (such as sales) and dividing by the total number of items. If there are two items (3 and 5), the average would be (3 + 5)/2.

The .map{Int($0.sales)}.reduce(0,+) adds up all the sales (.map) and reduces it to a single value.

The Set(mySalesArray.map({$0.sales})).count simply counts the total number of sales. The .foregroundStyle modifier then defines the color of the RuleMark.

Note   RuleMarks can be used to highlight any part of a chart.

To see how to display a RuleMark on a chart, follow these steps:

1. Create a new SwiftUI iOS App project and give it any name you wish such as "BarChartRuleMark."

2. Click the ContentView file in the Navigator pane. Add the Charts framework underneath the SwiftUI framework like this:

   ```
   import Charts
   ```

3. Add a structure underneath the "import Charts" line like this:

```
struct SalesPeople: Identifiable {
    var name: String
    var department: String
    var sales: Int
    var id = UUID()
}
```

4. Add an array underneath the structure like this:

```
var mySalesArray: [SalesPeople] = [
    .init(name: "Oscar", sales: 50),
    .init(name: "Mayer", sales: 43),
    .init(name: "George", sales: 62),
    .init(name: "Hormel", sales: 26)
]
```

5. Add a Chart inside a VStack like this:

```
var body: some View {
    VStack {
        Chart (mySalesArray) { x in

        }
    }
```

6. Add a BarMark inside the Chart like this:

```
    VStack {
        Chart (mySalesArray) { x in
            BarMark(x: .value("Name", x.name),
                    y: .value("Sales", x.sales))
        }
    }
```

The BarMark inside the Chart creates a simple bar chart.

7. Add the following two RuleMarks underneath the BarMark like this:

```
VStack {
    Chart (mySalesArray) { x in
        BarMark(x: .value("Name", x.name),
                y: .value("Sales", x.sales))

        RuleMark(y: .value("Average Sales", (mySalesArray.
        map{Int($0.sales)}).reduce(0, +)/Set(mySalesArray.
        map({$0.sales})).count))
            .foregroundStyle(.purple)

        RuleMark(y: .value("Sales must not go below this
        line",20))
            .foregroundStyle(.red)
    }
}
```

The entire ContentView file should look like this:

```
import SwiftUI
import Charts

struct SalesPeople: Identifiable {
    var name: String
    var sales: Int
    var id = UUID()
}

var mySalesArray: [SalesPeople] = [
    .init(name: "Oscar", sales: 50),
    .init(name: "Mayer", sales: 43),
    .init(name: "George", sales: 62),
    .init(name: "Hormel", sales: 26)
]
```

```
struct ContentView: View {
    var body: some View {
        VStack {
            Chart (mySalesArray) { x in
                BarMark(x: .value("Name", x.name),
                        y: .value("Sales", x.sales))

                RuleMark(y: .value("Average Sales", (mySalesArray.
                map{Int($0.sales)}).reduce(0, +)/Set(mySalesArray.
                map({$0.sales})).count))
                    .foregroundStyle(.purple)

                RuleMark(y: .value("Sales must not go below this
                line",20))
                    .foregroundStyle(.red)
            }
        }
    }
}

struct ContentView_Previews: PreviewProvider {
    static var previews: some View {
        ContentView()
    }
}
```

8. Click the Live icon in the Canvas pane. Notice that the purple line
   displays the average, while the red line appears at the arbitrary
   location of 20 as shown in Figure 16-6.

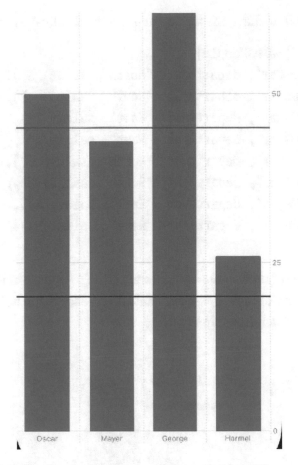

Figure 16-6. *RuleMarks display horizontal lines to identify specific values in a bar chart*

Creating a Stacked Bar Chart

A bar chart can track trends, but a stacked bar chart can let you see the parts of a whole, such as which products sold the most each quarter or which salesperson had the most sales each month. Creating a stacked bar chart involves three sets of data:

- The numeric data you want to define the marks (bars) (y value)

- The duplicate data that defines each stacked bar (x value)

- The category to separate each bar

To stack data in a bar chart, the x value needs to be duplicated like this:

```
var mySalesArray: [SalesPeople] = [
    .init(name: "Oscar", department: "North", sales: 50),
    .init(name: "Oscar", department: "South", sales: 43),
    .init(name: "Oscar", department: "East", sales: 62),
    .init(name: "Oscar", department: "West", sales: 26),
    .init(name: "Mayer", department: "North", sales: 67),
    .init(name: "Mayer", department: "South", sales: 38),
    .init(name: "Mayer", department: "East", sales: 47),
    .init(name: "Mayer", department: "West", sales: 53)
]
```

In this array, "name" represents a single stacked bar, "department" represents the separate colors of a single stacked bar, and "sales" represents the height of each separate color in the stacked bar as shown in Figure 16-7.

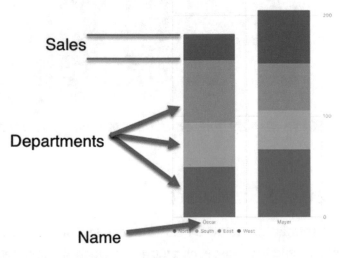

Figure 16-7. *How data defines a stacked bar chart*

To see how to create a stacked bar chart, follow these steps:

1. Create a new SwiftUI iOS App project and give it any name you wish such as "BarChartStacked."

2.   Click the ContentView file in the Navigator pane. Add the Charts framework underneath the SwiftUI framework like this:

```
import Charts
```

3.   Add a structure underneath the "import Charts" line like this:

```
struct SalesPeople: Identifiable {
    var name: String
    var department: String
    var sales: Int
    var id = UUID()
}
```

4.   Add an array underneath the structure like this:

```
var mySalesArray: [SalesPeople] = [
    .init(name: "Oscar", department: "North", sales: 50),
    .init(name: "Oscar", department: "South", sales: 43),
    .init(name: "Oscar", department: "East", sales: 62),
    .init(name: "Oscar", department: "West", sales: 26),
    .init(name: "Mayer", department: "North", sales: 67),
    .init(name: "Mayer", department: "South", sales: 38),
    .init(name: "Mayer", department: "East", sales: 47),
    .init(name: "Mayer", department: "West", sales: 53)
]
```

5.   Add a Chart inside a VStack like this:

```
    var body: some View {
        VStack {
            Chart (mySalesArray) { x in

            }
        }
```

6.   Add a BarMark inside the Chart like this:

```
VStack {
    Chart (mySalesArray) { x in
        BarMark(x: .value("Name", x.name),
                y: .value("Sales", x.sales))

        .foregroundStyle(by: .value("Department",
        $0.department))
    }.padding()
    Spacer()
    }
}
```

7.   Click the Live icon in the Canvas pane.

Creating a Line Chart

A line chart works like a bar chart in measuring values by height. The main difference is that a line chart makes it easier to spot upward or downward trends. To create any chart, just use the proper mark such as

- BarMark – Bar charts

- LineMark – Line charts

- PointMark – Point charts

- AreaMark – Area charts

- RectangleMark – Rectangle charts (also known as heat maps)

Line charts tend to look best when plotting several sets of data. On the other hand, bar charts still look useful when plotting just two sets of data as shown in Figure 16-8.

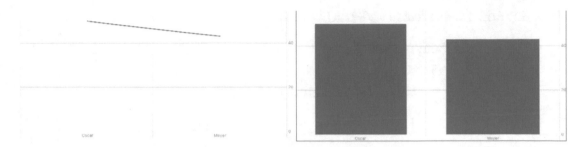

Figure 16-8. *Comparing a bar chart with a line chart*

To see how to create a line chart, follow these steps:

1. Create a new SwiftUI iOS App project and give it any name you wish such as "LineChart."

2. Click the ContentView file in the Navigator pane. Add the Charts framework underneath the SwiftUI framework like this:

```
import Charts
```

3. Add a structure underneath the "import Charts" line like this:

```
struct SalesPeople: Identifiable {
    var name: String
    var department: String
    var sales: Int
    var id = UUID()
}
```

4. Add an array underneath the structure like this:

```
var mySalesArray: [SalesPeople] = [
    .init(name: "Oscar", sales: 50),
    .init(name: "Mayer", sales: 43),
    .init(name: "George", sales: 62),
    .init(name: "Hormel", sales: 26),
    .init(name: "Jan", sales: 47),
    .init(name: "Lundy", sales: 53)
]
```

5. Add a Chart inside a VStack like this:

```
var body: some View {
    VStack {
        Chart (mySalesArray) { x in

        }
    }
```

6. Add a LineMark inside the Chart like this:

```
    VStack {
        Chart (mySalesArray) { x in
            LineMark(x: .value("Name", x.name),
                     y: .value("Sales", x.sales))
        }
    }
```

The entire ContentView file should look like this:

```
import SwiftUI
import Charts

struct SalesPeople: Identifiable {
    var name: String
    var sales: Int
    var id = UUID()
}

var mySalesArray: [SalesPeople] = [
    .init(name: "Oscar", sales: 50),
    .init(name: "Mayer", sales: 43),
    .init(name: "George", sales: 62),
    .init(name: "Hormel", sales: 26),
    .init(name: "Jan", sales: 47),
    .init(name: "Lundy", sales: 53)
]
```

```
struct ContentView: View {
    var body: some View {
        VStack {
            Chart (mySalesArray) { x in
                LineMark(x: .value("Name", x.name),
                          y: .value("Sales", x.sales))
            }
        }
    }
}

struct ContentView_Previews: PreviewProvider {
    static var previews: some View {
        ContentView()
    }
}
```

7. Click the Live icon in the Canvas pane. The line chart appears as shown in Figure 16-9.

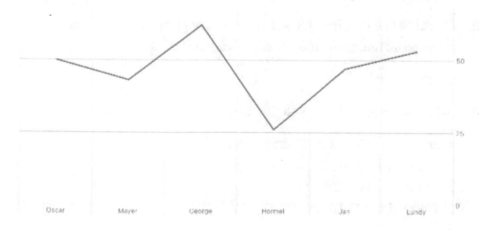

Figure 16-9. *A line chart can show trends over multiple sets of data*

Creating Area Charts

Area charts are essentially line charts but filled in to make them easier to read as shown in Figure 16-10.

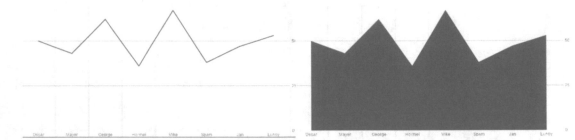

Figure 16-10. *An area chart can be easier to understand than a line chart*

Like line charts, area charts are best for plotting trends consisting of a large number of data points. That way you can easily see how the data changed over time.

To see how to create an area chart, follow these steps:

1. Create a new SwiftUI iOS App project and give it any name you wish such as "AreaChart."

2. Click the ContentView file in the Navigator pane. Add the Charts framework underneath the SwiftUI framework like this:

   import Charts

3. Add a structure underneath the "import Charts" line like this:

   ```
   struct SalesPeople: Identifiable {
       var name: String
       var sales: Int
       var id = UUID()
   }
   ```

4. Add an array underneath the structure like this:

   ```
   var mySalesArray: [SalesPeople] = [
       .init(name: "Oscar", sales: 50),
       .init(name: "Mayer", sales: 43),
       .init(name: "George", sales: 62),
   ```

```
        .init(name: "Hormel", sales: 56),
        .init(name: "Mike", sales: 27),
        .init(name: "Spam", sales: 38),
        .init(name: "Jan", sales: 33),
        .init(name: "Lundy",sales: 43)
    ]
```

5. Add a Chart inside a VStack like this:

```
    var body: some View {
        VStack {
            Chart (mySalesArray) { x in

            }
        }
```

6. Add an AreaMark inside the Chart like this:

```
        VStack {
            Chart (mySalesArray) { x in
                AreaMark(x: .value("Name", x.name),
                        y: .value("Sales", x.sales))
            }
        }
```

The entire ContentView file should look like this:

```
import SwiftUI
import Charts

struct SalesPeople: Identifiable {
    var name: String
    var sales: Int
    var id = UUID()
}

var mySalesArray: [SalesPeople] = [
    .init(name: "Oscar", sales: 50),
    .init(name: "Mayer", sales: 43),
    .init(name: "George", sales: 62),
```

```
            .init(name: "Hormel", sales: 56),
            .init(name: "Mike", sales: 27),
            .init(name: "Spam", sales: 38),
            .init(name: "Jan", sales: 33),
            .init(name: "Lundy",sales: 43)
    ]

    struct ContentView: View {
        var body: some View {
            VStack {
                Chart (mySalesArray) { x in
                    AreaMark(x: .value("Name", x.name),
                             y: .value("Sales", x.sales))
                }
            }
        }
    }

    struct ContentView_Previews: PreviewProvider {
        static var previews: some View {
            ContentView()
        }
    }
```

7. Click the Live icon in the Canvas pane.

Creating a Point Chart

Point charts are similar to line and area charts. The main difference is that point charts simply display data as dots on a chart. While this can make identifying trends harder than a line or an area chart, point charts can be especially useful to identify where groups of data appear. Once you know where data normally should appear, a point chart makes it easy to identify data that falls outside this normal range as shown in Figure 16-11.

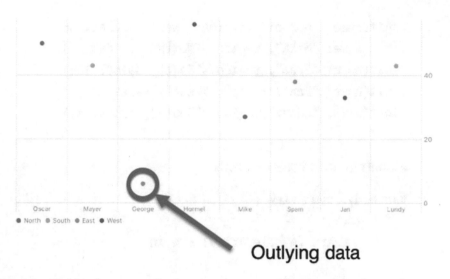

Outlying data

Figure 16-11. *Point charts make it easy to spot outlying data from the norm*

To see how to create an area chart, follow these steps:

1. Create a new SwiftUI iOS App project and give it any name you wish such as "PointChart."

2. Click the ContentView file in the Navigator pane. Add the Charts framework underneath the SwiftUI framework like this:

   import Charts

3. Add a structure underneath the "import Charts" line like this:

   ```
   struct SalesPeople: Identifiable {
       var name: String
       var region: String
       var sales: Int
       var id = UUID()
   }
   ```

4. Add an array underneath the structure like this:

   ```
   var mySalesArray: [SalesPeople] = [
       .init(name: "Oscar", region: "North", sales: 50),
       .init(name: "Mayer", region: "South", sales: 43),
       .init(name: "George", region: "East", sales: 6),
   ```

```
        .init(name: "Hormel", region: "West", sales: 56),
        .init(name: "Mike", region: "North", sales: 27),
        .init(name: "Spam", region: "East", sales: 38),
        .init(name: "Jan", region: "West", sales: 33),
        .init(name: "Lundy",region: "South", sales: 43)
    ]
```

5. Add a Chart inside a VStack like this:

```
var body: some View {
    VStack {
        Chart (mySalesArray) { x in

        }
    }
```

6. Add a PointMark inside the Chart like this:

```
    VStack {
        Chart (mySalesArray) { x in
            PointMark(x: .value("Name", x.name),
                    y: .value("Sales", x.sales))
                .foregroundStyle(by: .value("Region", x.region))
        }
    }
```

The entire ContentView file should look like this:

```
import SwiftUI
import Charts

struct SalesPeople: Identifiable {
    var name: String
    var region: String
    var sales: Int
    var id = UUID()
}
```

```
var mySalesArray: [SalesPeople] = [
    .init(name: "Oscar", region: "North", sales: 50),
    .init(name: "Mayer", region: "South", sales: 43),
    .init(name: "George", region: "East", sales: 6),
    .init(name: "Hormel", region: "West", sales: 56),
    .init(name: "Mike", region: "North", sales: 27),
    .init(name: "Spam", region: "East", sales: 38),
    .init(name: "Jan", region: "West", sales: 33),
    .init(name: "Lundy",region: "South", sales: 43)
]

struct ContentView: View {
    var body: some View {
        VStack {
            Chart (mySalesArray) { x in
                PointMark(x: .value("Name", x.name),
                          y: .value("Sales", x.sales))
                    .foregroundStyle(by: .value("Region", x.region))
            }
        }
    }
}

struct ContentView_Previews: PreviewProvider {
    static var previews: some View {
        ContentView()
    }
}
```

7. Click the Live icon in the Canvas pane.

Creating a Rectangle Chart

Rectangles essentially display the tops of a bar chart but without any colors underneath. That way it can be easy to see the values they represent without the distraction of additional graphics getting in the way as shown in Figure 16-12.

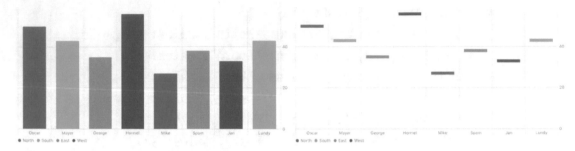

Figure 16-12. *Comparison of a rectangle chart with an equivalent bar chart*

To see how to create a rectangle chart, follow these steps:

1. Create a new SwiftUI iOS App project and give it any name you wish such as "RectangleChart."

2. Click the ContentView file in the Navigator pane.

3. Add the Charts framework underneath the SwiftUI framework like this:

   import Charts

4. Add a structure underneath the "import Charts" line like this:

```
struct SalesPeople: Identifiable {
    var name: String
    var region: String
    var sales: Int
    var id = UUID()
}
```

5. Add an array underneath the structure like this:

```
var mySalesArray: [SalesPeople] = [
    .init(name: "Oscar", region: "North", sales: 50),
    .init(name: "Mayer", region: "South", sales: 43),
    .init(name: "George", region: "East", sales: 35),
    .init(name: "Hormel", region: "West", sales: 56),
    .init(name: "Mike", region: "North", sales: 27),
    .init(name: "Spam", region: "East", sales: 38),
```

```
        .init(name: "Jan", region: "West", sales: 33),
        .init(name: "Lundy",region: "South", sales: 43)
    ]
```

6. Add a Chart inside a VStack like this:

```
var body: some View {
    VStack {
        Chart (mySalesArray) { x in

        }
    }
}
```

7. Add a RectangleMark inside the Chart like this:

```
VStack {
    Chart (mySalesArray) { x in
        RectangleMark(x: .value("Name", x.name),
                 y: .value("Sales", x.sales))
        .foregroundStyle(by: .value("Region", x.region))
    }
}
```

The entire ContentView file should look like this:

```
import SwiftUI
import Charts

struct SalesPeople: Identifiable {
    var name: String
    var region: String
    var sales: Int
    var id = UUID()
}

var mySalesArray: [SalesPeople] = [
    .init(name: "Oscar", region: "North", sales: 50),
    .init(name: "Mayer", region: "South", sales: 43),
    .init(name: "George", region: "East", sales: 35),
    .init(name: "Hormel", region: "West", sales: 56),
```

```
                .init(name: "Mike", region: "North", sales: 27),
                .init(name: "Spam", region: "East", sales: 38),
                .init(name: "Jan", region: "West", sales: 33),
                .init(name: "Lundy",region: "South", sales: 43)
        ]

    struct ContentView: View {
        var body: some View {
            VStack {
                Chart (mySalesArray) { x in
                    RectangleMark(x: .value("Name", x.name),
                            y: .value("Sales", x.sales))
                        .foregroundStyle(by: .value("Region", x.region))
                }
            }
        }
    }

    struct ContentView_Previews: PreviewProvider {
        static var previews: some View {
            ContentView()
        }
    }
```

8.   Click the Live icon in the Canvas pane.

Summary

Many apps rely on storing large amounts of data. Unfortunately, all that data means nothing if users can't understand it. That's why you may need charts to visualize data to spot trends, identify possible problems, or compare data. By making data easy to understand, charts can make data more useful.

Line charts can help identify trends such as falling or rising sales. Area charts can make such trends easier to see by filling in the empty space underneath a line.

Point charts can often be useful to spot outlying data that doesn't fit within normal clusters of data. Rectangle charts can be handy for highlighting values. Just as area charts are like line charts but filled in, bar charts are like rectangle charts but also filled in.

Stacking data in a chart, such as a bar chart, allows you to see proportions of a whole. Adding rule marks lets you draw lines to highlight specific values in a chart such as average sales.

Every chart has its pros and cons based on what people like, so experiment with different charts until you find the right one for your app and users.

CHAPTER 17

Using the Navigation Stack

Only the simplest apps consist of a single screen such as the Calculator app. However, most apps usually need two or more screens to display information. In SwiftUI, you can define each screen of your app's user interface by creating a separate structure. Then you need to provide a way to jump from one screen to another.

One of the simplest ways to jump from one screen to another is through a Navigation Stack, which displays multiple screens in sequential order. This Navigation Stack is commonly used in many iOS apps such as Settings to let users view different options as shown in Figure 17-1.

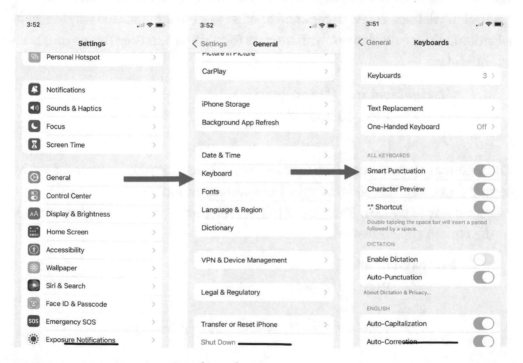

Figure 17-1. *A Navigation Stack makes it easy to jump from one screen to another*

© Wallace Wang 2023
W. Wang, *Beginning iPhone Development with SwiftUI*, https://doi.org/10.1007/978-1-4842-9541-0_17

In Figure 17-1, the user can tap the Settings icon on the Home screen to display the Settings screen. Tapping General opens the General screen. Then tapping Keyboard opens the Keyboards screen. Note that to go backward, you can just tap the Back button in the upper-left corner.

From the Keyboards screen, the Back button takes you back to the General screen. From the General screen, the Back button takes you back to the Settings screen. A Navigation Stack does nothing more than allow the user to jump from one screen to another in sequential order.

Using a Navigation Stack

A Navigation Stack can hold up to ten (10) views just like any other type of stack (VStack, HStack, ZStack). A Navigation Stack contains multiple views using code like this:

```
NavigationStack {
    // Put multiple views here
}
```

Within a NavigationStack, you need one or more NavigationLinks where each NavigationLink defines a view to click and another view to appear. One way to create a NavigationLink is to display text with no extra formatting and then define the view to appear like this:

```
NavigationLink ("Link text") {
    //  View to appear
}
```

The view that appears when the user selects the NavigationLink can vary from a single view (such as a Text view) to a stack containing multiple views.

A second way to create a NavigationLink lets you format the link's appearance and define the view to appear like this:

```
NavigationLink {
    //  View to appear
} label: {
    //  View that defines the navigation link
}
```

To see how to create a simple Navigation Stack with different ways of creating a NavigationLink, follow these steps:

1. Create a new SwiftUI iOS App project and give it any name you wish such as "NavigationStack."

2. Click the ContentView file in the Navigator pane.

3. Add a NavigationStack under the var body: some View line like this:

```
var body: some View {
    NavigationStack {

    }
}
```

4. Add four NavigationLinks inside the NavigationStack like this:

```
var body: some View {
    NavigationStack {
        NavigationLink {
            Text("The 1st view")
        } label: {
            Text("First link")
                .font(.largeTitle)
        }.padding()

        NavigationLink {
            Text("The 2nd view")
        } label: {
            Label {
                Text("Second link")
            } icon: {
                Image(systemName: "sun.and.horizon.circle")
            }
        }.padding()
```

```
            NavigationLink {
                Image(systemName: "ellipsis.message")
                    .font(.system(size: 125))
            } label: {
                VStack {
                    Text("Third view")
                    Image(systemName: "figure.archery")
                }.font(.largeTitle)
            }.padding()

            NavigationLink ("The 4th view") {
                VStack {
                    Image(systemName: "airplane.departure")
                        .font(.system(size: 120))
                    Text("Departure time is 12:15")
                        .font(.largeTitle)
                }
            }.padding()
        }
}
```

Notice that each NavigationLink defines a different way to create the navigation link and the view that appears when the user selects that particular navigation link.

The entire ContentView file should look like this:

```
import SwiftUI

struct ContentView: View {
    var body: some View {
        NavigationStack {
            NavigationLink {
                Text("The 1st view")
            } label: {
                Text("First link")
                    .font(.largeTitle)
            }.padding()
```

```
            NavigationLink {
                Text("The 2nd view")
            } label: {
                Label {
                    Text("Second link")
                } icon: {
                    Image(systemName: "sun.and.horizon.circle")
                }
            }.padding()

            NavigationLink {
                Image(systemName: "ellipsis.message")
                    .font(.system(size: 125))
            } label: {
                VStack {
                    Text("Third view")
                    Image(systemName: "figure.archery")
                }.font(.largeTitle)
            }.padding()

            NavigationLink ("The 4th view") {
                VStack {
                    Image(systemName: "airplane.departure")
                        .font(.system(size: 120))
                    Text("Departure time is 12:15")
                        .font(.largeTitle)
                }
            }.padding()
        }
    }
}

struct ContentView_Previews: PreviewProvider {
    static var previews: some View {
        ContentView()
    }
}
```

5.   Click the Live icon in the Canvas pane. All four NavigationLinks
     appear on the user interface.

6.   Click any of the displayed NavigationLinks. The view defined for
     that NavigationLink appears.

Adding a Title to a Navigation Stack

A Navigation Stack simply displays one or more NavigationLinks on the screen. However,
you may want to make sure users understand the purpose of these NavigationLinks by
adding a title over them. Titles can appear in one of two styles (.large or .inline) as shown
in Figure 17-2.

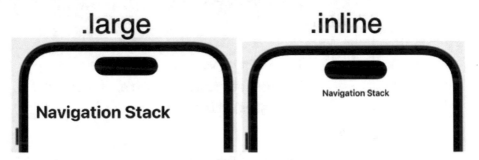

Figure 17-2. *Comparing the appearance of a .large and an .inline title above a*
Navigation Stack

To display a title above the Navigation Stack, use the following modifier:

```
.navigationTitle("Navigation Stack")
```

To change the appearance of a title, use the following modifier:

```
.navigationBarTitleDisplayMode(.inline)
```

Note   When adding the .navigationTitle and .navigationBarTitleDisplayMode modifiers to a NavigationStack, place the modifiers inside the last curly bracket of the NavigationStack like this:

```
NavigationStack {
    .navigationTitle("Navigation Stack Title")
    .navigationBarTitleDisplayMode(.inline)
}
```

The .navigationTitle modifier defines the text that will appear at the top of the screen, above the Navigation Stack. The .navigationBarTitleDisplayMode modifier defines how that title appears on the screen. The two options are .large and .inline (see Figure 17-2). If you do not define the .navigationBarTitleDisplayMode, .large is the default value.

To see how to display a title for a Navigation Stack and change its appearance, follow these steps:

1. Create a new SwiftUI iOS App project and give it any name you wish such as "NavigationStackTitle."

2. Click the ContentView file in the Navigator pane.

3. Add a State variable under the struct ContentView: View line like this:

    ```
    @State var titleType = NavigationBarItem.TitleDisplayMode.large
    ```

4. Add a NavigationStack inside the var body: some View like this:

    ```
    var body: some View {
        NavigationStack {

        }
    }
    ```

5. Add a NavigationLink inside the NavigationStack like this:

    ```
    var body: some View {
        NavigationStack {
            NavigationLink {
                Text("The 1st view")
    ```

```
        } label: {
            Text("First link")
                .font(.largeTitle)
        }.padding()
    }
}
```

6. Add the .navigationTitle and .navigationBarTitleDisplayMode modifiers like this:

```
var body: some View {
    NavigationStack {
        NavigationLink {
            Text("The 1st view")
        } label: {
            Text("First link")
                .font(.largeTitle)
        }.padding()
            .navigationTitle("Navigation Stack")
            .navigationBarTitleDisplayMode(titleType)
    }
}
```

Note   The .navigationTitle modifier not only defines the title above the Navigation Stack but also defines the text that appears in the Back button. If the .navigationTitle modifier does not exist, the Back button simply displays "Back."

---

7. Add an HStack with two Buttons inside like this:

```
var body: some View {
    NavigationStack {
        NavigationLink {
            Text("The 1st view")
        } label: {
            Text("First link")
                .font(.largeTitle)
```

```
    }.padding()
        .navigationTitle("Navigation Stack")
        .navigationBarTitleDisplayMode(titleType)

    HStack (spacing: 50) {
        Button (".large") {
            titleType = NavigationBarItem.
            TitleDisplayMode.large
        }

        Button (".inline") {
            titleType = NavigationBarItem.
            TitleDisplayMode.inline
        }
    }
  }
}
```

8. Click the Live icon in the Canvas pane.

9. Click the .large and .inline Buttons to see how the Navigation
    Stack title's appearance can change.

Adding Buttons to a Navigation Stack

Besides displaying a title above a Navigation Stack, you can also display one or more
buttons at the top of the screen. These buttons appear on a toolbar that you can add by
using the .toolbar modifier inside the Navigation Stack like this:

```
NavigationStack {

    .navigationTitle("Navigation Title")
    .toolbar {

    }
  }
```

By default, the color of any buttons or icons defined inside the .toolbar will be blue. If you want to define a different color, you can add the .accentColor modifier to the NavigationStack like this:

```
NavigationStack {

    .navigationTitle("Navigation Title")
    .toolbar {

    }
}.accentColor(.purple)
```

Inside the .toolbar modifier is where you can define one or more ToolbarItems. For each ToolbarItem you add, you can define its placement (in the upper-left corner as .navigationBarLeading or in the upper-right corner as .navigationBarTrailing). In addition, you must define the appearance of the button and the code to run if the user selects that button like this:

```
.toolbar {
    ToolbarItem(placement: .navigationBarLeading) {
        Button {
            //  Code to run
        } label: {
            //  Define button's appearance here
        }
    }

    ToolbarItem(placement: .navigationBarTrailing) {
        Button {
            //  Code to run
        } label: {
            //  Define button's appearance here
        }
    }
```

To see how to define buttons in a Navigation Stack, follow these steps:

1. Create a new SwiftUI iOS App project and give it any name you
    wish such as "NavigationStackButtons."

2. Click the ContentView file in the Navigator pane.

3. Add two State variables under the struct ContentView: View line
    like this:

    ```
    @State var titleType = NavigationBarItem.TitleDisplayMode.large
    @State var message = ""
    ```

4. Add a NavigationStack inside the var body: some View like this:

    ```
    var body: some View {
        NavigationStack {

        }
    }
    ```

5. Add the .accentColor modifier to the NavigationStack like this:

    ```
    var body: some View {
        NavigationStack {

        }.accentColor(.purple)
    ```

6. Add a NavigationLink inside the NavigationStack like this:

    ```
    var body: some View {
        NavigationStack {
            NavigationLink {
                Text("The 1st view")
            } label: {
                Text("First link")
                    .font(.largeTitle)
            }.padding()
                .navigationTitle("Navigation Stack")
    ```

```
                .navigationBarTitleDisplayMode(titleType)
        }.accentColor(.purple)
    }
```

7.   Add the .toolbar modifier like this:

```
var body: some View {
    NavigationStack {
        NavigationLink {
            Text("The 1st view")
        } label: {
            Text("First link")
                .font(.largeTitle)
        }.padding()
            .navigationTitle("Navigation Stack")
            .navigationBarTitleDisplayMode(titleType)
            .toolbar {
                ToolbarItem(placement: .navigationBarLeading) {
                    Button {
                        message = "iCloud icon tapped"
                    } label: {
                        Image(systemName: "icloud")
                    }
                }

                ToolbarItem(placement: .navigationBar
                Trailing) {
                    Button {
                        message = "Done button tapped"
                    } label: {
                        Text("Done")
                    }
                }
            }
    }.accentColor(.purple)
}
```

For each ToolbarItem, you can define the button's appearance with either a Text view or an Image view. The preceding code displays a cloud icon in the upper-left corner and the word "Done" in the upper-right corner as shown in Figure 17-3.

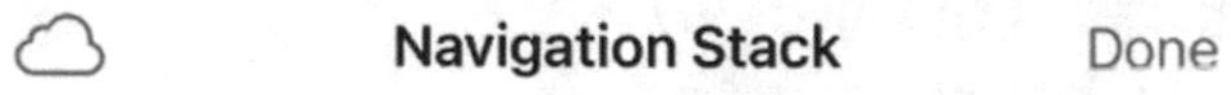

☁   **Navigation Stack**   Done

Figure 17-3. *The appearance of toolbar buttons with the .toolbar modifier*

8. Add a Text view and an HStack with two Buttons inside of them like this:

```
var body: some View {
    NavigationStack {
        NavigationLink {
            Text("The 1st view")
        } label: {
            Text("First link")
                .font(.largeTitle)
        }.padding()
            .navigationTitle("Navigation Stack")
            .navigationBarTitleDisplayMode(titleType)
            .toolbar {
                ToolbarItem(placement: .navigationBarLeading) {
                    Button {
                        message = "iCloud icon tapped"
                    } label: {
                        Image(systemName: "icloud")
                    }
                }

                ToolbarItem(placement: .navigationBar
                Trailing) {
                    Button {
                        message = "Done button tapped"
                    } label: {
                        Text("Done")
```

```
                            }
                        }
                    }
                Text(message)
                HStack (spacing: 50) {
                    Button (".large") {
                        titleType = NavigationBarItem.TitleDisplayMode
                        .large
                    }

                    Button (".inline") {
                        titleType = NavigationBarItem.TitleDisplayMode
                        .inline
                    }
                }
        }.accentColor(.purple)
}
```

The entire ContentView file should look like this:

```
import SwiftUI

struct ContentView: View {

    @State var titleType = NavigationBarItem.TitleDisplayMode
    .large
    @State var message = ""

    var body: some View {
        NavigationStack {
            NavigationLink {
                Text("The 1st view")
            } label: {
                Text("First link")
                    .font(.largeTitle)
            }.padding()
                .navigationTitle("Navigation Stack")
                .navigationBarTitleDisplayMode(titleType)
```

```
            .toolbar {
               ToolbarItem(placement: .navigationBarLeading) {
                  Button {
                     message = "iCloud icon tapped"
                  } label: {
                     Image(systemName: "icloud")
                  }
               }

               ToolbarItem(placement:
               .navigationBarTrailing) {
                  Button {
                     message = "Done button tapped"
                  } label: {
                     Text("Done")
                  }
               }
            }
         Text(message)
         HStack (spacing: 50) {
            Button (".large") {
               titleType = NavigationBarItem.
               TitleDisplayMode.large
            }

            Button (".inline") {
               titleType = NavigationBarItem.
               TitleDisplayMode.inline
            }
         }
      }.accentColor(.purple)
   }
}

struct ContentView_Previews: PreviewProvider {
   static var previews: some View {
      ContentView()
   }
}
```

9. Click the Live icon in the Canvas pane.

10. Click the buttons defined by ToolbarItems. Notice each time you click a toolbar button, a message appears in the Text view such as "iCloud icon tapped" or "Done button tapped."

Displaying Views from a Navigation Stack

Just displaying a single view like a Text or Image view within a Navigation Stack might be fine in some cases. However, many times you may want to display a completely different user interface altogether. Since you can define a user interface screen with a structure, you can create multiple screens using multiple structures that can appear within a Navigation Stack.

The simplest way to create a new structure is within the ContentView file. However, this can clutter the code, so a second way is to store the structure in a separate file.

To see how to create structures that define another user interface screen, follow these steps:

1. Create a new SwiftUI iOS App project and give it any name you wish such as "NavigationStackStructures."

2. Click the ContentView file in the Navigator pane.

3. Add a NavigationStack and a VStack inside the var body: some View line like this:

```
var body: some View {
    NavigationStack {
        VStack {

        }
    }
```

4. Add two NavigationLinks and a .navigationTitle modifier to the VStack like this:

```
var body: some View {
    NavigationStack {
        VStack {
```

```
NavigationLink(destination: FileView()) {
    Text("Link to structure in same file")
}

NavigationLink(destination: SeparateFileView()) {
    Text("Separate file link")
}
.navigationTitle("Navigation Title")
            }
        }
}
```

The first NavigationLink will display a structure called FileView.
The second NavigationLink will display a structure called
SeparateFileView. Since neither of these structures exists yet, we'll
need to create them.

5. Add the following structure underneath the entire struct
    ContentView: View structure like this:

```
struct FileView: View {
    var body: some View {
        HStack {
            Spacer()
            VStack {
                Spacer()
                Text("This is a separate structure")
                Text("that's stored in the same file")
                Spacer()
            }
            Spacer()
        }.background(Color.yellow)
    }
}
```

The entire ContentView file should look like this:

```swift
import SwiftUI

struct ContentView: View {
    var body: some View {
        NavigationStack {
            VStack {
                NavigationLink(destination: FileView()) {
                    Text("Link to structure in same file")
                }

                NavigationLink(destination: SeparateFileView()) {
                    Text("Separate file link")
                }
                .navigationTitle("Navigation Title")
            }
        }
    }
}

struct FileView: View {
    var body: some View {
        HStack {
            Spacer()
            VStack {
                Spacer()
                Text("This is a separate structure")
                Text("that's stored in the same file")
                Spacer()
            }
            Spacer()
        }.background(Color.yellow)
    }
}
```

```swift
struct ContentView_Previews: PreviewProvider {
    static var previews: some View {
        ContentView()
    }
}
```

We can keep adding new structures inside the ContentView file, but this risks cluttering up the file. A second way to create structures is to store them in a separate file, which the next steps will let us do. When creating a separate file to store a structure, we can use a completely blank Swift file or a SwiftUI View file.

We'll use a blank Swift file to see all the code needed to create a SwiftUI view, but a SwiftUI View file would work just as well too and provide the basic code needed to create a user interface.

6. Choose File ➤ New ➤ File. A dialog appears as shown in Figure 17-4.

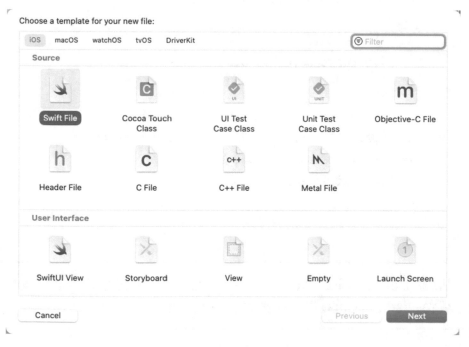

Figure 17-4. *A dialog for choosing a file to create*

7. Click iOS near the top of the dialog, click Swift File, and then click Next. Xcode asks for a name to give your newly created file.

8. Type SeparateFile and click Create. Xcode creates a new Swift file.

9. Delete all code currently in the SeparateFile and replace it with the following:

```swift
import SwiftUI

struct SeparateFileView: View {
    var body: some View {
        HStack {
            Spacer()
            VStack {
                Spacer()
                Text("This is another structure")
                Text("but stored in a separate file")
                Spacer()
            }
            Spacer()
        }.background(Color.orange)
    }
}

struct SeparateFileView_Previews: PreviewProvider {
    static var previews: some View {
        SeparateFileView()
    }
}
```

Note   When storing a structure in a separate file, you need a second structure (PreviewProvider) to display that user interface in the Canvas pane.

---

10. Click the ContentView file in the Navigator pane.

11. Click the Live icon in the Canvas pane.

12.   Click the "Link to structure in same file". Notice that this displays the FileView structure stored in the ContentView file.

13.   Click the Back button to return to the original screen.

14.   Click the "Separate file link". Notice that this displays the SeparateFileView structure stored in a file called SeparateFile.

If a structure is short, it might be more convenient to store it in the same file as the Navigation Stack. However, it's generally more useful to store structures in separate files to keep them better organized so each file is easier to read.

Passing Data Between Structures in a Navigation Stack

The previous project created two structures where one structure was stored in the ContentView file and a second structure was stored in a separate file. In both cases, the structures defined user interfaces that displayed static information unconnected to anything from the original structure (ContentView).

In many cases, you may want data from one structure to appear in a second structure. That means we must pass data from one structure to another.

Fortunately, this task is similar to passing data between functions. When a structure needs to receive data, we just need to declare a property by creating a variable, giving that variable a descriptive name, and defining the data type that variable can hold such as String or Double like this:

```
struct FileView: View {
    var choice: String
```

This defines a variable called "choice" that can hold a String. To pass data to this structure, we can load this structure by calling the structure name (FileView) followed by this "choice" variable as a parameter like this:

```
FileView(choice: "Heads")
```

When passing data to a structure stored in the same file, we just need to follow this two-step process:

• Declare one or more variables inside the structure to receive data.

• Call that structure using its variables as parameters.

However, when passing data to a structure stored in a separate file, there's an additional step necessary. Because a structure stored in a separate file also contains a second structure that displays the user interface in the Canvas pane, this preview structure must include the structure's parameter and pass it data as well like this:

```
struct SeparateFileView_Previews: PreviewProvider {
    static var previews: some View {
        SeparateFileView(passedData: "")
    }
}
```

To see how to pass data between structures, follow these steps:

1. Create a new SwiftUI iOS App project and give it any name you wish such as "NavigationStackPassData."

2. Click the ContentView file in the Navigator pane.

3. Edit the struct ContentView structure like this:

```
struct ContentView: View {
    var body: some View {
        NavigationStack {
            VStack (spacing: 26) {
                Text("Choose Heads or Tails")

                NavigationLink(destination: FileView(choice:
                "Heads")) {
                    Text("Heads")
                }

                NavigationLink(destination: SeparateFileView
                (passedData: "Tails")) {
                    Text("Tails")
                }
                .navigationTitle("Flip a Coin")
            }
        }
    }
}
```

The preceding code defines two NavigationLinks where one calls a structure called FileView with a parameter of "choice:" that gets passed "Heads". The second NavigationLink calls a structure called SeparateFileView with a parameter of "passedData:" that gets passed "Tails".

4. Add a new structure underneath the struct ContentView like this:

```
struct FileView: View {
    var choice: String

    var body: some View {
        HStack {
            Spacer()
            VStack {
                Spacer()
                Text("You chose = \(choice)")
                Spacer()
            }
            Spacer()
        }.background(Color.yellow)
    }
}
```

This FileView structure declares a "choice" variable that can hold a String. Then it displays this "choice" variable in a Text view that shows "You chose = ". The entire ContentView file should look like this:

```
import SwiftUI

struct ContentView: View {
    var body: some View {
        NavigationStack {
            VStack (spacing: 26) {
                Text("Choose Heads or Tails")
```

```
                    NavigationLink(destination: FileView(choice:
                    "Heads")) {
                        Text("Heads")
                    }

                    NavigationLink(destination: SeparateFileView
                    (passedData: "Tails")) {
                        Text("Tails")
                    }
                    .navigationTitle("Flip a Coin")
                }
            }
        }
    }

    struct FileView: View {
        var choice: String

        var body: some View {
            HStack {
                Spacer()
                VStack {
                    Spacer()
                    Text("You chose = \(choice)")
                    Spacer()
                }
                Spacer()
            }.background(Color.yellow)
        }
    }

    struct ContentView_Previews: PreviewProvider {
        static var previews: some View {
            ContentView()
        }
    }
```

This code creates a structure called FileView, but now we need to create a second structure called SeparateFileView that declares a passedData String variable.

5. Choose File ➤ New ➤ File. A dialog appears (see Figure 17-4).

6. Click iOS near the top of the dialog, click Swift File, and then click Next. Xcode asks for a name to give your newly created file.

7. Type SeparateFile and click Create. Xcode creates a new Swift file.

8. Delete all code currently in the SeparateFile and replace it with the following:

```swift
import SwiftUI

struct SeparateFileView: View {
    var passedData: String

    var body: some View {
        HStack {
            Spacer()
            VStack {
                Spacer()
                Text("You chose = \(passedData)")
                Spacer()
            }
            Spacer()
        }.background(Color.orange)
    }
}

struct SeparateFileView_Previews: PreviewProvider {
    static var previews: some View {
        SeparateFileView(passedData: "")
    }
}
```

This file creates a SeparateFileView structure that declares a passedData String variable. Because this SeparateFileView structure is stored in a separate file, it contains a struct PreviewProvider where we must use the passedData parameter as well.

9. Click ContentView in the Navigator pane to return to the ContentView structure.

10. Click the Live icon in the Canvas pane.

11. Click the Heads navigation link. The FileView structure appears, displaying "You chose = Heads".

12. Click the Back button in the upper-left corner.

13. Click the Tails navigation link. The SeparateFileView structure appears, displaying "You chose = Tails".

Changing Data Between Structures in a Navigation Stack

The previous project created two structures where one structure was stored in the ContentView file and a second structure was stored in a separate file. In both cases, the structures defined user interfaces that received data and displayed it.

What if we pass data to a structure and then allow that structure to modify that data? This will require several changes:

- Create a State variable.

- Use the NavigationLink to open another structure and pass that structure a binding to the State variable (using the $ symbol) such as

  FileView(choice: $message)

- Define a @Binding variable in the structure that will receive data.

- Change that Binding variable in the structure that received data.

To see how to change data between structures in a Navigation Stack, follow these steps:

1. Create a new SwiftUI iOS App project and give it any name you wish such as "NavigationStackBindingData."

2. Click the ContentView file in the Navigator pane.

3. Create a State variable under the struct ContentView: View line like this:

```
struct ContentView: View {
    @State var message = ""
```

4. Add a NavigationStack and a VStack inside the var body: some View line like this:

```
var body: some View {
    NavigationStack {
        VStack {

        }
    }
```

5. Add a Text view and two NavigationLinks inside the VStack like this:

```
NavigationStack {
    VStack (spacing: 26) {
        TextField("Type here", text: $message)

        NavigationLink(destination: FileView(choice:
        $message)) {
            Text("Send a message")
        }
```

```
        NavigationLink(destination: SeparateFileView
        (passedData: $message)) {
            Text("Separate file")
        }
        .navigationTitle("Passing Data")
    }
}
```

Notice that the first NavigationLink opens a structure called FileView and sends a binding variable ($message) to the "choice:" parameter. The second NavigationLink opens a structure called SeparateFileView and sends the same binding variable ($message) to the "passedData" parameter.

6. Add the following structure underneath the struct ContentView: View structure:

```
struct FileView: View {
    @Binding var choice: String

    var body: some View {
        HStack {
            Spacer()
            VStack {
                Spacer()
                TextField("Type here:", text: $choice)
                Spacer()
            }
            Spacer()
        }.background(Color.yellow)
    }
}
```

Notice that this structure declares a @Binding variable called "choice" that can hold a String. This structure uses a TextField to change this @Binding variable ($choice), which sends the changes automatically back to the ContentView structure.

7. Choose File ➤ New ➤ File. A dialog appears (see Figure 17-4).

8. Click iOS near the top of the dialog, click Swift File, and then click
   Next. Xcode asks for a name to give your newly created file.

9. Type SeparateFile and click Create. Xcode creates a new Swift file.

10. Delete all code currently in the SeparateFile and replace it with
    the following:

```swift
import SwiftUI

struct SeparateFileView: View {
    @Binding var passedData: String

    var body: some View {
        HStack {
            Spacer()
            VStack {
                Spacer()
                TextField("Type here", text: $passedData)
                Spacer()
            }
            Spacer()
        }.background(Color.orange)
    }
}

struct SeparateFileView_Previews: PreviewProvider {

    static var previews: some View {
        SeparateFileView(passedData: .constant(""))
    }
}
```

Notice that this structure declares a @Binding variable called
"passedData" that can hold a String. The TextField can change this
variable ($passedData) and automatically send the changes back
to the ContentView structure.

Also note that because this structure is stored in a separate file, the PreviewProvider structure must also include the "passedData" parameter by giving it a .constant("").

11. Click the ContentView file in the Navigator pane.

12. Click the Live icon in the Canvas pane.

13. Click in the TextField and type a phrase.

14. Click the "Send a message" navigation link that passes the string to the FileView structure stored in the ContentView file.

15. Click in the TextField displayed by the FileView structure and edit the data. Then click the Back button to return to the ContentView structure that displays the modified data.

16. Click the "Separate file" navigation link that passes the string to the SeparateFileView structure stored in a separate file.

17. Click in the TextField displayed by the SeparateFileView structure and edit the data. Then click the Back button to return to the ContentView structure that displays the modified data.

Sharing Data Between Structures in a Navigation Stack

Using @State and @Binding variables lets multiple views share and modify data. However, suppose you created a Navigation Stack that links four structures together in sequential order. If you change the data on the first structure and want to pass it to the fourth structure, you also have to pass that data through the second and third structures.

While this can work, it's clumsy. It's far better to pass data straight to the structures that need the data. To do this, SwiftUI offers another way to share data between structures. First, create an ObservableObject class that contains one or more variables to share. Each variable must be marked as @Published like this:

```
class ShareString: ObservableObject {
    @Published var message = ""
}
```

The structure that contains the NavigationStack (such as ContentView) needs to define a @StateObject variable that defines an object from the ObservableObject class like this:

```
@StateObject var showMe = ShareString()
```

Since we want to share this ObservableObject between all views within the Navigation Stack, we need to add the .environmentObject modifier to the NavigationStack along with the StateObject to share like this:

```
NavigationStack {


}.environmentObject(showMe)
```

Instead of passing data to each view, the NavigationLink just needs the name of the view to display such as

```
NavigationLink(destination: FileView()) {
    Text("Send a message")
}
```

Within each structure that needs to access the ObservableObject, we need to declare an @EnvironmentObject variable that uses the ObservableObject class like this:

```
@EnvironmentObject var choice: ShareString
```

Finally, within each structure that defines an @EnvironmentObject, we can access the actual data to share by using the @EnvironmentObject name plus the @Published property name to share like this:

```
$choice.message
```

In this case, "choice" is the @EnvironmentObject name, and "message" is the @Published property defined within the ObservableObject. To see how to share data using an ObservableObject, follow these steps:

1. Create a new SwiftUI iOS App project and give it any name you wish such as "NavigationStackObservable."

2. Click the ContentView file in the Navigator pane.

3. Create an ObservableObject class under the import SwiftUI line like this:

```
class ShareString: ObservableObject {
    @Published var message = ""
}
```

The @Published variable will contain the data to share between structures within the Navigation Stack.

4. Create a StateObject variable under the struct ContentView: View line like this:

```
struct ContentView: View {
    @StateObject var showMe = ShareString()
```

This creates a new object (showMe) based on the ShareString ObservableObject.

5. Add a NavigationStack and a VStack inside the var body: some View line like this:

```
var body: some View {
    NavigationStack {
        VStack (spacing: 26) {

        }
    }
```

6. Add a Text view, two NavigationLinks, and a .navigationTitle modifier inside the VStack like this:

```
NavigationStack {
    VStack (spacing: 26) {
        TextField("Type here", text: $showMe.message)

        NavigationLink(destination: FileView()) {
            Text("Send a message")
        }
```

```
NavigationLink(destination: SeparateFileView()) {
    Text("Separate file")
}
.navigationTitle("Sharing Data")
    }
}.environmentObject(showMe)
```

Make sure you add the .environmentObject(showMe) modifier at the end of the NavigationStack. This allows sharing of the showMe ObservableObject ShareString class. The preceding NavigationLinks open structures called FileView and SeparateFileView that we need to create.

7. Add the following structure underneath the struct ContentView structure like this:

```
struct FileView: View {
    @EnvironmentObject var choice: ShareString

    var body: some View {
        HStack {
            Spacer()
            VStack {
                Spacer()
                TextField("Type here:", text: $choice.message)
                Spacer()
            }
            Spacer()
        }.background(Color.yellow)
    }
}
```

Notice that this structure defines an @EnvironmentObject
variable that can hold a ShareString ObservableObject.
In the TextField, we must store the text in the "choice"
@EnvironmentObject that uses the "message" @Published
property ($choice.message). The entire ContentView file should
look like this:

```
import SwiftUI

class ShareString: ObservableObject {
    @Published var message = ""
}

struct ContentView: View {
    @StateObject var showMe = ShareString()

    var body: some View {
        NavigationStack {
            VStack (spacing: 26) {
                TextField("Type here", text: $showMe.message)

                NavigationLink(destination: FileView()) {
                    Text("Send a message")
                }

                NavigationLink(destination: SeparateFileView()) {
                    Text("Separate file")
                }
                .navigationTitle("Sharing Data")
            }
        }.environmentObject(showMe)
    }
}

struct FileView: View {
    @EnvironmentObject var choice: ShareString

    var body: some View {
        HStack {
            Spacer()
```

```
            VStack {
                Spacer()
                TextField("Type here:", text: $choice.message)
                Spacer()
            }
            Spacer()
        }.background(Color.yellow)
    }
}

struct ContentView_Previews: PreviewProvider {
    static var previews: some View {
        ContentView()
    }
}
```

8. Choose File ➤ New ➤ File. A dialog appears (see Figure 17-4).

9. Click iOS near the top of the dialog, click Swift File, and then click Next. Xcode asks for a name to give your newly created file.

10. Type SeparateFile and click Create. Xcode creates a new Swift file.

11. Delete all code currently in the SeparateFile and replace it with the following:

```
import SwiftUI

struct SeparateFileView: View {
    @EnvironmentObject var passedData: ShareString

    var body: some View {
        HStack {
            Spacer()
            VStack {
                Spacer()
                TextField("Type here", text: $passedData.message)
                Spacer()
            }
```

```
                Spacer()
            }.background(Color.orange)
        }
    }

    struct SeparateFileView_Previews: PreviewProvider {
        static var previews: some View {
            SeparateFileView()
        }
    }
```

Notice that this structure also declares an @EnvironmentObject that can hold a ShareString ObservableObject. Then the TextField uses the "passedData" @EnvironmentObject to access the "message" @Published property ($passedData.message).

12.   Click the ContentView file in the Navigator pane.

13.   Click the Live icon in the Canvas pane.

14.   Click in the TextField and type a phrase.

15.   Click the "Send a message" navigation link to open the FileView structure. Notice that what you typed in step 14 now appears in the FileView TextField.

16.   Edit the text in the TextField and then click the Back button. Notice that the modified text now appears in the ContentView TextField.

17.   Edit the text in the TextField and then click the "Separate file" navigation link. The edited text now appears in the SeparateFileView TextField.

18.   Edit the text in the TextField and click the Back button. Notice that the modified text now appears in the ContentView TextField. All this shows how the various structures can access the @Published property in the ObservableObject.

Using Lists in a Navigation Stack

Rather than display NavigationLinks individually, one common technique is to create a List (see Chapter 13) where each item in the List acts like a link. By selecting an item in a List, the Navigation Stack can then open a new view. This combination of lists within a Navigation Stack is commonly used in the Settings app on iOS.

When we created navigation links in previous projects, we defined the text to appear on the link along with the destination view to display like this:

```
NavigationLink {
    Text("Destination view")
} label: {
    Text("Text to appear on link")
}
```

However, when working with lists, it can be more convenient to separate the destination view from the navigation link. That way the navigation link simply defines its appearance. Then to define the destination view, we can use a navigationDestination modifier that defines what to display when the user selects a navigation link.

To see how to use a List within a Navigation Stack, follow these steps:

1. Create a new SwiftUI iOS App project and give it any name you wish such as "NavigationStackList."

2. Click the ContentView file in the Navigator pane.

3. Add the following structure under the import SwiftUI line like this:

    ```
    struct Books: Identifiable, Hashable {
        var id = UUID()
        var title: String
        var summary: String
    }
    ```

    Notice that this structure needs to be Identifiable to create a unique ID, and it must be Hashable so it can be used in the .navigationDestination modifier that will define the view to open after the user selects a navigation link.

415

4. Add an array of structures underneath the struct ContentView:
    View line like this:

```
let books: [Books] = [
    Books(title: "Fahrenheit 451", summary: "Dystopian novel about
    book burning"),
    Books(title: "The Martian Chronicles", summary: "Tales about
    the colonization of Mars"),
    Books(title: "Something Wicked This Way Comes", summary: "A
    sinister circus comes to town"),
    Books(title: "The Illustrated Man", summary: "Short stories
    revolving around a tattooed man")
]
```

5. Add the following structure above the struct
    ContentView_Previews: PreviewProvider line like this:

```
struct BookView: View {
    var bookInfo: Books
    var body: some View {
        VStack (spacing: 24) {
            Text("\(bookInfo.title)")
                .font(.largeTitle)
            Text("\(bookInfo.summary)")
                .font(.body)
        }
    }
}
```

This structure defines the view (user interface) that appears after
the user selects a navigation link. It needs to retrieve data from the
previously defined Books structure. Then it retrieves the title and
summary to display within two Text views inside of a VStack.

6. Add a NavigationStack, List, and NavigationLink inside the var body: some View like this:

```
var body: some View {
    NavigationStack {
        List(books) { book in
            NavigationLink("\(book.title)", value: book)
        }.navigationTitle(Text("Book List"))
        .navigationDestination(for: Books.self) { x in
            BookView(bookInfo: x)
        }
    }
}
```

The List retrieves the books array. Then it creates an arbitrarily named variable called "book" that it uses to display the book.title as a navigation link. Notice that the navigation link also defines a value (book), which is unique to each navigation link displayed.

The entire ContentView file should look like this:

```
import SwiftUI

struct Books: Identifiable, Hashable {
    var id = UUID()
    var title: String
    var summary: String
}

struct ContentView: View {

    let books: [Books] = [
        Books(title: "Fahrenheit 451", summary: "Dystopian novel
        about book burning"),
        Books(title: "The Martian Chronicles", summary: "Tales
        about the colonization of Mars"),
        Books(title: "Something Wicked This Way Comes", summary:
        "A sinister circus comes to town"),
```

```
            Books(title: "The Illustrated Man", summary: "Short
            stories revolving around a tattooed man")
        ]
    var body: some View {
        NavigationStack {
            List(books) { book in
                NavigationLink("\(book.title)", value: book)
            }.navigationTitle(Text("Book List"))
            .navigationDestination(for: Books.self) { x in
                BookView(bookInfo: x)
            }
        }
    }
}

struct BookView: View {
    var bookInfo: Books
    var body: some View {
        VStack (spacing: 24) {
            Text("\(bookInfo.title)")
                .font(.largeTitle)
            Text("\(bookInfo.summary)")
                .font(.body)
        }
    }
}

struct ContentView_Previews: PreviewProvider {
    static var previews: some View {
        ContentView()
    }
}
```

7. Click the Live icon in the Canvas pane. Notice that the List displays book titles as navigation links as shown in Figure 17-5.

Book List
Fahrenheit 451
The Martian Chronicles
Something Wicked This Way Comes
The Illustrated Man

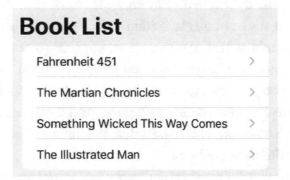

Figure 17-5. *A List of navigation links*

8. Click any book title (navigation link). The user interface defined by the struct BookView appears with a Back button in the upper-left corner as shown in Figure 17-6.

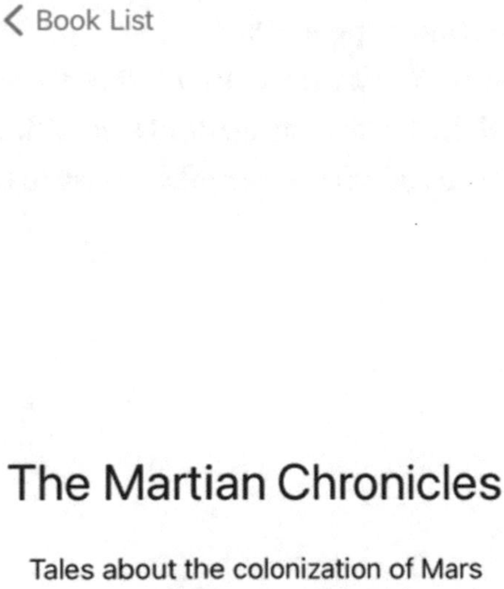

Book List
The Martian Chronicles
Tales about the colonization of Mars

Figure 17-6. *The user interface that appears after selecting a navigation link*

Lists can be a convenient way to create navigation links within a Navigation Stack. Since lists typically rely on arrays for data, you'll likely need to create a structure to store in an array.

Summary

A Navigation Stack is a handy way to display multiple views. One structure defines a Navigation Stack with one or more NavigationLinks. These NavigationLinks open views that can be as simple as Text or Image views, but more often are views defined by structures. These structures can be stored in the same file or in a separate file.

A NavigationLink can pass data to another view, much like passing data to a function. This other view needs to define a property, and then the NavigationLink can pass data to that property. If you want to pass data to another view that can modify the data, you can use two different methods.

The first method uses @State and @Binding variables and forces the NavigationLink to pass data to each view that it opens. The second method uses ObservableObjects, StateObjects, and EnvironmentObjects to share data among multiple views.

Navigation stacks are often used with lists. By tapping an item in a List, users can jump to a new view. Lists typically retrieve data stored in an array. That array can store individual data types like strings, but more often the array stores structures to group related data together. Items in a List can naturally create navigation links to another view such as items found in the Settings app in iOS.

When creating a Navigation Stack with a List, it's often easier to use navigation links to define the link and then use the .navigationDestination modifier to define the destination view to display. Navigation stacks make it easy to display successive screens of data.

CHAPTER 18

Using the Tab View

Most apps consist of multiple screens. Chapter 17 explained how to create apps that use a Navigation Stack that lets users jump from one screen to another in sequential order. This can be handy for showing more details such as the Settings app in iOS that lets you pick various options and then view multiple screens to choose different settings.

However, one problem with the Navigation Stack is that if you link too many screens together, navigation becomes cumbersome since you must navigate from the first screen to the second to the third just to get to the fourth screen. Then you have to reverse the entire process to get back from the fourth screen to the first screen.

To provide an alternate way of jumping from one screen to another, you can use the Tab View, which displays icons and/or text at the bottom of the screen. Selecting a tab (icon and/or text) then jumps to a new screen. For example, the Clock app displays icons/text at the bottom of the screen to let you jump to different features as shown in Figure 18-1.

© Wallace Wang 2023
W. Wang, *Beginning iPhone Development with SwiftUI*, https://doi.org/10.1007/978-1-4842-9541-0_18

Figure 18-1. *A Tab View makes it easy to jump from one screen to another*

Since the tab bar appears at the bottom of the screen no matter which screen you're viewing, tab views make it easy to jump to the screen you want to see at any time.

Using a Tab View

A Tab View contains multiple views using code like this:

```
TabView {
    // Put multiple views here
}
```

Each view stored within a Tab View can be as simple as an individual view (such as a Text or Image view) or more detailed such as a structure that defines a view. The first part of creating a Tab View is simply listing all the views you want to use within the Tab View like this:

```
TabView {
    Text("One")
    Text("Two")
    Text("Three")
    Text("Four")
}
```

After you've defined the views to display within a Tab View, the next step is to define an icon and/or text to represent each view. To do this, add a .tabItem modifier to each view that uses an Image and a Text view like this:

```
Text("One")
    .tabItem {
        Image(systemName: "heart.fill")
        Text("Tab1")
    }
```

By attaching a .tabItem modifier to each view and using an Image and a Text view to define its contents, you can create a tab bar that appears at the bottom of the screen as shown in Figure 18-2.

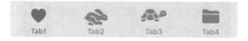

Figure 18-2. *A typical tab bar displays icons and text*

The Image view can display any image but typically displays an icon that you can view inside of the SF Symbols app (https://developer.apple.com/sf-symbols).

Note   Tabs can appear as an image and text, just an image, or just text. For clarity, it's usually best to define a tab as both an image and text.

To see how to create a simple Tab View, follow these steps:

1. Create a new SwiftUI iOS App project and give it any name you wish such as "TabViewSimple."

2. Click the ContentView file in the Navigator pane.

3. Add the following views inside the var body: some View like this:

```
var body: some View {
    TabView {
        Text("One")
        Text("Two")
        Text("Three")
        Text("Four")
    }

}
```

To create a tab bar at the bottom of the screen, we need to add the .tabItem modifier that uses an Image and a Text view.

4. Add the following .tabItem modifiers to each view like this:

```
var body: some View {
    TabView {
        Text("One")
            .tabItem {
                Image(systemName: "heart.fill")
                Text("One")
            }
        Text("Two")
            .tabItem {
                Image(systemName: "hare.fill")
                Text("Two")
            }
        Text("Three")
            .tabItem {
                Image(systemName: "tortoise.fill")
                Text("Three")
```

```
                }
        Text("Four")
            .tabItem {
                Image(systemName: "folder.fill")
                Text("Four")
            }
    }
}
```

Feel free to use different SF Symbol icons and text to customize the buttons in the tab bar at the bottom of the screen. Rather than use a combination of an Image and a Text view, you can also use a single Label view like this:

```
Label("Four", systemImage: "folder.fill")
```

5. Click the Live icon in the Canvas pane.

6. Click the different tabs at the bottom of the screen to see the different views.

Note   Since a Tab View represents each view as an icon/text, tab views can only display a maximum of five (5) items at the bottom of the screen. If you store more than five views in a Tab View, the Tab View automatically creates a More icon that hides any additional views in a second tab bar.

To see how a Tab View automatically creates a More button in the tab bar if you display more than five views in the Tab View, follow these steps:

1. Open the previous Xcode project ("TabViewSimple") that you created earlier.

2. Edit the ContentView file so the entire code looks like this:

```
import SwiftUI

struct ContentView: View {
    var body: some View {
        TabView {
```

```
            Text("One")
                .tabItem {
                    Image(systemName: "heart.fill")
                    Text("One")
                }
            Text("Two")
                .tabItem {
                    Image(systemName: "hare.fill")
                    Text("Two")
                }
            Text("Three")
                .tabItem {
                    Image(systemName: "tortoise.fill")
                    Text("Three")
                }
            Text("Four")
                .tabItem {
                    Image(systemName: "folder.fill")
                    Text("Four")
                }
            Text("Five")
                .tabItem {
                    Image(systemName: "internaldrive.fill")
                    Text("Five")
                }
            Text("Six")
                .tabItem {
                    Image(systemName: "cloud.drizzle.fill")
                    Text("Six")
                }
        }.accentColor(.purple)
    }
}
```

```
struct ContentView_Previews: PreviewProvider {
    static var previews: some View {
        ContentView()
    }
}
```

Notice that the .accentColor modifier on the Tab View lets you define a color for the tab bar.

3. Click the Live icon in the Canvas pane. The tab bar appears, but now a More icon appears on the far right as shown in Figure 18-3.

Figure 18-3. *The More icon automatically appears when a Tab View contains more than five tabs*

4. Click the More icon. Notice that a Navigation Stack appears, listing your additional tabs in a list as shown in Figure 18-4.

Figure 18-4. *The More icon displays a Navigation Stack*

5.   Click the Five or Six item in the Navigation Stack to see that
particular Text view.

Because the tab bar can only show a maximum of five icons, it's best to limit the
number of options to five or fewer.

Selecting Buttons Programmatically in a Tab Bar

To select a different view, users can simply select a tab in the tab bar. By default, the first
tab on the far left appears highlighted. However, sometimes you may want to select a tab
through code. In that case, you need to identify each .tabItem using the .tag modifier.

The .tag modifier lets you identify each tab with a fixed value such as 2. When each .tabItem has a unique .tag value, then you can use Swift code to choose a particular tab by referencing its .tag value.

To see how to access tabs in a Tab View through Swift code, follow these steps:

1. Create a new SwiftUI iOS App project and give it any name you wish such as "TabViewTag."

2. Click the ContentView file in the Navigator pane.

3. Add a State variable under the struct ContentView: View line like this:

```swift
struct ContentView: View {
    @State var selectedView = 1
```

4. Add a VStack and an HStack under the var body: some View line, and add four Buttons inside the HStack like this:

```swift
var body: some View {
    VStack {
        HStack {
            Button ("1") {
                selectedView = 1
            }
            Button ("2") {
                selectedView = 2
            }
            Button ("3") {
                selectedView = 3
            }
            Button ("4") {
                selectedView = 4
            }
        }
    }
}
```

5. Add a Tab View inside the VStack and underneath the HStack
    like this:

```
TabView (selection: $selectedView){
    Text("One")
        .tabItem {
            Image(systemName: "heart.fill")
            Text("One")
        }.tag(1)
    Text("Two")
        .tabItem {
            Image(systemName: "hare.fill")
            Text("Two")
        }.tag(2)
    Text("Three")
        .tabItem {
            Image(systemName: "tortoise.fill")
            Text("Three")
        }.tag(3)
    Text("Four")
        .tabItem {
            Image(systemName: "folder.fill")
            Text("Four")
        }.tag(4)
}
```

The entire ContentView file should look like this:

```
import SwiftUI

struct ContentView: View {
    @State var selectedView = 1
    var body: some View {
        VStack {
            HStack {
                Button ("1") {
                    selectedView = 1
                }
```

```
        Button ("2") {
            selectedView = 2
        }
        Button ("3") {
            selectedView = 3
        }
        Button ("4") {
            selectedView = 4
        }
    }
    TabView (selection: $selectedView){
        Text("One")
            .tabItem {
                Image(systemName: "heart.fill")
                Text("One")
            }.tag(1)
        Text("Two")
            .tabItem {
                Image(systemName: "hare.fill")
                Text("Two")
            }.tag(2)
        Text("Three")
            .tabItem {
                Image(systemName: "tortoise.fill")
                Text("Three")
            }.tag(3)
        Text("Four")
            .tabItem {
                Image(systemName: "folder.fill")
                Text("Four")
            }.tag(4)
    }
  }
 }
}
```

```
struct ContentView_Previews: PreviewProvider {
    static var previews: some View {
        ContentView()
    }
}
```

This code creates a Tab View and four Buttons at the top of the screen labeled 1, 2, 3, and 4.

6.   Click the Live icon in the Canvas pane.

7.   Click the numbered Buttons at the top of the screen. Notice that if you click the 2 Button, the second tab in the tab bar gets selected. If you click the 4 button, the fourth tab in the tab bar gets selected. The .tag modifier gives you a way to access a specific tab through Swift code.

Displaying a Page View

Normally a Tab View displays tabs at the bottom of the screen so users can select a tab and jump to a different view. As an alternative, you can turn a Tab View into a Page View. A Page View displays tab bar icons at the bottom middle of the screen that represent different screens. Then the user can scroll right and left to view each screen in sequential order.

To turn a Tab View into a Page View, just add the .tabViewStyle modifier to a Tab View and specify .page like this:

```
TabView {

}.tabViewStyle(.page)
```

Now instead of selecting a tab from the bottom of the screen to open a view, users can scroll left and right to open each view in sequential order. To provide a visual map of how many views are available, you can add the .indexViewStyle modifier and specify .always for the backgroundDisplayMode like this:

```
TabView {

}.tabViewStyle(.page)
 .indexViewStyle(PageIndexViewStyle(backgroundDisplayMode: .always))
```

To see how to a Page View works, follow these steps:

1. Create a new SwiftUI iOS App project and give it any name you
   wish such as "PageView."

2. Click the ContentView file in the Navigator pane.

3. Add a Tab View inside the var body: some View line like this:

```
TabView {
    Text("One")
        .tabItem {
            Image(systemName: "heart.fill")
        }
    Text("Two")
        .tabItem {
            Image(systemName: "hare.fill")
        }
    Text("Three")
        .tabItem {
            Image(systemName: "tortoise.fill")
        }
    Text("Four")
        .tabItem {
            Image(systemName: "folder.fill")
        }
    Text("Five")
        .tabItem {
            Image(systemName: "tray.fill")
        }
    Text("Six")
        .tabItem {
            Image(systemName: "keyboard.fill")
        }
}
```

433

Feel free to choose different text for each Text view and different SF Symbol icons for each Image view. Notice that you only need to add an Image view and do not need a Text view for each .tabItem.

4.   Add a .tabViewStyle and an .indexViewStyle modifier to the Tab View like this:

```
TabView {
    Text("One")
        .tabItem {
            Image(systemName: "heart.fill")
        }
    Text("Two")
        .tabItem {
            Image(systemName: "hare.fill")
        }
    Text("Three")
        .tabItem {
            Image(systemName: "tortoise.fill")
        }
    Text("Four")
        .tabItem {
            Image(systemName: "folder.fill")
        }
    Text("Five")
        .tabItem {
            Image(systemName: "tray.fill")
        }
    Text("Six")
        .tabItem {
            Image(systemName: "keyboard.fill")
        }
}.tabViewStyle(.page)
.indexViewStyle(PageIndexViewStyle(backgroundDisplayMode:
.always))
```

This displays each Image as a list of icons in the bottom middle of the screen as shown in Figure 18-5.

Figure 18-5. *The icon bar at the bottom of a Page View*

The entire ContentView file should look like this:

```swift
import SwiftUI

struct ContentView: View {
    var body: some View {
        TabView {
            Text("One")
                .tabItem {
                    Image(systemName: "heart.fill")
                }
            Text("Two")
                .tabItem {
                    Image(systemName: "hare.fill")
                }
            Text("Three")
                .tabItem {
                    Image(systemName: "tortoise.fill")
                }
            Text("Four")
                .tabItem {
                    Image(systemName: "folder.fill")
                }
            Text("Five")
                .tabItem {
                    Image(systemName: "tray.fill")
                }
            Text("Six")
                .tabItem {
                    Image(systemName: "keyboard.fill")
                }
```

```
                    }
            }.tabViewStyle(.page)
            .indexViewStyle(PageIndexViewStyle(backgroundDisplayMode:
            .always))
        }
    }

    struct ContentView_Previews: PreviewProvider {
        static var previews: some View {
            ContentView()
        }
    }
```

5.   Click the Live icon in the Canvas pane.

6.   Drag the mouse from right to left (and left to right) to swipe from one view to the next. Notice that each time you do this, a different icon at the bottom of the screen appears highlighted to let you know which view you're currently on and how many additional views may be before and after the currently displayed view.

Displaying Structures in a Tab View

While a Tab View can display a single view like a Text or Image view, many times you may want to display a new user interface altogether. Since you can define a user interface screen with a structure, you can create multiple screens using multiple structures that can appear within a Tab View.

The simplest way to create a new structure is within the ContentView file. However, this can clutter the code, so a second way is to store the structure in a separate file.

To see how to create structures that define another user interface screen, follow these steps:

1.   Create a new SwiftUI iOS App project and give it any name you wish such as "TabViewStructures."

2.   Click the ContentView file in the Navigator pane.

3. Add a TabView inside the var body: some View line like this:

```
var body: some View {
    TabView {

    }
}
```

4. Add the following inside the TabView like this:

```
var body: some View {
    TabView {
        FileView()
            .tabItem {
                Image(systemName: "heart.fill")
                Text("First")
            }
        SeparateFileView()
            .tabItem {
                Image(systemName: "hare.fill")
                Text("Second")
            }
    }
}
```

The preceding code displays two views called FileView() and SeparateFileView(), which we'll need to define using a structure.

5. Add the following structure underneath the entire struct ContentView: View structure like this:

```
struct FileView: View {
    var body: some View {
        HStack {
            Spacer()
            VStack {
                Spacer()
                Text("This is a separate structure")
                Text("that's stored in the same file")
```

```
                      Spacer()
                }
                Spacer()
           }.background(Color.yellow)
      }
}
```

The entire ContentView file should look like this:

```
import SwiftUI

struct ContentView: View {
    var body: some View {
        TabView {
            FileView()
                .tabItem {
                    Image(systemName: "heart.fill")
                    Text("First")
                }
            SeparateFileView()
                .tabItem {
                    Image(systemName: "hare.fill")
                    Text("Second")
                }
        }
    }
}

struct FileView: View {
    var body: some View {
        HStack {
            Spacer()
            VStack {
                Spacer()
                Text("This is a separate structure")
                Text("that's stored in the same file")
                Spacer()
            }
```

```
            Spacer()
        }.background(Color.yellow)
    }
}

struct ContentView_Previews: PreviewProvider {
    static var previews: some View {
        ContentView()
    }
}
```

We can keep adding new structures inside the ContentView file, but this risks cluttering up the file. A second way to create structures is to store them in a separate file, which the next steps will let us do.

6. Choose File ➤ New ➤ File. A dialog appears.

7. Click iOS near the top of the dialog, click Swift File, and then click Next. Xcode asks for a name to give your newly created file.

8. Type SeparateFile and click Create. Xcode creates a new Swift file.

9. Delete all code currently in the SeparateFile and replace it with the following:

```
import SwiftUI

struct SeparateFileView: View {
    var body: some View {
        HStack {
            Spacer()
            VStack {
                Spacer()
                Text("This is another structure")
                Text("but stored in a separate file")
                Spacer()
            }
            Spacer()
```

```
            }.background(Color.orange)
        }
    }

    struct SeparateFileView_Previews: PreviewProvider {
        static var previews: some View {
            SeparateFileView()
        }
    }
```

Note   When storing a structure in a separate file, you need a second structure (PreviewProvider) to display the user interface in the Canvas pane.

---

10.   Click the ContentView file in the Navigator pane.

11.   Click the Live icon in the Canvas pane. Notice that the FileView structure appears because the First icon in the tab bar is selected by default.

12.   Click the Second icon in the tab bar. Notice that this displays the SeparateFileView structure defined in the SeparateFile.

It's far more common to display views defined by a structure within a Tab View. You can store structures that define a view in the same file or in separate files.

Passing Data Between Structures in a Tab View

The previous project created two structures where one structure was stored in the ContentView file and a second structure was stored in a separate file. In both cases, the structures defined user interfaces that displayed static information unconnected to anything from the original structure (ContentView).

In many cases, you may want data from one structure to appear in a second structure. That means we must pass data from one structure to another.

Fortunately, this task is similar to passing data between functions. When a structure needs to receive data, we just need to declare a property by creating a variable, giving that variable a descriptive name, and defining the data type that variable can hold such as String or Double like this:

```
struct FileView: View {
    var choice: String
```

This defines a variable called "choice" that can hold a String. To pass data to this structure, we can load this structure by calling the structure name (FileView) followed by this "choice" variable as a parameter like this:

```
FileView(choice: "Heads")
```

When passing data to a structure stored in the same file, we just need to follow this two-step process:

- Declare one or more variables inside the structure to receive data.

- Call that structure using its variables as parameters.

However, when passing data to a structure stored in a separate file, there's an additional step necessary. Because a structure stored in a separate file also contains a second structure that displays the user interface in the Canvas pane, this preview structure must include the structure's parameter and pass it data as well like this:

```
struct SeparateFileView_Previews: PreviewProvider {
    static var previews: some View {
        SeparateFileView(passedData: "")
    }
}
```

To see how to pass data between structures in a Tab View, follow these steps:

1. Create a new SwiftUI iOS App project and give it any name you wish such as "TabViewPassData."

2. Click the ContentView file in the Navigator pane.

3. Edit the struct ContentView structure like this:

```
struct ContentView: View {
    @State var message = ""
    var body: some View {
        TabView {
            TextField("Type here", text: $message)
                .tabItem {
                    Image(systemName: "house.fill")
                    Text("Home")
                }
            FileView(choice: message)
                .tabItem {
                    Image(systemName: "heart.fill")
                    Text("First")
                }
            SeparateFileView(passedData: message)
                .tabItem {
                    Image(systemName: "hare.fill")
                    Text("Second")
                }
        }
    }
}
```

The preceding code defines a structure called FileView with
a parameter of "choice:" that gets passed the State variable
"message". The second structure is called SeparateFileView with
a parameter of "passedData:" that gets passed the State variable
"message" as well.

4.   Add a new structure underneath the struct ContentView like this:

```
struct FileView: View {
    var choice: String
    var body: some View {
        HStack {
            Spacer()
            VStack {
                Spacer()
                Text("You typed = \(choice)")
                Spacer()
            }
            Spacer()
        }.background(Color.yellow)
    }
}
```

This FileView structure declares a "choice" variable that can hold a String. Then it displays this "choice" variable in a Text view that shows "You typed = ". The entire ContentView file should look like this:

```
import SwiftUI

struct ContentView: View {
    @State var message = ""
    var body: some View {
        TabView {
            TextField("Type here", text: $message)
                .tabItem {
                    Image(systemName: "house.fill")
                    Text("Home")
                }
            FileView(choice: message)
                .tabItem {
                    Image(systemName: "heart.fill")
                    Text("First")
                }
```

```
                SeparateFileView(passedData: message)
                    .tabItem {
                        Image(systemName: "hare.fill")
                        Text("Second")
                    }
            }
        }
    }
}

struct FileView: View {
    var choice: String
    var body: some View {
        HStack {
            Spacer()
            VStack {
                Spacer()
                Text("You typed = \(choice)")
                Spacer()
            }
            Spacer()
        }.background(Color.yellow)
    }
}

struct ContentView_Previews: PreviewProvider {
    static var previews: some View {
        ContentView()
    }
}
```

This code creates a structure called FileView, but now we need to create a second structure called SeparateFileView that declares a passedData String variable.

5. Choose File ➤ New ➤ File. A dialog appears.

6. Click iOS near the top of the dialog, click Swift File, and then click Next. Xcode asks for a name to give your newly created file.

7. Type SeparateFile and click Create. Xcode creates a new Swift file.

8. Delete all code currently in the SeparateFile and replace it with the following:

```swift
import SwiftUI

struct SeparateFileView: View {
    var passedData: String
    var body: some View {
        HStack {
            Spacer()
            VStack {
                Spacer()
                Text("String from text field = \(passedData)")
                Spacer()
            }
            Spacer()
        }.background(Color.orange)
    }
}

struct SeparateFileView_Previews: PreviewProvider {
    static var previews: some View {
        SeparateFileView(passedData: "")
    }
}
```

This file creates a SeparateFileView structure that declares a passedData String variable. Because this SeparateFileView structure is stored in a separate file, it contains a struct PreviewProvider where we must use the passedData parameter as well.

9. Click ContentView in the Navigator pane to return to the ContentView structure.

10. Click the Live icon in the Canvas pane. The TextField appears.

11. Click in the TextField and type a word or short phrase.

12. Click the Heart icon in the tab bar. This passes the string that you typed in the TextField and displays it in the FileView structure.

13. Click the Hare icon in the tab bar. This passes the string that you typed in the TextField and displays it in the SeparateFileView structure.

Changing Data Between Structures in a Tab View

The previous project created two structures where one structure was stored in the ContentView file and a second structure was stored in a separate file. In both cases, the structures defined user interfaces that received data and displayed it.

What if we pass data to a structure and then allow that structure to modify that data? This will require several changes:

- Create a State variable.

- Open another structure and pass that structure a binding to the State variable (using the $ symbol) such as

    ```
    FileView(choice: $message)
    ```

- Define a @Binding variable in the structure that will receive data.

- Change that Binding variable in the structure that received data.

To see how to change data between structures in a Tab View, follow these steps:

1. Create a new SwiftUI iOS App project and give it any name you wish such as "TabViewBindingData."

2. Click the ContentView file in the Navigator pane.

3. Create a State variable under the struct ContentView: View line like this:

    ```
    struct ContentView: View {
        @State var message = ""
    ```

4. Add a TabView inside the var body: some View line like this:

```
var body: some View {
    TabView {
        TextField("Type here", text: $message)
            .tabItem {
                Image(systemName: "house.fill")
                Text("Home")
            }
        FileView(choice: $message)
            .tabItem {
                Image(systemName: "heart.fill")
                Text("First")
            }
        SeparateFileView(passedData: $message)
            .tabItem {
                Image(systemName: "hare.fill")
                Text("Second")
            }
    }
}
```

Notice that the FileView sends a binding variable ($message)
to the "choice:" parameter. The second structure called
SeparateFileView sends the same binding variable ($message) to
the "passedData" parameter.

5. Add the following structure underneath the struct ContentView:
    View structure:

```
struct FileView: View {
    @Binding var choice: String

    var body: some View {
        HStack {
            Spacer()
            VStack {
                Spacer()
                TextField("Type here:", text: $choice)
```

```
                    Spacer()
                }
                Spacer()
        }.background(Color.yellow)
    }
}
```

Notice that this structure declares a @Binding variable called "choice" that can hold a String. This structure uses a TextField to change this @Binding variable ($choice), which sends the changes automatically back to the ContentView structure.

The entire ContentView file should look like this:

```
import SwiftUI

struct ContentView: View {
    @State var message = ""
    var body: some View {
        TabView {
            TextField("Type here", text: $message)
                .tabItem {
                    Image(systemName: "house.fill")
                    Text("Home")
                }
            FileView(choice: $message)
                .tabItem {
                    Image(systemName: "heart.fill")
                    Text("First")
                }
            SeparateFileView(passedData: $message)
                .tabItem {
                    Image(systemName: "hare.fill")
                    Text("Second")
                }
        }
    }
}
```

```
struct FileView: View {
    @Binding var choice: String

    var body: some View {
        HStack {
            Spacer()
            VStack {
                Spacer()
                TextField("Type here:", text: $choice)
                Spacer()
            }
            Spacer()
        }.background(Color.yellow)
    }
}

struct ContentView_Previews: PreviewProvider {
    static var previews: some View {
        ContentView()
    }
}
```

6. Choose File ➤ New ➤ File. A dialog appears.

7. Click iOS near the top of the dialog, click Swift File, and then click Next. Xcode asks for a name to give your newly created file.

8. Type SeparateFile and click Create. Xcode creates a new Swift file.

9. Delete all code currently in the SeparateFile and replace it with the following:

```
import SwiftUI

struct SeparateFileView: View {
    @Binding var passedData: String

    var body: some View {
        HStack {
            Spacer()
```

```
            VStack {
                Spacer()
                TextField("Type here", text: $passedData)
                Spacer()
            }
            Spacer()
        }.background(Color.orange)
    }
}

struct SeparateFileView_Previews: PreviewProvider {

    static var previews: some View {
        SeparateFileView(passedData: .constant(""))
    }
}
```

Notice that this structure declares a @Binding variable called "passedData" that can hold a String. The TextField can change this variable ($passedData) and automatically send the changes back to the ContentView structure.

Also note that because this structure is stored in a separate file, the PreviewProvider structure must also include the "passedData" parameter by giving it a .constant("").

10. Click the ContentView file in the Navigator pane.

11. Click the Live icon in the Canvas pane.

12. Click in the TextField and type a phrase.

13. Click the Heart icon to pass the string to the FileView structure stored in the ContentView file.

14. Click in the TextField displayed by the FileView structure and edit the data. Then click the Home tab to return to the ContentView structure that displays the modified data.

15. Edit this data.

16. Click the Hare tab that passes the string to the SeparateFileView structure stored in a separate file. Notice that your edited data now appears in the SeparateFileView structure.

17. Click in the TextField displayed by the SeparateFileView structure and edit the data. Then click the Home tab to return to the ContentView structure that displays the modified data.

Sharing Data Between Structures in a Tab View

Using @State and @Binding variables lets multiple views share and modify data. However, SwiftUI offers another way to share data between structures. First, create an ObservableObject class that contains one or more variables to share. Each variable must be marked as @Published like this:

```
class ShareString: ObservableObject {
    @Published var message = ""
}
```

The structure that contains the Tab View (such as ContentView) needs to define a @StateObject variable that defines an object from the ObservableObject class like this:

```
@StateObject var showMe = ShareString()
```

Since we want to share this ObservableObject between all views within the Tab View, we need to add the .environmentObject modifier to the TabView along with the StateObject to share like this:

```
        TabView {

        }.environmentObject(showMe)
```

Within each structure that needs to access the ObservableObject, we need to declare an @EnvironmentObject variable that uses the ObservableObject class like this:

```
@EnvironmentObject var choice: ShareString
```

Finally, within each structure that defines an @EnvironmentObject, we can access the actual data to share by using the @EnvironmentObject name plus the @Published property name to share like this:

```
$choice.message
```

In this case, "choice" is the @EnvironmentObject name, and "message" is the @Published property defined within the ObservableObject. To see how to share data using an ObservableObject, follow these steps:

1. Create a new SwiftUI iOS App project and give it any name you wish such as "TabViewObservable."

2. Click the ContentView file in the Navigator pane.

3. Create an ObservableObject class under the import SwiftUI line like this:

```
class ShareString: ObservableObject {
    @Published var message = ""
}
```

The @Published variable will contain the data to share between structures within the Tab View.

4. Create a StateObject variable under the struct ContentView: View line like this:

```
struct ContentView: View {
    @StateObject var showMe = ShareString()
```

This creates a new object (showMe) based on the ShareString ObservableObject.

5. Add a TabView inside the var body: some View line like this:

```
var body: some View {
    TabView {
        TextField("Type here", text: $showMe.message)
            .tabItem {
                Image(systemName: "house.fill")
                Text("Home")
```

```
            }
        FileView()
            .tabItem {
                Image(systemName: "heart.fill")
                Text("First")
            }
        SeparateFileView()
            .tabItem {
                Image(systemName: "hare.fill")
                Text("Second")
            }
    }.environmentObject(showMe)
}
```

Make sure you add the .environmentObject(showMe) modifier
at the end of the TabView. This allows sharing of the showMe
ObservableObject ShareString class. The preceding TabView
opens structures called FileView and SeparateFileView that we
need to create.

6. Add the following structure underneath the struct ContentView
   structure like this:

```
struct FileView: View {
    @EnvironmentObject var choice: ShareString

    var body: some View {
        HStack {
            Spacer()
            VStack {
                Spacer()
                TextField("Type here:", text: $choice.message)
                Spacer()
            }
            Spacer()
        }.background(Color.yellow)
    }
}
```

Notice that this structure defines an @EnvironmentObject variable that can hold a ShareString ObservableObject. In the TextField, we must store the text in the "choice" @EnvironmentObject that uses the "message" @Published property ($choice.message). The entire ContentView file should look like this:

```swift
import SwiftUI

class ShareString: ObservableObject {
    @Published var message = ""
}

struct ContentView: View {
    @StateObject var showMe = ShareString()

    var body: some View {
        TabView {
            TextField("Type here", text: $showMe.message)
                .tabItem {
                    Image(systemName: "house.fill")
                    Text("Home")
                }
            FileView()
                .tabItem {
                    Image(systemName: "heart.fill")
                    Text("First")
                }
            SeparateFileView()
                .tabItem {
                    Image(systemName: "hare.fill")
                    Text("Second")
                }
        }.environmentObject(showMe)
    }
}

struct FileView: View {
```

```
    @EnvironmentObject var choice: ShareString

    var body: some View {
        HStack {
            Spacer()
            VStack {
                Spacer()
                TextField("Type here:", text: $choice.message)
                Spacer()
            }
            Spacer()
        }.background(Color.yellow)
    }
}

struct ContentView_Previews: PreviewProvider {
    static var previews: some View {
        ContentView()
    }
}
```

7. Choose File ➤ New ➤ File. A dialog appears.

8. Click iOS near the top of the dialog, click Swift File, and then click Next. Xcode asks for a name to give your newly created file.

9. Type SeparateFile and click Create. Xcode creates a new Swift file.

10. Delete all code currently in the SeparateFile and replace it with the following:

```
import SwiftUI

struct SeparateFileView: View {
    @EnvironmentObject var passedData: ShareString

    var body: some View {
        HStack {
            Spacer()
            VStack {
```

```
                    Spacer()
                    TextField("Type here", text: $passedData.message)
                    Spacer()
                }
                Spacer()
            }.background(Color.orange)
        }
    }
}

struct SeparateFileView_Previews: PreviewProvider {
    static var previews: some View {
        SeparateFileView()
    }
}
```

Notice that this structure also declares an @EnvironmentObject
that can hold a ShareString ObservableObject. Then the TextField
uses the "passedData" @EnvironmentObject to access the
"message" @Published property ($passedData.message).

11. Click the ContentView file in the Navigator pane.

12. Click the Live icon in the Canvas pane.

13. Click in the TextField and type a phrase.

14. Click the Heart tab. Notice that what you typed in step 13 now
     appears in the FileView TextField.

15. Edit the text in the TextField and then click the Home tab. Notice
     that the modified text now appears in the ContentView TextField.

16. Edit the text in the TextField and then click the Hare tab. The
     edited text now appears in the SeparateFileView TextField.

17. Edit the text in the TextField and click the Home tab. Notice that
     the modified text now appears in the ContentView TextField. All
     this shows how the various structures can access the @Published
     property in the ObservableObject.

Summary

A Tab View offers another way to display multiple views where each view can be represented by a tab at the bottom of the screen. Tab views can open views as simple as Text or Image views, but more often use views defined by structures. These structures can be stored in the same file or in a separate file.

A Tab View can pass data to another view, much like passing data to a function. This other view needs to define a property, and then the Tab View can pass data to that property. If you want to pass data to another view that can modify the data, you can use two different methods.

The first method uses @State and @Binding variables and forces the Tab View to pass data to each view that it opens. The second method uses ObservableObjects, StateObjects, and EnvironmentObjects to share data among multiple views.

Tab views can display a maximum of five tabs at the bottom of the screen. If you define more than five tabs, SwiftUI automatically creates a More tab and displays all additional tabs in a Navigation Stack.

Since tab views can only display five tabs at the bottom of the screen, you can turn a Tab View into a Page View. That way you can display more than five icons at the bottom of the screen. Unlike a Tab View, a Page View forces users to navigate between screens sequentially. Tab Views are convenient any time users need to jump to a different screen on your app's user interface.

CHAPTER 19

Using Grids

A Text view is fine for displaying strings, and an Image view is perfect for displaying graphics. However, what if you want to display multiple chunks of data on the screen? That's when you can use a grid that can display data in rows (horizontally) or columns (vertically) as shown in Figure 19-1.

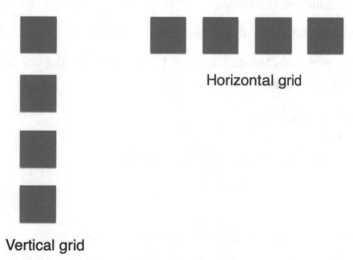

Figure 19-1. *Grids can display data horizontally or vertically*

Creating a grid requires three items:

- The data you want to display

- An array of GridItem that defines how to arrange data in a grid

- A LazyVGrid or LazyHGrid that places your data in the array of GridItem

The term "Lazy" refers to the way the grid loads data. If a grid needs to display 1000 items, it could load all 1000 items in memory even though most of those items can't be shown on the screen. Since this wastes memory, "Lazy" grids only load those items

© Wallace Wang 2023
W. Wang, *Beginning iPhone Development with SwiftUI*, https://doi.org/10.1007/978-1-4842-9541-0_19

that need to be displayed. The moment the user scrolls to view more data, the Lazy grid immediately loads those items. By waiting until the last second to load data, Lazy grids use far less memory and allow an app to run more efficiently at the slight tradeoff of running slightly slower.

Note   Lazy grids are commonly embedded inside of a Scroll View to let users scroll to see more data stored in the grid.

To see how to create a simple horizonal and vertical grid, follow these steps:

1. Create a new SwiftUI iOS App project and give it any name you wish such as "GridSimple."

2. Click the ContentView file in the Navigator pane.

3. Add a VStack and create an array of GridItem inside the var body: some View like this:

```
var body: some View {
    VStack {
        let gridItems = [GridItem()]
    }
}
```

GridItem is a structure in SwiftUI that allows you to define the spacing between columns and rows. For now, we'll just use default values by leaving the GridItem parameter list empty.

4. Add a ScrollView and a LazyHGrid underneath the gridItems array like this:

```
ScrollView(Axis.Set.horizontal, showsIndicators: true, content: {
    LazyHGrid(rows: gridItems) {
        Image(systemName: "1.circle")
        Image(systemName: "2.circle")
        Image(systemName: "3.circle")
        Image(systemName: "4.circle")
        Image(systemName: "5.circle")
        Image(systemName: "6.circle")
```

```
        Image(systemName: "7.circle")
        Image(systemName: "8.circle")
        Image(systemName: "9.circle")
        Image(systemName: "10.circle")
    }.font(.largeTitle)
})
```

This code defines a horizontal Scroll View (Axis.Set.horizontal) with a LazyHGrid inside that displays a row of data. The LazyHGrid can hold a maximum of ten (10) views, so we fill it with ten Image views displaying a different number inside the circle. Since the circle icons are small, the .font(.largeTitle) modifier makes them larger and easier to see.

5. Add a second ScrollView with a LazyVGrid underneath the other Scroll View like this:

```
ScrollView(Axis.Set.vertical, showsIndicators: true, content: {
    LazyVGrid(columns: gridItems) {
        Image(systemName: "1.square")
        Image(systemName: "2.square")
        Image(systemName: "3.square")
        Image(systemName: "4.square")
        Image(systemName: "5.square")
        Image(systemName: "6.square")
        Image(systemName: "7.square")
        Image(systemName: "8.square")
        Image(systemName: "9.square")
        Image(systemName: "10.square")
    }.font(.largeTitle)
})
```

This code defines a vertical Scroll View (Axis.Set.vertical) with a LazyVGrid inside that displays a column of data. That data consists of ten Image views that display a different number inside of a square. The .font(.largeTitle) modifier makes these square icons larger and easier to see. The entire ContentView file should look like this:

```
import SwiftUI

struct ContentView: View {
    var body: some View {
        VStack {

            let gridItems = [GridItem()]

            ScrollView(Axis.Set.horizontal, showsIndicators: true,
            content: {
                LazyHGrid(rows: gridItems) {
                    Image(systemName: "1.circle")
                    Image(systemName: "2.circle")
                    Image(systemName: "3.circle")
                    Image(systemName: "4.circle")
                    Image(systemName: "5.circle")
                    Image(systemName: "6.circle")
                    Image(systemName: "7.circle")
                    Image(systemName: "8.circle")
                    Image(systemName: "9.circle")
                    Image(systemName: "10.circle")
                }.font(.largeTitle)
            })

            ScrollView(Axis.Set.vertical, showsIndicators: true,
            content: {
                LazyVGrid(columns: gridItems) {
                    Image(systemName: "1.square")
                    Image(systemName: "2.square")
                    Image(systemName: "3.square")
                    Image(systemName: "4.square")
                    Image(systemName: "5.square")
                    Image(systemName: "6.square")
                    Image(systemName: "7.square")
                    Image(systemName: "8.square")
                    Image(systemName: "9.square")
                    Image(systemName: "10.square")
```

```
            }.font(.largeTitle)
        })
    }
  }
}

struct ContentView_Previews: PreviewProvider {
    static var previews: some View {
        ContentView()
    }
}
```

6. Click the Live icon in the Canvas pane.

7. Scroll the horizontal grid left to right or right to left to see all the numbered circles as shown in Figure 19-2.

Figure 19-2. *Displaying a horizontal grid on top of a vertical grid*

8. Scroll the vertical grid up and down to see all the numbered squares.

Defining Multiple Rows/Columns

The previous project created a single row in the LazyHGrid and a single column in the LazyVGrid. These single row and column were defined by the array of GridItem like this:

```
let gridItems = [GridItem()]
```

If you want to create multiple rows or columns, just define the array with more than one GridItem like this:

```
let gridItems = [GridItem(),
                 GridItem()
]
```

This will create two rows in a LazyHGrid or two columns in a LazyVGrid. Each time you add an additional GridItem to the array, you increase the number of rows or columns in the grid.

To see how to change the number of rows or columns in a grid, follow these steps:

1. Make sure to load the previous project in Xcode ("GridSimple").

2. Edit the array as follows to define three rows in the LazyHGrid and three columns in the LazyVGrid:

```
let gridItems = [GridItem(),
                 GridItem(),
                 GridItem()
]
```

The entire ContentView file should look like this:

```
import SwiftUI

struct ContentView: View {
    var body: some View {
        VStack {

            let gridItems = [GridItem(),
                             GridItem(),
                             GridItem()
            ]
```

```
ScrollView(Axis.Set.horizontal, showsIndicators: true,
content: {
    LazyHGrid(rows: gridItems) {
        Image(systemName: "1.circle")
        Image(systemName: "2.circle")
        Image(systemName: "3.circle")
        Image(systemName: "4.circle")
        Image(systemName: "5.circle")
        Image(systemName: "6.circle")
        Image(systemName: "7.circle")
        Image(systemName: "8.circle")
        Image(systemName: "9.circle")
        Image(systemName: "10.circle")
    }.font(.largeTitle)
})

ScrollView(Axis.Set.vertical, showsIndicators: true,
content: {
    LazyVGrid(columns: gridItems) {
        Image(systemName: "1.square")
        Image(systemName: "2.square")
        Image(systemName: "3.square")
        Image(systemName: "4.square")
        Image(systemName: "5.square")
        Image(systemName: "6.square")
        Image(systemName: "7.square")
        Image(systemName: "8.square")
        Image(systemName: "9.square")
        Image(systemName: "10.square")
    }.font(.largeTitle)
})
    }
  }
}
```

```
struct ContentView_Previews: PreviewProvider {
    static var previews: some View {
        ContentView()
    }
}
```

3. Click the Live icon in the Canvas pane.

4. Scroll the horizontal grid left to right or right to left to see all the numbered circles as shown in Figure 19-3.

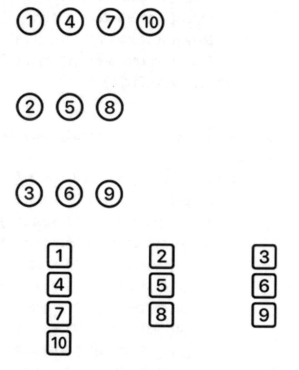

Figure 19-3. *Displaying a grid with three rows and three columns*

5. Scroll the vertical grid up and down to see all the numbered squares.

Notice that when filling out a LazyHGrid, SwiftUI places each item in a separate row. That's why circle 1 appears in the top row, circle 2 appears in the second row, circle 3 appears in the third row, and circle 4 appears back in the top row again.

The same holds true when filling out the LazyVGrid except SwiftUI places each item in a separate column. Square 1 appears in the first column, square 2 appears in the second column, square 3 appears in the third column, and square 4 appears back in the first column again.

Note   The scroll indicator only appears when the grid cannot show all items at the same time. When displaying three rows or three columns, all items can be visible, so the scroll indicator does not need to appear.

Adjusting Spacing Between Rows/Columns

By creating an array of GridItem, we can define the number of rows/columns in a grid. For additional customization, we can also define the spacing between rows and columns. Three ways to define spacing between rows/columns in a grid include

- .fixed

- .flexible

- .adaptive

The .fixed option lets you define a decimal value (CGFloat data type) that creates a specific spacing amount. Figure 19-4 shows different fixed spacing options and how they affect the appearance of rows and columns in grids.

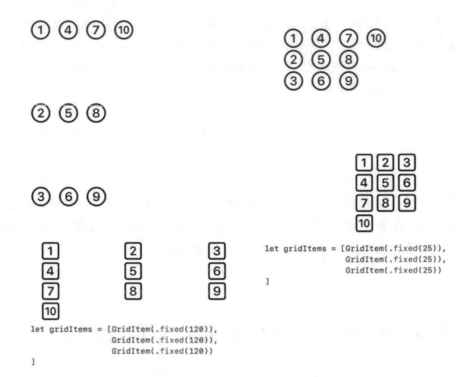

Figure 19-4. *Various .fixed spacing options for a grid*

Note   In Figure 19-4, all GridItem elements in the array use the same .fixed size value, but you can give each GridItem different size values if you want.

Defining a .fixed value for spacing rows and columns in a grid will give predictable results on any iOS device. However, a .fixed value may not always look good on smaller or larger iOS device screens. In case you want to create grids that can change based on different screen sizes, use .flexible or .adaptive instead.

The .flexible option tries to expand spacing between rows/columns as much as possible. On the other hand, the .adaptive option tries to shrink spacing between rows/ columns as much as possible. Both the .flexible and .adaptive options let you define a minimum and a maximum value. This defines the range of values the grid spacing can use.

If no option is chosen, the default value is .flexible with a maximum value of .infinity. To see how the .fixed, .flexible, and .adaptive options work, follow these steps:

1. Make sure to load the previous project in Xcode ("GridSimple").

2. Edit the array as follows to define three rows in the LazyHGrid and three columns in the LazyVGrid:

```
let gridItems = [GridItem(.fixed(120)),
                 GridItem(.fixed(120)),
                 GridItem(.fixed(120))
]
```

Notice that this separates the rows and columns in the grid by a fixed amount (see Figure 19-4).

3. Edit the array as follows to define three rows in the LazyHGrid and three columns in the LazyVGrid:

```
let gridItems = [GridItem(.flexible(minimum: 20, maximum: 450)),
                 GridItem(.flexible(minimum: 20, maximum: 450)),
                 GridItem(.flexible(minimum: 20, maximum: 450))
]
```

4. Comment out the second Scroll View like this:

```
//              ScrollView(Axis.Set.vertical, showsIndicators: true,
                content: {
//                  LazyVGrid(columns: gridItems) {
//                      Image(systemName: "1.square")
//                      Image(systemName: "2.square")
//                      Image(systemName: "3.square")
//                      Image(systemName: "4.square")
//                      Image(systemName: "5.square")
//                      Image(systemName: "6.square")
//                      Image(systemName: "7.square")
//                      Image(systemName: "8.square")
```

```
//                          Image(systemName: "9.square")
//                          Image(systemName: "10.square")
//              }.font(.largeTitle)
//          })
```

Notice that without the second Scroll View, the LazyHGrid can now expand the spacing between rows as shown in Figure 19-5.

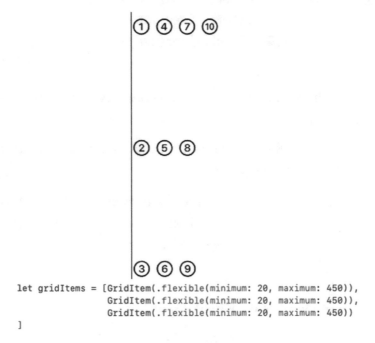

```
let gridItems = [GridItem(.flexible(minimum: 20, maximum: 450)),
                 GridItem(.flexible(minimum: 20, maximum: 450)),
                 GridItem(.flexible(minimum: 20, maximum: 450))
]
```

Figure 19-5. *The LazyHGrid expands the spacing between rows*

5. Edit the array as follows to define three rows in the LazyHGrid and three columns in the LazyVGrid:

```
let gridItems = [GridItem(.adaptive(minimum: 20, maximum: 45)),
                 GridItem(.adaptive(minimum: 20, maximum: 450)),
                 GridItem(.adaptive(minimum: 20, maximum: 450))
]
```

Notice that the .adaptive option shrinks the spacing to the minimum as shown in Figure 19-6.

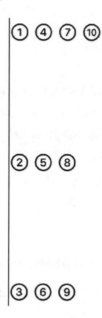

Figure 19-6. *The .adaptive option shrinks spacing to the minimum possible*

Creating Tables Using GridRows

Oftentimes data can be organized in rows and columns similar to a spreadsheet or a table. To mimic tables in SwiftUI, there's a special GridRow that lets you define rows of data organized within a grid as shown in Figure 19-7.

Movies	Distributer
The Martian	20th Century
E.T.	Universal
Raiders of the Lost Ark	Paramount
Toy Story	Buena Vista Pictures
Dunkirk	Warner Brothers

Figure 19-7. *A grid and GridRow can create a table*

To create a table, you must first define a grid like this:

```
var body: some View {
    Grid() {

    }
```

Then within the Grid(), define multiple GridRows. Within each GridRow, define a separate view for each column you want to create. So if you wanted to create a row divided into two columns, the GridRow might consist of two Text views like this:

```
        GridRow {
            Text("The Martian")
            Text("20th Century")
        }
```

To see how to create a table using GridRows, follow these steps:

1. Create a new SwiftUI iOS App project and give it any name you wish such as "GridRows."

2. Click the ContentView file in the Navigator pane.

3. Add a Grid() inside the var body: some View like this:

```
var body: some View {
    Grid() {

    }
```

4. Add GridRows inside the Grid(). The number of GridRows defines the number of rows. The number of different views within a GridRow defines the number of columns:

```
var body: some View {
    Grid() {
        GridRow {
            Text("Movies")
            Text("Distributer")
        }.bold()
            .font(.largeTitle)
        GridRow {
```

```
            Text("The Martian")
            Text("20th Century")
        }
        GridRow {
            Text("E.T.")
            Text("Universal")
        }
        GridRow {
            Text("Raiders of the Lost Ark")
            Text("Paramount")
        }
        GridRow {
            Text("Toy Story")
            Text("Buena Vista Pictures")
        }
        GridRow {
            Text("Dunkirk")
            Text("Warner Brothers")
        }
    }
```

Notice that you can format individual GridRows. In the preceding example, the first GridRow is formatted in bold and in .largeTitle to define a heading for the table (see Figure 19-7).

The entire ContentView file should look like this:

```
import SwiftUI

struct ContentView: View {
    var body: some View {
        Grid() {
            GridRow {
                Text("Movies")
                Text("Distributer")
            }.bold()
                .font(.largeTitle)
```

```
                GridRow {
                    Text("The Martian")
                    Text("20th Century")
                }
                GridRow {
                    Text("E.T.")
                    Text("Universal")
                }
                GridRow {
                    Text("Raiders of the Lost Ark")
                    Text("Paramount")
                }
                GridRow {
                    Text("Toy Story")
                    Text("Buena Vista Pictures")
                }
                GridRow {
                    Text("Dunkirk")
                    Text("Warner Brothers")
                }
            }
        }
    }
}

struct ContentView_Previews: PreviewProvider {
    static var previews: some View {
        ContentView()
    }
}
```

5. Click the Live icon in the Canvas pane.

    Two additional ways to format the appearance of a grid is by using
    dividers and alignment. Dividers display a horizontal line between
    each GridRow, while alignment lets you define how data appears
    within each GridRow such as .center (the default), .leading (left-
    aligned), or .trailing (right-aligned) as shown in Figure 19-8.

Movies	Distributer	Movies	Distributer	Movies Distributer
The Martian	20th Century	The Martian	20th Century	The Martian 20th Century
E.T.	Universal	E.T.	Universal	E.T. Universal
Raiders of the Lost Ark	Paramount	Raiders of the Lost Ark	Paramount	Raiders of the Lost Ark Paramount
Toy Story	Buena Vista Pictures	Toy Story	Buena Vista Pictures	Toy Story Buena Vista Pictures
Dunkirk	Warner Brothers	Dunkirk	Warner Brothers	Dunkirk Warner Brothers

.leading   .center   .trailing

Figure 19-8. *Different ways to align data in a GridRow*

To see how to use dividers and alignment in a grid and GridRows, follow these steps:

1. Open the previous project you created called "GridRows."

2. Click the ContentView file in the Navigator pane.

3. Edit the ContentView file to add alignment to the grid and dividers in between the GridRows like this:

```
Grid(alignment: .leading) {
    GridRow {
        Text("Movies")
        Text("Distributer")
    }.bold()
        .font(.largeTitle)
    GridRow {
        Text("The Martian")
        Text("20th Century")
    }
    Divider()
    GridRow {
        Text("E.T.")
        Text("Universal")
    }
    Divider()
    GridRow {
        Text("Raiders of the Lost Ark")
        Text("Paramount")
    }
    Divider()
```

```
        GridRow {
            Text("Toy Story")
            Text("Buena Vista Pictures")
        }
        Divider()
        GridRow {
            Text("Dunkirk")
            Text("Warner Brothers")
        }
    }
}
```

The entire ContentView file should look like this:

```
import SwiftUI

struct ContentView: View {
    var body: some View {
        Grid(alignment: .leading) {
            GridRow {
                Text("Movies")
                Text("Distributer")
            }.bold()
                .font(.largeTitle)
            GridRow {
                Text("The Martian")
                Text("20th Century")
            }
            Divider()
            GridRow {
                Text("E.T.")
                Text("Universal")
            }
            Divider()
            GridRow {
                Text("Raiders of the Lost Ark")
                Text("Paramount")
            }
```

```
            Divider()
            GridRow {
                Text("Toy Story")
                Text("Buena Vista Pictures")
            }
            Divider()
            GridRow {
                Text("Dunkirk")
                Text("Warner Brothers")
            }
        }
    }
}

struct ContentView_Previews: PreviewProvider {
    static var previews: some View {
        ContentView()
    }
}
```

4. Click the Live icon in the Canvas pane. The table should now look as shown in Figure 19-9.

Movies	Distributer
The Martian	20th Century
E.T.	Universal
Raiders of the Lost Ark	Paramount
Toy Story	Buena Vista Pictures
Dunkirk	Warner Brothers

Figure 19-9. *Aligning a grid (.leading) and adding dividers between GridRows*

Summary

Grids offer another way to display views on the user interface. LazyHGrids can display views horizontally in rows, while LazyVGrids can display views vertically in columns. To use grids, you need the data you want to display, an array of GridItem that defines how to arrange data in a grid, and a LazyHGrid or LazyVGrid.

The number of GridItem defined in the array determines the number of rows/columns displayed in the grid. With each GridItem, you can define a spacing option such as .fixed, .flexible, or .adaptive.

The .fixed option lets you define a decimal value for spacing such as 25.7. The .flexible option tries to expand spacing as much as possible, while the .adaptive option tries to shrink spacing as much as possible. You can apply different spacing options to each GridItem in an array.

By using grids, you can display data in rows and columns. Grids are often embedded in a Scroll View to allow users to scroll up/down or left/right to view data that might not be visible due to the size of the grid and the iOS device screen.

If you want to display data in a table, use a grid to define the table, and then use multiple GridRows to define the number of rows. Within each GridRow, define one or more views where the total number of views defines the number of columns in the table. Grids are simply a convenient way to organize and display related data so it's easy for users to read.

CHAPTER 20

Using Animation

Animation can move items on a user interface to provide feedback or just add an aesthetic touch. Unlike traditional animation created by hand where cartoonists had to draw every single frame but slightly differently, animation in SwiftUI works by simply defining a starting and an ending state. Then SwiftUI takes care of animating an item in between those starting and ending states.

The three most common types of animation involve

- Moving – Changing the x and y position of an item on the user interface

- Scaling – Changing the size of an item by shrinking or enlarging it

- Rotating – Changing the angle of an item in either a clockwise or counterclockwise direction

Creating animation involves defining what to animate, how to animate it (move, scale, rotate), and when to animate it. Animation typically occurs when the user does something (such as tap a button) or when a specific event occurs (such as a numeric value reaching a certain point).

Moving Animation

To move a view, we must define an x, y starting location and an x, y ending location. The two modifiers that specify location are .position and .offset.

The .position modifier places a view at a specific x and y position away from the upper-left corner of an iOS device screen, which is considered the origin (0,0). The .offset modifier places a view at a specific x and y position away from where it would normally appear on the user interface.

© Wallace Wang 2023
W. Wang, *Beginning iPhone Development with SwiftUI*, https://doi.org/10.1007/978-1-4842-9541-0_20

The .position modifier defines fixed locations on the screen. The .offset modifier defines locations relative to where it would normally appear if its .offset modifier x and y values were 0. In both cases, positive x values move a view to the right, and positive y values move a view down as shown in Figure 20-1.

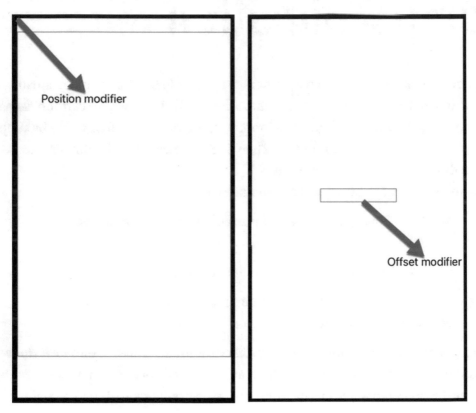

Figure 20-1.   *The difference between the .position modifier and the .offset modifier*

Note   With both the .position and .offset modifiers, it's possible that extreme x or y values could place a view off the screen.

To see how to move a view using the .position and .offset modifiers, follow these steps:

1. Create a new SwiftUI iOS App project and give it any name you wish such as "AnimationMove."

2. Click the ContentView file in the Navigator pane.

3. Add a State variable under the struct ContentView: View line like this:

```
@State var move = true
```

4. Add a Text view and a Toggle inside the VStack like this:

```
var body: some View {
    VStack {
        Text("A Text view")
            .offset(x: move ? 100 : 0, y: move ? 100 : 0)

        Toggle(isOn: $move) {
            Text("Toggle me")
        }
    }
}
```

The entire ContentView file should look like this:

```
import SwiftUI

struct ContentView: View {
    @State var move = true

    var body: some View {
        VStack {
            Text("A Text view")
                .offset(x: move ? 100 : 0, y: move ? 100 : 0)

            Toggle(isOn: $move) {
                Text("Toggle me")
            }
        }
```

```
        }
    }

    struct ContentView_Previews: PreviewProvider {
        static var previews: some View {
            ContentView()
        }
    }
```

5. Click the Live icon in the Canvas pane.

6. Click the Toggle. Notice that the .offset modifier moves the Text view away from its normal position.

7. Edit the ContentView file and replace .offset with .position like this:

```
.position(x: move ? 100 : 0, y: move ? 100 : 0)
```

8. Make sure Live is still turned on and click the Toggle. Notice that the Text view now moves based on the origin (0,0) in the upper-left corner of the screen.

   Both the .offset and .position modifiers cause the Text view to jump from one location to another. Now it's time to add the .animation modifier to the Text view so the movement appears smoother.

9. Add the .animation modifier to the Text view so the entire ContentView should look like this:

```
import SwiftUI

struct ContentView: View {
    @State var move = true

    var body: some View {
        VStack {
            Text("A Text view")
                .position(x: move ? 100 : 0, y: move ? 100 : 0)
                .animation(.default, value: move)
```

```
            Toggle(isOn: $move) {
                Text("Toggle me")
            }
        }
    }
}

struct ContentView_Previews: PreviewProvider {
    static var previews: some View {
        ContentView()
    }
}
```

10. Make sure Live is still turned on and click the Toggle. Notice that the Text view now appears animated as it moves based on the origin (0,0) in the upper-left corner of the screen.

11. Replace the .position modifier with the .offset modifier.

12. Make sure Live is still turned on and click the Toggle. Notice that the Text view now appears animated as it moves based on its normal location.

In this project, the .animation modifier provides the transition between the two different x and y locations of the Text view. Each time the Toggle changes the Boolean State variable, the animation runs again.

The .animation modifier requires defining the type of animation you want (such as .default) and the variable that will trigger the animation. In this case, each time the "move" variable changes, we want animation, so that's why the .animation modifier displays "move" in its value parameter like this:

```
@State var move = true
.animation(.default, value: move)
```

Scaling Animation

Another way to create animation is to define two different sizes for a view, known as scaling. To define the starting and ending states for a view's size, use the .scaleEffect modifier and define the relative size changes to make. For example, a .scaleEffect(1) represents the view's current size. A .scaleEffect value greater than 1 defines a greater size or scale, while a .scaleEffect value less than 1 defines a smaller size or scale.

To see how to animate a view by scaling it to different sizes, follow these steps:

1. Create a new SwiftUI iOS App project and give it any name you wish such as "AnimationScale."

2. Click the ContentView file in the Navigator pane.

3. Add a State variable under the struct ContentView: View line like this:

```
@State private var changeMe = false
```

4. Add an Image view inside the var body: some View like this:

```
var body: some View {
    Image(systemName: "tortoise.fill")
        .font(.system(size:100))
        .foregroundColor(.red)
        .scaleEffect(changeMe ? 1.75 : 1)
}
```

This displays a tortoise icon on the screen at a size of 100 to make it easier to see. Then it colors the tortoise icon red and uses the .scaleEffect modifier to alternate the size of the tortoise from 1.75 times its normal size back to its original size.

5. Add the following modifiers to the Image view like this:

```
.animation(.default, value: changeMe)
.onTapGesture {
    changeMe.toggle()
}
```

This adds the .animation modifier to the Image view so its size changes appear animated. Then the .onTapGesture modifier detects a tap gesture to toggle the changeMe State variable from true to false (or false to true). The entire ContentView file should look like this:

```
import SwiftUI

struct ContentView: View {
    @State private var changeMe = false

    var body: some View {
        Image(systemName: "tortoise.fill")
            .font(.system(size:100))
            .foregroundColor(.red)
            .scaleEffect(changeMe ? 1.75 : 1)
            .animation(.default, value: changeMe)
            .onTapGesture {
                changeMe.toggle()
            }
    }
}

struct ContentView_Previews: PreviewProvider {
    static var previews: some View {
        ContentView()
    }
}
```

6. Click the Live icon in the Canvas pane.

7. Click the tortoise image. Notice that each time you click the tortoise image, it alternates between shrinking and expanding in size.

Rotating Animation

Animating rotation involves changing the angle of a view using the .rotationEffect modifier. A .rotationEffect value of 0 displays no rotation, while a rotation less than or greater than 0 rotates the view either counterclockwise or clockwise.

To see how to animate a view by rotating it by different angles, follow these steps:

1. Create a new SwiftUI iOS App project and give it any name you wish such as "AnimationRotate."

2. Click the ContentView file in the Navigator pane.

3. Add two State variables under the struct ContentView: View line like this:

```
@State var myDegrees: Double = 0.0
@State var flag = false
```

4. Add a Text view inside the VStack like this:

```
var body: some View {
    VStack {
        Text("Hello, world!")
            .padding()
            .rotationEffect(Angle(degrees: flag ? myDegrees : 0))
            .animation(.default, value: flag)
```

This Text view uses the .rotationEffect to define the starting and ending angles. Then it uses the .animation modifier to animate the Text view as it rotates between the starting and ending angles. The .animation modifier displays animation whenever the "flag" variable changes.

5. Add a Button and a Slider under the Text view inside the VStack like this:

```
var body: some View {
    VStack {
        Text("Hello, world!")
            .padding()
```

```
        .rotationEffect(Angle(degrees: flag ? myDegrees : 0))
        .animation(.default, value: flag)

    Button("Animate now") {
        flag.toggle()
    }

    Slider(value: $myDegrees, in: -180...180, step: 1)
        .padding()
    }
}
```

The Slider lets you choose between an angle of –180 degrees and 180 degrees. The entire ContentView file should look like this:

```
import SwiftUI

struct ContentView: View {
    @State var myDegrees: Double = 0.0
    @State var flag = false

    var body: some View {
        VStack {
            Text("Hello, world!")
                .padding()
                .rotationEffect(Angle(degrees: flag ?
                myDegrees : 0))
                .animation(.default, value: flag)

            Button("Animate now") {
                flag.toggle()
            }

            Slider(value: $myDegrees, in: -180...180, step: 1)
                .padding()
        }
    }
}
```

```
struct ContentView_Previews: PreviewProvider {
    static var previews: some View {
        ContentView()
    }
}
```

6. Click the Live icon in the Canvas pane.

7. Drag the Slider left or right to define an ending angle. (The starting angle is 0.)

8. Click the Button. Notice the .animation modifier animates the Text view as it rotates to its new angle.

Animation Options

So far, we've used the .default setting for the .animation modifier. While this works, there are several other animation options you can choose:

- .easeIn – Starts the animation slower and then speeds up

- .easeOut – Slows the animation near the end

- .easeInOut – Starts the animation slower, speeds up, and then slows down near the end (same as .default)

- .linear – Maintains a constant speed for the animation from start to finish

By choosing a different .animation option, you can adjust how the animation appears when it runs. To compare these different .animation options, follow these steps:

1. Create a new SwiftUI iOS App project and give it any name you wish such as "CompareAnimation."

2. Click the ContentView file in the Navigator pane.

3. Add a State variable under the struct ContentView: View line like this:

   @State private var start = false

4. Add a VStack in the var body: some View.

5. Add a Button inside the VStack like this:

```
var body: some View {
    VStack {
        Button("Start animation") {
            start.toggle()
        }
```

6. Add an HStack with four Text views underneath the Button
    like this:

```
HStack {
    Text("easeIn")
        .offset(x: 0, y: start ? 450 : 0)
        .animation(.easeIn, value: start)
    Text("easeOut")
        .offset(x: 0, y: start ? 450 : 0)
        .animation(.easeOut, value: start)
    Text("easeInOut")
        .offset(x: 0, y: start ? 450 : 0)
        .animation(.easeInOut, value: start)
    Text("linear")
        .offset(x: 0, y: start ? 450 : 0)
        .animation(.linear, value: start)
}.position(x: 150, y: 10)
```

Notice that the .position modifier initially places the entire HStack
and all four Text views near the top of the screen. The entire
ContentView file should look like this:

```
import SwiftUI

struct ContentView: View {
    @State private var start = false
    var body: some View {
        VStack {
            Button("Start animation") {
```

```
                        start.toggle()
                }
                HStack {
                    Text("easeIn")
                        .offset(x: 0, y: start ? 450 : 0)
                        .animation(.easeIn, value: start)
                    Text("easeOut")
                        .offset(x: 0, y: start ? 450 : 0)
                        .animation(.easeOut, value: start)
                    Text("easeInOut")
                        .offset(x: 0, y: start ? 450 : 0)
                        .animation(.easeInOut, value: start)
                    Text("linear")
                        .offset(x: 0, y: start ? 450 : 0)
                        .animation(.linear, value: start)
                }.position(x: 150, y: 10)
            }
        }
    }

    struct ContentView_Previews: PreviewProvider {
        static var previews: some View {
            ContentView()
        }
    }
```

7. Click the Live icon in the Canvas pane.

8. Click the Button. Notice that all four Text views drop to the bottom
    of the screen, but because they all use different .animation
    options, the animation appears slightly different even though they
    all start and stop at the same time.

Using Delays and Duration in Animation

Two ways to modify animation by time include delays and duration. A delay lets you specify how many seconds to wait before starting the animation. A duration lets you specify how long the animation should last. Larger time values make the animation run slower, while shorter time values make the animation run faster.

To define a delay, add the .delay modifier to the .animation option you want such as

```
.animation(.linear.delay(2.5), value: yourVariableNameHere)
```

To see how delays work, follow these steps:

1. Load the previous "CompareAnimation" Xcode project.

2. Add the .delay modifier to each .animation option like this:

```
HStack {
    Text("easeIn")
        .offset(x: 0, y: start ? 450 : 0)
        .animation(.easeIn.delay(0.5))
    Text("easeOut")
        .offset(x: 0, y: start ? 450 : 0)
        .animation(.easeOut.delay(1.0))
    Text("easeInOut")
        .offset(x: 0, y: start ? 450 : 0)
        .animation(.easeInOut.delay(1.5))
    Text("linear")
        .offset(x: 0, y: start ? 450 : 0)
        .animation(.linear.delay(2.5))
}.position(x: 150, y: 10)
```

The entire ContentView file should look like this:

```
import SwiftUI

struct ContentView: View {
    @State private var start = false
    var body: some View {
        VStack {
            Button("Start animation") {
```

```
                    start.toggle()
                }
                HStack {
                    Text("easeIn")
                        .offset(x: 0, y: start ? 450 : 0)
                        .animation(.easeIn.delay(0.5), value: start)
                    Text("easeOut")
                        .offset(x: 0, y: start ? 450 : 0)
                        .animation(.easeOut.delay(1.0), value: start)
                    Text("easeInOut")
                        .offset(x: 0, y: start ? 450 : 0)
                        .animation(.easeInOut.delay(1.5),
                        value: start)
                    Text("linear")
                        .offset(x: 0, y: start ? 450 : 0)
                        .animation(.linear.delay(2.5), value: start)
                }.position(x: 150, y: 10)
            }
        }
    }

    struct ContentView_Previews: PreviewProvider {
        static var previews: some View {
            ContentView()
        }
    }
```

3. Click the Live icon in the Canvas pane.

4. Click the Button. Notice that each Text view now animates at
    different times if each of them has a different .delay value.

To define a duration, add the duration to the .animation option you want such as

```
.animation(.easeIn(duration: 0.7), value: start)
```

Note   You can combine a duration with a delay like this: `.animation(.linear (duration: 3.1).delay(1.2), value: start)`.

While a delay temporarily keeps an animation from starting, a duration defines how long that animation actually runs. To see how durations work, follow these steps:

1. Load the previous "CompareAnimation" Xcode project.

2. Add a duration to each .animation option like this:

```
HStack {
    Text("easeIn")
        .offset(x: 0, y: start ? 450 : 0)
        .animation(.easeIn(duration: 0.7),
        value: start)
    Text("easeOut")
        .offset(x: 0, y: start ? 450 : 0)
        .animation(.easeOut(duration: 1.7),
        value: start)
    Text("easeInOut")
        .offset(x: 0, y: start ? 450 : 0)
        .animation(.easeInOut(duration: 2.6),
        value: start)
    Text("linear")
        .offset(x: 0, y: start ? 450 : 0)
        .animation(.linear(duration: 3.1),
        value: start)
}.position(x: 150, y: 10)
```

The entire ContentView file should look like this:

```
import SwiftUI

struct ContentView: View {
    @State private var start = false

    var body: some View {
        VStack {
```

```
                    Button("Start animation") {
                        start.toggle()
                    }
                    HStack {
                        Text("caseIn")
                            .offset(x: 0, y: start ? 450 : 0)
                            .animation(.easeIn(duration: 0.7),
                            value: start)
                        Text("easeOut")
                            .offset(x: 0, y: start ? 450 : 0)
                            .animation(.easeOut(duration: 1.7),
                            value: start)
                        Text("easeInOut")
                            .offset(x: 0, y: start ? 450 : 0)
                            .animation(.easeInOut(duration: 2.6),
                            value: start)
                        Text("linear")
                            .offset(x: 0, y: start ? 450 : 0)
                            .animation(.linear(duration: 3.1),
                            value: start)
                    }.position(x: 150, y: 10)
                }
            }
        }

        struct ContentView_Previews: PreviewProvider {
            static var previews: some View {
                ContentView()
            }
        }
```

3. Click the Live icon in the Canvas pane.

4. Click the Button. Notice how the different duration values modify the various animations.

Using an Interpolating Spring in Animation

To provide even more ways to customize how an animation works, you can also define an .interpolatingSpring modifier to an animation. An .interpolatingSpring lets you define one or more of the following:

- Mass – Low values animate slower with less damping; high values animate faster with more damping.

- Stiffness – Low values animate slower; high values animate faster.

- Damping – Low values create more "bounce"; high values dampen the "bounce."

- InitialVelocity – Low values animate slowly in the beginning; high values animate faster in the beginning.

To see how stiffness and damping work, follow these steps:

1. Load the previous "CompareAnimation" Xcode project.

2. Change all the Text views to display the same string such as "spring".

3. Add an .interpolatingSpring modifier to each Text view like this:

```
HStack {
    Text("spring")
        .offset(x: 0, y: start ? 450 : 0)
        .animation(.interpolatingSpring(stiffness: 1,
        damping: 1), value: start)
    Text("spring")
        .offset(x: 0, y: start ? 450 : 0)
        .animation(.interpolatingSpring(stiffness: 1.8,
        damping: 1), value: start)
    Text("spring")
        .offset(x: 0, y: start ? 450 : 0)
        .animation(.interpolatingSpring(stiffness: 0.5,
        damping: 1), value: start)
```

```
    Text("spring")
        .offset(x: 0, y: start ? 450 : 0)
        .animation(.interpolatingSpring(stiffness: 2, damping: 1),
        value: start)
}.position(x: 150, y: 10)
```

Make sure the damping parameter is identical for every
.animation modifier and make sure the stiffness parameter is
different for every .animation modifier. The entire ContentView
file should look like this:

```
import SwiftUI

struct ContentView: View {
    @State private var start = false

    var body: some View {
        VStack {
            Button("Start animation") {
                start.toggle()
            }
            HStack {
                Text("spring")
                    .offset(x: 0, y: start ? 450 : 0)
                    .animation(.interpolatingSpring(stiffness: 1,
                    damping: 1), value: start)
                Text("spring")
                    .offset(x: 0, y: start ? 450 : 0)
                    .animation(.interpolatingSpring(stiffness:
                    1.8, damping: 1), value: start)
                Text("spring")
                    .offset(x: 0, y: start ? 450 : 0)
                    .animation(.interpolatingSpring(stiffness:
                    0.5, damping: 1), value: start)
                Text("spring")
                    .offset(x: 0, y: start ? 450 : 0)
```

```
            .animation(.interpolatingSpring(stiffness: 2,
                damping: 1), value: start)
        }.position(x: 150, y: 10)
    }
}
}

struct ContentView_Previews: PreviewProvider {
    static var previews: some View {
        ContentView()
    }
}
```

4. Click the Live icon in the Canvas pane.

5. Click the Button. Notice how the different stiffness values alter the
    way each Text view animates.

6. Edit the .animation modifier so the stiffness value is identical but
    the damping value is different.

7. Click the Button. Notice how the different damping values alter
    the way each Text view bounces up and down before coming
    to a stop.

Besides stiffness and damping, you can also define a mass and an initial velocity. By
experimenting with different values for all four parameters, you can further customize
the animation.

To see how mass and initial velocity affect animations, follow these steps:

1. Load the previous "CompareAnimation" Xcode project.

2. Add an .interpolatingSpring modifier to each Text view like this:

```
HStack {
    Text("spring")
        .offset(x: 0, y: start ? 450 : 0)
        .animation(.interpolatingSpring(mass: 1, stiffness: 1,
        damping: 1, initialVelocity: 1), value: start)
    Text("spring")
```

497

```
        .offset(x: 0, y: start ? 450 : 0)
        .animation(.interpolatingSpring(mass: 1.9, stiffness: 1,
        damping: 1, initialVelocity: 1), value: start)
    Text("spring")
        .offset(x: 0, y: start ? 450 : 0)
        .animation(.interpolatingSpring(mass: 2.5, stiffness: 1,
        damping: 1, initialVelocity: 1), value: start)
    Text("spring")
        .offset(x: 0, y: start ? 450 : 0)
        .animation(.interpolatingSpring(mass: 3.5, stiffness: 1,
        damping: 1, initialVelocity: 1), value: start)
}.position(x: 150, y: 10)
```

Make sure the initialVelocity is the same for every .animation modifier but that the mass value is different for every .animation modifier. The entire ContentView file should look like this:

```
import SwiftUI

struct ContentView: View {
    @State private var start = false

    var body: some View {
        VStack {
            Button("Start animation") {
                start.toggle()
            }
            HStack {
                Text("spring")
                    .offset(x: 0, y: start ? 450 : 0)
                    .animation(.interpolatingSpring(mass: 1,
                    stiffness: 1, damping: 1, initialVelocity: 1),
                    value: start)
                Text("spring")
                    .offset(x: 0, y: start ? 450 : 0)
                    .animation(.interpolatingSpring(mass: 1.9,
                    stiffness: 1, damping: 1, initialVelocity: 1),
                    value: start)
```

```
            Text("spring")
                .offset(x: 0, y: start ? 450 : 0)
                .animation(.interpolatingSpring(mass: 2.5,
                stiffness: 1, damping: 1, initialVelocity: 1),
                value: start)
            Text("spring")
                .offset(x: 0, y: start ? 450 : 0)
                .animation(.interpolatingSpring(mass: 3.5,
                stiffness: 1, damping: 1, initialVelocity: 1),
                value: start)
        }.position(x: 150, y: 10)
    }
  }
}

struct ContentView_Previews: PreviewProvider {
    static var previews: some View {
        ContentView()
    }
}
```

3. Click the Live icon in the Canvas pane.

4. Click the Button. Notice how higher mass values affect the animation compared with lower mass values.

5. Edit the .animation modifier so the mass value is identical but the initialVelocity value is now different.

6. Click the Button. Notice how the different initialVelocity values alter the way each Text view starts animating.

By altering the mass, stiffness, damping, and initialVelocity values, you can find the perfect animation effect for your user interface.

Using withAnimation

By using the .animation modifier, you can define which views you want to animate. One problem with the .animation modifier is that if you have five views that you want to animate identically, you have to add the same .animation modifier to all five views like this:

```
HStack {
    Text("One")
        .offset(x: 0, y: start ? 450 : 0)
        .animation(.default, value: start)
    Text("Two")
        .offset(x: 0, y: start ? 450 : 0)
        .animation(.default, value: start)
    Text("Three")
        .offset(x: 0, y: start ? 450 : 0)
        .animation(.default, value: start)
    Text("Four")
        .offset(x: 0, y: start ? 450 : 0)
        .animation(.default, value: start)
    Text("Five")
        .offset(x: 0, y: start ? 450 : 0)
        .animation(.default, value: start)
}
```

To solve this problem, SwiftUI offers a second way to animate views. The withAnimation lets you specify a State variable that can animate views. Rather than write multiple .animation modifiers on separate views, you can just define the State variable to affect, and when that State variable changes, it automatically animates any view that uses that State variable like this:

```
withAnimation {
    start.toggle()
}
```

To see how withAnimation works, follow these steps:

1. Create a new SwiftUI iOS App project and give it any name you wish such as "WithAnimation."

2. Click the ContentView file in the Navigator pane.

3. Add a State variable under the struct ContentView: View line like this:

```
@State private var start = false
```

4. Add a VStack and a Button under the var body: some View line like this:

```
var body: some View {
    VStack {
        Button("Start animation") {
            start.toggle()
        }
```

5. Add an HStack with five Text views underneath the Button like this:

```
HStack {
    Text("One")
        .offset(x: 0, y: start ? 450 : 0)
        .animation(.default, value: start)
    Text("Two")
        .offset(x: 0, y: start ? 450 : 0)
        .animation(.default, value: start)
    Text("Three")
        .offset(x: 0, y: start ? 450 : 0)
        .animation(.default, value: start)
    Text("Four")
        .offset(x: 0, y: start ? 450 : 0)
        .animation(.default, value: start)
    Text("Five")
        .offset(x: 0, y: start ? 450 : 0)
        .animation(.default, value: start)
}.position(x: 150, y: 10)
```

Notice that each Text view has the identical .animation modifier.
The entire ContentView file should look like this:

```
import SwiftUI

struct ContentView: View {
    @State private var start = false

    var body: some View {
        VStack {
            Button("Start animation") {
                start.toggle()
            }
            HStack {
                Text("One")
                    .offset(x: 0, y: start ? 450 : 0)
                    .animation(.default, value: start)
                Text("Two")
                    .offset(x: 0, y: start ? 450 : 0)
                    .animation(.default, value: start)
                Text("Three")
                    .offset(x: 0, y: start ? 450 : 0)
                    .animation(.default, value: start)
                Text("Four")
                    .offset(x: 0, y: start ? 450 : 0)
                    .animation(.default, value: start)
                Text("Five")
                    .offset(x: 0, y: start ? 450 : 0)
                    .animation(.default, value: start)
            }.position(x: 150, y: 10)
        }
    }
}

struct ContentView_Previews: PreviewProvider {
    static var previews: some View {
        ContentView()
    }
}
```

6. Click the Live icon in the Canvas pane.

7. Click the Button to make all five Text views animate identically.

8. Comment out (or delete) all the .animation modifiers on each Text view.

9. Edit the Button code in the ContentView file to include the withAnimation block like this:

```
Button("Start animation") {
    withAnimation {
        start.toggle()
    }
}
```

The entire ContentView file should look like this:

```
import SwiftUI

struct ContentView: View {
    @State private var start = false

    var body: some View {
        VStack {
            Button("Start animation") {
                withAnimation {
                    start.toggle()
                }
            }
            HStack {
                Text("One")
                    .offset(x: 0, y: start ? 450 : 0)
//                    .animation(.default, value: start)
                Text("Two")
                    .offset(x: 0, y: start ? 450 : 0)
//                    .animation(.default, value: start)
                Text("Three")
                    .offset(x: 0, y: start ? 450 : 0)
```

```
//                          .animation(.default, value: start)
                Text("Four")
                    .offset(x: 0, y: start ? 450 : 0)
//                          .animation(.default, value: start)
                Text("Five")
                    .offset(x: 0, y: start ? 450 : 0)
//                          .animation(.default, value: start)
            }.position(x: 150, y: 10)
        }
    }
}

struct ContentView_Previews: PreviewProvider {
    static var previews: some View {
        ContentView()
    }
}
```

10. Click the Button and notice that all five Text views animate exactly
    as before when each Text view had its own .animation modifier.

    In case you want to add a delay and duration, you can use code
    like this:

```
withAnimation(.easeOut(duration: 2.1).delay(1.2)) {

}
```

    You can also use .interpolatingSpring to define stiffness and
    damping like this:

```
withAnimation(.interpolatingSpring(stiffness: 2.4,
damping: 1.6)) {

}
```

To include parameters for mass and initialVelocity, you can use
code like this:

```
withAnimation(.interpolatingSpring(mass: 25, stiffness: 1.5,
damping: 2.3, initialVelocity: 1.7)) {


}
```

Anything you can do with the .animation modifier you can also do with the
withAnimation block. You can use one method instead of the other or both methods
within the same code.

Summary

Animation can make your user interface come to life by providing visual feedback to
the user or simply offering fun visual images that engage the user. As a general rule,
use animation sparingly because too many visual changes happening at once can
be confusing and distracting. The best animation highlights an action but doesn't
overwhelm the user in the process.

Animation involves defining a starting and an ending state whether you're moving,
resizing, or rotating a view. Then you need some kind of trigger to define a new state.
Finally, you need to use the .animation modifier. If you're going to animate multiple
views using the exact same .animation modifier, you could reduce duplication of code by
using withAnimation instead.

To customize animation, you can define delay and duration values to slow down the
amount of time before the animation begins and set how long it takes to complete. For
greater customization, use the .interpolatingSpring modifier and define mass, stiffness,
damping, and initialVelocity. By using animation, you can make your user interface fun
and more interesting to use.

CHAPTER 21

Using GeometryReader

User interfaces for iOS devices must adapt to different screen sizes. Not only are there different-size screens for the iPhone and iPad, but there are also different screen sizes among different iPhone and iPad models on the market. To solve this problem, SwiftUI centers user interface items, but what if you need to precisely place user interface items in specific locations?

Specific X and Y coordinates won't work because what might look good on a large screen won't look right on a much smaller screen and vice versa. When you need to the place user interface items in specific locations on the screen, a safer approach is to use the GeometryReader.

The GeometryReader acts like a container that automatically adapts to different screen sizes. After adding a GeometryReader, you can then place user interface items using the GeometryReader's relative coordinates instead of the exact coordinates of different-size screens. That way when an app runs on different-size screens, the GeometryReader adapts its relative coordinates as well.

Understanding the GeometryReader

The GeometryReader can hold multiple views like a stack. The key difference is that the GeometryReader expands to take up as much space as possible. In addition, the GeometryReader can retrieve its width and height. The code to define a GeometryReader looks like this:

```
GeometryReader { geometry in
    // Views defined here
}
```

© Wallace Wang 2023
W. Wang, *Beginning iPhone Development with SwiftUI*, https://doi.org/10.1007/978-1-4842-9541-0_21

The GeometryReader uses an arbitrarily named variable such as "geometry" in the preceding example, although this variable can be named anything. Then to retrieve the width and height of the GeometryReader, you can retrieve the size.width and size.height properties like this:

```
geometry.size.width
geometry.size.height
```

To see how a GeometryReader works, follow these steps:

1. Create a new SwiftUI iOS App project and give it any name you wish such as "BasicGeometryReader."

2. Click the ContentView file in the Navigator pane.

3. Add a GeometryReader inside var body: some View like this:

```
var body: some View {
    GeometryReader { geometry in

    }.background(Color.yellow)
}
```

The .background modifier colors the GeometryReader to make it easy to see its boundaries.

4. Add a VStack inside the GeometryReader.

5. Add two Text views inside the VStack like this:

```
var body: some View {
    GeometryReader { geometry in
        VStack {
            Text("Width = \(geometry.size.width)")
            Text("Height = \(geometry.size.height)")
        }
    }.background(Color.yellow)
}
```

The entire ContentView file should look like this:

```
import SwiftUI

struct ContentView: View {
    var body: some View {
        GeometryReader { geometry in
            VStack {
                Text("Width = \(geometry.size.width)")
                Text("Height = \(geometry.size.height)")
            }
        }.background(Color.yellow)
    }
}

struct ContentView_Previews: PreviewProvider {
    static var previews: some View {
        ContentView()
    }
}
```

Notice that the geometry.size.width and geometry.size.height properties define the height and width of the GeometryReader within the current iOS device such as an iPhone SE as shown in Figure 21-1.

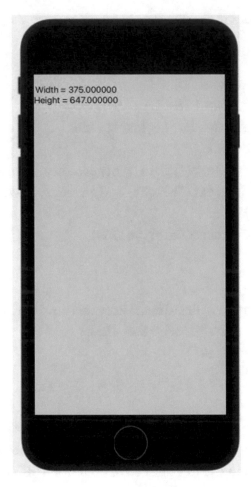

Figure 21-1. *The GeometryReader defines its width and height within an iPhone SE*

6. Click ContentView() inside the struct ContentView_Previews: PreviewProvider. The Inspector pane appears on the right side of the Xcode window.

7. Click the Device popup menu and choose a different-size screen such as a larger or smaller iPhone or iPad as shown in Figure 21-2.

Figure 21-2. *The Device popup menu in the Inspector pane*

8. Choose a different-size iPhone or iPad. Notice that the
    GeometryReader expands or shrinks to fit within the boundaries
    of the new iOS screen size and displays a different width and
    height as shown in Figure 21-3.

Figure 21-3. *Displaying the width and height of the GeometryReader in a different-size iOS screen*

Try experimenting with different iOS devices such as a small-screen iPhone or a large-screen iPad. No matter which size iOS device screen you choose, the GeometryReader can expand or shrink and return its width and height.

Understanding the Differences Between Global and Local Coordinates

Once you've seen how the GeometryReader can shrink or expand to fit the width and height of different iOS screen sizes, the next step is to understand how the GeometryReader's coordinates work. Coordinates within the GeometryReader are known as local coordinates.

On the other hand, global coordinates refer to the entire iOS screen. While global coordinates always differ between different iOS device screens, local coordinates within a GeometryReader always remain consistent.

To see the differences between local and global coordinates, follow these steps:

1. Create a new SwiftUI iOS App project and give it any name you wish such as "GeometryReaderCoordinates."

2. Click the ContentView file in the Navigator pane.

3. Add a GeometryReader inside var body: some View like this:

```
var body: some View {
    GeometryReader { geometry in

    }.background(Color.yellow)
}
```

4. Add a VStack inside the GeometryReader and add four Text views and a Divider like this:

```
GeometryReader { geometry in
    VStack {
        Text("Local X origin = \(geometry.frame
        (in: .local).origin.x)")
        Text("Local Y origin = \(geometry.frame
        (in: .local).origin.y)")
        Divider()
        Text("Global X origin = \(geometry.frame
        (in: .global).origin.x)")
        Text("Global Y origin = \(geometry.frame
        (in: .global).origin.y)")
    }
}.background(Color.yellow)
```

First, notice that the Divider() simply draws a horizontal line in a VStack (and a vertical line in an HStack). Second, the frame returns coordinates. When using .local coordinates, the x and y origin of a GeometryReader is always (0,0). When using .global coordinates, the x and y origin of a GeometryReader is based on the distance from the upper-left corner of the iOS screen.

The entire ContentView file should look like this:

```
import SwiftUI

struct ContentView: View {

    var body: some View {
        GeometryReader { geometry in
            VStack {
                Text("Local X origin = \(geometry.frame
                (in: .local).origin.x)")
                Text("Local Y origin = \(geometry.frame
                (in: .local).origin.y)")
                Divider()
                Text("Global X origin = \(geometry.frame
                (in: .global).origin.x)")
                Text("Global Y origin = \(geometry.frame
                (in: .global).origin.y)")
            }
        }.background(Color.yellow)
    }
}

struct ContentView_Previews: PreviewProvider {
    static var previews: some View {
        ContentView()
    }
}
```

Notice that the local origin is (0,0) because it starts in the upper-left corner of the iOS screen. However, the global origin appears at (0,59). That's because the GeometryReader actually appears underneath the notch of the iPhone 14 Pro model as shown in Figure 21-4.

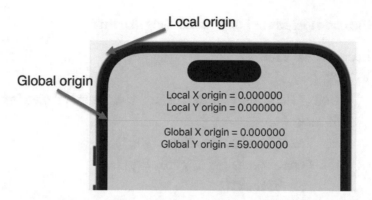

Figure 21-4. *The local origin appears in the upper left corner while the global origin appears in the upper-left corner of the Geometry Reader*

5. Add an .ignoreAllSafeAreas() modifier after the .background(Color.yellow) modifier like this:

```
}.background(Color.yellow)
    .ignoresSafeArea()
```

This ignores the area around the notch, so the global y origin now appears in the upper-left corner of the screen, just like the local y origin as shown in Figure 21-5.

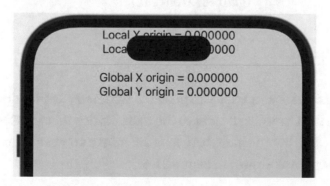

Figure 21-5. *The .ignoresSafeArea() modifier pushes the GeometryReader to the top of the screen so the local and global origins are identical*

6. Edit the code inside var body: some View like this:

```
var body: some View {
    VStack {
        Text("This Text view pushes the GeometryReader down")
        HStack {
            Text("Pushes to the right")
            GeometryReader { geometry in
                VStack {
                    Text("Local X origin = \(geometry.frame(in:
                    .local).origin.x)")
                    Text("Local Y origin = \(geometry.frame(in:
                    .local).origin.y)")
                    Divider()
                    Text("Global X origin = \(geometry.frame(in:
                    .global).origin.x)")
                    Text("Global Y origin = \(geometry.frame(in:
                    .global).origin.y)")
                }
            }.background(Color.yellow)
                .ignoresSafeArea()
        }
    }
}
```

The preceding code uses a VStack to push the GeometryReader down and then uses an HStack to push the GeometryReader to the right. Notice that the GeometryReader's local origin is still (0,0), but the global origin is different as measured from the upper-left corner of the iOS screen as shown in Figure 21-6.

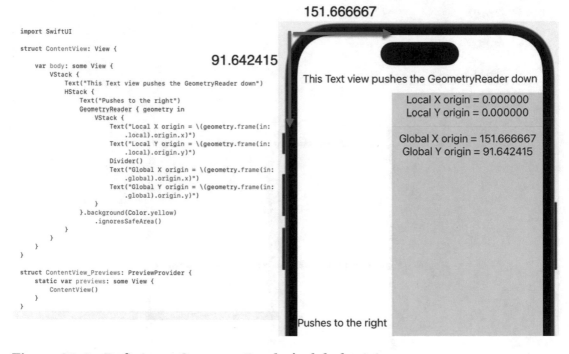

Figure 21-6. *Defining a GeometryReader's global origin*

Identifying Minimum, Mid, and Maximum Values of a GeometryReader

Global coordinates depend on the current iOS screen size. The maximum X and Y coordinates on smaller iOS screens will be different than the maximum X and Y coordinates on a much larger iOS screen. As a result, using global coordinates to position views on the screen could move a view entirely off the screen or cut part of it off.

On the other hand, using local coordinates within a GeometryReader will always adapt to different screen sizes automatically. Since a GeometryReader's width or height will vary depending on the iOS screen size, it's important not to use fixed values but minimum and maximum values instead.

The GeometryReader lets you access the following defined properties as shown in Figure 21-7:

- minX

- minY

- midX

- midY

- maxX

- maxY

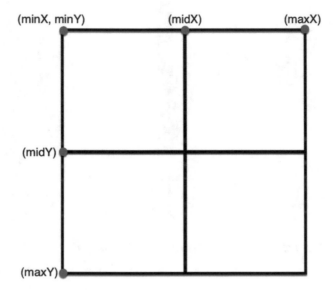

Figure 21-7. *The minimum, mid, and maximum X and Y values of a GeometryReader*

To see how the minimum, mid, and maximum X and Y values of the GeometryReader work, follow these steps:

1. Create a new SwiftUI iOS App project and give it any name you wish such as "GeometryReaderValues."

2. Click the ContentView file in the Navigator pane.

3. Add a GeometryReader inside var body: some View like this:

```
var body: some View {
    GeometryReader { geometry in

    }.background(Color.yellow)
}
```

4. Add a VStack inside the GeometryReader and add six Text views
    and a Divider like this:

```
var body: some View {
    GeometryReader { geometry in
        VStack {
            Text("minX = \(geometry.frame(in: .local).minX)")
            Text("midX = \(geometry.frame(in: .local).midX)")
            Text("maxX = \(geometry.frame(in: .local).maxX)")
            Divider()
            Text("minY = \(geometry.frame(in: .local).minY)")
            Text("midY = \(geometry.frame(in: .local).midY)")
            Text("maxY = \(geometry.frame(in: .local).maxY)")
        }
    }.background(Color.yellow)
}
```

The entire ContentView file should look like this:

```
import SwiftUI

struct ContentView: View {

    var body: some View {
        GeometryReader { geometry in
            VStack {
                Text("minX = \(geometry.frame(in: .local).minX)")
                Text("midX = \(geometry.frame(in: .local).midX)")
                Text("maxX = \(geometry.frame(in: .local).maxX)")
                Divider()
                Text("minY = \(geometry.frame(in: .local).minY)")
                Text("midY = \(geometry.frame(in: .local).midY)")
                Text("maxY = \(geometry.frame(in: .local).maxY)")
            }
        }.background(Color.yellow)
    }
}
```

```
struct ContentView_Previews: PreviewProvider {
    static var previews: some View {
        ContentView()
    }
}
```

Notice that the maxX and maxY properties are just another way to measure the width and height of the GeometryReader.

5. Click ContentView() inside the struct ContentView_Previews: PreviewProvider. The Inspector pane appears on the right side of the Xcode window.

6. Click the Device popup menu and choose a different-size screen such as a larger or smaller iPhone or iPad (see Figure 21-2).

7. Choose a different-size iPhone or iPad. Notice that the GeometryReader expands or shrinks to fit within the boundaries of the new iOS screen size and displays a different maxX and maxY value.

Summary

The GeometryReader is a unique container that can hold multiple views. By using the GeometryReader's local coordinates, you can place different views on the user interface that can automatically adapt to different iOS screen sizes.

The GeometryReader can expand to fill an entire screen or can share a screen with other views within a stack. Two ways to identify the GeometryReader's width and height are either to retrieve the size.height and size.width properties or to retrieve the maxX and maxY properties.

By using local coordinates within a GeometryReader, you always know the origin (0,0) appears in the upper-left corner of the GeometryReader no matter where the GeometryReader appears. By using global coordinates, you always know the origin (0,0) appears at the upper-left corner of the screen.

The GeometryReader is just one more way to position different views on the screen using specific X and Y coordinates.

APPENDIX

An Introduction to Swift

While there are numerous programming languages and tools you can use to create iOS apps, the most popular tool is Xcode, which allows you to write iOS apps using two languages: Objective-C or Swift. Originally Objective-C was the only language that Xcode supported, but in 2014, Apple introduced Swift. Two crucial advantages of Swift over Objective-C are that Swift is easier to read and write and Swift is faster than Objective-C. While many older iOS apps are written in Objective-C, Swift is the programming language of the future for not only iOS but also macOS, tvOS, watchOS, and any future operating systems Apple may develop in the future.

The best way to learn Swift is to use a special feature of Xcode called a playground. A playground lets you write and experiment with Swift code without worrying about a user interface. By doing this, a playground helps you focus solely on learning how to write Swift commands.

To open a playground, follow these steps:

1. Choose File ➤ New ➤ Playground, as shown in Figure A-1, or click the Get started with a playground on the opening Xcode window. A window appears displaying different types of playgrounds you can create as shown in Figure A-2.

521

© Wallace Wang 2023

W. Wang, *Beginning iPhone Development with SwiftUI*, https://doi.org/10.1007/978-1-4842-9541-0

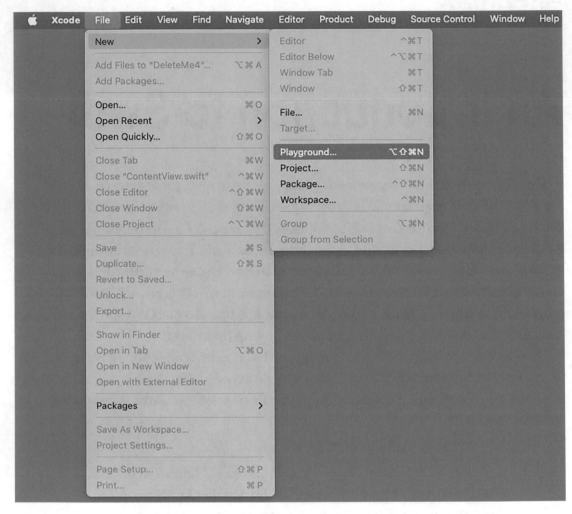

Figure A-1. *Creating a playground in Xcode*

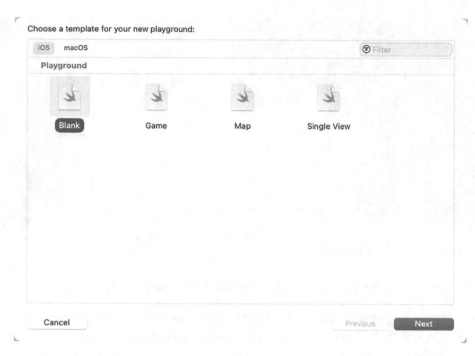

Figure A-2. *Choosing a playground template*

2.   Click Blank under the iOS category and click the Next
     button. A dialog appears where you can choose where to
     save your playground and give it a name beyond the generic
     MyPlayground name.

3.   Choose a folder to store your playground and give it a descriptive
     name if you wish. Then click the Create button. Xcode displays the
     playground as shown in Figure A-3.

Figure A-3. *An iOS playground*

Notice that in Figure A-3, Xcode colors all Swift code in the following ways:

- Magenta (purple) – Identifies keywords of the Swift language. In Figure A-3, "import" tells the code to access a software framework called UIKit. By replacing UIKit with another name or adding another import statement, you can access as many software frameworks as you wish. A second keyword is "var," which stands for variable.

- Black – Identifies arbitrarily named text. In Figure A-3, UIKit is a software framework name.

- Greenish-blue – Identifies variable names such as "greeting".

- Red – Identifies a text string bracketed by double quotation marks such as "Hello, playground".

When typing Swift code, use color-coding to help identify possible mistakes. For example, if you're typing a string, it should appear in red. If it does not, chances are good you're missing a beginning or an ending quotation mark.

You can create as many different playgrounds as you wish to experiment with different features of Swift. Once you get Swift code to work correctly, then you can copy and paste it into an Xcode project.

Note   Every iOS Swift playground begins with the "import UIKit" line, which allows access to Apple's UIKit framework for iOS devices.

Storing Data

Every programming language needs a way to store data. In Swift, you can store data in two ways:

- As a constant

- As a variable

A constant lets you store data in it exactly once. A variable lets you store data multiple times over and over again. Each time you store data in a variable, it deletes any data already stored in that variable.

Every constant or variable needs a name that begins with a letter, although it can use numbers as part of its name such as "Fred2" or "jo903tre." Ideally, the name should be descriptive of the type of data it holds such as "taxReturn" or "Age."

Although not required, Swift programmers typically create names using something known as camel case. That's where a name is made up of two or more words where the first letter is lowercase and the first letter of each additional word is uppercase. Some examples of camel case names are

- nameToDelete

- fly2MoonTomorrow

- sleepLatePlayHard

Apple uses camel case throughout its software frameworks, so you should get familiar with camel case and use it for your own code as well.

Each time you create a new Swift playground, it creates a default line that creates or declares a variable called "greeting" and stores or assigns it a text string "Hello, playground" as shown in Figure A-4.

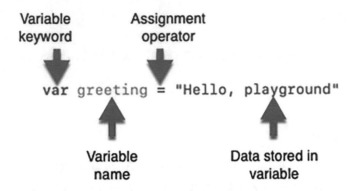

Figure A-4. *The parts of a variable declaration*

Every variable (or constant) declaration begins with the keyword "var" (for a variable) or "let" (for a constant). The second part of a variable or constant declaration is the name, which can be any descriptive name you want to use.

Next is the equal sign that assigns data to that name. Finally, the data itself appears on the right side of the equal sign. In this case, the text string "Hello, playground" gets stored in the variable named "greeting".

To see the difference between constants and variables, follow these steps in the Swift playground:

1. Add the following line in the playground underneath the variable declaration:

   ```
   print (greeting)
   ```

2. Click the Run button in the left column as shown in Figure A-5.

Figure A-5. *Viewing the output of the print statement*

3. Choose View ➤ Debug Area ➤ Show Debug Area, click the Show/ Hide Debug Area icon in the lower-left corner of the playground window, or click the Show/Hide Debug Area icon in the lower-right corner of the playground window. The playground window displays the text "Hello, playground" in the right column and the debug area at the bottom of the window.

The variable declaration simply stores "Hello, playground" into the "greeting" variable. Then the print statement prints the contents of that "greeting" variable, displaying "Hello, playground" in the right column and in the debug area at the bottom of the screen.

Right now, all we've done is store data in a variable once and print it out. Modify the code as follows and then click the Run button:

```
import UIKit

var greeting = "Hello, playground"
print (greeting)
greeting = "Swift is a great language to learn"
print (greeting)
```

Notice that the preceding code first stores the string "Hello, playground" into the "greeting" variable. Then it prints out the data currently stored in the "greeting" variable.

Then it stores a new string "Swift is a great language to learn" into the "greeting" variable and prints the "greeting" variable content out again, which is now "Swift is a great language to learn".

You can store data in a variable as many times as you wish. The limitations are that

- A variable can only hold one chunk of data at a time.

- A variable can only hold one type of data.

Storing Different Data Types

We've already seen how the "greeting" variable can only hold one string at a time. The first time we store data in a variable, we need to define what type of data that variable can hold. By storing a string in that "greeting" variable, we've told the "greeting" variable that it can only hold strings but cannot hold any other type of data such as integers or real numbers (decimal numbers such as 3.14 or 49.082).

527

Modify the code to store a number into the "greeting" variable a second time as follows and then click the Run button:

```
import UIKit

var greeting = "Hello, playground"
print (greeting)
greeting = 54
print (greeting)
```

Notice that Xcode flags the line assigning the number 54 to the "greeting" variable as an error as shown in Figure A-6.

Figure A-6. *An error occurs when you try to store a number into a variable that can only hold string values*

The problem occurs because the first time we store data in the "greeting" variable, it holds a text string. From now on, that "greeting" variable can only hold string data. Let's rewrite the code to make the "greeting" variable hold an integer. Modify the code as follows and then click the Run button:

```
import UIKit

var greeting = 7
print (greeting)
greeting = 54
print (greeting)
```

In the preceding code, we first store the number 7 into the "greeting" variable. From that point on, the "greeting" variable can only hold numbers, so when we store 54 into the "greeting" variable a second time, there is no error message.

Note   The first time you store data in a variable, Swift tries to guess the type of data it's storing in a variable, which is called "inference."

In the previous examples, we've created a variable and stored two different strings in it and then two different integers. Let's change the "greeting" from a variable to a constant by replacing the "var" keyword with "let" as follows:

```
import UIKit

let greeting = 7
print (greeting)
greeting = 54
print (greeting)
```

Notice that this also creates an error. That's because a constant can only store data exactly once. The first time we stored the number 7 in the "greeting" constant, which is fine. The problem is that we tried to store 54 into the "greeting" constant, and that's not allowed because "greeting" is now declared a constant.

If you only need to store data once, use a constant. If you need to store different data over and over again, use a variable.

You might be tempted to simply use a variable all the time, even if you only store data in it once. While this is technically allowed, Xcode will suggest that you use a constant instead. That's because constants use less memory than variables and will make your app run more efficiently. In addition, using constants can help prevent errors by making sure a value never changes by mistake.

When creating a variable, you must define the data type you want that variable to hold. The simplest method is to store any data into a variable and let Swift infer the data type. However, inference can sometimes be confusing when it's not clear what type of data is being stored in a variable. Modify the code as follows:

```
import UIKit

var greeting = 7.0
print (greeting)
greeting = 54
print (greeting)
```

When you click the Run button, the playground prints the numbers 7.0 and 54.0, yet we stored the value of 54 in the "greeting" variable as shown in Figure A-7.

Figure A-7. *Swift infers that all data must be floating-point decimal numbers*

Modify the code to store an integer (7) in the "greeting" variable first, and then try storing a decimal number (54.0) in the "greeting" variable later. The first time we store the number 7 in the "greeting" variable, Swift infers that we'll be storing integer data types from now on. Then when we try storing a decimal number (54.0) in the same "greeting" variable, Swift raises an error message as shown in Figure A-8.

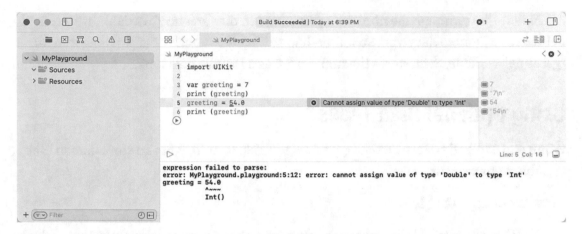

Figure A-8. *Swift raises an error if you try to store different data types in the same variable*

While it's often easier to simply store data in a variable, you might want to make it clear what data type a variable can store. Some common data types include

- Int – Integers or whole numbers such as 8, 92, and 102

- Float – Decimal or floating-point numbers such as 2.13, 98.673, and 0.3784 that store 32 bits of data

- Double – Decimal or floating-point numbers such as 2.13, 98.673, and 0.3784 except offering greater precision by storing 64 bits of data

- String – Text enclosed by double quotation marks such as "Hello, playground" or "78.03"

- Bool – Represents a true or false value

To see how to make the data type of a variable clear, modify the code as follows:

```
import UIKit

var greeting: Double = 7
print (greeting)
greeting = 54.0
print (greeting)
```

Notice that although the number 7 gets stored in the "greeting" variable, it's explicitly defined as a Double data type. So rather than storing the number 7 as an integer in the "greeting" variable, Swift stores the number 7.0 as a Double data type.

Using Optional Data Types

When you explicitly declare a data type for a variable to hold, you can store data in that variable right away like this:

```
var greeting: Double = 7
```

Another alternative is to define the data type without storing any data in that variable right away like this:

```
var greeting: Double
```

The preceding line means the "greeting" variable can only hold Double (decimal) numbers. However, it currently contains nothing. If you create a variable without storing any data in it initially, you cannot use that variable because it contains nothing. Trying to do so will create an error, which you can see by modifying the code as follows:

```
import UIKit

var greeting: Double
print (greeting)
greeting = 54.0
print (greeting)
```

To avoid this problem, you have two options. One, you can declare a variable and store data in it right away. Two, you can declare an optional variable by adding a question mark at the end of the data type like this:

```
var greeting: Double?
```

An optional variable initially has a value of nil, so using a variable with a nil value won't cause an error. To see the difference, modify the code as follows and click the Run button:

```
import UIKit

var greeting: Double?
print (greeting)
greeting = 54.0
print (greeting)
```

Notice that the first print statement prints nil, but the second print statement prints Optional(54.0) as shown in Figure A-9.

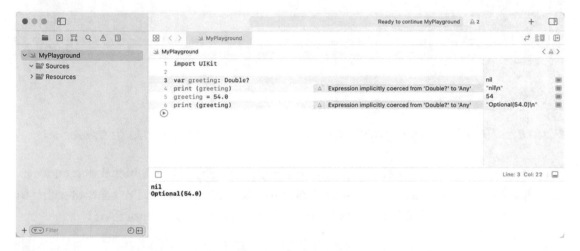

Figure A-9. *Optional variables can be used without data in them.*

To access values stored in an optional variable, you can unwrap the data using the exclamation mark symbol (!). To see how to unwrap data, modify the code as follows and click the Run button:

```
import UIKit

var greeting: Double?
print (greeting)
greeting = 54.0
print (greeting!)
```

Notice that unwrapping optional variables with an exclamation mark retrieves the data as shown in Figure A-10.

Figure A-10. *Unwrapping optional variables can access the data in them*

However, an error will occur if you try unwrapping optional variables that contain a nil value. Modify the code as follows and click the Run button to see the error of trying to unwrap an optional variable that contains a nil value as shown in Figure A-11.

Figure A-11. *You cannot unwrap an optional variable if it contains a nil value*

When using an optional variable, you should always check if it contains a nil value first before trying to access its contents. One way to do this is to use an if statement that uses an optional variable only if it does not contain a nil value. To see how this works, modify the code as follows and click the Run button:

```
import UIKit

var greeting: Double? = 9
if greeting != nil {
    print (greeting!)
}
greeting = 54.0
print (greeting!)
```

The first print statement runs because the "greeting" variable does not contain a nil value. Change the variable declaration like this:

```
var greeting: Double?
```

Now the "greeting" variable contains a nil value, so the first print statement will no longer run.

Making sure an optional variable does not contain a nil value is one way to safely use optional variables. A second way is to assign a constant to an optional variable and then use that constant. This method, called optional binding, is often a preferred method rather than checking if an optional variable does not equal nil. To see how this works, modify the code as follows and click the Run button:

```
import UIKit

var greeting: Double? = 9
if let myConstant = greeting {
    print (myConstant)
}
greeting = 54.0
print (greeting!)
```

Both methods let you check if an optional variable contains a nil value first before trying to access it. The first method (making sure an optional variable is not equal != to nil) requires you to unwrap the optional variable to use it.

The second method (assigning a constant to an optional variable) lets you use the constant without adding exclamation marks to unwrap the data, so this method looks cleaner and is used most often by Swift programmers.

Optional variables are commonly used in Swift, so make sure you're familiar with using them. The basics behind optional variables are as follows:

- Optional variables avoid errors when using variables that do not contain any data.

- You must declare an optional variable using a question mark such as

  var greeting: Double?

- You must unwrap an optional variable to access its data.

Using Comments

One crucial feature of every programming language, including Swift, is the ability to add comments to code. Comments are descriptive text meant for humans to read but the computer to ignore. Programmers often add comments to their code for several reasons:

- To identify who wrote the code and when it was last modified

- To define any assumptions in the code

- To explain what the code does

- To temporarily disable code

You can add as many comments as you wish because the computer just ignores them. There are two ways to create comments:

- To comment out a single line of text, type // in front of the text you want to turn into a comment.

- To comment out blocks of text, type /* at the beginning of the text and */ at the end of text.

```
// This is a single line comment

/* This is a multi-line
 comment because the slash
 and asterisk define the
 beginning of a comment
```

```
while the asterisk and
slash characters define
the end of a comment
*/
```

To comment out multiple lines of text quickly, you can follow these steps:

1. Select the text you want to turn into a comment.

2. Choose Editor ➤ Structure ➤ Comment Selection, or press Command+/.

If you repeat the preceding steps, you can convert comments back into code again.

As a general rule, use comments generously. Every programmer has their own style, so add comments to your code to make sure someone else can understand what your code means if you aren't around to explain it to someone in person.

Mathematical and String Operators

The whole purpose of any program is to manipulate data and create a useful result. Spreadsheets calculate large amounts of formulas, word processors manipulate text, and even games display animation to challenge the user. The simplest way to manipulate numeric data is to use a mathematical operator. The most common types of mathematical operators are

- + (addition)

- – (subtraction)

- / (division)

- * (multiplication)

When performing mathematical calculations, all data types must be the same. That means you can't add an integer (Int) with a decimal (Double) number. Instead, all numbers must be of the same data type.

To convert one numeric data type into another, you just need to define the data type you want followed by the value inside parentheses as shown in Figure A-12.

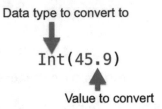

Data type to convert to

Int(45.9)

Value to convert

Figure A-12. *Converting numeric data types*

Note   When converting a decimal number to an integer, Swift will drop the decimal value, so the integer value of 45.9 is simply 45.

To see how to use mathematical operators, modify the code as follows and then click the Run button to see the results as shown in Figure A-13:

```
import UIKit

var x : Int
var y : Double
var z : Float

x = 90 + Int(45.9)

y = Double(x) - 6.25

z = Float(y) * 4.2

y = Double(z) / 7.3

print (x)
print (y)
print (z)
```

Figure A-13. *Using all four mathematical operators*

Note   When using division, make sure you never divide by zero because this will cause an error.

The addition (+) operator can also be used to concatenate two strings. To see how this works, modify the code as follows and click the Run button:

```
import UIKit

var name = "Swift"
var term : String

term = name + " is a great language"

print (term)
```

The + operator joins two strings together into a single string. Notice that you need to leave a space between two strings when concatenating them, or else Swift will jam the two strings together incorrectly like this: "Swiftis a great language", where there should be a space between "Swift" and "is."

If you ever need to add, subtract, multiply, or divide a variable by a fixed value, the straightforward way to do so is like this:

```
x = x + 5 // Add by five
x = x - 3 // Subtract by three
x = x * 2 // Multiply by two
x = x / 6 // Divide by six
```

While this is perfectly fine, you may see shortcuts like this:

```
x += 5 // Add by five
x -= 3 // Subtract by three
x *= 2 // Multiply by two
x /= 6 // Divide by six
```

The first method is longer but easier to understand. The second method is shorter but slightly harder to understand. Experienced programmers often use the shorter method that takes less time to type.

Branching Statements

The simplest program runs through a single list of commands and then stops when it reaches the last command. However, more complicated programs typically offer two or more different sets of commands to follow based on the value of certain data. For example, a program might offer two sets of commands when asking a user to type a password.

One set of commands would run if the user types in a valid password, while a second set of commands would run if the user types an incorrect password. To decide which set of commands to run requires the following:

- A branching statement that offers two or more different sets of commands to run

- A condition to determine which set of commands to run

Using Boolean Values

One data type used in branching statements is the Boolean data type, which can hold one of two values: true or false. At the simplest level, you can simply declare a Boolean variable like this:

```
var flag : Bool = true
```

Of course, declaring a Boolean variable as either true or false can be limiting. A more flexible way to create a Boolean variable is to use comparison operators that compare two values. Then based on the result of that comparison operator, it returns a value of true or false.

The most common types of comparison operators include

- Equal to (==)

- Not equal to (!=)

- Greater than (>)

- Greater than or equal to (>=)

- Less than (<)

- Less than or equal to (<=)

Comparison operators return a true or false Boolean value depending on the comparison. Technically, you could compare two values that will always return a true or false value such as

```
5 > 98      // Always false
20 == 20    // Always true
```

However, it's far more useful to compare a value to a variable or compare two variables such as

```
5 > x      // Only true if x is 4 or less
x == y     // Only true if x is exactly equal to y
```

To see how comparison operators evaluate to either true or false, modify the code as follows and click the Run button:

```
import UIKit

var x = 7
```

```
print (5 > x)      // Only true if x is 4 or less
print (x <= 6)     // Only true if x is 6

x = 2

print (5 > x)      // Only true if x is 4 or less
print (x <= 6)     // Only true if x is 6
```

The first two print statements evaluate to false and false, but the next two print statements evaluate to true and true as shown in Figure A-14.

Figure A-14. *Comparison operators evaluate to either true or false*

Using Boolean Operators

Boolean operators let you manipulate Boolean values. The three different types of Boolean operators include

- && – Represents the And operator

- || – Represents the Or operator

- ! – Represents the Not operator

The And operator compares two Boolean values and returns true only if both Boolean values are true. The Or operator compares two Boolean values and returns false only if both Boolean values are false. The Not operator simply changes a true value to false (and vice versa).

To see how these Boolean operators work, modify the code as follows and click the Run button:

```
import UIKit

var x = 7

// And operator
print ((x > 10) && (x <= 15))    // false && true = false
print ((x > 1) && (x <= 5))      // true && false = false
print ((x > 45) && (x <= 1))     // false && false = false
print ((x > 3) && (x <= 15))     // true && true = true

// Or operator
print ((x > 10) || (x <= 15))    // false || true = true
print ((x > 78) || (x <= 15))    // true || false = true
print ((x > 10) || (x <= 1))     // false || false = false
print ((x > 3) || (x <= 15))     // true || true = true

// Not operator
print (!(x > 6))     // !true = false
print (!(x > 9))     // !false = true
```

Using if Statements

Boolean values and Boolean operators are most often used to determine which set of commands to choose in a branching statement. The most common type of branching statement is an if statement. The basic structure of an if statement checks if a single Boolean value evaluates to true, and then it runs one or more commands. If the Boolean value evaluates to false, then it does not run one or more commands.

An if statement looks like this:

```
if (Boolean value) {
    // Run one or more commands
}
```

If the Boolean value is true, then the if statement runs the commands inside its curly brackets. If the Boolean value is false, then the if statement does not run any commands.

A variation of the if statement is called the if-else statement, which creates exactly two mutually exclusive sets of commands to run. If its Boolean value is true, then one set of commands runs, but if its Boolean value is false, then a different set of commands runs. The if-else statement looks like this:

```
if (Boolean value) {
    // Run one or more commands
} else {
    // Run one or more commands
}
```

The if statement either runs a set of commands or does nothing. The if-else statement offers exactly two different sets of commands and always runs one set of commands.

A commonly used shortcut for the if-else statement looks like this:

```
x > 9 ? print ("It's true") : print ("It's false")
```

This shortcut first evaluates a Boolean expression $(x > 9)$. If this Boolean expression is true, then it runs the command immediately following the question mark (?). If this Boolean expression is false, then it runs the command immediately following the colon (:).

If you want to offer more than two different sets of commands, you can use another variation called an if-elseif statement. An if-elseif statement looks like this:

```
if (Boolean value) {
    // Run one or more commands
} else if (Boolean value) {
    // Run one or more commands
} else if (Boolean value) {
    // Run one or more commands
}
```

The if-elseif statement can offer more than two sets of commands and checks a different Boolean value each time. Even with so many sets of commands, it's still possible that an if-elseif statement won't run any commands at all.

The three variations of the if statement are

- The if statement – Only runs one set of commands if a Boolean value is true.

- The if-else statement – Offers exactly two different sets of commands and runs one set of commands if a Boolean value is true and a second set of commands if a Boolean value is false.

- The if-elseif statement – Can offer two or more sets of commands and compares a Boolean value before running any commands. Depending on its different Boolean values, it's possible that an if-elseif statement won't run any commands at all.

To see how different if statements work, modify the code as follows and click the Run button:

```swift
import UIKit

var x = 7

if (x > 0) {
    print ("If statement running")
}

if (x > 10) {
    print ("First half of if-else statement running")
} else {
    print ("Second half of if-else statement running")
}

if (x > 10) {
    print ("First if-elseif commands running")
} else if (x > 5) {
    print ("Second if-elseif commands running")
} else if (x <= 0) {
    print ("Third if-elseif commands running")
}
```

Change the value of x from 7 to 12 and then to –4 to see how the different if statements react when their Boolean values change.

Using switch Statements

The if-elseif statement offers multiple sets of commands to run depending on different Boolean conditions. However, an if-elseif statement that offers too many different sets of commands can be confusing to read. As an alternative to the if-elseif statement, Swift offers a switch statement.

A switch statement is a cleaner, more organized version of the if-elseif statement. The basic structure of a switch statement looks like this:

```swift
switch (Variable) {
case (Boolean Value1):
    // Run commands here
case (Boolean Value2):
    // Run commands here
default:
    // Run commands here
}
```

The switch statement makes it easy to provide multiple sets of mutually exclusive commands that run only if a specific Boolean condition becomes true. It's possible that no Boolean conditions in a switch statement will ever be true, so every switch statement must always end with a default set of commands.

A switch statement's Boolean values can represent the following types of conditions:

- Equality – A variable is exactly equal to a specific value.

- Comparison – A variable is less than, less than or equal to, greater than, or greater than or equal to a specific value.

- Range – A variable falls within a range of two values.

In an if statement, we can test for equality like this:

```swift
if x == 1 {
    print ("x = 1")
}
```

In a switch statement, we can test for equality like this:

```
switch x {
case 1:
    print ("x = 1")
default:
    print ("x is not equal to 1")
}
```

In an if statement, we can compare a variable to a value using a comparison operator ($<$, $<=$, $>$, or $>=$). In a switch statement, we must define a new constant and check this constant using a comparison operator such as

```
switch x {
case let y where y < 9:
    print ("x < 9")
default:
    print ("x is not less than 9")
}
```

A switch statement is especially useful to check if a variable falls within a range of two values. If you want to check if a variable is equal to or greater than 1 and equal to or less than 10, you could do the following:

```
switch x {
case 1...10:
    print ("x is within the range of 1 - 10")
default:
    print ("x is not within the range of 1 - 10")
}
```

Besides checking if a value falls within a range, Swift offers an alternative that checks if a variable is equal to or greater than one value but only less than (not equal) to a second value. This range check looks like this:

```
switch x {
case 1..<10:
    print ("x is within the range of 1 - 9")
```

```
default:
    print ("x is not within the range of 1 - 9")
}
```

To see how the switch statement works, modify the code as follows and click the Run button:

```
import UIKit

var x = 1 // Change this to 4, 7, and 10

switch x {
case 1:
    print ("x is 1")
case let y where y < 0:
    print ("x is a negative number")
case 2...5:
    print ("x is a number from 2 - 5")
case 6..<10:
    print ("x is a number from 6 - 9")
default:
    print ("None of the Boolean values matched")
}
```

Change the value of x from 1 to 4, 7, and 10 and click the Run button each time to see a different result.

Looping Statements

Branching statements like the if or switch statement allow a program to run different sets of commands based on Boolean conditions. Another type of programming statement is called a loop statement. With a loop statement, a program runs a set of commands multiple times until a Boolean value becomes true such as repeating exactly five times or repeating until the user enters a valid password.

> **Note**   Looping statements must always have a way to stop. A loop that fails to stop is called an endless loop, which makes a program stuck running commands but failing to respond to the user. Whenever you use a looping statement, always make sure there's a way to make that loop stop running by changing its Boolean value somehow.

Swift offers the following different looping statements:

- for loops

- while loops

- repeat-while loops

You can use loops interchangeably, but some loops are easier for certain types of tasks. For example, a for loop makes it easy to repeat commands a fixed number of times, but you can duplicate that behavior using any of the other loops instead. By learning what each loop does best, you can write more efficient and understandable code.

Using the for Loop

The for loop is best for running a fixed number of times such as five or sixteen times. This assumes that you know ahead of time exactly how many times you need to repeat a set of commands that will never change. The basic structure of a for loop requires a variable and a range such as

```
for variable in range {
    // Run commands here
}
```

If you want to count from 1 to 10, you could define a range like this:

```
for i in 1...10 {
    print (i)
}
```

The preceding code simply prints the numbers 1 through 10 sequentially. If you only wanted to count from 1 to 9, you could define a range up to but not including 10 like this:

```
for i in 1..<10 {
    print (i)
}
```

The preceding code prints the numbers 1 through 9 sequentially. Notice that the preceding code defines a variable (i) that counts between a range of numbers. Then a print statement uses this (i) variable. What if you don't need to use this counting variable inside the for loop? Then you can simply use an underscore like this:

```
for _ in 1...4 {
    print ("test")
}
```

The preceding code prints "test" four times and then stops. The for loop is best to use whenever you know ahead of time exactly how many times to run a loop.

Normally a for loop counts from a lower value to a higher value such as from 1 to 10. If you want to count backward, you can use the reversed() method like this:

```
for i in (1...4).reversed() {
    print (i)
}
```

This code prints the numbers 4, 3, 2, and 1 in that order, reversing the range from 1 to 4 and changing it to 4 to 1.

Besides counting from an arbitrary range of numbers, the for loop can also count the number of items within an array or string. Rather than define a numeric range, you define an item to count such as

```
for i in "Hello" {
    print (i)
}
```

This for loop runs five times and prints each letter from the string "Hello" on a separate line like this:

```
H
e
l
l
o
```

Using the while Loop

The for loop always runs a fixed number of times. However, sometimes you may want a loop that does one or both of the following:

- May not run at all

- May run a different number of times

A while loop checks a Boolean condition first. If this Boolean condition is true, then the loop runs. If this Boolean condition is false, then the while loop won't run at all. The basic structure of a while loop looks like this:

```
while Boolean condition {
    // Run commands here
}
```

A while loop needs two commands. One command must appear before the while loop and define the Boolean condition to either true or false. A second command must appear inside the while loop and change that Boolean condition to false eventually.

Note   A while loop absolutely must include a command that can change the Boolean condition to false inside the while loop. Failure to do so can create an endless loop.

Modify the code as follows and click the Run button to see how both a for loop and a while loop can count and repeat the same number of times:

```
import UIKit

for i in 1...4 {
    print (i)
}

var x = 1

while (x <= 4) {
    print (x)
    x = x + 1
}
```

Notice that although the for loop and while loop perform the exact same task (counting from 1 to 4), the for loop is much simpler and shorter. On the other hand, the while loop requires an additional line to define its Boolean condition and another additional line to eventually change its Boolean condition, which creates a greater chance of mistakes.

Using the repeat Loop

The while loop checks a Boolean condition before running, which means if that Boolean condition is false, the while loop won't run at all. The repeat loop is like an upside-down while loop because it runs at least once and then checks a Boolean condition. If this Boolean condition is false, then it stops running after running at least once. The main features of a repeat loop are

- Always runs at least once

- May run a different number of times

The basic structure of a repeat loop looks like this:

```
repeat {
// Run commands here
} while (Boolean condition)
```

Like the while loop, the repeat loop also needs two additional commands. One command needs to appear before the repeat loop and help define its Boolean condition. Then a second command needs to appear inside the repeat loop to change the Boolean condition eventually.

To make a repeat loop run four times just like the previous example using the for loop and while loop, modify the code as follows and click the Run button:

```
import UIKit

var x = 1

repeat {
    print (x)
    x = x + 1
} while (x <= 4)
```

The preceding repeat loop simply prints the numbers 1 through 4 sequentially. As a general rule, use for loops to repeat commands a fixed number of times, use while loops in case you may want the loop to run zero or more times, and use repeat loops to run at least once.

Functions

The more your program needs to do, the longer it will get. While you could write an entire program in one long list of commands, it's far easier to divide a large program into smaller parts called functions. Functions act like building blocks that allow you to create a large, complicated program by solving one task at a time.

Besides breaking a large program into smaller pieces, functions also let you create reusable code that different parts of your program can run. Without functions, you would have to make copies of code. Then if you modified that code, you would have to modify it in every copy.

A far simpler solution is to store your code in a function. Now if you need to modify that code, you just modify it once in a single location. This improves efficiency and reliability.

The simplest function consists of a name followed by a list of commands as follows:

```
func name() {
    // Commands here
}
```

To run or call a function, you simply use the function name as a command like this:

```
name()
```

To see how a simple function can work, modify the code as follows and click the Run button:

```
import UIKit

func greeting() {
    print ("Hello")
}

greeting()
```

This code defines a function called "greeting," which simply prints "Hello". To run or call this function, you simply need the greeting() line, which makes the function actually run.

In case you noticed the empty parentheses after the function name, those empty parentheses define parameters. Parameters let you pass data to a function so the function can use that data somehow. To create parameters to pass, you need to give each parameter a descriptive name and define its data type like this:

```
func name(parameterName: dataType) {
    // Commands here
}
```

To run or call a function with parameters, you must specify the function name along with all parameter names such as

```
name(parameterName: dataType)
```

To see how a function with parameters can work, modify the code as follows and click the Run button:

```
import UIKit

func greeting(name: String) {
    print ("Hello, " + name)
}

greeting(name: "Fred")
```

The preceding code calls the greeting function and passes it the string "Fred". The greeting function retrieves this passed parameter and uses it in the print statement to print "Hello, Fred".

Functions can have zero or more parameters. Another variation of a function returns a value where the function name represents that value. A function that returns a value needs to define the data type of the returned value plus define the value to return like this:

```
func name() -> dataType {
    // Commands here
    return value
}
```

To see how to return a value in a function, modify the code as follows and click the Run button:

```
import UIKit

func greeting(name: String) -> String {
    let message = "Hello, " + name
    return message
}

print (greeting(name: "Jack"))
```

This code passes the name "Jack" to the greeting function, which adds the name "Jack" to "Hello, " and returns the entire string back as "Hello, Jack".

Ideally, functions should focus on performing a single task. This keeps the function short, which makes it easy to write and debug. The shorter your code, the easier it will be to debug, which increases the reliability of your overall program.

Data Structures

Earlier you learned about storing data in variables. The problem with using variables to store data is that you need a separate variable for each chunk of data you want to store. Even worse, if you need to store numerous amounts of data, the data gets stored in separate variables, which means there's no connection between related data. To solve this problem, Swift offers different ways to store related data together in what are called data structures. Some common types of data structures include

- Arrays

- Tuples

- Dictionaries

- Structures

- Enumerations

Storing Data in Arrays

While variables store data in separate chunks, arrays store data in a list as shown in Figure A-15.

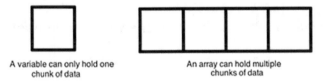

A variable can only hold one chunk of data

An array can hold multiple chunks of data

Figure A-15. *Arrays act like a single variable that can hold multiple chunks of data*

The simplest way to declare an array is to store a list of items in square brackets like this:

```
var myArray = [3, 54, 90, 1, 83]
```

This creates an array of integers. If you use an array with a for loop, you can sequentially retrieve each item stored in an array. Modify the code as follows and click the Run button to print each number in the array:

```
import UIKit
```

```swift
var myArray = [3, 54, 90, 1, 83]

for x in myArray {
    print (x)
}
```

Another way to create an array is to define its data type only like this:

```swift
var arrayName = [dataType]()
```

So if we wanted to create an array to hold only strings, the declaration would look like this:

```swift
var arrayName = [String]()
```

Just as you can explicitly declare data types for variables, you can also explicitly define array data types like this:

```swift
var arrayName: [String] = [String]()
```

Whether you have an array filled with data or just created an empty array, you may want to add new items to that array. To add a new item at the end of an array, you can use the append or insert command.

The append command always adds data to the end of an array where the beginning of an array is considered the far left and the end of the array is considered the far right. To see how the append command works, modify the code as follows and click the Run button:

```swift
import UIKit

var myArray = [Int]()

for x in 1...4 {
    myArray.append(x)
    print(myArray)
}
```

The preceding code prints the following:

> **[1]**
>
> **[1, 2]**
>
> **[1, 2, 3]**
>
> **[1, 2, 3, 4]**

Another way to add items to an array is through the insert command. While the append command always adds a new item to the end of an array, the insert command lets you define where to insert a new item based on an index value.

The index value of an array defines the position of each item where the first item in an array has an index of 0, the second item has an index of 1, and so on. So if you want to always insert new items at index position 0 (the beginning of the array), you could use the insert command. Modify the code as follows and click the Run button:

```swift
import UIKit

var myArray = [Int]()

for x in 1...4 {
    myArray.insert(x, at: 0)
    print(myArray)
}
```

The preceding code prints the following:

> **[1]**
>
> **[2, 1]**
>
> **[3, 2, 1]**
>
> **[4, 3, 2, 1]**

To delete an item from an array, you can use the remove command and specify the index position of the item you want to remove. So if you want to remove the third item in an array, you would remove the item at index position 2.

To see how to use the remove command, modify the code as follows and click the Run button:

```
import UIKit

var myArray = [Int]()

for x in 1...4 {
    myArray.insert(x, at: 0)
    print(myArray)
}

myArray.remove(at: 2)
print(myArray)
```

The preceding code prints the following:

[1]

[2, 1]

[3, 2, 1]

[4, 3, 2, 1]

[4, 3, 1]

One useful command is counting the total number of items in an array using the count command. To see how the count command works, modify the code as follows and click the Run button:

```
import UIKit

var myArray = [Int]()

for x in 1...4 {
    myArray.insert(x, at: 0)
    print(myArray)
}

print(myArray.count)
```

The preceding code prints the following:

[1]

[2, 1]

[3, 2, 1]

[4, 3, 2, 1]

4

Arrays make it easy to store similar data in one location. Once you create an array, you can add new items to the end (append) or anywhere by specifying an index position (insert). To delete an item from an array, you must specify the index position (remove). Finally, you can use the count command to count the total number of items in an array.

Storing Data in Tuples

If you have two different types of data, such as a name (string) and an age (integer), you would normally need to store them in two separate variables. However, it makes more sense to store related data together. To store related data in a single variable, even if they are of different data types, you can use something called a tuple.

To create a tuple, you just need to group all data together and assign it to a variable name such as

```
var myTuple = ("Joe", 42)
```

You can store two or more chunks of data in a tuple. To retrieve data from a tuple, you need to identify the data position where the first item in a tuple is at position 0, the second item is at position 1, and so on. To see how to create and retrieve data from a tuple, modify the code as follows and click the Run button:

```
import UIKit

var myTuple = ("Joe", 42)

print (myTuple.0)
print (myTuple.1)
```

The first print statement retrieves "Joe" (myTuple.0), and the second print statement retrieves 42 (myTuple.1). Since identifying data in a tuple by its position can be awkward, Swift also allows you to give each position in a tuple a distinct name. That way instead of retrieving data using its position number, you can retrieve data using its name instead.

To see how to use named elements in a tuple, modify the code as follows and click the Run button:

```
import UIKit

var myTuple = (name: "Joe", age: 42)

print (myTuple.name)
print (myTuple.age)
```

The preceding code does the exact same thing as the previous tuple example that references data using its position in the tuple such as myTuple.0 or myTuple.1. Use tuples whenever you need to store related information of different data types in a single variable.

Storing Data in Dictionaries

When you store data in an array, each item gets assigned an index number that represents its position in the array. The first item in the array has an index of 0, the second item has an index of 1, and so on. To retrieve data from an array, you need to know its index number (position) in the array.

So what happens if you want to search for an item but don't know its index number? Then you'll need to exhaustively search the entire array until you find the item you want. For a small array, this won't be a problem, but for a larger array, this can slow down your program.

As an alternative to storing data in an array, Swift gives you the option of storing data in a dictionary. A dictionary acts like an array except that you identify each stored item with an identifying key value. Now to retrieve a value from a dictionary, you just need to know its key. To declare a dictionary, you can use the following:

```
var myDictionary: [keyDataType: valueDataType]
```

Both the keyDataType and valueDataType can be any data type such as String, Int, or Double. When you store data in a dictionary, you must also assign a unique key value to that data value as well. If you have a list of employees, each employee can be assigned a unique employee ID number such as

```
import UIKit

var myDictionary: [Int: String] = [
    10: "Bob",
    15: "Lucy",
    20: "Kyle",
    25: "Jackie",
    30: "Gile"]

print (myDictionary.count)

for (key, value) in myDictionary {
    print("\(key): \(value)")
}
```

The myDictionary.count command returns the total number of items stored in the dictionary where a single key:value pair is considered one item. Thus, myDictionary. count returns a value of 5.

The for-in loop goes through the dictionary and returns each key:value pair stored in the dictionary. Note that the order of data stored in a dictionary doesn't matter. That means the for-in loop does not print 10: Bob first and 15: Lucy second, but may print the data in a wildly different order such as

25: Jackie
10: Bob
30: Gile
20: Kyle
15: Lucy

To add new data to a dictionary, you need to define a new key and assign it new data like this:

```
myDictionary[35] = "Tom"
```

The preceding code assigns the data "Tom" to a new key 35. If you want to replace data with a key that's already used, you can use the updateValue method to define new data and the existing key for that data such as

```
myDictionary.updateValue("Howard", forKey: 10)
```

Finally, if you want to remove data from a dictionary, you can use the removeValue method and define the key of the data you want to remove such as

```
myDictionary.removeValue(forKey: 10)
```

Modify the code as follows and click the Run button:

```
import UIKit

var myDictionary: [Int: String] = [
    10: "Bob",
    15: "Lucy",
    20: "Kyle",
    25: "Jackie",
    30: "Gile"]

print (myDictionary.count)

for (key, value) in myDictionary {
    print("\(key): \(value)")
}

print ("*****")

myDictionary[35] = "Tom"

print (myDictionary.count)

for (key, value) in myDictionary {
    print("\(key): \(value)")
}

print ("*****")

myDictionary.updateValue("Howard", forKey: 10)

for (key, value) in myDictionary {
    print("\(key): \(value)")
}

print ("*****")
```

```
myDictionary.removeValue(forKey: 10)

for (key, value) in myDictionary {
    print("\(key): \(value)")
}
```

This will create output similar to the following (the exact order that the for-in loop prints out data may differ on your computer):

5
20: Kyle
25: Jackie
10: Bob
15: Lucy
30: Gile
*****
6
35: Tom
20: Kyle
25: Jackie
10: Bob
15: Lucy
30: Gile
*****
35: Tom
20: Kyle
25: Jackie
10: Howard
15: Lucy
30: Gile
*****
35: Tom
20: Kyle
25: Jackie
15: Lucy
30: Gile

Storing Data in Structures

If you need to store someone's name, age, and email address, you could use three separate variables. However, using separate variables won't show you the relationship between all the variables. When you need to group different variables together to show that they're related to each other and should be treated as a single chunk of data, you can use a structure.

A structure lets you group related variables together like this:

```swift
struct myStructure {
    var name: String
    var age: Int
    var email: String
}
```

Every structure needs a distinct name such as myStructure. Then inside the structure you can define as many variables as you want. After defining variables, you need to give each variable an initial value such as

```swift
struct myStructure {
    var name: String = ""
    var age: Int = 0
    var email: String = ""
}
```

A structure is simply a data type, so you don't use a structure directly. Instead, you create a variable and assign the structure to that variable such as

```swift
var myContacts = myStructure()
```

To store data in a structure, you need to use the variable name (that represents the structure) followed by the structure variable like this:

```swift
import UIKit

struct myStructure {
    var name: String = ""
```

```
    var age: Int = 0
    var email: String = ""
}

var myContacts = myStructure()

myContacts.name = "Flora"
myContacts.age = 30
myContacts.email = "flora@yahoo.com"

print (myContacts.name)
print (myContacts.age)
print (myContacts.email)
```

The preceding code simply prints the following:

Flora
30
flora@yahoo.com

Structures are often used with other data structures such as an array that holds a structure rather than a single string or number.

Defining Your Own Data Type with an Enumeration

If you need to store someone's name, you'll most likely use a String data type. However, any valid string could be stored as someone's name such as "jhnewm4jd", "294", or "#$^@". While these are all valid strings, they aren't valid names.

Rather than use basic data types like String, Int, Double, or Float, you can define your own data type along with a list of valid data for that enumeration. An enumeration needs a name (that typically begins with an uppercase letter) followed by one or more valid data options defined by a "case" keyword like this:

```
enum Directions {
    case north
    case south
    case east
    case west
}
```

Since an enumeration is a data type, we can declare any variable to hold this enumeration data type like this:

```
var whichWay: Directions
```

The "whichWay" variable can only hold Directions data types, and the only valid options are north, south, east, or west.

To assign enumeration data to a variable, we can explicitly list the enumeration name followed by the data like this:

```
whichWay = Directions.east
```

As a shortcut, most Swift programmers omit the enumeration name and just type the data itself like this:

```
whichWay = .north
```

Although an enumeration's list of valid options might look like text (such as a String data type), an enumeration's data does not represent any common data type like String, Double, or Float. To convert an enumeration's options into String data types, there's a two-step process.

First, define the data type for the enumeration like this:

```
enum Directions: String {
    case north
    case south
    case east
    case west
}
```

Declaring : String after the enumeration name defines every option in the enumeration as a String data type. To retrieve the String data type from an enumeration, we need to access its .rawValue property like this:

```
enum Directions: String {
    case north
    case south
    case east
    case west
}
```

```
var whichWay: Directions
```

```
whichWay = .north
print ("I am going in this direction = " + whichWay.rawValue)
```

This prints "I am going in this direction – north". Omit the .rawValue property, and the enumeration data type cannot be treated as a String, which gives an error as shown in Figure A-16.

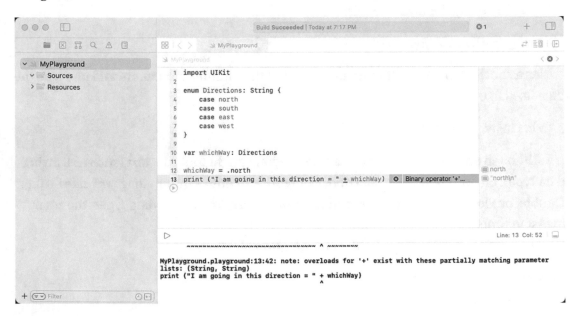

Figure A-16. *Without the .rawValue property, Swift cannot treat an enumeration data type as a String*

The options listed in an enumeration can be any data type. It's possible to define non-String data types for an enumeration, but that means assigning each option with a value. If we wanted an enumeration to represent Int data types, we could define an enumeration like this:

```
enum Directions: Int {
    case north = 15
    case south = 27
    case east = 85
    case west = 102
}
```

Now we could assign a variable as a Directions data type and access the .rawValue property of that enumeration's option like this:

```
var whichWay: Directions

whichWay = .north
print (whichWay.rawValue + 70)
```

This would print 85, adding 70 to the .rawValue of .north (which is assigned a value of 15).

Classes and Object-Oriented Programming

Modern programming languages like Swift support object-oriented programming. Objects are defined by a class file, which determines the following:

- Properties – Variables that allow an object to store data or share it with other objects

- Methods – Functions that perform some action on data

You can treat an object's properties like a variable. To assign a value to an object's property, you just need to specify the object's name and the property you want to access, separated by a period as shown in Figure A-17.

Figure A-17. *Accessing an object's property*

In Figure A-17, we're creating a new object named myButton, based on the UIButton class. Then we can use the backgroundColor property. Object-oriented programming offers three features:

- Encapsulation

- Inheritance

- Polymorphism

Understanding Encapsulation

Encapsulation means that objects can define private and public variables. Private variables can only be accessed and modified by code within that object, which prevents other parts of a program from accidentally modifying a variable used by a different part of a program. Public variables allow an object to share data with other parts of a program.

Note   Encapsulation is meant to eliminate the problem of global variables that allow any part of a program to store and modify data in a variable. If multiple parts of a program can modify the same variable, it can be difficult to identify problems when one part of a program modifies a variable incorrectly.

Public variables are usually called properties and need an initial value. When creating class names, it's customary to start with an uppercase letter such as MyClass instead of myClass. To see how to create a class with properties you can access, modify the code as follows and click the Run button:

```
import UIKit

class MyClass {
    var name: String = ""
    var age: Int = 0
}

var person = MyClass()
person.name = "Kate"
person.age = 32

print (person.name)
print (person.age)
```

The preceding code defines a class named MyClass and defines two properties with initial values. Then it creates an object based on that class and stores data in the name and age properties. Finally, it prints out this data ("Kate" and 32).

Besides defining properties, class files typically also define methods, which are functions that manipulate data. Methods typically accept data through parameters. To see how to create and use a method in a class, modify the code as follows and click the Run button:

```swift
import UIKit

class MyClass {
    var name: String = ""
    var age: Int = 0

    func greeting(human: String) {
        print ("Hello, " + human)
    }
}

var person = MyClass()

person.greeting(human: "Mary")
```

The preceding code calls the greeting method and passes it the string "Mary". The greeting method then prints "Hello, Mary".

Understanding Inheritance

The main idea behind object-oriented programming is to reuse code. Suppose you're making a video game that displays a race car and obstacles such as rocks on the road. A rock needs to store data like a location and size, while a car needs to store data like a location, size, speed, and direction.

You could write one chunk of code to define a rock and a second chunk of code to define a car, but this essentially duplicates code. Now if you need to modify the code that defines location or size, you'll have to do it for both the rock and car, which increases the risk of making a mistake or having two different versions of the same code.

Inheritance solves this problem by letting you write code for one object (such as a rock) and inherit that code for a second object (such as a car). Instead of copying code, inheritance points to the code it wants to use. That way there's only one copy of code that can be reused by multiple classes.

Without inheritance, you might define two classes like this:

```swift
class MyPerson {
    var name: String = ""
```

```
    var age: Int = 0

    func greeting(human: String) {
        print ("Hello, " + human)
    }
}

class MyDog {
    var name: String = ""
    var age: Int = 0
    var legs: Int = 0

    func greeting(human: String) {
        print ("Hello, " + human)
    }
}
```

Notice the duplication of code in both classes with the properties age and name and the method greeting. By using inheritance, we can eliminate this duplication of code and just focus on adding properties and methods unique to the second class like this:

```
class MyPerson {
    var name: String = ""
    var age: Int = 0

    func greeting(human: String) {
        print ("Hello, " + human)
    }
}

class MyDog : MyPerson {
    var rabies: Bool = false
}
```

To inherit code from another class, notice that the MyDog class includes a colon (:) and the MyPerson name. This tells the MyDog class to inherit code from the MyPerson class.

To see how inheritance works, modify the code as follows and click the Run button:

```swift
import UIKit

class MyPerson {
    var name: String = ""
    var age: Int = 0

    func greeting(thing: String) {
        print ("Hello, " + thing)
    }
}

class MyDog : MyPerson {
    var rabies: Bool = false
}

var person = MyPerson()
person.greeting(thing: "Mary")

var pet = MyDog()
pet.name = "Lassie"
pet.age = 3
pet.rabies = true
pet.greeting(thing: pet.name)
```

The preceding code prints "Hello, Mary" and "Hello, Lassie". Even though the MyDog class does not explicitly define a name and an age property or a greeting method, it's still possible to use the name and age properties along with the greeting method through inheritance.

Understanding Polymorphism

Even though one class can inherit from another class, there still might be a problem with the names of methods stored in each class. In a video game, there might be a method called move() that defines how different objects move. However, a race car can only move in two dimensions, while a bird can move in three dimensions.

Ideally, you'd want to move both a race car and a bird using the same method named move(). However, the code within each move() method needs to be different. A clumsy solution is to create different method names such as move() for a race car and fly() for a bird, but if the bird class inherits from the car class, the bird class will still inherit the move() method anyway.

Polymorphism solves this problem by letting you use the same method name but fill it with different code. When you want to reuse a method name but use different code, you have to use the override command in front of the method name. To see how polymorphism works, modify the code as follows and click the Run button:

```swift
import UIKit

class MyPerson {
    var name: String = ""
    var age: Int = 0

    func greeting(thing: String) {
        print ("Hello, " + thing)
    }
}

class MyDog : MyPerson {
    var rabies: Bool = false
    override func greeting(thing: String) {
        print ("Barking at you, " + thing)
    }
}

var person = MyPerson()
person.greeting(thing: "Mary")

var pet = MyDog()
pet.name = "Lassie"
pet.age = 3
pet.rabies = true
pet.greeting(thing: pet.name)
```

Notice that the MyDog class overrides the greeting method it inherited from the MyPerson class. The MyPerson class greeting method prints "Hello, Mary", while the MyDog greeting method prints "Barking at you, Lassie". So even though the greeting method name remains the same, the result can be different because of polymorphism.

You'll be using object-oriented programming extensively when creating an iOS app. User interface objects are derived from different classes that inherit from each other. If you browse through Apple's documentation for their various software frameworks, you'll see how different classes inherit from others as shown in Figure A-18.

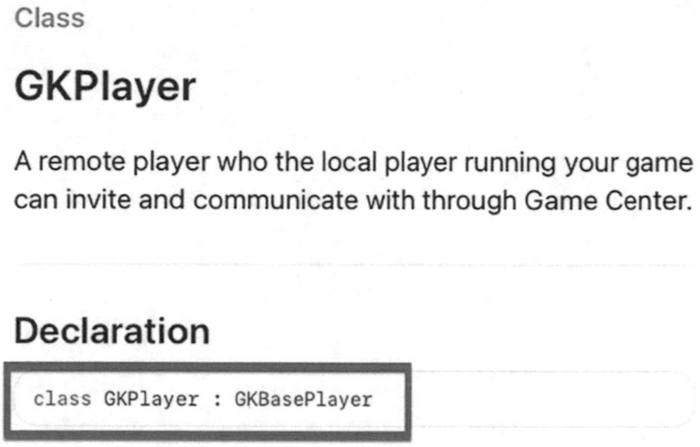

Class

GKPlayer

A remote player who the local player running your game can invite and communicate with through Game Center.

Declaration

```
class GKPlayer : GKBasePlayer
```

Figure A-18. *Identifying inheritance in different classes used by a framework*

Summary

Since 2014, Swift has been Apple's official programming language. Swift is designed to be simpler, easier to read and write, and faster than Apple's previous programming language, Objective-C. While many older apps are still written in Objective-C, most newer apps are written in Swift. If you're going to learn iOS programming, learn Swift first because that's the future of programming for all of Apple's devices including the Macintosh (macOS), Apple Watch (watchOS), Apple TV (tvOS), and Vision Pro (visionOS).

If you're familiar with other programming languages, you'll find Swift easy to learn. If you've never programmed before, learn Swift by using Xcode's playgrounds. A playground gives you a safe way to experiment with Swift without the additional distraction of designing an iOS user interface.

Besides letting you learn about Swift in a safe environment, playgrounds also give you a way to experiment with different Swift features before using them in an actual project. That way you can make sure your Swift code works before you rely on it.

By learning Swift and iOS programming, you'll be able to program all of Apple's products now and in the future.

Index

© Wallace Wang 2023
W. Wang, *Beginning iPhone Development with SwiftUI*, https://doi.org/10.1007/978-1-4842-9541-0

M

N

V, W

Vertical stack (VStack), 10

X, Y, Z

Xcode
  design user interface, 4
  organize folders, 5

project, 5
  choosing template, 7
  ContentView, 10
  ContentView_Previews, 10
  Editor/Canvas pane, 10, 11
  navigator pane, 9
  organization name/organization
    identifier, 8
  welcoming screen, 6

Printed in the United States
by Baker & Taylor Publisher Services